# LEARNING DISORDERS & DISORDERS OF THE SELF

## IN

## CHILDREN & ADOLESCENTS

A NORTON PROFESSIONAL BOOK

# LEARNING DISORDERS &
# DISORDERS OF THE SELF

IN

# CHILDREN &
# ADOLESCENTS

**Joseph Palombo**

*Institute for Clinical Social Work, Chicago*

**W. W. NORTON & COMPANY**
New York • London

For information about permission to reproduce selections
from this book, write to Permissions, W. W. Norton & Company, Inc.,
500 Fifth Avenue, New York, NY 10110

The text of this book is composed in Garamond
Composition by TechBooks
Manufacturing by Haddon Craftsmen
Production Manager: Leeann Graham

**Library of Congress Cataloging-in-Publication Data**

Palombo, Joseph, 1928-
  Learning disorders and disorders of the self in children and adolescents / Joseph
Palombo.
       p.     cm.
  "A Norton professional book."
  Includes bibliographical references and index.
  **ISBN 0-393-70377-0**
  1. Learning disabilities. 2. Learning disabled children—Education. 3. Personality
disorders. 4. Object relations (Psychoanalysis) 5. Self psychology. I. Title.

LC4704.5 .P35 2001
618.9'85889—dc21        2001024007

W. W. Norton & Company, Inc., 500 Fifth Avenue, New York, N.Y. 10110
www.wwnorton.com

W. W. Norton & Company Ltd., Castle House, 75/76 Wells St., London W1T 3QT

*To Dottie, whose steadfast*
*support made the*
*completion of this work possible*

# CONTENTS

# FOREWORD

The issue of learning disorders in children is at the forefront of both education and child mental health. With the delineation of a diagnosis of attention deficit disorder, pediatricians, psychiatrists, and educators alike have focused on the problems of children who seem to be unable to adjust to life in the classroom. These children find it difficult to concentrate on what the teacher is presenting or to remain in their seats, wander about the classroom provoking classmates trying to do their work, and only rarely comply with the demands of classwork and homework. While often of above average intelligence, they usually receive poor grades. At home these children have trouble keeping their rooms in order, misplace their homework assignments, and disrupt everyday family routines.

The discovery that some specific pharmacologic agents appear to have miraculous effects, leading to profound changes in these children's ability to concentrate and to organize their lives, has led to wide-scale medicating of children. The tragedy is that too often we stop with the recognition of the neurological foundation of the disorder and presume that medication alone will solve the child's problems. In this book a wise and sophisticated child psychotherapist shows the importance of an integrated perspective that takes into account neuropsychological problems and the context in which children with learning disorders cope with their difficulties.

Joseph Palombo provides a refreshingly sensible and comprehensive understanding of learning disorders and the development of the self. Drawing upon more than three decades of clinical study, Palombo shows that learning disorders reflect a complex interplay of constitutional givens and the nature of the child's experience at home and at school. He observes that biologically based problems may interfere with the child's sense of caregiving as good enough to form a solid basis of self-confidence and sense of personal vitality. Emerging from early childhood lacking the ability to provide for adequate self-regulation, the child with a learning disorder may be ill-equipped to deal with the reality of problems in concentrating at home and at school. These children feel unable to realize tension regulation and consequently experience others as unable to be of help to them.

Using theoretical insights on the emergence of self-esteem from psychoanalyst Heinz Kohut and his colleagues, Palombo makes sense of the child's experience of self as deficient in tension regulation, leading to consequent behavioral disruption. He also uses self psychology to help parents, teachers, pediatricians, and psychotherapists understand the child's experience of self and others and includes specific ways of working with these children and adolescents. Palombo emphasizes the importance of planning for intervention only after careful neuropsychological evaluation and of engaging parents, educators, physicians, and mental health professionals as collaborators with children having problems in learning. At the same time, he makes an important contribution to psychoanalytic theories of development. This book is among the very few efforts to apply Kohut's theory of self and its development to understanding behavioral disorders of children and adolescents.

Readers will find a comprehensive and readable overview of the most common learning disorders in childhood and adolescence, approached both from the perspective of neuropsychology and from the study of personality development, together with important clinical observations regarding the contributions of both mental health professionals and parents in fostering the child's progress. The child's ability to tolerate frustration, as well as feelings of futility, must be carefully considered in planning for intervention. Palombo provides careful guidelines for mental health and educational specialists to consider in planning for optimal intervention. The goal of this effort is to foster a new sense of personal coherence or integrity, so that the child is able to make effective use of various resources.

Palombo takes advantage of the tradition of psychoanalytic understanding of childhood, informed by long experience in working with young people, in leading the reader to a new and more comprehensive perspective on children and adolescents with learning disorders than has previously been presented. He attends to the particular problems posed for the therapist and parents alike by children with learning disorders, who desperately seek to make others feel their distress. The result is a book that not only contributes to the study of psychological development across the years of childhood and adolescence, but also provides detailed and useful means of working with these psychologically vulnerable children at home, at school, and in the therapist's office. Palombo's discussion shifts the focus from the otherwise inevitable cycle of disappointment and despair experienced by both these children and those who care for them, to the effort to repair the child's damaged sense of self-esteem and to increasing competence and the capacity to bear and resolve tension states. This book is must reading both for all those who share the lives of children with learning disorders and also for those interested in the contributions of contemporary psychoanalytic perspectives in understanding psychological development. It is a wise book for parents, educators, physicians, and mental health professionals.

*Bertram J. Cohler, Ph.D.*
*William Rainey Harper Professor of Social Sciences*
*University of Chicago*

# PREFACE

This book addresses the concerns of two audiences: psychotherapists who treat children and adolescents with learning disorders and professionals, such as clinical psychologists, neuropsychologists, school psychologists, and learning disabilities specialists, who are involved in the assessment or remediation of children's learning disorders.

The major thesis is that neuropsychological deficits or weaknesses play a critical role in the development of the sense of self and in the creation of a self-narrative. Psychopathology, in the form of a disorder of the self, may arise as a result of the presence of a learning disorder. Three areas are opened for exploration from the child's subjective perspective:

- How do these children experience their learning disorder and how does that experience affect their interactions with others?
- What factors contribute to the development of disorders of the self in some children but not in others?
- How does the knowledge of the presence of a learning disorder affect the treatment process?

The book is not intended as a manual on how to treat patients with learning disorders. As I emphasize in the chapters that follow, the treatment methods used with these patients in many ways are no different from those used with any other type of patient. What is different is the therapist's perspective as to the origins and nature of the patient's difficulties. Situating the origins of those difficulties within the context in which the patient developed helps therapists appreciate the contributions of both endowment and the environment.This perspective not only highlights what the patient, as a child, brings to the interaction with caregivers but also underscores the reasons for caregivers' responses to the patient.

I hope educators concerned with the training of professionals involved with this population will also take an interest in this work. Few programs that train psychotherapists include courses on this topic. This gap has serious consequences for the welfare of our patients. By the same token, few programs that prepare specialists who deal with this population emphasize sufficiently the contribution made by learning disorders to the child's subjective responses and nonacademic problems. Students alerted early in their training to the impact of neuropsychological deficits on development will be in a better position to assist those whom they are charged to help.

The book is divided into three sections. Following the introductory chapter that sets the theoretical and historical setting of the problems, Section I details the conceptual framework I use. Psychoanalytic self psychology, as proposed by Heinz Kohut, provides a perspective that starts with self-experience. By focusing on the child's sense of self, the empathic/introspective perspective provides an approach to understanding the child's subjective experience as it is filtered through his or her particular neuropsychological deficits. The child's self-narrative supplements this subjective view by addressing the meanings the child assigns to those experiences. The juxtaposition of the two perspectives provides insights into the patient's world and provides clues as to why some children develop a disorder of the self while others do not. Because of the special problems that this population presents, the section includes a chapter on adolescence. Section II deals with the five specific disorders I have chosen as exemplars of the range of actual learning disorders. These are dyslexia, attention-deficit/hyperactivity disorder, executive function disorder, nonverbal learning disability, and Asperger's disorder. Compared to other learning disorders, more is known about the disorders highlighted here and they are more likely to be encountered by clinicians. I have excluded disorders such as autism and mental retardation, as well as disorders that have their origins in acquired brain changes, such as those resulting from strokes, closed head injuries, or brain lesions. All of these require special treatment. Section III provides a framework for applying the information in Sections I and II to the therapeutic process.

## Acknowledgments

Special thanks to Charles Saltzman, Amy Eldridge, Karen Pierce, John Watkins, and John Mitchell for taking on the task of reading and commenting on the entire first draft of the book. I profited immensely from their assistance. A special thanks to Anne Berenberg, who as coauthor of two papers has helped me think through many of the ideas that are contained in this work. Thanks also Ghita Lapidus for her valuable help with the chapter on dyslexia, to Betty Fish for her comments on Section I of the first draft, and to James Monaco for his comments on the introductory chapter. I also owe a debt of gratitude to the staff of the Rush Neurobehavioral Center and its Director, Dr. Meryl Lipton, for support and valuable comments and to the Los Angeles study group on neuroscience and psychoanalysis for helping clarify for me the role of memory during development. Thanks to my patients*, my students, and the many colleagues who have participated in my study groups. My gratitude also goes to Susan Munro, my editor at W. W. Norton, who made numerous suggestions that helped clarify and improve my text. The final product reflects views for which I take responsibility.

Without the support and encouragement I received from my wife, Dottie Palombo, I might never have undertaken the arduous task of devoting the time to write this work, time from which she was deprived of my presence.

## Permissions

I am grateful to the following for permission to include sections of previously published materials. In most cases, the material has been edited and modified to make it coherent with the context in which it is used:

Chapter 6, The cohesive self, the nuclear self, and development in late adolescence. In S. C. Feinstein (Ed.), *Adolescent psychiatry* (Vol. 17, pp. 338-359). Chicago: University of Chicago Press. 1990. (© 1990 by the University of Chicago. All rights reserved.)

Chapter 10, A disorder of the self in an adult with a nonverbal learning disability. In A. Goldberg (Ed.), *Progress in self psychology* (Vol. 16, pp. 311-335). Hillsdale, NJ: The Analytic Press.

Chapter 14, Palombo, J., & Berenberg, A. (1999). Working with parents of children with nonverbal learning disabilities. In J. A. Incorvia, B. S. Mark-Goldstein, & D. Tesmer (Eds.), *Understanding, diagnosing, and treating AD/HD in children and adolescents: An integrative approach* (Vol. 3, pp. 389-441). Northvale, NJ: Aronson.

---

*All references to patients have been altered to conceal their identity and protect their privacy.

# LEARNING DISORDERS & DISORDERS OF THE SELF

IN

# CHILDREN & ADOLESCENTS

# 1

# INTRODUCTION: THEORETICAL AND HISTORICAL SETTING

IN SOME RESPECTS, ALL CHILDREN are alike, yet in other respects each child is unique and different from every other child. In this work, the focus is on the *differences* between children rather than on their similarities. Specifically, it is on the differences that result from having a learning disorder. By a learning disorder, I mean a neuropsychological deficit or weakness in one or more of the domains of perception, attention, memory, executive function, verbal and nonverbal language, affect regulation, or social functioning.

The profile of an individual child's neuropsychological strengths and weaknesses is analogous to the topography of a landscape. For some children, the terrain is fairly flat; that is, their competencies are evenly distributed. Other children's profiles looks like a terrain filled with prominent peaks. These children are gifted in multiple areas. Yet the valleys between the ridges indicate that their gifts are rarely uniformly distributed across the entire terrain. Gifted children may also have learning disorders (Vail, 1989). For children with learning disorders the terrain is highly variable. There are peaks and valleys that are notable for the contrast they present. The valleys between the peaks are much deeper than one would expect, indicating a great disparity between the areas of strength and those of weakness.

Some children appear unaffected by their learning disorders. In fact, the presence of a deficit may remain undetected either because the child has learned to compensate for it or because the environment has not placed a demand on her* to demonstrate competence in that area. However, for those children who manifest symptoms, the learning disorder produces academic underachievement, psychological disturbances, or both. I will refer to these psychological disturbances as disorders of the self. Such disorders of the self may manifest as failures to attain or maintain a sense of self-cohesion or as an inability to construct a coherent self-narrative, or both.

A disorder of the self may manifest as dysfunctional behaviors, emotional problems, or as both. The dysfunctional behaviors may range from the absence of motivation to perform academically to disruptive behaviors at home and in the classroom. The children's emotional problems may present as low self-esteem, depression, anxiety, or difficulties in affect regulation. Dysfunctional behaviors may manifest as an inability to cope with the environment or an impairment in the ability to form positive relationships to caregivers, to respond appropriately to peers, or to function in school settings. For some children the emotional problems manifest as intense shame, because they feel that they cannot be as successful as they want to be. They realize that they are smart but find themselves unable to demonstrate their competence in academic work. Their self-image is deeply affected. The net result of these dysfunctional behaviors and emotional problems is that these children's development takes a different course than it would have taken had they not been impaired. The extent to which children are affected, as I will discuss, depends on many factors. Among these is the severity of the learning disorder, the demands and expectations made of the child, the child's capacity to compensate for the disorder, opportunities and resources available to the child for the remediation of the disorder, and the parents' responses to the problems the child presents, which in circular fashion affect how the child will react and respond.

Learning disorders do not occur in a vacuum. Children with learning disorders exist in an environment that has a significant impact on their functioning. I refer to that environment as the *context* in which the child is found. My preference for the term context instead of environment grows out of my desire to emphasize the child's social and emotional

---

*I have chosen to alternate with each chapter the use of gender of the child so as to represent both sexes in my discussions. The feminine pronoun is used in odd-numbered chapters; the masculine in even-numbered. Since I was the therapist in most of the cases discussed, I refer to the therapist as male, unless otherwise specified.

milieu rather than simply the physical location in which the child is raised. Caregivers as well as other aspects of the context provide psychological nurture that is as important as the physical care the child receives. This context may complement deficits in endowment by providing protective factors, which may explain how the context can, at times, mitigate the impact of deficits in endowment (Cohler, 1987). At the other extreme, the context may amplify the effects of a deficit and overwhelm the child. While endowment may help overcome the deprivations that exist in some contexts, endowment can also act as a constraint that limits the child's development in a way for which no context can compensate.

The relationship between learning disorders and disorders of the self is complex. Disorders of the self may interfere with the acquisition of knowledge, but they do not cause learning disorders, since the latter are neurologically based. The impression derived from clinical experience is that children with learning disorders appear to suffer psychologically more than their peers who do not have learning disorders. Their psychological suffering cannot be measured through manifest symptoms alone, as many do not display such symptoms. Epidemiological data, which look at overt symptoms, do not deal with the children's subjective responses to their learning disorder. Most of the children seen clinically seem to suffer at a minimum from self-esteem problems, anxiety, or depression. Some have, in addition, psychiatric problems—comorbid conditions—such as mood disorders, anxiety disorders, obsessive-compulsive disorders, and adjustment problems. But no single pattern of problems is associated with all learning disorders. Some subtypes of learning disorders produce specific identifiable configurations of behavioral and emotional problems, while others do not seem to be associated with any pattern of such problems (Brown, 2000a; Rourke & Furerst, 1991).

The complex interplay among the neuropsychological deficits or strengths and weaknesses, the context, and the compensations a child utilizes leads to a variety of outcomes. While it is probable that no one is totally unaffected by the presence of a learning disorder, the manifestation of the impairment in the form of successful or unsuccessful adaptation or functioning can range from mild to severe. In the milder cases, the mark left may take the form of personality traits that uniquely identify the person. In the middle range, the combination of factors may lead to self-esteem problems or to narcissistic vulnerabilities to particular situations. In the severe cases, the child's functioning can be seriously impaired.

## Major Themes of This Book

In this book, I explore the association between learning disorders and disorders of the self. I offer a developmental perspective based on psychoanalytic self psychology, as elaborated by Heinz Kohut (1959, 1971, 1977, 1978, 1984; Lichtenberg & Wolf, 1997; Rosenberger, 1988). This perspective enables us to understand the subjective experience of the child, the impact that learning disorders have on development, and their contribution to personality formation. A strength of this perspective is that it provides an explanatory framework that encompasses the role of motivation, affect, and social relationships in development. It complements neuropsychological theories that limit themselves to cognitive and academic functioning. I take two paths in exploring the child's subjective experience, tracking both the *development of the sense of self* and the *emergence of the self-narrative*. The former reveals the child's experience, while the latter provides a view of the child's integration of the meanings of those experiences. A simple way to begin to think about the relationship between the sense of self and the self-narrative is that the former provides a way, through empathy, to enter into the patient's experience, while the latter provides an explanation of how the child has integrated those experiences. These explanations, however, are not pure cognitive statements devoid of feelings; rather, they incorporate within them the feelings associated with the experiences. Another way to conceive of the relationship is that it represents two metaphorical ways of addressing the same phenomena. The perspective of the sense of self deals very effectively with the domain of human experience while the perspective of the self-narrative deals with the explanations both therapist and patients give to those experiences. Much as a set of maps may represent the same terrain in different ways, highlighting one set of features rather than another, so it is with self psychology and the narrative perspective.

Three themes organize the discussion:

- effects of neuropsychological deficits or weaknesses on a child's development
- factors that give rise to a disorder of the self when a child has such deficits or weaknesses
- modifications of the way the treatment process is conceptualized when a child has a learning disorder

The emphasis in the literature on learning disabilities has been largely on the children's behaviors, their social responses to other children, and their self-assessment (see, for example, Cosden, Elliott, Noble, & Kelemen, 1999; Morvitz & Motta, 1992; Pickar, 1986; Vaughn & Haager, 1994). Insufficient attention has been paid to the way neuropsychological deficits affect a child's experience of the world. By highlighting the two lenses of the sense of self and self-narrative, I propose to shift attention from the external to the internal state of the child. The discussion of the development of the sense of self emphasizes the affective dimension of the developmental process, while the discussion of the self-narrative deals with the autobiographical constructions to which the child arrives.

Children's subjective experiences are filtered through their neuropsychological deficits and the context in which they are raised. Each of these has a direct bearing on the child's experience. The deficits restrict, modify, or impose constraints on the child's experiences, while the caregivers influence the child's interpretations of those experiences. A pattern of reciprocal and circular interchanges between the child, the deficits, and the context is the hallmark of the interactions that ensue. As we will see, the child with a learning disorder evokes responses from caregivers and others around her that are different from the responses that a child without such a disorder evokes. But that is only the beginning of a complex set of interactions. The child responds to those responses in ways that often heighten the sense of difference. These responses lead to further responses that, at times, reinforce the vicious cycle of negative interactions. Even if the responses from the context are, on the whole, positive, a set of circular interactions may be unavoidable. The course of the child's development is inevitably altered by the presence of the learning disorder.

The second theme of the book relates to the conditions under which the presence of a learning disorder leads to a disorder of the self. The child's sense of self provides a window into her subjective world. It also provides a view of the psychological needs that must be filled to maintain a sense of cohesion or integration. When the conditions necessary to maintain the sense of cohesiveness are not met, the child will develop a disorder of the self. On the other hand, the child's self-narrative provides a view of the meanings the child has drawn from her experiences. Explicating the ways in which this process takes place provides an understanding of the ways in which verbal and nonverbal language systems contribute to the content and structure of the child's self-narrative. If successful, the process leads to a coherent self-narrative; failure results in an incoherent self-narrative and a disorder of the self. Self-cohesion and narrative coherence are two interrelated factors that provide insight into the child's subjective state and the origins of a disorder of the self. A learning disorder may disrupt the sense of self-cohesion, contribute to the incoherence of a self-narrative, or produce both disorders. A goal of this work is to specify the conditions under which such disorders occur.

It is important to keep in mind that there is no simple relationship between a child's subjective experience and the overt symptoms the child displays. Children respond differently to inner stresses and conflicts. Commonalities may emerge that are associated directly with neuropsychological deficits that produce specific dysfunctions. But this is not true of disorders of the self, where the same psychodynamics can generate different overt symptoms. Conversely, different psychodynamics may produce the same symptoms. For example, a child with dyslexia may be aggressive in school because she feels embarrassed by her inability to read, while similar embarrassment, in a different child, might lead to shyness and withdrawal. Conversely, a child's aggressive behavior may be the product of dyslexia or of AD/HD.

The third theme of the book concerns the modifications in the way we conceptualize the therapeutic process in treating children with a learning disorder. When asked by colleagues whether therapy with a patient who has a learning disorder is any different from therapy with a patient who does not have such a disorder, my first inclination has been to say that it is not significantly different. But, on reflection, I have come to realize that the answer to the question is that there are important differences.

While the technique of child therapy remains the same, the treatment process with these children must be conceptualized differently from traditional child psychotherapy. It cannot be structured as a process with a beginning, a middle, and an end, in which a set of transferences is worked through and resolved. Rather, the process is an open-ended one, in which many transactions occur between the therapist and the child. These transactions can be defined as "moments" (Pine, 1985) in which important interchanges take place. We can identify three types of moments: *concordant moments, complementary moments*, and *disjunctive moments*. During concordant moments, the therapist's attunement to the child's subjective experience is meant to help the child feel understood and supported. During the complementary moments, aspects of the transference/countertransference are played out, but with the difference that a distinction is made between those occasions when a child is displacing feelings about others onto the therapist and those in which the child is displaying the effects of the learning disorder through her behavior. During disjunctive moments, a rupture has occurred between the child and the therapist either because the negative transference has been activated or because the therapist's countertransference has gotten in the way. The therapist must then attempt to restore the concordant moments.

Several differences between the treatment of children with and without learning disorders are now revealed. First, the therapist must be aware of the effects of the learning disorder on the child and the symptoms the child displays. Second, during the complementary moments, the therapist must clearly distinguish between thoughts and behaviors that are caused by the learning disorder and those that are motivated by the child's reaction to the learning disorder. Children with learning disorders are commonly misunderstood because caregivers and therapists fail to consider the children's thoughts and behaviors as neurologically driven rather than motivated by psychological factors. Simply put, there is a failure to distinguish between "she won't" and "she can't." A child with dyslexia does not fail to learn to read because she *does not want* to learn but because she *cannot* learn.

Once I learned to think in these terms my work as a child therapist changed. Both my attitude toward the child and my responses to the caregivers were affected. Traditional psychodynamic developmental theories—including the early works by self psychologists—carried with them a subtle accusatory tone toward caregivers. They were blamed for their responses to the child, which were seen as causing the child's difficulties instead of being understood as caused by the child's difficulties. While clinicians claimed never to blame parents for their children's problems, they rationalized their understanding of the psychodynamics as resulting from the parent's own unconscious conflicts (cf. Miller, 1981).

In my practice now, the first things I want to know are the child's developmental history, the milestones, schooling, peer relationships, and the nature of the interaction within the family. To that end, I engage the parents as partners in the therapeutic process. I want their input. I also want to inform or educate them about the child's condition, so that they can collaborate in the child's treatment. In this partnership, I extend myself by getting information from teachers about the child's context. If there is any suggestion of academic or behavioral problems, I insist on neuropsychological or psychoeducational testing. It is imperative to detect learning disorders, since ignoring them raises the risk of not providing the patient with optimal interventions and of perpetuating a situation in which the environment continues to make demands that the child cannot meet.

It is only after I have gathered this information that I feel myself to be in a position to make a recommendation. That does not mean that I do not see the child. Of course I do. The child is the central character in the diagnostic process; her input is critical to what is to follow.

The conceptual framework I offer is meant to facilitate clinicians' approach to the clinical process in the treatment of patients with learning disorders. It is not intended as a comprehensive clinical theory or as a novel way to treat patients. It is an attempt to integrate the metapsychology of self psychology with a neuropsychological perspective. By clarifying the complex relationship between a child's learning disorders and the disorders of the self that at times emerge, I hope to shed light on aspects of the treatment process with these patients that may have been obscured by other paradigms. This framework can also assist those involved in the remediation of the child's deficits. For them, the obverse of what was said about child therapists applies, that is, they are only too aware of the child's neuropsychological deficits, but less so of the child's emotional condition. Keeping in mind the child's subjective experiences will help maximize the outcomes of their interventions.

## Psychoanalysis and Learning Disorders

### The Psychoanalytic Perspective

In my initial training, the existence of learning disorders as contributors to psychopathology was largely ignored. I was taught the traditional approach of Anna Freud (1962, 1965) and trained to apply her developmental profile to every child patient I saw. I learned to look at each child's ego functions, developmental lines (looking for arrests or regressions), defenses, and superego development. This perspective placed great emphasis on the caregiving role in the development of psychopathology. Spitz's (1945, 1946, 1951) psychotoxic factors were primarily factors in the environment that paved the way for a child's mental health or illness. His studies of hospitalism underscored the devastating impact of early separations on children's lives.

At the time, histories provided by parents were often considered suspect because they were biased by the parents' own psychopathology. No school reports were obtained. The outside world was left out as a context in which the child lived. It was recommended that parents be referred to another therapist so that they would not interfere with the therapeutic work. The issue of whether children formed transferences was vigorously debated, but eventually that battle was conceded to Melanie Klein. There was no doubt in our minds that children were capable of forming intense transferences and that it was in those areas that the work needed to be done.

When Mahler's (Mahler, Pine, & Bergman, 1975) work came along, I believed that I had found a comprehensive developmental framework in which to place my diagnostic thinking. The separation-individuation schema gave an organizing framework within which to see children's psychopathology. Her only acknowledgment of innate factors as contributory to psychopathology was in cases of autism, although she lumped those cases with those of symbiotic attachments (Mahler, 1968). I had been exposed to Kohut's work shortly before, but the full impact of that work was not immediately felt by me. In the long run, his influence was decisive for many reasons. First, it brought me even closer to the children's experience than I was able to get previously. His concept of empathy articulated what I had learned to do intuitively with children, knowing nothing about their lives outside the clinical setting. Of greatest importance was the shift that occurred in my view of parents and their role in the child's disturbance. Rather than simply seeing parents as intruders into the therapeutic process, I began to see them as potential allies. I could empathize with their distress and their struggles at coping with a difficult child.

Lichtenberg's *Psychoanalysis and Infant Research* (1983) opened the way to an empirical approach to child development. Although Mahler had sought to establish such an approach in her own work, she did not overcome the limitation of a reconstructive method in organizing her observations. Ultimately, her schema, based on regressive states of adults in analysis, was overlaid on her observations. In his book, Lichtenberg went beyond the reconstructive method by presenting an amplification of ego psychology. He sought for evidence in infancy research to support some of the tenets of ego psychology.

Stern's (1985) work represented a sharp break with traditional psychoanalytic developmental theories. By rejecting the assumption that a model of development could be established from the observation of regressed states of adult patients, he gave prominence to the body of infancy research. His work is a triumph of empirical observation in the establishment of a psychoanalytic developmental theory. His proposal of the emergent self as the first domain of development made it possible to integrate the findings of neuropsychology into a psychoanalytic perspective.

It is interesting to note that the seminal work of Chess and Thomas (1977, 1986) on temperament was never fully integrated into the psychodynamic perspective. While there was an acknowledgment of the contributions that a child's temperament makes to the fit between child and caregiver, its overall significance was never formally integrated into a psychoanalytic paradigm.

With the exception of proposals made by Weil (1970, 1973a, 1973b, 1977, 1978, 1985) and Greenspan (1981, 1988, 1989a, 1989b; Greenspan & Meisels, 1993), psychoanalytic theories have generally attributed learning disturbances to psychodynamic factors other than those of endowment. Weil took an ego psychological approach to the issue of differences in endowment and their effect on development. She conceptualized a "basic core" as constituting the child's primary autonomous ego apparatus. Variations in the basic core could result from a child's biological-genetic makeup and/or from neurophysiological immaturities or dysfunctions. She suggested that differences in perception, motility, and language development contribute significantly to ego functions and structures. In her terms, a learning disorder may be thought of as a deficit in "the primary autonomous ego apparatus." It represented an organically based deficit that manifested as an impaired psychological apparatus. Deficits affect the child's interaction with caregivers and influence caregivers' responses to the child. The psychopathology that emerges in these children is conceived as being the result of both sets of factors.

Greenspan is the only psychodynamic researcher who includes a theory of cognition in his theory of development. He takes a structural/ developmental approach that combines Piaget's cognitive theories with ego psychology. He proposes six stages of ego development and states, "the interplay between age-appropriate experiences and maturation of the central nervous system (CNS) ultimately determines the characteristics of the organizational capacity of each phase" (1989b, p. 4). According to Greenspan, infants organize their experiences along the interrelated dimensions of sensory and affective experience. For him, as for Piaget, the capacity for representational thought emerges around 18 months of age, at the time when language acquisition begins. The phase prior to 18 months is a preverbal and a pre-representational phase.

Weil's and Greenspan's fundamental assumptions are that, while ego development is contingent upon caregivers' emotional nurturing of the child, primary autonomous ego functions are part of each child's endowment. Deficits in endowment interfere with caregivers' ability to nurture the child, and the resulting psychopathology is attributed to that interference. For them, ego deficits interfere with learning, which in turn cause secondary conflicts in the child related to parental investment and expectations. A weakness of both these theories is their failure to incorporate a neuropsychological perspective into their explanations of the child's development. Weil, of course, did not have the data available to provide such integration. However, Greenspan, because of his preference for Piaget, has missed an opportunity to provide a more comprehensive view of development than the one he provides. Recognition should be given to Greenspan, for his work on early childhood disorders through his Zero to Three project, as well as the recently published *Clinical Practice Guidelines* of the Interdisciplinary Council on Developmental and Learning Disorders, which he chairs (Greenspan, 2000).

Rothstein and her associates (Rothstein, Benjamin, Crosby, & Eisenstadt, 1988) have sought to integrate neuropsychological concepts with psychoanalytic theory. They included a valuable comprehensive critical review of the psychoanalytic literature on learning disorders, recently updated in *Learning Disabilities and Psychic Conflict: A Psychoanalytic Casebook*, by Rothstein and Glenn (1999). This book is a compilation of the analyses of nine patients presumed to have a learning disability. Rothstein and Glenn demonstrate an appreciation of the importance of learning disabilities in personality development. They emphasize that patients' learning disabilities become entwined with their psychodynamics, in particular with the psychic conflicts associated with oedipal problems. While they recognize that the deficits have an impact on the child's relationships to others and to the context, it is their view that the focus of treatment should be the resolution of the conflicts associated with the child's symptoms (see also Egan & Kernberg, 1984).

In my own work, I initially tried to establish a link between the manifestation of a borderline disorder in a child and the presence of a severe learning disability. A careful reading of the psychoanalytic literature published through the early 1980s describing children identified as having a borderline disorder led me to conclude that in many instances the children had an undiagnosed learning disability (Palombo, 1983; Palombo & Feigon, 1984). It was my impression that often the symptoms the child displayed were the direct result of the learning disability. The most common cases were those of children with evident reading problems whose learning disability was interpreted as due to some form of inhibition. I stated:

> The etiology of borderline disorders is generally presumed to lie in a developmental arrest at an early age. Factors of poor or improper nurturance have been implicated as contributing to the disturbance. This view may not take sufficiently into account possible biogenetic or congenital factors. A growing body of evidence is developing that begins to support the hypothesis that such factors may, indeed, play a significant role in the development of the disturbance. (Palombo, 1982, p. 247)

This led me to suggest a redefinition of the childhood form of borderline disorders. I hypothesized that such disorders are best understood as related to developmental deficits in the child's primary autonomous ego apparatus. I proposed a consensus definition derived from the literature, which would limit the diagnosis of borderline conditions in childhood to those with severe learning disorders, discontinuing its use as a wastebasket category into which children whose symptoms derived from many different etiologies were tossed. In the preface of a book he edited titled *The Borderline Child*, Robinson (1983) stated: "In my opinion, ultimately most borderline children described in the literature and this volume will turn out to be at biogenetic risk for major mental illness and their variants." However, neither of these suggestions gained acceptance in the broader psychiatric community, nor were they reflected in the subsequent DSM manuals (see also Andrulonis, Glueck, Stroeble, Vogel, & Shapiro, 1980; Berg, 1992; Chethic, 1979; Famularo, Kinscherff, & Fenton, 1991; Fries, Nelson, & Woolf, 1980; Lofgren, Bemporad, King, Lindem, & O'Driscoll, 1991). In other publications, I have addressed the issues of transference and countertransference in the treatment of these children (Palombo, 1985, 1987, 1991, 1992, 1993, 1994).

More recently, my interest has turned to the emotional problems of children with nonverbal learning disabilities. In a first paper, I discussed the diagnostic and psychodynamic issues presented by these children (Palombo, 1995). In two subsequent papers, my colleague Anne Berenberg and I (Palombo & Berenberg, 1997, 1999) addressed treatment approaches with those children and working with their parents. In this series of papers, we attempted to integrate some neuropsychological constructs with psychodynamics. While these papers introduced some of the ideas that form the conceptual framework for this book, their focus was primarily on the developmental sequelae of learning disorders and their manifestations during treatment.

## *The Neuropsychological Perspective*

Paralleling the developments in psychoanalytic theory described above, equally significant developments occurred in pediatric neurology and neuropsychology. The concept of learning disabilities began with the identification of specific dysfunctional states that were analogous to the states of people who had suffered brain injuries. These states were labeled "minimal brain dysfunctions" (MBD) (Giffin, 1965; Wender, 1972). However, when symptoms could not be associated with specific anatomical brain changes, the term was replaced with the label "perceptual handicap." It was assumed that the source of the difficulty was a dysfunction in the perceptual system. This definition was also unsatisfactory, as it excluded many children whose dysfunctions were unrelated to their perceptual system (Bryan & Bryan, 1986). Since the concept of learning disorders is central to this work, I turn to a discussion of the definition of this term.

If we conceive of a hierarchy of neuropsychological disorders in children, we may posit that the set of *neurobehavioral disorders* is the broadest category of disorders, *learning disorders* are a subset of these disorders, and *learning disabilities* are a subset of learning disorders. *Neurobehavioral disorders* are generally defined by pediatric neurologists and neuropsychologists to include learning disorders, learning disabilities, as well as neurological conditions such as autism, mental retardation, Tourette's syndrome, and those resulting from acquired brain changes, such as strokes, lesions, and closed head injuries (see Figure 1.1).

*Learning disorders.* Learning disorders are a subset of the category of neurobehavioral disorders. Neuropsychologists tend to link their findings from testing with concepts that attempt to correlate behaviors with brain systems. They regard learning disorders as related to problems in motor, perceptual, memory, attention, executive function, language, or socioemotional functioning. Their findings are interpreted as indicating that, for example, a child has problems with gross or fine coordination (motor), visual or auditory discrimination (perception), visual or auditory memory (memory), distractibility or inattention (attention), disorganization (executive function), verbal or written expression (language), or peer relationship or affect processing problems (socioemotional).

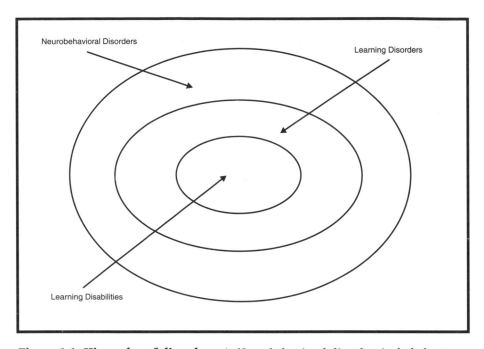

**Figure 1.1. Hierarchy of disorders:** A. *Neurobehavioral disorders* include learning disorders, learning disabilities, and a wide range of brain-based disorders, such as autism, mental retardation, Tourette's syndrome, genetic disorders, and disorders that result from head injuries or infections of the brain. B. *Learning disorders* include learning disabilities such as language-based learning disabilities, AD/HD, executive function disorders, nonverbal learning disabilities, Asperger's disorder, and motor problems that involve problems of large and small muscle coordination. Excluded are autism, mental retardation, Tourette's syndrome, genetic disorders, and disorders that result from head injuries or infections of the brain. C. *Learning disabilities* include language-based learning disabilities: problems in language reception, such as dyslexia and central auditory processing problems; expressive language problems, such as problems in verbal or written expression.

Learning disorders are defined as neuropsychological deficits, or weakness due to genetic, heritable, or environmental disruption in brain function, that are found in children with at least average intelligence. These deficits must be unrelated to a brain dysfunction caused by lesions, head injuries, or other physical impairments of the brain (Coplin & Morgan, 1988, p. 614). The dysfunction interferes with the child's capacity to perform in the social, academic, or emotional context or in more than one of these domains. Deficits may be found in (a) *sensorimotor function*, such as impairments in fine or gross motor coordination; (b) *perceptual functions*, such impairments in visual or auditory perception; (c) *mem-*

*ory function*, such as problems in short- or long-term memory, explicit or implicit memory; (d) *attention*, such as problems with distractibility or deficits in the capacity for attention; (e) *executive functions*, such as difficulties in organization or the capacity to initiate and implement goals or plans; (f) *language*, such as difficulties in receptive or expressive language; (g) *nonverbal organization and communications*, such as difficulties with new situations and problem solving or understanding nonverbal social cues; and (h) *social-emotional*, such as problems in interaction with peers and in the regulation of affect states. Based on a profile of the child's neuropsychological strengths and weaknesses, the diagnosis of a learning disorder is made.

Pennington (1991) discusses five subtypes of learning disorders, each of which he believes is correlated with a specific set of the brain systems:

1. *Phonological processing difficulties*: These are related to the ability to produce different phonemes that emerge in the babbling phase of speech development. Included are difficulties in the perception and the production of discrete phonemic segments. The disorder that characterizes this processing difficulty is dyslexia.

2. *Spatial cognition difficulties*: These involve difficulties in the visual and spatial systems and include functions such as spatial imagery, spatial construction, object localization and identification, and short- and long-term visual or spatial memory. Disorders most often associated with these dysfunctions are specific difficulties in mathematics and handwriting.

3. *Social cognition difficulties*: These appear as problems in the recognition and perception of emotional expression in social contexts. Included are problems in the recognition of social cues and prosody, which is the ability to recognize the meaning of feelings as expressed through vocal inflections and intonations. The disorders commonly associated with these difficulties are, in the extreme form, autism, and in less extreme form, Asperger's syndrome.

4. *Executive function difficulties*: These disorders indicate problems in the areas of organization, self-monitoring, and goal-setting that interfere with the capacity to perform complex tasks that involve planning. The disorder most commonly associated with this dysfunction is attention-deficit.

5. *Acquired long-term memory disorders*: These are disorders that affect implicit (procedural memory), that is, memory for skills

like driving a car, hitting a tennis ball, or riding a bicycle, as well
as disorders in explicit (declarative memory), that is, to memory
for word meanings, word retrieval, and memory of specific
events in one's personal past. The disorders commonly associated with this dysfunction are the amnesias.

Pennington contends that these five domains account for "all or nearly
all the learning disorders encountered by most clinicians" (p. 5). He excludes motor problems because they manifest primarily as handwriting
problems. I use Pennington's framework for defining learning disorders
but exclude acquired memory problems because they are encountered
infrequently by most practitioners.

An important distinction needs to be made between a *deficit* in a domain of cognition and a set of *strengths and weaknesses* in those domains. A deficit implies that the particular module associated with a brain
system is impaired or damaged and therefore dysfunctional. On the other
hand, the description of strength or weakness in a module implies that
a continuum of functioning exists within and across modules, that is, as
measured and compared to other children of the same age, the child's
functioning in that domain may be one or more standard deviations above
or below the mean for that age. In this work, I will refer to both dysfunctions as neuropsychological deficits, even though this usage of the
term may simplify what is a highly complex set of issues.

*Learning disabilities.* Learning disabilities are a subcategory of learning disorders. Educators, educational psychologists, and neuropsychologists use the term *learning disabilities* in their assessments of children
eligible for school special education services. The term is generally defined as a neurologically based condition in which a discrepancy exists
between a person's competence and performance in specific areas of academic functioning as measured by standardized tests. For a child to be
considered to have a learning disability, the child must be of at least average intelligence and should not have a medically diagnosed brain dysfunction (Strang & Casey, 1994).

Public Law 94-142, Education for All Handicapped Children (EHA), enacted in 1975, mandated services for all children with learning disabilities. A definition was then adopted that was thought to cover all conditions; however, that definition proved to have limitations and was
eventually broadened and replaced (Abrams, 1987; Hammill, 1993; Hammill, Leigh, McNutt, & Larsen, 1987; Kavale & Forness, 2000). In 1990,
Congress reauthorized PL 94-142 as the Individuals with Disabilities Ed-

ucation Act (IDEA), PL 101-476. In the process the concept was redefined. The latest definition incorporated in that act reads as follows:

> The term "specific learning disability" means a disorder in one or more of the basic psychological processes involved in understanding or in using language, spoken or written, which disorder may manifest itself in imperfect ability to listen, think, speak, read, write, spell, or do mathematical calculations. Such a term includes such conditions as perceptual disabilities, brain injury, minimal brain dysfunction, dyslexia, and developmental aphasia. Such a term does not include a learning problem that is primarily the result of visual, hearing, or motor disabilities, of mental retardation, of emotional disturbance, or of environmental, cultural, or economic disadvantage. (Individuals with Disabilities Education Act Amendments of 1997, PL 105-17, June 4, 1997, 11 stat. 37 [codified as amended at 20 U.S.C. ~ 1401 (26)]) (Hammill & Bryant, 1998, p. 3)

With regard to the incidence of learning disabilities, the National Information Center for Children and Youth with Disabilities states:

> Many different estimates of the number of children with learning disabilities have appeared in the literature (ranging from 1% to 30% of the general population). In 1987 the Interagency Committee on Learning Disabilities concluded that 5% to 10% is a reasonable estimate of the percentage of persons affected by learning disabilities. The U.S. Department of Education (1998) reported that more than 5% of all school-aged children received special education services for learning disabilities and that in the 1996-97 school year over 2.6 million children with learning disabilities were served. Differences in estimates reflect variations in the definition. (1999)

Often only children with severe learning disabilities are identified while most of those who suffer milder forms of disability remain unidentified. Most commonly, emotional and behavioral problems mask the deficit, leaving educators and caregivers in the dark as to the cause of the child's underachievement. Those children are often labeled as unmotivated or as having a conduct disorder. A different standard is often applied to boys than to girls. Boys are often overrepresented in this population, and because they often present with behavior problems that cloud their difficulties, the focus shifts to their conduct rather than to their academic performance. Learning disabilities in girls are often overlooked because the expectations for achievement in some academic subjects, such as mathematics, are generally lower than they are for boys. (The definition of learning disorders used in this work is broader than the definition of learning disabilities used in arriving at the estimates given above. Consequently, the number of children affected is certainly greater, although no specific data are available.)

Most educational and school psychologists use some variant of an information-processing paradigm in their diagnostic work. The basic assumption of the paradigm is that all knowledge is represented, stored, and processed through a set of mental codes. It presumes that there is an input register through which the information is obtained, a central processor, and an output or response system (Daelhler & Bukatko, 1985, p. 87).

Diagnosticians who use this approach to testing examine the child's performance in various academic tasks. Following the definition above, they examine the child's ability to *listen, speak, read, write, do mathematics*, and *reason*. A school psychologist may find that a child has problems with auditory discrimination (listening), that is, is unable to distinguish between two words that have similar sounds, or has a speech problem (speaking), or cannot decode printed words (reading), or has poor handwriting or cannot express herself in written language (writing), or has problems with multiplication or long division (mathematics), or finally, has problems organizing her thoughts (reasoning).

Finally, the definition given in *DSM-IV* (APA, 1994) compounds the confusion around definitions by avoiding a definition of learning disabilities and referring only to learning disorders and communication disorders. The definition of learning disorders is narrower than the conditions that, by law, are defined as learning disabilities, while the definition of communication is more inclusive than the disorders allowed by law. Consequently, the *DSM-IV* definitions are restricted in their usefulness to professionals in the learning disabilities field because of the scope of diagnostic options it offers, although these definitions form the basis for most of the research on comorbidity conducted by investigators in psychiatry.

In actual practice and in school settings, both legal and psychiatric definitions are applied differently in different settings. Some settings rely on what is called the *discrepancy criterion*, while others rely on *deficit models*. State law often mandates these criteria. Those that rely on the discrepancy criterion determine the existence of a learning disability in a number of ways. A learning disability is found if the child is underachieving in a specific academic area as compared to other children that child's age. For example, a child behind peers in reading by two grade levels would be considered to have a learning disability and be eligible for services. A discrepancy may also be found to exist if the findings in a test battery indicate that the child is underperforming on some tests while performing at a higher level on other tests, again as compared to the norms established for the age group. Finally, a discrepancy may be found to exist if the child's performance on standardized tests differs from classroom achievement. The *DSM-IV* definition is based on this last criterion.

Why focus on learning disorders? There are several reasons for my choice of learning disorders over learning disabilities in this work. First, I believe it to be essential to anchor our understanding of these disorders in a paradigm that can provide brain-based explanations for the symptoms the children manifest. Neuropsychological theories, at this time, provide the best explanatory linkages between hypothesized brain dysfunctions and those symptoms. While the discrepancy criterion, based on information theory, is useful in making practical decisions as to which child should receive services, it does not further the scientific end of finding causal relationships for the disorders. Second, the definition of learning disability has, in the past, excluded such disorders as attention-deficit/hyperactivity disorder (AD/HD) (see Chapter 8). It currently does not permit the inclusion of executive function disorders or of nonverbal learning disabilities. This restriction not only excludes disorders that legitimately belong under that definition but also denies services to some children who ought to receive them (Gregg, 2000). Third, the status of Asperger's disorder, which is currently designated as a psychiatric disorder, might be clarified. The inclusion of this disorder under learning disorders would anticipate consolidation, in the future, of several entities, such as nonverbal learning disabilities and conduct disorders. These entities all identify problems in children's social relationships that may come under an inclusive designation of *social learning disability* (Denckla, 1983).

## Integrating the Psychoanalytic and Neuropsychological Perspectives

One way to think about integrating the psychoanalytic perspective with the neuropsychological is to see the problem much as Freud saw it in his early work over a century ago (1895). When his patients presented him with a set of symptoms, Freud, as a neurologist, first looked for possible causes in brain dysfunctions. When he excluded patients who obviously suffered from neurological disorders, he was left with a group of patients who displayed symptoms that appeared to be caused by other factors. He did not assume that brain function made no contribution to the symptoms they manifested; he simply had no way of associating the symptoms to any known neurological condition. Freud's *Project* was an early attempt to carry out a neuroscience project that would provide a framework to explain the basis for all thoughts and behaviors, whether they originated from brain dysfunctions or from psychodynamic factors.

As Basch (1975) pointed out, the objective in the *Project* was to provide a neurological explanation for psychological events; it failed in part because the neurology of the time was not sufficiently advanced to explain some of the phenomena Freud observed. In particular, it failed, according to Basch, because Freud could not find an explanation for what is called today the defense of disavowal. He could not explain how people who had no specific brain dysfunction and who were not delusional could fail to see reality and could have beliefs that were contrary to reality. Freud then shifted to making a distinction between neurology and psychology to explain neurotic symptoms. He distinguished motivated behaviors or symptoms that did not have a neurological basis from those that seemed to stem from unmotivated behavior, such as those associated with aphasia, a disorder that is neurologically based.

Interestingly, Freud was mindful of the immense role genetic heritage plays in development. He chose not to address its impact because he took its significance for granted and felt it would be more productive to attend to an aspect of development to which insufficient attention had been given.

> I take this opportunity of defending myself against the mistaken charge of having denied the importance of innate (constitutional) factors because I have stressed that of infantile impressions. A charge such as this arises from the restricted nature of what men look for in the field of causation; in contrast to what ordinarily holds good in the real world, people prefer to be satisfied with a single causative factor. Psychoanalysis has talked a lot about the accidental factors in aetiology and little about the constitutional ones; but this is only because it was able to contribute something fresh to the former, while, to begin with, it knew no more than was commonly known about the latter. We refuse to posit any contrast in principle between the two sets of etiological factors; on the contrary, we assume that the two sets regularly act jointly

in bringing about the observed result. . . . [Endowment and chance] determine a man's fate—rarely or never one of these powers alone. The amount of etiological effectiveness to be attributed to each of them can only be arrived at in every individual case separately. These cases may be arranged in a series according to the varying proportions in which the two factors are present, and the series will no doubt have its extreme cases. (Freud, 1912, p. 99, footnote #2)

In recent years, great strides have been made in the direction of integrating the findings of the neurosciences into psychoanalytic theory. These efforts may be divided into two approaches (Palombo, 1996b). One explains mental activity through the use of information theory, i.e., the functions of the mind may be modeled on the workings of a computer— it is like a machine. Basch, for one, posited a computational theory of mind. Mental activity, he believed, reflects brain function, with the brain serving as an information-processing organ (Basch, 1976). Others have proposed a model premised on the belief that minds are best understood as functioning like organisms. In *Mapping the Mind*, Levin (1991) attempts to correlate specific psychological/psychoanalytic variables with neuroanatomical-neurophysiological events. Hadley, in her epilogue to Lichtenberg's book, *Psychoanalysis and Motivation*, attempts to demonstrate that brain systems undergird Lichtenberg's five motivational systems. Schore, in his monumental work, *Affect Regulation and the Origin of the Self: The Neurobiology of Emotional Development*, attempts to integrate "psychological studies of the critical interactive experiences that influence development of the socioemotional functions and neurobiological studies of the ontogeny of postnatally maturing brain structures that come to regulate these same functions." Finally, Pally, in an excellent series of papers written for psychoanalysts, outlines the functions of different brain systems, such as perception, memory, and emotional processing (Pally, 1997a, 1997b, 1997c, 1998a, 1998b).

While each of these authors has addressed the problem using different assumptions, a consensus is emerging among psychoanalytic theorists that the basic assumptions of an evolutionary psychology perspective should underlie all future attempts at explaining mental activities. A good example is found in Kandel (1998), who states that we have evolved a set of brain systems that allow us to adapt to the environment in which we live.

Furthermore, increasingly psychoanalytic investigators have paid attention to the contributions that genetic and heritable factors make to the normal development and psychopathology of children. Robust evidence exists to support the hypothesis that autism and schizophrenia are strongly linked to genetic factors. Affective disorders, panic disorders, and obsessive-compulsive disorders are similarly suspected of having a genetic basis. In addition, factors such as temperament and neuropsychological deficits are now thought to be heritable. The integration of knowledge from other disciplines, particularly the neurosciences, into psychoanalysis presents major challenges to psychodynamic theory. The challenge is to conceptualize the interface between brain function (and brain dysfunctions) and behavior in a way that is compatible with our psychological understanding of development. In the case of learning disorders, the task is to create a theory that integrates the impact of neurological deficits on a child's development and on the ultimate shape of the adult's personality.

Recent developments in neurobiology and our understanding of brain function have changed our perspective on the limits that endowment imposes on the development of our competencies. Not long ago endowment was viewed as fixed, much like the wiring and hardware of a computer. This view colored the anticipation of the possible changes that could occur both during development and as a result of interventions. Innate factors were thought to set a ceiling on what a person could attain. While as practitioners we knew that we were very poor at predicting our patients' future outcomes, we were surprised when some of them overcame to a remarkable extent what at first appeared to be serious limitations. In those instances, we fell back on explanations such as the capacity to compensate or the brain's malleability and plasticity. But now, the findings of molecular biology open new avenues to explain these phenomena and give greater hope to those affected, confirming the validity of our vague explanations. The brain's capacity to adapt appears much greater than was previously thought. Context is now thought to play a significant role in development. Since brain function is affected and modified by the context, a contextual interactional approach seems best suited to explain the developmental phenomena we observed.

In conclusion, for too long psychoanalysis remained isolated from other disciplines (Palombo, 2000). This isolation resulted in the impoverishment of the explanatory power of the paradigm and was detrimental to patients who required the knowledge possessed by other disciplines for a full understanding of their problems. Fortunately, now doors have been opened to other bodies of knowledge that will enrich psychoanalytic theory. This book takes a step in the direction of such an integration by incorporating the larger body of knowledge encompassed by neuropsychology (Kandel, 1998; Olds & Cooper, 1997; Shane, 1984).

# I

# DEVELOPMENTAL
# CONSIDERATIONS

# 2

# LEARNING DISORDERS AND THE SENSE OF SELF

THE SELF IS REGARDED BY self psychologists as the psychological structure that undergirds the totality of a person's experiences, both conscious and unconscious. It represents the subjective dimension of the
person's psychic organization. The cohesive self is enduring and stable.
It represents a sense of intactness, wholeness, and vitality. Once firmly
established, it embodies the person's values and world view (Kohut, 1971;
Palombo, 1976; Wolf, 1988).

It is important to distinguish the concepts of "sense of self" and "self."
When we speak of the "self," it brings to mind an entity. We are, in fact,
referring to "the person" (Basch, 1983). By "the sense of self," I mean the
experience of *being a self* or *being a person*. In what follows, I will
refer to the sense of self or to being a self in order to maintain the focus on the patient's subjective experience. In speaking of disorders of
the self, I am referring to disturbances in the sense of self or the self-
narrative (see Table 2.1).

The development of the sense of self may be regarded as a set of
phase-specific experiences that reflect the intersection of the child's endowment and his responses to the community's expectations. Each child
brings to the world a set of competencies that represent his endowment.
Among these are neuropsychological strengths and weaknesses. Other
competencies are the capacity to feel, to think, to learn and to act; the
capacity to generate and interpret signs; the capacity for self-awareness,

**TABLE 2.1**
**Learning Disorders and the Sense of Self**

---

1. THE SENSE OF SELF
   a. The "self" refers to the person, while the "sense of self" or "being a self" refers to the person's subjective experience.
   b. Being a self consists of having a set of endowments that are embedded in a context. The context constitutes the physical and emotional milieu in which the child lives.
   c. Each person's experiences are filtered through his endowment and the context in which he exists.

2. THE SENSE OF SELF-COHESION
   a. Human beings are motivated to maintain a sense of self-cohesion in order to maintain a sense of well-being.
   b. A set of positive affect states, such as feelings of well-being, wholeness, and vitality, are associated with the sense of self-cohesion.
   c. For children with neuropsychological deficits, the presence of complementary or compensatory functions may help preserve the sense of self-cohesion and can act as protective factors against the loss of self-cohesion.

3. THE CONTEXT
   a. The context provides complementary functions that enhance or help maintain self-cohesion. These functions may be provided in the form of:
      i. Selfobject functions that facilitate the integration of affects into the sense of self.
      ii. Adjunctive functions that can
         (1) Complement immature or deficient neuropsychological modules,
         (2) Enhance or extend a person's capacity to successfully complete specific tasks.
   b. Within the context the child may develop compensations. These take the form of self-complementing functions that may permit the child to:
      i. Utilize selfobjects functions in the service of self-regulation and cohesion maintenance,
      ii. Utilize cognitive strengths or strategies to enhance the attainment of goals or completion of tasks.

---

self-criticism, self-control, and self-interpretation; and the capacity for attachment to others. Furthermore, people are capable of a sense of privacy, of being in error, of having motives of which they are unconscious. These competencies are grounded in each person's endowment and result in the accrual of learned habits, as well as defenses, compensatory structures, and aggregated functions. These functions may find expression in beliefs, desires, feelings, or actions. In referring to learning disorders, I refer to deficits in a particular area of these neuropsychological competencies.

Since each person is endowed with different capacities for cognition, perception, affectivity, memory, motor function, linguistic, and other abilities, in a sense each person's experience is unique and unlike that of any other person. Yet endowment cannot be isolated from the context in which the person emerges. Alone, it does not define the totality of the person's experiences. The child's endowment also interpenetrates the child's experience. Conceptualizing development in this way represents a paradigm shift from traditional models of development. Such a model "of gene-environment interaction emphasize[s] a dialectic between genetically timed events and biological substrate with environment and experience such that each influences the other, and the ensuing development is neither so linear or staged nor so intrinsically progressive and predictable" (Mayes, 1999, p. 171).

To be a self is to be a member of a human community that constitutes the context in which the child is raised. A person in the absence of a community that represents the context within which the person exists is a meaningless abstraction. In contrast to Mahler's view that maturity entails both separation and individuation, I maintain that the mature person, while distinguishable from others, is not separable from others (Colapietro, 1989, p. 78). That is, a person cannot be separated from the context within which he is embedded, even though he can certainly be distinguished from others by the individuality and uniqueness of his personality.

The context in which each child is raised interpenetrates his experiences. It is constituted of the social, cultural, and historical milieu that complements each person's immature or deficient capacity to function independently. Complementary functions are functions that others, in the child's context, provide so that the child can maintain a sense of self-cohesion. Among these complementary functions are the *selfobject* and *adjunctive* functions that significant others provide. Selfobject functions include approval, admiration, regulation of affect states, or a sense of

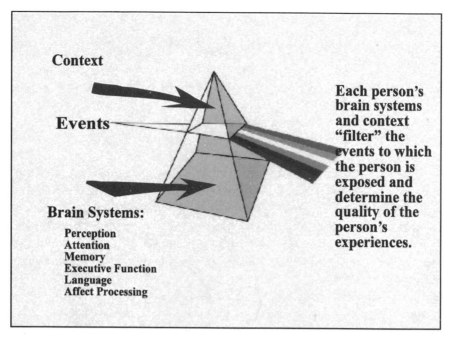

**Figure 2.1.** The context and the child's brain systems act as a prism through which experiences pass or are filtered. The result is that what the child encodes about the experience has a uniqueness that makes it distinct from what others exposed to the same event encode.

belonging to a community of like-minded others. Adjunctive functions are part of the supports the child needs in order to survive.

Before turning to a discussion of these functions, let me comment on self-experience and self-cohesion.

## The Sense of Self and Self-experience

To be a self entails more than being a passive recipient of external inputs, a simple register or wax tablet on which experience is inscribed. Each child's context and neuropsychological strengths and weaknesses act as filters of self-experience or as a prism through which events pass (see Figure 2.1). Each child's experience of the world is different from that of every other child; the greater the neuropsychological differences the more different the experience will be. Much as a prism breaks up light into different colors of the spectrum, so the child's context and neuropsychological endowment color his experiences. The material out of which the prism is made has a refractive index that affects the colors that emerge. For the child with cognitive or affective deficits, events are refracted so that some are highlighted while others are ignored or discounted. In a sense, a child with a learning disorder will fail to "see" some events to which he is exposed or will process them differently from his peers. Such a child does not acquire the information necessary to view the world as others do. His view will be discordant from that of his peers. As I will discuss later, the child with a learning disorder does not necessarily distort the reality to which he is exposed; rather, his experience of that reality is discordant because neuropsychological givens lead him to process the event differently from others. Consequently, the meanings he draws from those experiences will be different from those of his peers.

Recent studies on the way the mind encodes and stores information into memory lend support to the view that each person's experience is determined by his state of mind at the time it is encoded. The principle involved was formulated by Tulving, a prominent researcher on memory. Called the *encoding specificity principle*, it states in part that "the specific way a person thinks about, or encodes, an event determines what 'gets into' the engram" (Schacter, 1996, p. 60). The engram is the memory trace left of the experience. This memory trace is not found in a single location; instead it is widely distributed among different regions of the brain. It is formed by linking together what Damasio calls "convergence zones" that bind together fragments of perceptual experience (Schacter, 1996, p. 86). I propose that the intersection of the context and the neuropsychological differences that children with learning disorders bring to their experiences accentuate the uniqueness of the encoded experiences. Ultimately, both contribute to the shape of the sense of self and to whether the child develops a cohesive sense of self.

## The Sense of Self and Self-cohesion

A primary motive that engages a person's sense of self is the desire for self-cohesion. Kohut (1978) proposed that infants are generally endowed with a capacity for a *cohesive sense of self*. Some do not have this capacity because of serious deficits in their endowment. These infants may go on to develop schizophrenia or autism or may suffer from severe neurological disorders.

The concept of self-cohesion is used descriptively to characterize a state of self-consolidation (Stolorow, Brandchaft, & Atwood, 1987, p. 90). Self-cohesion is not a static state but a dynamic one that represents the organizing capacities that are always in play to synthesize and integrate self-experiences.Across the life cycle, the sense of cohesion is maintained as a result of the success a person has in synthesizing new experiences with old ones, in reworking old experiences, in reinterpreting them in the light of new ones, and in maintaining a level of attachment to those who provide selfobject functions. Maintaining self-cohesion does not involve striving for a stable homeostatic or nirvana-like state. Rather, it is a dynamic, active process of continual movement from destabilization to restabilization.

Learning disorders may disrupt the sense of self-cohesion in several ways.The child's sense of self-cohesion may be disrupted by his responses to his learning disorder, or the learning disorder itself may interfere with the capacity for self-cohesion. The movement from destabilization to restabilization is complicated by neuropsychological strengths and deficits. Depending on the nature and severity of the deficits and of the context's responses to those deficits, the swings between stability and instability may be much greater than in children without those deficits. For example, a child with a sensorimotor problem whose sense of balance is tenuous will have more difficulty learning to walk than a child who is agile and well endowed in that area. For the former child, the first steps will be halting and tentative. This child will not venture out into the world feeling physically confident and self-assured. His poor coordination may form a nucleus of hesitancy and uncertainty at facing life tasks that will be central to this child's personality. The resulting sense of instability, however, may later be counterbalanced by good intellectual capacities that lead to academic successes. Restabilization may then occur as the child finds his footing in the arena of academic accomplishments.

## Complementary Functions

Viewed from the perspective of the child's subjective experience, the context provides three types of complementary functions that are essential for the development of a sense of cohesion: *selfobject functions, adjunctive functions,* and *compensatory functions.*These functions may act as protective factors that prevent a child with a learning disorder from developing a disorder of the self or, if absent, may place the child at risk for the development of a disorder of the self (Anthony, 1987; Cohler, 1987).

The concept of "complementarity" has its roots in several intellectual traditions. In psychoanalysis the concept was suggested by Racker to describe an aspect of the transference patients form to a therapist (Racker, 1968, 1972). It is the aspect of the therapeutic relationship in which the therapist responds to the patient in a manner that replicates an old relationship. In the cognitive literature, Vygotsky refers to the "zone of proximal development" as a region in which adults provide the child with the support he needs to accomplish a task (Vygotsky, 1986, p. 187). Similarly, Bruner speaks of the "Language Acquisition Support System" (LASS) that caregivers provide a child to permit the acquisition of language (Bruner, 1983, p. 39).

In this work, I use the concept of complementarity to cover all of these senses. However, my focus is on the child's subjective perception of the effects these supports have. The child may or may not be aware of the presence of the supports. In fact, it is likely that most often the child will be unaware of them. What he will experience is a sense of self-cohesion when they are present and discomfort or failure in their absence. I consider three types of complementary functions: selfobject functions, adjunctive functions, and compensation.

### Selfobject Functions

At its simplest level, the concept of a selfobject provides a mode of thinking about one form of complementarity. In self psychology the concept of "selfobject" has been useful in delineating the ways in which others provide psychological functions necessary for a person to maintain a sense of self-cohesion. In other words, the human context becomes a part of the person's sense of self. Most often those functions operate silently and outside the person's awareness. Even though they are provided by another person, the subject experiences them as within and part of the sense of self.

"Selfobject," one of Kohut's (1991) most seminal concepts, was introduced to describe a particular aspect of the relationship between caregivers and child. The child experiences the caregiver as a selfobject as long as the caregiver is empathically responsive to the child's psychic needs. It is in the nature of selfobject experiences that so long as an empathic connectedness exists through which requisite functions are performed, the child experiences a sense of wholeness and intactness. The child has no awareness that any function is being performed, much less any awareness of the source or location of the performing agent. Only when the functions are absent do discomfort and awareness that something is amiss occur. Eventually, some selfobject functions are internalized and the capacity to maintain internal harmony is developed, although one can never totally dispense with the need for selfobject functions.

Selfobject functions, therefore, are psychological functions that are experienced as part of or within the self. People are not born with these functions but aspects of them are eventually internalized into the matrix of the self as structures. These structures within the self represent enduring functions that accrue to the self as a result of the internalization of experiences with significant others. They are essential for a child to sustain the sense of self-cohesion and integration. Kohut drew an analogy between the human need for selfobject functions and the human need for an environment that includes oxygen. Without oxygen, people suffocate. The awareness of the need for the function is most urgently felt when a person is deprived of it. It is then that the means to sustain a sense of well-being ceases to exist. At other times, as with oxygen, when the function is available, it is taken for granted.

There is a duality in the use of the concept of the selfobject functions as discussed below. In the first sense, it describes the complementary psychological functions caregivers provide. In the second sense, it specifies a narrative theme that organizes the child's experience. In the first sense, it describes phenomena that may be universal and that characterize all caregiver-child relationships; in the second, it gives a culture-bound thematic content to the child's self-experience. Other cultures or social/religious groups may assign other meanings to these experiences and incorporate them as themes in their myths. Three common selfobject functions are *idealizing, mirroring*, and *alter-ego*.

*Idealizing selfobject functions: The caregivers as idealized objects.* Children require caregivers to function psychologically as protectors and as providers of emotional support. Caregivers are responsible for seeing to it that the child not only feels safe from external dangers but is also protected from being overwhelmed by internal emotional upheavals. For the child to experience such feelings of safety, he must have faith that the caregivers are sufficiently powerful to assure him that he is safe. The success of the caregivers in providing that context is experienced by the child as resulting from the caregivers' omnipotence. When the caregivers' interventions are successful, the child experiences them as powerful and effective and feels soothed, comforted, and calmed.

In addition, caregivers make sure that the child's excitement and over-stimulation do not lead him to become overwhelmed. Their efforts are directed at modulating and regulating the child's affect states. These interventions can result in the internalization of self-control, self-discipline, and self-regulation. An extension of this function is the caregivers' transmission of the content of the culture's values and ideals, which also regulate conduct. Transmission is mediated by the respect and admiration that caregivers expect of their children. When internalized, multiple experiences around cultural expectations become consolidated into a value system and a set of ideals that serve as guides in the child's life. They give a sense of purpose to the pursuit of goals and a joyous vitality in the manner in which they are pursued.

The specific ways in which children with learning disorders experience their caregivers will vary depending on the type and severity of the deficit. Some caregivers may have problems similar to those of their children, or their capacity to empathize with the child may be limited. The impact of their unavailability will be felt by the child as a failure in the caregivers" capacity to have empathy with the child's experiences. However, what is often the case with children with learning disorders is that their caregivers are able and willing to provide for the child's needs, but the child is prevented from making use of their caregiving functions by the learning disorder. For example, a child with problems in affect regulation because of an AD/HD may be in desperate need of a firm but kind, idealizable adult who can impose limits by soothing, calming, and modulating the child's mood swings. The caregiver may try to intervene, sensing the child's need, but the child may experience the intervention as harsh, controlling, or punitive. The caregiver is aware that the child may be endangering himself by getting out of control, but the child feels driven to behave as he does. When the caregiver feels compelled to intervene massively, by either physically containing the child or threatening punishment, the child becomes convinced that the adult is unfair or arbitrary. The connection between the child and the caregiver is lost. The child can no longer experience the caregiver in a positive way and any hope of a selfobject function being performed is lost. The subsequent de-idealization of the caregiver by the child leads to a perception of the caregiver as arbitrary or cruel. In such situations, a caregiver's capacity to remain empathic with the child's experience is often dependent upon the caregiver's understanding of the motives for the child's behaviors. Often caregivers do not understand or lose sight of the fact that the child's behavior is not motivated by a desire to be difficult or oppositional but instead reflects the neuropsychological deficit. The child may end up feeling frustrated and unable to understand the motives behind the caregivers' intervention.

*Mirroring selfobject functions: The child is cherished by caregivers.* For self-esteem to develop, children require that their caregivers cherish and affirm their unique specialness and treat them as if they were the center of the caregivers' universe. When these responses are successful, the child experiences a sense of worth and of positive self-regard. Having been respected and approved of by caregivers, the child can receive their praises and compliments as authentic. These experiences result in a sense of dignity and self-respect. They may result in a sense of poise, self-confidence, and self-assurance. The child is then able to pursue novel experiences and feel encouraged to attempt to master challenges that stretch his reach. What results is a sense of self-cohesion and self-respect that is the hallmark of positive self-regard.

Here again, the experiences of a child with a learning disorder are variable. Some children develop early on an awareness of the deficits in their functioning. For these children, caregivers' praise and admiration have little effect. Having compared themselves to other children whom they perceive as more capable than themselves, these children develop the conviction that they are flawed. This conviction results not only from other children's teasing and taunting comments but also from a tendency to be self-critical and to view themselves negatively. For these children, caregivers' praise and support are discounted because they feel their caregivers wish to be kind and to spare them the harsh reality of how defective they truly are. If a child can find an area in which to excel in a way that feels authentic and be recognized by those whom he considers to really count, that experience may undo some of those feelings. If not, no amount of praise from the caregiver can produce the intended positive experience.

Another variation of mirroring in children with learning disorders is seen in those children who cling to their parents' adoration of them in the face of failure. These children, whose infantile grandiosity is overinflated, do not feel that they are out of step with their peers; rather, their peers are thought to be out of step with them. The reality of their failure is attributed to the incompetence of others. We shall see this variation in the case of Joel,* a seven-and-a-half-year-old boy with dyslexia, an

*See Chapter 7, p. 134.

only child who was adored and indulged by his parents. His view was that the teachers were dumb because they could not teach him to read.

*Alter-ego selfobject functions. The child's bond to others.* Finally, the experience of a common bond with others that ties all human beings together and that leads to feelings of kinship with others is critical to the healthy development of all children, but particularly to the child with a learning disorder. The experiences of being intact, of feeling healthy and complete in one's endowment, provide a sense of well-being and wholesomeness without which we can feel dehumanized. The acquisition of alter-ego self-object functions is most problematic for children with learning disorders.

We derive our sense of humanity by feeling a kinship with others to whom we are connected and whom we experience to be like us. But when we are thrown into a context where we feel ourselves to be so different, so unlike others, our sense of the humanity is devastatingly threatened. Such experiences are common to refugees who arrive in a country and a culture that is totally foreign to them. Children with learning disorders have similar experiences. Although at first their experience of the world around them appears to them to be similar to those of others, they soon discover that others respond differently—not only to the world but also to them. A sense of estrangement sets it. The child begins to pay attention to critical comments made to him. He is puzzled by the disparities between his behaviors and those of others. He soon begins to wonder about those differences. The seeds are planted for feeling different from others and for seeing that difference as a negative attribute. As experiences pile up, the child may conclude that he is quite unlike all others in his community. His sense of being different from other children is experienced negatively. To be different means to be an outsider or to be rejected by the group. To be an outsider also means being "weird," an alien in a foreign culture. This feeling may result in feeling dehumanized, or worse, sub-human.

If the child requires assistance with tasks that his peers master without help, or if he needs remediation or is placed in special education, he sees this as confirmation that his sense of difference is negatively valued. The stigma attached to being labeled as having a learning disability may lead to feelings of shame or humiliation, reinforcing the sense of alienation, of being "out of this world!" Various defenses mustered to ward off and cope with these feelings often make the child's experience of this situation even worse than it is. If behavior problems develop, as they often do in children with learning disorders, reprimands and criticism by others will magnify the sense of alienation.

These dynamics can get even more complex. When a child is threatened with exclusion from the group, the experience may lead him to hide his sense of difference in order to be accepted. Subsequently, a series of defensive deceptions may lead to a variety of outcomes. If the child is successful in his efforts, he may be accepted but at the cost of feeling that he has deceived the others and that he cannot be who he truly is. If he is unsuccessful, then other children's ridicule of his efforts can lead to greater devastation.

These concepts of self psychology lead us to appreciate the significance selfobjects have in the development of children with learning disorders. The empathic approach permits us to understand people's experiences of the events that shape their lives. It opens a window on the meanings those events have for them and to their specific interpretations.

### Adjunctive Functions

There is another group of phenomena that appear to operate in a manner similar to selfobject functions in that they serve to complement the sense of self, but they must be conceptualized differently. I designate these as adjunctive functions.

While all selfobject functions provide complementarities to the sense of self, not all complementary functions can be identified as selfobject functions. Some examples may help clarify this distinction. Children often need to be reminded to perform a task or to prepare themselves for school in the morning. Sometimes directions must be repeated to them, either because they were inattentive or because their auditory processing of verbal information is weak, e.g., they may have poor auditory memory skills. In performing these functions caregivers are providing adjunctive cognitive functions for the child. They are complementing an area of deficit, but are not necessarily providing selfobject functions.

A different set of examples involves "prosthetic devices" we use to extend our capacity to perform tasks. Computers are increasingly being used to complement functions for many people. We use spell-checking functions of word processors to make up for our deficits in spelling. We use computer dictation programs not only to increase the efficiency of our output but also to bypass problems of poor or illegible handwriting. Hand-held gadgets now serve as auxiliary memories by keeping our calendars and helping us to be organized. The computer is an example of an adjunctive function that is task specific, in contrast to a caregiver who responds generatively to a child's needs. An example that blurs the distinction between selfobject and adjunctive functions is that of a blind person's seeing eye dog, which provides a critical function the blind person does not possess. In this case, the line between a creature substituting for a missing sensory modality and being a selfobject to its master cannot be clearly drawn. The dog may be both.

Contrivances or prostheses that extend people's capacities to perform tasks can be conceived of as tools that complement some aspect of the person. These tools may have meaning to the person or they may be no more than the means to an end. Such tools, I suggest, perform adjunctive functions. Even when what is complemented is in the neuropsychological sphere, these tools would not necessarily qualify as selfobject functions. Nevertheless, without such appliances we would all be seriously "handicapped."

It is difficult to make a clear-cut distinction between selfobject and adjunctive functions when people are involved in the performance of these functions. Children with neurocognitive deficits tend to draw from caregivers adjunctive functions to complement their immature or deficient psyches, functions that are not usually identified as part of the parenting process. Sometimes it is impossible to identify specific delays or deficits early in infancy. Parents are then left in the dark as to what that the child requires. Some caregivers respond intuitively. Through their empathic capacities they may be able to fill in the child's neuropsychological deficits. In fact, these parents, if they have had other children, recognize the differences in the child and feel they must respond as they do or cause the child serious distress. When parents either cannot or do not complement the child's deficits, the child suffers. The reason for the child's distress is seldom clearly evident early on. Parents often feel much puzzlement and guilt, since they assume that they are the cause of the problem.

When a caregiver devotes herself to complementing a child's deficits, a complex relationship evolves between the two that at times may be identified as "symbiotic." The child's needs evoke responses from the caregiver that the caregiver finds impossible to ignore. The child's initial realistic dependence is furthered by the parent's anxiety. As the relationship evolves, the child may become fearful and feel helpless. These fears may manifest as "separation anxiety" or a symbiotic attachment. The child desperately needs what the parent provides and may feel unable to survive psychologically without the caregiver's response. However, the caregiver's view of the interaction is clouded by the inability to distinguish between the child's realistic needs and the child's simple enjoyment of the dependence. Many parents, in those circumstances, feel torn between their intuitive perceptions of the child's needs and their desire to enhance the child's growth, which they feel may be impaired by their catering to his demands. Caregivers at times are made to feel guilty and are criticized for their responses to the child because their responses are viewed as fostering dependence and impeding the child's developmental progression. Such condemnation of caregivers is unwarranted in the absence of a clear understanding of the motives behind the interaction. In the case of children with learning disorders, the motives for the reciprocal interaction must be understood as arising from the survival needs of the child and not necessarily from some unconscious destructive need on the parent's part to maintain the child's helpless state. I will discuss this issue further in Chapter 14 on working with parents.

### Compensation

Compensation consists of strategies a child uses to achieve the desired goal without the mediating intervention of another person or tool. It may seem odd to think of compensation as a form of complementarity until we look at it as a way people have of complementing themselves for deficits or weakness they have. In this respect we may speak of compensation as it relates to selfobject functions as well as adjunctive functions.

Kohut (1977) wrote of compensatory functions in the area of selfobject functions as a way of delineating the ways in which psychological functions are used to maintain a sense of self-cohesion. His use of the concept of compensation is narrower than mine. I include the way in which people gain from drawing strength from sources other than selfobjects. Compensation for missing selfobject functions occurs when a child can turn away from a desire for responses from a caregiver who cannot provide for the child's emotional needs and instead substitutes a relationship with someone else who may provide the emotional response or an emotional response that satisfies a different need (Kohut, 1977).

CASE ILLUSTRATION: BRAD

**Brad was a 14-year-old eighth grader with a language-based learning disability that impaired his capacity to express himself both verbally and in written form. In addition, he had a serious spelling problem. Brad's**

gift lay in the area of the visual arts. He was a gifted artist who produced remarkable work through the graphic medium. However, his father was a down-to-earth businessman who had no use for any occupation where success could not be measured monetarily. He was derisive
of his son's work and disparaged any recognition he got, characteriz-
ing it as "people are being nice, but they don't mean it!" Although he
longed for his father's approval, Brad despaired that he would ever get
it. In seventh grade, his art teacher immediately recognized his talent
and gave Brad the support to pursue it. Brad entered several competi-
tions, which he won with high praise. Eventually, Brad gave up on ever
having his father recognize his gift and discounted the disparagement.
What became important was the critical acclaim he got from those who
valued his work.

The brain's plasticity and the capacity of some areas to take over functions to make up for dysfunctions in other parts is well-known. The phenomenon of compensation for physical handicaps is also well documented. When it comes to compensations for neuropsychological
deficits, similar phenomena may be observed, although these are less well
documented in the literature. For example, since verbal expressive capacities are often an area of strength for children with nonverbal learning disabilities, these children can learn to "verbally mediate" nonverbal
tasks. They achieve the goal of completing a task by "talking their way"
through the nonverbal steps. Some children learn to do this for themselves, while others can gain from being taught the strategy. These cognitive strategies offer compensatory functions that serve the child well.

The compensatory strategies children develop are limited only by their
creativity. Some children develop strategies other than those of verbal me-
diation. Some learn to structure their environment to minimize their reliance on areas of weakness. Others, with help, learn to anticipate and avoid
encounters with situations that would expose their weaknesses. When a
child is capable of using such compensatory strategies, the negative impact of the disability is attenuated, as are the psychological problems.

Clearly, not all children compensate for deficits in their development.
Some do very well while others do not. For reasons that are not clear,
some children do not acquire compensatory functions. These children
may learn to rely on others to complement their deficient functioning
or they may fail to be effective in dealing with life tasks (Miller, 1991,
1992). The capacity to use adjunctive functions and the reasons why some
children do not or cannot use them are not well understood.

Generally, most children whose deficits are not in the serious to severe range manage to compensate for their deficits by the time they reach adulthood. Some who do not compensate arrange their lives in such a way as to avoid the pitfalls they would confront were they to undertake tasks that they could not manage. Some children who are confronted with tasks they find insurmountable in one area and who have marked strengths in other areas turn to the latter areas to find successes. They then appear to cope much better with areas of deficiencies. At times, they even challenge themselves to undertake what is most difficult for them. However, they are seldom able to perform these tasks with the ease and comfort seen in endowed persons.

Compensation then does not mean that the child "outgrows" a deficit. It means that the child has been able to get around the problems created by the deficit by strengthening areas of weakness or using areas of strength to attain the goals he desires. At times, some children take a perspective through denial or through acceptance that permits them to function quite adequately. They may depreciate or devalue what is difficult and therefore neutralize the negative effects of the deficit. Some transform the meanings of the deficit, making it into a badge to be displayed, joked about, or used as a source of pride. In all of these cases the child turns to other areas of competence to obtain satisfaction. Compensation results in a greater sense of coherence, a stronger sense of cohesiveness, and less vulnerability to others' estimation of them.

## CASE ILLUSTRATION: JOSH

Josh, a 15-year-old high school freshman, was referred because he was on the verge of failing all his classes. Josh had a long history of serious difficulties in reading, spelling, and math. He had been identified early in third grade as having dyslexia and had received tutorial help for many years. The impending failure in almost all academic subjects was the result of his inability to do the work on his own. When he entered high school, he refused all tutoring, insisting that he had to make it on his own or not at all. His parents had reluctantly acquiesced, feeling they had little choice.

When seen diagnostically, Josh was extremely resistive to becoming involved in therapy. He described himself as not needing any help, as having lots of friends, being a star on the lacrosse team, and being pursued by a number of girls who wished to date him. He gave a description of his family as warm, caring, and concerned. His mother had a wide social circle, while his father, a successful businessman, was actively involved in sports with his children.

It was clear that in this family, social skills and sports were as valued as academic achievement. While academic failure was not acceptable, being a sports star and having valued friends were considered signs of success. Josh took from his parents the values that fit with his strengths; this was his way of compensating for his academic underachievement. The problem he confronted was that in his adolescent desire to no longer be dependent on others for academic success, which he did not value as highly, he refused the help he needed to make it in high school.

Josh and I agreed that he really did not need "therapy" as he stereotyped it, i.e., as something that kids with serious emotional problems need. What he needed was someone who understood the choices he was making and who could facilitate his struggles to achieve independence from his tutors. We agreed that he needed to learn to make it on his own, but that it would take time for him to make the transition.

Josh was seen once a week on and off during the next four years until he went to college. His compensations in the social and athletic areas were supported. Arrangements were made with the school for him to stay on the athletic team in spite of his low academic scores. They had to be convinced that this activity was of immense value to him in sustaining his self-esteem and in his eventual success as a person. In therapy he formed an ambivalent relationship, partly because he felt affronted by having to be in therapy and partly because accepting help had so many negative meanings for him. Eventually he was accepted into a small college with a good lacrosse team that welcomed him for the contribution he could make to their team.

Many years later, in a chance encounter with his father, I was told that Josh took hold academically in his junior year in college when he decided he wanted to become a lawyer. He worked incredibly hard to attain a B average. In the summer he worked for a law office where he formed close relationships with some of the young attorneys. He came to be valued for his social skills and his work ethic. Eventually he made it through law school, being closely supported by a group of friends who verbally rehearsed with him all of his assignments. He had recently taken and passed the state bar exam and was in a committed relationship with a woman.

To summarize, we can distinguish three types of complementary functions, two of which caregivers and the context provide, and a third, compensations, that the child provides for himself. Selfobject functions are functions that address the child's emotional needs and are necessary for the child to attain or maintain a sense of self-cohesion. Providers of these functions are not interchangeable, since the person performing the function assumes a special value to the child that makes the relationship distinctive.

The second type of complementary function is that of being an adjunct to the child's cognitive and physical capacities. Here we distinguish two classes of phenomena, those associated with physical objects (tools) and those associated with caregivers. I would designate the former as *prosthetic devices* that extend our competencies to perform tasks. The second are more difficult to classify because they may contain elements of selfobject functions. Caregivers may extend a child's cognitive capacities by operating in the "zone of proximal development" (Vygotsky, 1986, p. 187) or providing scaffolding that permits the child to accomplish tasks that he could not accomplish without the assistance of these adjunctive functions. But since the caregiver is a feeling, empathic human being, it seems inevitable that the child will experience the caregiver's empathy as providing for selfobject needs.

Finally, compensatory functions are functions that the child creates to self-complement. They serve to make up deficits in his sense of self, but do not require the intervention of others.

# 3

# LEARNING DISORDERS AND SELF-NARRATIVES

CHILDREN'S SELF-NARRATIVES provide us with a second window into their subjective experiences (Klitzing, 2000). The self-narrative focuses on the *meanings* the child construes from her experience, on how others in the child's context *confer meanings* on those experiences, and on how the child *organizes those meanings* into thematic units within the narrative to create a coherent story. Interpretations a child makes of her experiences are determined by the neuropsychological strengths and weaknesses she brings to the process and by the community or context in which she is raised. As the child integrates and synthesizes these meanings, the self-narrative acquires a structure and content. Cohler states:

> The life-history construct, like all historical accounts within our own culture, may be understood as a narrative ... that is composed of a sequence of events reflecting particular intentions and covering a presently remembered past, experienced present, and expected or assumed future and that is organized according to socially constructed understandings of time and space. (1993, p. 112)

By self-narrative,* I refer to the broad set of communications through which children tell us about themselves that reflect the organization of

---

*While others, such as Brandell (2000), Bruner (1987, 1990), Cohler (1982), Saari (1991), Schafer (1980, 1981, 1983, 1992), Spence (1982, 1986a, 1986b, 1987, 1990),

43

their experiences. These communications include explicit autobiographical statements, fantasies, play sequences, stories, as well as nonverbal enactments that give behavioral expression to their desires, beliefs, and emotions. In a manner of speaking, everything children say and do is an
expression of who they are. The challenge for therapists is to interpret
the significance of the communication as it reflects the child's experience. Ordinarily, the themes of the self-narrative are descriptively unconscious; that is, they are not available to the person without reflection
and introspection. A person may be able to give an account of her life,
but may not have direct access to major motifs or themes that organize
her life. The unavailability of these motifs is due simply to their being
transparent to the child, not necessarily to their being unacceptable or
repressed. There is much about ourselves that we cannot see because of
our immersion in who we are. This is, of course, all the more true of children. In this discussion of self-narrative, I address three major issues: the
development of the self-narrative, the organization of some experiences
into themes or motifs within the self-narrative, and the vital role that narrative coherence plays in sustaining a sense of cohesion (see Table 3.1).

We can conceive of normal development as a process through which
an infant, born within the context of devoted caregivers, assigns meanings to experiences in ways that permit feelings of coherence, continuity, and intactness to become prevalent from phase to phase. Development is the process by which a child gradually accrues an evolving
self-narrative (Cohler & Freeman, 1993). It represents an ongoing series
of changes in the direction of more complex levels of organization of
the narrative. As the child is exposed to new experiences, the motifs—
the themes within the narrative—are reworked into the old narrative.
New meanings can emerge and old experiences may be seen in a new
light. Continuity in the self-narrative exists as these meanings are integrated into a whole. The progression may include a return to old themes
as well as a suspension of ways of interpreting the past and present.

---

and Stern (1985, 1989a, 1989b), have written about narrative, I have turned to the
concept self-narrative to supplement traditional psychoanalytic metapsychological
explanations. I have chosen Stern's approach because he is a clinician with a developmental perspective and because of his close links to Nelson's work on children's memory (Aaron, Phillips, & Larsen, 1988; Nelson, 1992, 1993, 1994, 2000). I
am also indebted to Cohler for the concept of narrative coherence and for his psychoanalytic developmental perspective on what he calls the "life-story construct"
and "personal narrative" (Cohler, 1993, 1996, 1998; Cohler & Freeman, 1993; Cohler
& Galatzer-Levy, 1988).

## TABLE 3.1
## Learning Disorders and the Self-narrative

1. THE SELF-NARRATIVE
   a. The self-narrative is constituted of memories of life events that are stored in both implicit (procedural, associative) and explicit (semantic, episodic) memories.
   b. The communications through which children tell us about themselves reveal their self-narrative. These include autobiographical statements, fantasies, play sequences, and nonverbal enactments of their desires, beliefs and feelings.
   c. Developmentally, the self-narrative is formed from the scripts that emerge shortly after birth. Scripts encode both the event and the associated affects. These scripts are encoded as implicit memories. Some become organizing themes or motifs within the self-narrative. By age five, a child is capable of making explicit autobiographical statements.

2. NARRATIVE COHERENCE
   a. Human beings are motivated to make sense of their experiences. They attempt to do so by creating a coherent self-narrative that organizes the meanings of experiences stored in implicit and explicit memory.
   b. A set of positive affects is associated with having a coherent self-narrative.
   c. For children with neuropsychological deficits, the integration of the shared meanings of experiences may enhance their ability to attain a coherent self-narrative. This coherence is contingent upon the concordance of the self-narrative with the context in which they are raised and the community's beliefs and values.

3. THE CONTEXT
   a. The context may provide children with the means through which personal meanings are translated into shared meanings.
   b. The context may impose constraints on children with neuropsychological deficits, leading them to conventionalize their self-narratives in order to conform with others' expectations of them, or to allow themselves to be emplotted or ensnared in others' self-narratives through a wish to please others.

Novel ways of understanding meanings are thus created. A rhythmic and characteristic set of patterns emerges for every individual.

When given expression verbally, the self-narrative becomes an auto-biographical statement that reveals the patient to herself and to others. In the clinical setting, such autobiographical statements may be viewed much as a dream told to the therapist that includes both conscious and unconscious content. The manifest content is but the tip of an iceberg; the latent content remains beneath the surface. As further details of the life story are revealed, more of the unconscious content emerges. Gaps, distortions, and self-serving statements all point to dimensions that, once explored, offer areas for greater understanding of the child. Autobio-graphical statements present one component of the self-narrative; an-other component includes nonverbal contents enacted in the interac-tions with others.

By focusing on the self-narratives of children with learning disor-ders we can obtain an intimate understanding of the ways in which they experience the events in their lives, organize them into scripts or episodes, and store them for later retrieval. As we will see, the en-coding of these episodes into scripts that are stored in memory is in-fluenced by the circumstances in which the event occurs, the feelings stirred up by the event, the state of mind of the child at the time of the occurrence, and the child's particular configuration of neuropsy-chological strengths and weakness. Some of these episodes acquire much greater significance than others. They become themes or motifs that organize the child's perceptions and shape her responses to peo-ple and to events in her life. Such themes become the plot that struc-tures the child's self-narrative and shapes how she acts and whom she is perceived to be.

Finally, coherence, in the sense in which I will be using the term, does not relate to logical coherence and consistency; it relates to the idio-syncratic integration made by a child of the meanings of her experiences. As Justice Oliver Wendell Holmes wrote over a century ago:

> [T]he life of the law has not been logic, it has been experience. The felt necessities of the time, the prevalent moral and political theories, intuitions of public policy, avowed or unconscious, even the prejudices which judges share with their fellow men, have a good deal more to do than the syllogism in determining the rules by which men shall be governed. (quoted in Murphy, 1990, p. 38)

## The Development of the Self-narrative

The process through which the self-narrative evolves has its origins in infancy. It is closely tied to the developing brain structures that are involved in the formation and retention of memories. We can identify two periods, the preverbal—roughly prior to 18 months of age—and the verbal—after language acquisition has occurred. In the preverbal period, when the child communicates primarily through gestures and nonspecific sounds, memories are encoded and stored as implicit, nonverbal memories. This is the period Piaget calls the sensorimotor phase of development, during which sensorimotor schemas are laid down. Implicit memories continue to be encoded and stored throughout a person's life. A rich nonverbal domain continues to influence people's communications, as well as their behaviors (Nelson, 1993).

At about the time that children acquire language, the brain systems involved in the encoding and storage of explicit memories begin to mature, making it possible for the child to retain and retrieve semantic and episodic knowledge. The schemas and scripts are stored in semantic memory, while events associated with life episodes are kept in episodic memory (Farrar & Goodman, 1990). By about age of four or five,* the child, with the help of a supporting adult, can produce autobiographical memories that constitute the explicit part of the self-narrative (Nelson, 1992, 2000). Influenced by Nelson's work, Stern (1989a, 1989b) has proposed a fifth domain to be added to the four domains he had previously outlined in the development of the infant (emergent, core, subjective, and verbal selves). This is the domain of "the narrative self," whose development follows that of the verbal self (Stern, 1985). For Stern the narrative self is the culmination of the series of "lived experiences" (episodes) that are remembered.

The need to express ourselves in narrative form is probably due to the unique nature of our memory system. Our memory system is organized into implicit and explicit or nondeclarative and declarative memories. These terms replace the old terminology of short- and long-term memory, as researchers have not found support for that distinction. The categories of implicit and explicit memory have proven more useful (Gathercole, 1998). Implicit memory contains, among other things, the

---

*In her earlier work (1992), Nelson gives four as the age when children can retrieve autobiographical memories, but in a later publication she assigns that age as five (2000, p. 276).

nonverbally encoded habits and procedures we use in our daily lives, such as the routines we follow and the motor skills we use in swimming, dancing, and riding bicycles. Explicit or declarative memory is divided into semantic memory and episodic memory. Semantic memory is that system in which we place word definitions and other facts, such as dates or trivia that we call upon periodically. Episodic memory is the system in which we store information as meaningful events connected to one another (Schacter, 1996). Our autobiographical memory forms part of our episodic memory (Nelson, 1992). Self-narratives incorporate both implicit and explicit memories.

Three points must be kept in mind in this discussion. First, what the child retains, whether in implicit or explicit memory, is never totally isolated from the context in which the events occurred. The imprint of the social and cultural milieu forms part of every memory the child stores (Nelson, 1993). Second, what the child stores is not a replica of the event but the experience of the event, a representation that is colored by the child's endowment. Third, the memories a child retrieves are not like replays of a videotape of the events; rather, they are constructions that may bear a strong resemblance to the occurrence the child reports, but that also contain elements that represent personal interpretations, secondary elaborations, or biases that serve the child's purpose at that moment.

## Themes or Motifs as Organizers of the Self-narrative

A central tenet of all psychodynamic theories is that past experience shapes present and future responses to others. Freud named this principle the *repetition compulsion*; Melanie Klein referred to it as *projective identification*; Kohut attributed this phenomenon to *deficits in the sense of self*; and Stolorow (Atwood & Stolorow, 1984) used the concept of *invariant organizing principle* to refer to it. What each of these concepts addresses is the clinical phenomenon of transference in its broadest sense, that is, that each of us reshapes our perceptions of current situations so that they conform to past experiences. Of utmost importance is the fact that in the process of reshaping these perceptions part of the current reality is made to conform to a bias or belief about similar situations from our past. In the view I offer of the organization of the self-narrative, I reframe this concept to make it conform to the narrative metaphor. It becomes the *theme or motif* that provides the central plot of the narrative. In the discussion that follows, I suggest that by taking seriously the view that learning disorders influence the meanings that children construe from their experiences, we may be able to explain not just the presence of organizing themes but also the reasons behind the choice themes. To arrive at this conclusion, I discuss Stern's concept of Representation of Interactions Generalized (RIGs), Tomkins' concept of scripts, and the distinction between personal and shared meanings.

### Representation of Interactions Generalized (RIGs)

Stern refers to the invariant components of such episodes as Representation of Interactions Generalized (RIGs). The invariant components or RIGs represent the common denominator in a set of interactions with significant others. They may be thought of as building blocks that serve to organize these interactions. The child stores the RIGs in episodic memory; they are later recalled as scenarios and internal working models. For Stern, each RIG is the product of multiple interactions with another person. From the perspective of the child, the following factors may be said to be involved in the experience of a specific episode: (1) the *uniqueness of the context* in which the episode takes place, (2) the *uniqueness of the object* with whom the interaction takes place, and (3) the *uniqueness of the child's competencies* (i.e., endowments) through which she filters her experiences.

Stern's concept of RIG is helpful as a starting point from which to view the effects of individual differences in the encoding of experiences. Through the concept of RIGs Stern highlights the *invariant*, i.e., the commonalities within a set of interactions that are retained and generalized. To understand children with learning disorders, we must focus on the *differences* that each child brings to her experiences, in addition to the invariant aspects of the experience. We need to understand the ways in which learning disorders or specific neuropsychological strengths and weaknesses shape an infant's or child's experience and lead her to assign to it a meaning different from the meanings that others might derive from similar experiences.

### Scripts

As stated earlier, during the preverbal period infants encode and store their experiences as implicit memories. Sensorimotor schemas, as described by Piaget (1972), consist of a set of nonconscious procedures through which the child is primed to respond to specific stimuli. While Piaget regarded those schemas as purely cognitive mental structures, the work of Tomkins guides us in understanding how these schemas are translated into scripts—a term he uses in a different sense from that used by Nelson—and how they incorporate the child's affect states.

The concept of scripts as formulated by Tomkins provides a key for understanding the contributions of differences in one's competencies to the construal of meanings. For Tomkins (1979, 1987), scripts are ordered sets of scenes derived from experience. He proposed that there are two types of scripts, innate scripts and learned scripts. The innate scripts constitute the nine categorical affects: excitement, joy, surprise, fear, distress, anger, disgust, dismell (reaction to offensive odors), and shame. Learned scripts originate from innate scripts and incorporate within them the affect state recruited by the event to which the child was exposed. Both sets of scripts become templates through which experiences may be shaped and become self-fulfilling, in the sense that they are used to anticipate and predict what is to happen.

Tomkins (1979) suggested that the affects recruited by each experience are analogues of the experience itself. Affects parallel the interactions with others but do not precisely mirror or necessarily accurately reflect the occurrences to which the child is exposed. He also maintained that affects make "good things better and bad things worse" by amplifying and magnifying the impact of the person's experiences. An experience of great importance to one child may be insignificant to others. In part this is because of the differences in children's capacities to modulate affect states or in their thresholds for experiencing affect states. For example, two children exposed as infants to the experience of separation from a caregiver or to hospitalization will respond quite differently. For one child, the experience has minimal impact and is soon forgotten, while for the other child, who is much more reactive and emotionally labile, the experiences of being exposed to an unfamiliar environment, being handled by strangers or comforted differently from the ways she is accustomed, assume traumatic proportions. Each nuance of feeling is magnified, so as to leave an indelible imprint in her memory.

Children with problems in the area of affect regulation, such as children with nonverbal learning disabilities, will experience the world differently from their peers. At one end of the spectrum are children whose experience of affect states is flattened by the overregulation of their feelings. For them experience is covered over by a gray haze. At the other end of the spectrum are those children for whom what would be considered average disruptions are experienced as overstimulating and traumatic. Their oversensitivity and inability to regulate their feelings make them see each experience in magnified form.

The amplified and magnified experiences are retained in implicit memory as scripts or thematic models that serve as filters of subsequent experiences. Some of these scripts serve as major organizers of how events are perceived. The child's appraisal of the affect-laden experiences will reflect her distinctive cognitive competencies. Other scripts encode the events and the interactions that made a lasting impression on the child and that are considered prototypical of a set of experiences. When a child's cognitive competencies are impaired, her scripts will have idiosyncratic features. The extent to which these features differ from those of others will depend on the extent and severity of the impairment.

Some scripts become "motifs" or themes in self-narratives. Motifs are a form of bias or belief about the future (Eichenbaum & Bodkin, 2000; Nelson, 2000) that is retained because of the significance it had for the child at the time it was formed. These motifs acquire such importance that they become impervious to modification by subsequent events or knowledge. They are organizing principles or motives that both actively shape interactions and predict future encounters.

For example, a child may interpret her inability to spell as related to her being lazy or as meaning that she does not try hard enough to memorize the words. She may believe her spelling problem to be caused by those factors, even though we have evidence that it is caused by a poor visual and auditory memory. Her belief that she is lazy may then act as a motive that causes her to feel discouraged when faced with difficult academic tasks. Her diminished efforts, motivated by that belief, may lead to academic failure. In addition, others may also view her lack of effort as evidence of her laziness, a conclusion that would reinforce her belief, so that in a vicious cycle causes and beliefs become indistinguishable.

## Personal and Shared Meanings

Another way to think of scripts is as implicit memories that encode a child's personal meanings of events to which she is exposed. Personal meanings are unique meanings or meanings that are discordant from those given to those events by others. Children with neuropsychological deficits often hold such meanings. In a sense, all experience has its origin as personal experience. By personal experience I refer to the realm of "subjective experience" to which no one but the person has access. In this sense, no one can know another person's experiences. We can only assume that because of our common humanity what we feel is similar to what others feel, but we can have no direct knowledge of that realm of experience. The meaning of the experience, while communicable to others and transmitted in meaningful terms to others, retains some of its distinctiveness and uniqueness for the child; its meaning has a personal dimension. Introspection recovers what has been encoded in memory and therefore what has already been represented in some form.

While children encode their experiences in the language of their caregivers, the concepts that children with learning disorders use contain areas of meaning not fully shared by others. Communication with others involves articulation through language with a common denominator understandable by all. To the extent that an overlap exists between what a person desires to express and what the member of the community to whom the communication is directed understands, communication will have occurred. The area in which little or no overlap exists is an area of vagueness or indeterminacy that may be clarified only through further explanation. Complete understanding of the exact meaning of another person's experience may be impossible. We understand what others try to convey by approximating what we believe their communications mean. Thus, as I write, trying to explain my thoughts, there is much that I cannot fully articulate. Yet I hope that readers will grasp what I intend to say through the pale words I use to communicate. If I were to continue writing for an indefinite period, elaborating on these thoughts, it is possible that the common denominator between what I mean to say and what a reader understands would increase. However, there are limits both to my ability to express myself and to the reader's patience in trying to understand my thoughts. At some point the process stops and we are left with a shared experience that is sufficient for practical purposes.

The universe of *personal (i.e., subjective) meanings* is complemented by the universe of the *shared (i.e., objective) meanings*. Personal meanings possess a unique dimension because they are stamped by the child's neuropsychological strengths and weaknesses, while shared meanings are defined, in part, by others in the child's context. These meanings are *conferred* upon the child's experience. These universes are organized as hierarchies of meaning with their own coherence, consistency, and level of comprehensiveness. Both contribute to the self-narrative.

Shared meanings provide the "reality" that children confront every day. The term reality as used here has two meanings. The first is that which is independent of our thoughts and cannot be changed by our thinking of it as different from what it is, such as snow falling outside a window. The second is the product of the shared meanings in the context in which a person lives. This latter reality, often referred to as a "constructed" reality, may best be called our version of what is "our world." It is linked to the former reality as signs are linked to their referents. It reflects a particular version of what we have represented through our attempts to communicate to others; e.g., you look pale and are shivering, you must have a fever!

This interpretation of what constitutes "our world" is contextual in the scnsc that wc grasp "facts" not in isolation from each other but in contexts that relate meanings to each other. The constructed or shared world (as personal reality) is therefore a narrative that is given coherence through the linkages provided by the culture. We can talk about such narratives in terms of the mores, values, myths, and other phenomena expressed through social institutions from which the fabric of society is made.

It is important to note that, while all meaning has its genesis within the context of a dialogue with another, not all meanings are created from within the dialogue or are sustained through interactions with others. Once a set of meanings is established, it forms a foundation upon which an infant begins to roam, at times freely, in different directions. It is as though, once an infant has formulated the rule or principle through which experience becomes meaningful, then, much as the discovery of syntax permits the generation of an infinite number of syntactically correct sentences, the child can generate new sets of meanings from experience.

This capacity brings to our attention the fact that children, in their eagerness to find explanations for their experiences, will at times latch onto explanations they give themselves or that others give to them, even though those explanations may be untenable or may later be found to be without foundation. The following quotation states this point better than I can:

> Our interpretative mind is always attributing a cause to felt states of mind, and we now know that these interpretations are frequently irrelevant to the true underlying causes of a felt state. Our mind's explanations become more relevant only as we come to believe our own theories about the cause of a state like anxiety. The fact appears to be that some people are genetically disposed to an anxious response while

others are not. Those who are anxious search for a theory to explain their anxiety and commonly seize on the number of decisions they make a day as a likely source of their state of mind. As we see from the example of the surgeon, this explanation is most likely spurious. Yet as the anxious person comes to believe his own theory, he begins to change his life pattern in ways that can easily be imagined. (Gazzaniga, 1988, p. 98).

## Memory and Motifs

A different way to think about narrative themes or motifs is to discuss the way these are stored in memory. Implicit memories are retained as a set of biases or beliefs that are not conscious, such as the motifs in the self-narratives, while explicit memories store the knowledge we acquire and the sense we make of the world around us (Eichenbaum & Bodkin, 2000). Stern's RIGs and Tomkins' scripts are encoded in implicit memory. But this alone does not explain the fact that children also give themselves explanations for their difficulties. For that we must understand another function of explicit memory.

As mentioned earlier, explicit memory consists of semantic and episodic memory. The difference between semantic and episodic memory is analogous to the differentiation that historians make between a chronicle and a history. A chronicle consists of simple lists of dates or events that are not connected to one another. A history, on the other hand, attempts to establish a relationship between dates and events by embedding them in a narrative. When we remember an episode, we do more than just recall the facts, thoughts, or feelings as we bring these into the present. We also recall the relationships that were established between the facts, thoughts, or feelings when they occurred. The associations we make may be causal or circumstantial. For example, we may remember that at our last vacation we were delayed getting to our destination because we missed our flight as a result of the traffic jam that interfered with our getting to the airport on time. We establish a causal relationship between the disparate events. On the other hand, if we recall that our last child patient destroyed a puppet during a particularly violent play sequence, we may be reminded that we should buy a replacement prior to her return. The relationship between the destruction of the toy and our need to replace it is circumstantial.

The connections we make between events are superimposed on the facts themselves. The result is the recall of an episode. By the age of three children achieve the capacity to retain such episodes and are capable of retelling what occurred in schematic form with the assistance of an adult. By the age of four or five, they are capable, again with the support of an adult, of giving autobiographical accounts of past experiences. What is important is to distinguish the association made between events within an episode that are causal and those that are circumstantial. When children assign personal meanings to events, they assign a causal relationship when the relationship was circumstantial, misattributing causes and motives where none existed.

The self-narrative, therefore, includes within it both implicit and explicit memories. The motifs encoded in implicit memory serve to organize the contents of the episodes the child explicitly remembers. In other words, as the child searches for coherence among the events in her life, her motifs are superimposed on the contents of her explicit memories. What she reconstructs during recall is heavily colored by the biases and beliefs she arrived at in previous encounters. The self-narrative is, therefore, broader that any autobiographical statement the child makes, because the self-narrative contains nonconscious elements of implicit memory.

## CASE ILLUSTRATION: ALICE

**Alice is an eight-year-old with severe AD/HD. She is impulsive, lacks any ability to manage frustration, and jumps from one topic to the next during conversations, maintaining a dizzying pace of verbalization. She often alienates her peers by her intrusive insensitivity, which they regard as rude.**

**Until recently, Alice's mother had devoted herself to managing Alice's life. She had taken her for therapy when she was an infant regarding problems with attachment. She actively participated in the therapeutic process, often modifying her style of relating to Alice in order to facilitate Alice's development. She comforted Alice and helped to modulate her deregulated outbursts; she planned and orchestrated small group activities so that Alice might benefit from these experiences of socialization.**

**After doing this for eight years and seeing little in return, Alice's mother felt burned out and decided to go to work. Alice's response was to feel bereft of the one person who helped her mediate her environment. She interpreted her mother's going to work as a desertion, even though her mother left home after Alice went to school and returned**

from work before school ended. She was as available to Alice as she had always been. The experience of mother's seeming detachment was magnified by Alice's own inability to modulate her affect states. Rather than coping in some constructive way with this turn of events, Alice went on a campaign to make her mother's life miserable. Her interpretation of the events was that mother was responsible for her inability to modulate her feelings. She held her mother responsible for that inability because she felt her mother had constantly interfered with her activities. From Alice's perspective it was because of mother's intrusion into her life that she had no friends, that she had problems in school, and that she got into trouble with her father.

In part, Alice's acquisition of this theme of her narrative was based on the many reinforcing responses she got from teachers and peers. Many times she had heard them say that Alice should stop behaving so childishly and grow up. She was accused by peers of being a "mommy's girl" who did nothing without her mother. She felt that if only she could be more independent she would not have these problems.

Alice's contribution to the relationship with her mother was not evident to outside observers. When she began verbally attacking her mother, they saw that as a healthy effort at asserting herself and breaking away from an overly dependent relationship with her mother. To understand what Alice drew from these experiences, we must look at the meanings she attached to her experiences and how those meanings became organized as themes in her self-narrative.

As a child, Alice could not be introspective enough to note her impulsivity. Her only understanding was that people were critical of her behavior. Only her mother had been kind and appreciative of her. This meant that, while others saw her as a problem child, her mother was the source of good feelings and self-esteem. It also meant that, as long as she had her mother as an ally, she could discount what others said about her.

When her mother went to work, Alice's world was turned topsy-turvy. Her feelings of abandonment grew totally out of proportion to the reality. Her mother was still available to her after school hours. But now the views of others assumed much greater significance than they had previously been given. Since Alice now needed to give herself an explanation for the changes she was experiencing, she began to construct her own interpretation of the events around her. Much like someone trying to formulate a hypothesis about a set of disconnected events, she put the beads of her experiences onto a string in a sequence that fit

**with her context and her disability. A different child might have strung the beads of her experience together differently.**

## *Narrative Coherence*

Many people in our society do not arrive at fully integrated narratives that have coherence and continuity (Cohler, 1982). Children with learning disorders are at particular risk for not developing a coherent self-narrative.

Coherence represents the integration of the *personal* and *shared* meanings patients have drawn from their experience into the self-narrative. It is a product of the relationships of the motifs to the whole. Concordance between the personal and shared meanings is an essential component of coherence. A self-narrative may be coherent to a person who excludes communal meanings. Such exclusion, at one extreme, produces a paranoid delusional system. At the other extreme, it is perceived by the community as a singularity, that is, the self-narrative of a person who views him or herself as having a vision that goes beyond what others perceive; such persons become prophets or leaders of cults.

At times the need for connectedness and coherence leads to a narrative that is less logical and formal than it is contingent upon the accidental events to which the child has been exposed. In this sense coherence and consistency are related to each other and contribute to the meanings that arise from the reading of the text. The capacity for organization contributes to the establishment of a coherence that leads to experiences of self-understanding and therefore to internal regulation. That is, when integrated, self-experience may lead to further coherence and self-regulation. However, other motifs can reinforce regulation in the absence of integration. This view of development maintains that the components within this whole are identifiable and play a significant role as motifs within the narrative. These components are marshaled together in a fashion that permits an orderly or an incoherent narrative to unfold. In the same way that the genetic code encased in the fertilized egg is thought to determine the direction of fetal development, organizing motifs set the course for each person's personality development.

With some modifications, the same may be said of each person's self-narrative. By logical standards the narratives configured by people are hardly coherent and/or consistent. A self-narrative that appears coherent to one person may appear totally incoherent to another. When Freud struggled to make the irrational rational, he was attempting to solve the

problem of the apparent incoherence of people's dreams and their neurotic symptoms. He believed that rational explanations of these phenomena were possible. He postulated the unconscious as the construct
that would allow for the bridging of the two worlds of the rational and
the irrational.

As we will see, most children with learning disorders come to treatment with incoherent narratives. The incoherence may stem from their
puzzlement at their lack of success or from their inability to come to
grips with the limitations their deficits produce. But not all these children have incoherent narratives. Some have arrived at personal explanations that appear to satisfy them. These explanations may or may not
conflict with the communal explanations for their difficulties. What
stands out is that they have reached a satisfactory balance between the
personal and shared meanings of their learning disorder.

## CASE ILLUSTRATION: LARRY

**Larry was six-and-a-half years old at the time of referral. He was an only
child living with his mother, who had divorced his father when Larry
was three. The social worker from the therapeutic nursery he was at-
tending was making discharge plans because Larry would be starting
public school and so would need to be in individual therapy. He was to
be placed in a self-contained special education classroom for emotionally disturbed children.**

**At the time of his placement two years earlier, the psychiatric con-
sultant to the nursery concluded that Larry, who was presenting disruptive and uncooperative behavior, was symbiotically attached to his
divorced mother. His mother was thought to have displaced her intensely ambivalent feelings about her former husband onto Larry. Concurrent psychological testing, which the psychologist found difficult to
administer, revealed him to be functioning at the high end of the average range on the I.Q. test, although there was a significant discrepancy,
of 21 points, between verbal and performance scores, with the performance score lower than the verbal. At the time, the psychologist concluded that emotional factors played a large part in the poor performance of the child. But he wondered whether the erratic behavior might
be the result of neurological, seizure-like activity, and for that reason
he recommended that Larry be given a neurological exam. However,
this recommendation was not implemented. A second evaluation, conducted a year later, described Larry as having improved somewhat as a**

result of the milieu provided by the therapeutic nursery. He was less disorganized and somewhat more related. No specific diagnosis of a learning disorder was made. Reexamination of the test results today leads me to conclude that Larry had a nonverbal learning disability, a diagnosis unknown at the time of the prior two evaluations and unknown to me at the time I treated Larry, in the early 1980s.

When I first saw Larry, I described him as a chaotic, disorganized child who attacked his environment in a most disruptive way. He immediately became a management problem, even in the diagnostic sessions, but when limits were set and controls imposed on him, he readily accepted them. I noticed little overt anxiety in him, although much anxiety in myself in response to the bewilderment and disorganization that he experienced.

At the time, I concluded that he was "a classically borderline child with marked neurological problems which were never clearly diagnosed." After two years of treatment, I continued to be puzzled by Larry's lack of progress in therapy and encouraged his mother to obtain the neurological examination recommended earlier by the psychologist. I was able to refer Larry to an excellent medical facility for a full workup. The center diagnosed a "sensory integrative dysfunction" and a borderline personality disorder. It recommended occupational therapy as well as continued psychotherapy. Sensory integration problems are related to motor problems in areas such as sensory processing, fine- or gross-motor control, motor planning or bilateral coordination. They affect the capacity to translate sensory inputs across modalities, as well as the ability to synthesize the various sensory messages received into coherent meaningful concepts (Ayres, 1977). In Larry's case the problem consisted of an inability to process motor tasks and to coordinate them with their concurrent psychological meanings. Crudely speaking, it was as though his body were detached from his mind. His school provided the occupational therapy the center recommended, while I recommended twice-a-week therapy in hopes that the greater frequency would help. His mother, feeling too burdened to bring him that frequently, agreed to continue once-a-week treatment.

The vignette I am about to relate in part illustrates Larry's problem. It also exemplifies the way in which he was able to play out a major theme in his self-narrative. This play sequence developed spontaneously at the midpoint of the third year of his once-a-week treatment. Up to that point, there were no organizing themes to any of his play. Much of the time was spent in containing his behavior to prevent his becoming completely overstimulated and fragmented. There were many struggles around limits to behaviors that I considered to be destructive. In preparation for each session I had to clear the top of my desk and "child-proof" my office by removing all objects he could throw. On occasion, when his behavior became completely unmanageable, I would ask his mother to join us and to restrain him.

The session in which the play sequence I am about to describe occurred began with his usual disruptive behavior. I had gotten up from my chair to protect some item that he was about to destroy. He quickly jumped into my chair, smiling triumphantly. This had happened many times before. I never objected to his sitting in my chair, but this time the quality of the interaction was different. I smiled back, acknowledging that he enjoyed sitting in my chair. He twirled around happily and, because of his lack of coordination, suddenly fell off the chair. I rushed over to check that he was all right. He was lying on the floor smiling. I feigned concern and asked if he was OK. He smiled and said, "I am broken!" I picked up his cue and asked what was broken. He responded by saying, "I'm a broken statue!" I replied in a serious tone that we must put the pieces together. He asked, "How?" I said that maybe I could glue the pieces together until we found a better way to do it. He then happily allowed me to pretend to gather up the pieces. I picked up his hand and, holding each joint, I pretended to glue the fingers, then the hands, then the arms. He then reminded me that I needed to do the same to his feet and legs. I repeated the process with his toes, feet, and legs. By the time we were through, the session had ended and it was time for him to leave. For the first time he walked out quietly and happily.

The following session, he practically ran into the office saying, "Let's play the broken statue game!" I agreed. He lay down on the floor while I methodically pretended to glue the various parts of his body together. Although I took my time doing this, he seemed quite contented and happy. I introduced one variation, which was to culminate the process by taking his head in my hands and firmly placing it on his shoulders. I managed to stretch the game to the full length of the session so that he could walk out feeling whole.

This game continued over a period of months. He introduced a subtle set of variations from time to time. The first variation occurred when he decided that he didn't like being a statue but wanted to pretend to be a robot. This required a different metaphor to repair what was wrong. He still wanted me to manipulate each body part, but now I needed to use tools to put them together. We had an imaginary workshop to help us.

One day, in the midst of the repair, he said that I was not doing it correctly. The arm I was working on was a bionic arm. It needed a different kind of tool to repair it. Soon he was transformed from a mechanical robot to a bionic man. I made the necessary adjustments in the imaginary workshop to permit the repairs to continue. Now he felt that he had superhuman powers and could perform feats no other child could equal. Those were the days of the TV program called "The Six Million Dollar Man," whose hero was a test pilot who had crashed and whose body had been rebuilt with bionic parts.

Weeks went by; then once more in the midst of the game he said that I had forgotten something. I asked what that was. He responded by saying that I did not do a heart transplant. This was the first I had heard of his needing a new heart. I quickly adjusted and became a heart surgeon. He beamed as I pretended to place a new heart into his chest. I reassured him that he would certainly feel better with his new heart.

In spite of the repetitiveness, the game never became ritualized and we both were having a great deal of fun. I certainly felt relieved at not having to deal with the constant pressure of containing his behavior and he seemed to be more content in treatment. The constant component of the game remained the climactic moment when I would take his head in my hands and pretend to firmly fix it on his shoulders, making whatever repairs were necessary to assure that it would remain there.

Larry surprised me one day when, as I was taking his head in my hands, he asked if Einstein's brain was in one of the jars in the local museum he had visited. His class had gone for a field trip to an exhibit on biology. Among the items exhibited were body parts in formaldehyde. He had seen brains kept in jars and wondered where Einstein's brain was being kept. I picked up his cue, saying that I wasn't sure, but was he thinking that he might like to have a brain transplant? I added that if he could have Einstein's brain a lot of things would be different. He responded with a loud, "Yeah! I could get rid of my broken brain!" We both laughed and I agreed to see what I could do about this.

The game continued. I now included the critical brain transplant. He seemed the happiest I had seen him. His behavior at home and at school had improved somewhat, though it was hard to tell whether this was the result of the therapy or because of some of the other interventions he was receiving. It was now June and he was soon to go to summer camp.

Unfortunately, the interruption during the summer was followed by events that did not permit us to build on the gains made in the spring. A new teacher was assigned to his special education classroom, one determined to use strict behavioral methods to correct Larry's conduct.

He responded violently to her efforts and the gains he had made evaporated. He did not return to the game but settled on stopping by the candy machine before coming to his sessions. He then sat quietly playing with the candy while he ate it, creating a gooey mess. He volunteered little as to what was going on and seemed to retreat quietly to a defeated, regressed state.

I saw Larry for another year, until his mother's situation changed so that she could not bring him regularly. By the end of the school year she decided that therapy had not been helpful and, against my advice, discontinued Larry's treatment.

*Discussion*: I present this vignette to illustrate two points that flow from my theoretical discussion. First, the case exemplifies the clinical manifestations of Larry's experience of the world and his sense of self. Second, the play sequence exemplifies the articulation of the central theme in his self-narrative. Had the therapy continued along these lines, the theme might have led to the development of a coherent narrative.

As far as the clinical manifestations of Larry's sense of self, it is possible to hypothesize that the level of fragmentation he presented was at least partially related to his learning disability. While there were other significant factors in his environment and in his relationship with his mother that might account for his symptoms, these were insufficient to explain the extent of his disturbance. Unless one retains the old bias that the early mother-infant interaction determines exclusively a child's psychopathology, it is impossible to ignore the contribution of constitutional factors. Even the extensive interventions introduced from the early age of four-and-a-half were insufficient to reverse the effects of the neuropsychological factors. The disorganized, chaotic behavior he presented in the sessions was accompanied by anxiety that was covered over with excitement and action. Consequently, Larry did not acquire selfobject functions that would have allowed him to regulate his excitement and comfort himself. Unfortunately, he had not learned to use others to provide him with the functions he lacked or to complement his deficits. Perhaps it is in this area that the environment failed him. Once he found a metaphor through which to express his distress in therapy, a metaphor that I could understand, his anxiety dissipated in the sessions and he became more cohesive. The metaphor became the vehicle through which he conveyed a central theme of his self-narrative. It constituted a statement of how he saw himself. Interestingly, the more Larry could elaborate on the theme, the more human he felt he became. This greater integration led to a sense of humanity. Ultimately, he found an explanation for what was wrong with him: his brain was broken.

His self-narrative became more coherent as the play progressed. He realized there was something "broken" in him that needed to be repaired. I became the vehicle through which the repair could take place. Had we been able to continue our work together, eventually we might have reached the point where I could have explained to him the nature of the difficulties that led him to feel that his brain, which was broken at one point, was now restored. We might have worked on how he could use people to help him complement what he did not have. He might then have begun to make use of others as selfobjects, forming meaningful attachments and a more coherent narrative.

## Self-cohesion and Narrative Coherence

The sense of coherence is related to the sense of self-cohesion. Coherence results from the integration of life's occurrences into a set of meanings that are unique to each person. It is the product of the organization and integration of these meanings, their synthesis into preexisting meanings. These systems of meanings are the product of the dialogue with caregivers who provide selfobject function and of the factors contributed by the infant's endowment.

Psychologically, the human struggle is to maintain coherence and to defend against the loss of the sense of self-cohesion (Cohler, 1993). Conflict results from the attempt to reconcile the irreconcilable, to bring together opposites in experience. It also stems from the difficulty of finding a unitary "truth" that is all encompassing and coherent. Conflict need not be equated with pathology. It is the level of incoherence or the disruption created by the conflict that can produce psychopathology.

The sense of cohesion may be thought of as the experience that results from being in a context in which selfobject needs are satisfied and limitations that result from deficits are either complemented by others or compensated for. When associated with a coherent self-narrative, it produces what may be described as a state of self-consolidation. Such a state is present in persons who can endure psychological stresses or nar-

cissistic injuries without suffering from fragmentation, and who have sufficient resiliency, endurance, and strength to tolerate insults without major difficulties. This capacity to tolerate potentially traumatic stresses is
related to the coherence of the self-narrative in tandem with a cohesive
sense of self. The cohesive sense of self is reciprocally related to the sense
of having a coherent self-narrative.

The relationship between coherence and cohesiveness is complex.
There are several possibilities. A person may be *cohesive and coherent,*
*cohesive and incoherent, non-cohesive and coherent*, and *non-cohesive*
*and incoherent.* A child with a learning disorder may feel cohesive because she is in a context that complements her deficits and also have a
coherent narrative in that she understands that she has a learning disorder that requires someone or something to complement her in order
to function satisfactorily. Such is the case when a child who understands
and accepts that she must use the spell-check of her word processor because she has a spelling problem. A different child with a similar learning disorder may feel cohesive because of the support she gets from her
family and tutors, but may not understand the nature of her learning disorder and may not understand the nature of her deficit. She would not
be able to generate a coherent narrative to explain her difficulties. It is
unlikely that a child lacking a sense of cohesiveness can simultaneously
explain the lack of cohesiveness, although some children in great distress, feeling overwhelmed by what they confront, my be able to explain
the sources of their discomfort. Finally, a child may be both distressed
and on the verge of fragmentation as a result of the learning disorder,
but have no idea of what is producing the distress.

Clearly the relationship is complex and one factor is not conditional
for the other. It is an interactive relationship. Understanding may counteract the discomfort of an experience that is threatening, and an experience of being cared for may counteract the child's lack of understanding of what is occurring.

In summary, to be a self is to have a self-narrative that includes having a sense of agency—being a locus of activity, power, and control—and
having the capacity for intentionality, volition, and a sense of coherence.
It also includes having a sense of history, a sense of continuity of experience, a sense of integration and integrity that may be experienced as
cohesiveness, as well as a sense of privacy within the context of intersubjective experiences (Stern, 1985). These specific themes of the sense
of self do not represent universal phenomena, but reflect our particular
culture. In some cultures, where the position of children is not as valued

as it is in ours, the course of development would be entirely different. The components of the sense of self would reflect the values of that specific cultural context.

The child acquires implicit memories that include scripts that become motifs in the child's self-narrative. The facts stored as events in explicit memory are organized into episodes that form the core of autobiographical memory. Scripts constitute biases or beliefs because the child has assigned personal meanings to her experiences. These meanings may differ from the meanings others give to the same event, because the experience of the child with neuropsychological deficits is shaped by those deficits. Episodes are constituted from shared meanings that are consensual within the child's context, i.e., shared by the community.

Children with learning disorders face problems of integrating the meanings of their experiences into the themes within their self-narratives. They ask themselves: "Why am I having so much trouble in school?" "Why do my parents hate me? They keep criticizing me for not doing well in school." "Why don't I have any friends?" At a different level they are aware and puzzled by their own neuropsychological strengths and weaknesses. They ask themselves: "Why can't I be as good in sports as I am in math?" "Why am I so good in sports but can't read?" These questions set the stage for the enactment of themes in the clinical arena. They also provide an opportunity for revision or replacement.

A complex relationship exists between the sense of self-cohesion and the coherence of the self-narrative. Understanding can counter the effects of the loss of cohesion, but the loss of cohesion can also disrupt attempts at understanding. On the other hand, failure to comprehend a set of experiences can be countered by beliefs that help retain the sense of self-cohesion. Such are religious beliefs. But it is also possible that a person can understand what is happening to him but still feel devastated by the occurrence. In other words, a child with social difficulties because of a nonverbal learning disability may understand the sources of his difficulties. This understanding can either be devastating to his sense of self or it can help him maintain his sense of self-cohesion. This same child can feel devastated by the treatment he receives at the hands of his peers and turn to scholarly pursuits while discounting what others do to him.

# 4

## LEARNING DISORDERS AND DISORDERS OF THE SENSE OF SELF: DISORDERS OF SELF-COHESION

As we have seen, disorders of the self result from the loss of self-cohesion, from incoherences in the self-narrative, or both. In this chapter, I begin with a discussion of developmental psychopathology as a way of uncovering the relationship between a child's subjective state and overt symptoms. I examine the complexity that is introduced into this discussion when we consider children with learning disorders. The related topic of comorbidity or of coexisting psychiatric conditions requires clarification and is dealt with briefly. The rest of the chapter is devoted to a discussion of the disorders that result from the loss of self-cohesion in children with learning disorders. In the next chapter, I address the disorders that result from incoherences in the self-narrative and the relationship between these incoherences and the sense of self-cohesion.

### Developmental Psychopathology

The concept of "developmental psychopathology" is central to psychoanalytic theories of psychopathology (Freud, 1983). This view states that all psychological disturbances are understandable within a developmental context, that is, some behaviors that are age-appropriate at a younger

66

age are considered symptomatic if present at an older age. Early psychoanalytic theorists maintained that pathology represented either a fixation in or a regression to a prior phase of drive development, that is, the development of the libidinal or aggressive drives either failed to progress or retreated in the face of interferences from the environment. Ego psychologists enlarged this view by adding the concept of ego deficits. Severe ego deficits, such as those caused by mental retardation, brain syndromes, or physical handicaps, could also produce psychological problems (Fraiberg, 1964, 1977; Freedman, 1981). Self psychologists displaced these explanations by maintaining that disorders of the self are caused by empathy failures during development. These failures produce deficits in the sense of self. As discussed in Chapter 1, all these theories gave insufficient attention to the role of neuropsychological deficits in the development of psychopathology. An account of developmental psychopathology from an evolutionary perspective may come closer to the one espoused here than that of traditional psychoanalysis. However, evolutionary accounts "are typically population-based and fail to account for why a particular individual is affected" (Leckman & Mayes, 1998, p. 1011).

All children's problems must be understood within a developmental context. In addition, they must be viewed as resulting from the intersection of the dual axes of the complementary functions that the context provides and the neuropsychological strengths and weaknesses the child brings to that context. Furthermore, the perspective of the child's subjective experience is critical to a deep understanding of the problems. What the child tells us about the meanings of his experiences provides greater insight into what occurred than does a categorization of the overt symptoms he manifests.

Before continuing, let me dispose of a basic assumption that most psychoanalytic developmental theories make. These theories assume that all children, excepting those with severe deficits, are similarly endowed in all neuropsychological areas. The distinctive differences between children are insufficiently stressed. These theories describe a construct of what might be called a "generic child."* Such a generic child is presented as the norm, to which all children are compared. He becomes the exemplar by which deviations from the norm are evaluated. This approach may be useful for the study of sequential stages through which all children traverse; however, the approach reaches its limits when individual

---

*I am indebted to Laura Segal, Psy.D., for this term, which she coined in the course of one of our many fruitful conversations.

differences among children must be taken into account. My view focuses precisely on the differences rather than on the similarities between the children. A major variable in the differences is the age of the child and his reactions to the stresses he endures. Another variable is that of the protective factors that operate to prevent a child from developing a disorder of the self.

### Relationship between Complementary Functions and Neuropsychological Competencies

I now return to the interrelationship between complementary functions and neuropsychological competencies to explain the circumstances under which a disorder of the self can emerge. Three assumptions underlie these explanations:

1. The complementary functions the context provides exist along a continuum from fully available to totally absent.
2. The child may have neuropsychological deficits or may have a range of strengths and weaknesses in specific areas of neuropsychological functions.
3. The context may make available functions to complement the child's deficits, but the child may be either unable or unwilling to utilize those functions.

The accompanying diagram (see Figure 4.1) serves a useful heuristic function in approaching this discussion. The values along the *x-axis* represent the profile of the complementary functions the context provides the child (as discussed in Chapter 2, these would include whatever compensations the child is able to make for his deficits), and those on the *y-axis* represent the profile of the child's neuropsychological competencies. Let us assume that it were possible to assign a value to represent the amount of support the child receives or fails to receive through complementary functions and a value for the overall profile of the child's measured neuropsychological strengths and weaknesses. The zero value on the *x-axis* would represent what might be called a "good enough" context or an "average expectable environment." The positive values would represent contexts in which supports were available and the child was capable of utilizing them. Conversely, the negative values would represent a context in which the supports were not available or the child could not utilize the supports that were available. Along the *y-axis* the zero value would represent an average set of endowments as measured through testing.

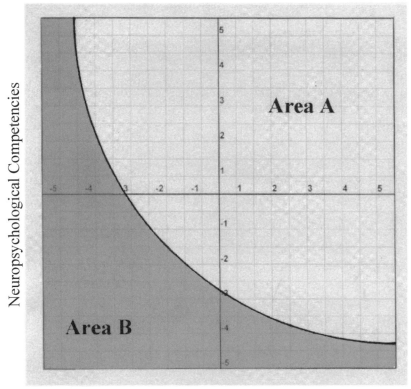

Complementary Functions

**Figure 4.1. Relationship between neuropsychological competencies and complementary functions:** In this graph, the *x-axis* (the horizontal line) represents a hypothetical value assigned to the complementary functions the context provides the child. In both axes the zero value represents an average profile or context. The *y-axis* (the vertical line) represents a hypothetical value assigned to a child's profile of measured neuropsychological strengths and weakness. Any point that falls in Area A would be interpreted as meaning that the child is able to maintain a cohesive sense of self and/or a coherent self-narrative. In contrast, any point that falls in Area B would be interpreted as meaning that the child is unable to maintain or prevented from maintaining a cohesive sense of self and/or coherent self-narrative.

This could be a composite score from several tests or a single score from a comprehensive test. A positive value would represent an above-average composite score of neuropsychological strengths and weaknesses, and a negative value would represent a below-average composite score.

It would now be possible to plot as a point on this graph the intersection of the two values for a given child. In the case of a gifted child in a supportive context with a score of (4,4), the point would fall in Area A. A less well endowed child whose problems interfere with his use of the supports available might have a score of (−4, −4), falling in Area B. Area A covers the scores attained by children who would not have disorders of the self; they would have an adequate sense of self-cohesion and a reasonably coherent self-narrative. Area B represents the converse, scores of children who would suffer from disorders of the self. The imaginary line dividing A and B is the border between children with and those without disorders of the self.*

Consideration of some cases may help clarify the heuristic value of this diagram. A child with a score of 4 (*x-axis*) and −4.5 (*y-axis*) would fall into Area B. That is, a child living within a highly supportive context but having serious neuropsychological deficits could not attain a sense of self-cohesion or a coherent self-narrative in spite of the caregivers' best efforts. The context could not make up for the deficits in endowment. On the other hand, a child with a score of −4 (*x-axis*) and 4.5 (*y-axis*) would also have problems, the reason being that even exceptional endowment cannot make up for a severely depriving social context. Of course, the values set for any child should not be considered as fixed or as predictive of the child's future. These will vary as conditions change and as the child moves forward developmentally. Keeping this diagram in mind during the discussion that follows may help clarify the dynamic role of the two factors in the development of disorders of the self. But first, before turning to that topic, let me briefly address the complex issue of comorbidity.

## Comorbidity

Comorbidity, as used here, refers to the coexistence of one or more *DSM-IV* diagnoses in a child with a learning disorder. *DSM-IV* distinguishes between categorical and dimensional classificatory systems. A categorical system "divides mental disorders into types based on criteria sets with defining features. . . . A categorical approach to classification works best when all members of a diagnostic class are homogeneous, when there are clear boundaries between classes, and when the different classes are

---

*It should be emphasized that this diagram leaves out of consideration the contribution of other important variables, such as physical illness or trauma, to the development of disorders of the self.

mutually exclusive" (APA, 1994, p. xxii). A dimensional system "classifies presentations based on quantification of attributes rather than the assignment to categories and works best in describing phenomena that are distributed continuously and that do not have clear boundaries" (p. xxii). Dyslexia is an example of a categorical disorder, while AD/HD and executive function disorders belong more appropriately to a dimensional classificatory system. *DSM-IV* subscribes to a categorical system. In referring to comorbidity, we refer to the coexistence of one or more distinct psychiatric disorders with a learning disorder. In fact, it is possible to say that a learning disorder can coexist with one or more other learning disorders.

*DSM-IV* also specifies the discrepancy between I.Q. and achievement as the criterion by which to establish the presence of a learning disorder. It is generally recognized that children with learning disorders have a higher prevalence rate of psychiatric conditions than the general population. Studies indicate that about 50 percent of children with a language or learning disorder have a comorbid Axis I psychiatric disorders (AACAP, 1998, p. 46S). However, studies have not established the co-occurrence of a specific Axis I diagnosis and a specific learning disorder. It appears that only a subset of children with a specific learning disorders have the same Axis I coexisting condition, while a different subset has a different coexisting condition (Osman, 2000). A recent book (Brown, 2000b) contains chapters on some of the following coexisting conditions in children with attention deficit disorders: mood disorders, anxiety disorders, oppositionality and aggression, obsessive compulsive disorders, executive function disorders, substance use, sleep/arousal problems, and developmental coordination disorders. No such compendium exists for the other learning disorders discussed in this book, and no data exist as to the frequency with which a given psychiatric disorder co-occurs with a given learning disorder. Dyslexia has received a good deal of attention in this regard through federally funded research (Lyon, 1990), but findings have not supported the hypothesis that a specific comorbid condition or set of conditions is found across a wide sample of children with the same learning disorder. The literature on conditions that coexist with executive function disorders, nonverbal learning disabilities, and Asperger's disorder is practically nonexistent. It is likely that this area will receive increased attention in the future.

In addition, aside from the fact of their coexistence, the relationship between the psychiatric conditions and the learning disorders remains unexplained. It is recognized that learning disorders have different etiologies from psychiatric conditions, but whatever overlap may exist in their etiologies remains to be discovered.

From the perspective taken in this book, the issue of comorbidity raises an important question: How do we view psychopathology from the child's subjective perspective? The psychiatric classifications of *DSM-IV* are intentionally phenomenological; they focus on observable signs and symptoms. This approach permits research to be conducted by investigators at different sites without the introduction of ambiguities inherent in different interpretations of the child's condition. In contrast, my view focuses on the subjective experiences of the child. These subjective experiences can seldom be correlated with the overt manifest behaviors. The child's sense of self and self-narrative are not necessarily reflected in a set of uniform overt symptoms. In fact, the manifest symptoms vary considerably with each subjective state. Furthermore, the same symptoms can be found to reflect different subjective states. This is not to say that the underlying neuropsychological deficits manifest differently from child to child. There are common manifestations that permit the diagnosis and identification of syndromes, but no parallel is found for the relationship between subjective conditions and objective signs and symptoms.

Perhaps the distinction is best made by looking at situations where a learning disorder co-occurs with an Axis II rather than an Axis I diagnosis. In contrast to Axis I disorders, Axis II disorders have multiple etiologies. When we refer to comorbidity, we refer to Axis I disorders, but the symptoms that accompany a disorder of the self are more closely related to some Axis II disorders, such as narcissistic, dependent, and avoidant personality disorders. Some of these disorders of the self do not fully meet the criteria for an Axis II diagnosis. It is possible that the study of neuropsychological strengths and weaknesses will someday provide insight into their contribution to personality development and establish closer ties to the emergence of some Axis II disorders in these children. There is no doubt in my mind that the traits associated with some of the learning disorders described in Section II are also found in patients with diagnosed Axis II personality disorders. The danger lies in making a leap to the obverse of this proposition, that is, that individuals with Axis II personality disorders all suffer from some neuropsychological deficit. No doubt some do, but there are no data to support the proposition that they all might have such deficits.

A different way to approach the relationship between children's symptoms, i.e., their disorder of the self, and their learning disorder is to examine their self-narrative for the meanings they have assigned to their experiences. The motifs in their self-narratives become motives for their thoughts and actions; that is, they become active organizers of the child's thoughts and behaviors. Since the motifs vary widely, the overt symptoms will vary equally. The overt behaviors reflect the child's interpretation of the events to which he has been exposed. These interpretations are as variable as the profile of each child.

A further complexity in the relationship between the learning disorder and the disorder of the self must be kept in mind. Whatever the original cause of the deficits in the child's sense of self or the incoherence in the child's self-narrative, other factors may be responsible for sustaining the child's symptoms. The child's personality continues to unfold with maturation. Other life events contribute to the child's effort at adaptation.* A simplistic linear view of the relationships is misplaced.

In summary, the co-occurrence of learning disorders and some Axis I disorders is not in question. I am raising two questions: What is the relationship between learning disorders and some Axis II disorders? And, what is the relationship between learning disorders and some of the disorders of the self described in this book? A third question that is even more difficult to address is that of the relationship between Axis II disorders and disorders of the self. This last question must be set aside for future discussion.

The first two questions approach the issue of coexistence of maladaptive personality traits and specific learning disorders. There is clinical evidence that some children with AD/HD are generally impulsive, a trait that at times creates serious relationship problems; some children with executive function disorder create chaos in their lives and those of others; some children with nonverbal learning disabilities have serious social problems; almost all these children have self-esteem problems. There appears to be a close relationship between the learning disorder and the personality traits of these children. Since the coexistence of learning disorders has generally been overlooked in the diagnosis of some Axis II disorders and disorders of the self, I propose that we might gain a better understanding of these personality disorders if, as diagnosticians, we remain alert to the presence of a learning disorder as a contributing factor.

## Learning Disorders and the Loss of Self-cohesion

Disruptions in the sense of self manifest as the loss of self-cohesion (see Table 4.1). Anxiety and defenses against it are a general response to impending or actual loss of self-cohesion. Developmental considerations en-

*I am indebted to Jeffrey Weinberg for this observation.

TABLE 4.1
**Learning Disorders and the Loss of the
Sense of Self-cohesion**

1. THE LOSS OF SELF-COHESION
   a. It is a condition in which the child is unable to maintain a sense of inner organization and self-continuity.
   b. It is characterized by anxiety, defenses against anxiety, and a variety of symptoms.
   c. It occurs when complementary functions are unavailable to a child with a learning disorder, when the child is unable to utilize those functions even when available, or when the child cannot compensate for his deficits.
2. THE EMERGENCE OF A DISORDER OF THE SELF
   a. A disorder of the self emerges when negative self-evaluations result in loss of self-esteem.
   b. A disorder of the self emerges when complementary functions such as:
      i. Selfobject functions are unavailable or if available the child's learning disorder interferes with their utilization.
      ii. Adjunctive functions are insufficient to help the child
         (1) maintain self-cohesion or the child is unable to use them.
         (2) attain the intended goal in a task or the child is unable to use these functions.
      iii. Compensations are unavailable or insufficient to prevent the child from a loss of self-cohesion.

ter into those responses, as the tolerance for anxiety varies with the age of the child, as does the repertoire of available defenses. Anxiety that may be tolerable to an adolescent may be experienced by a five-year-old as catastrophic. The range of responses to the anxiety is equally variable. An adolescent is capable of running away from home or going to a friend's house to spend the night, while a five-year-old might feel trapped, with the only options available being to withdraw or have a temper outburst. It would be simple to generalize and say that the younger the child, the more immature, and hence the more brittle the child's sense of self. Such a generalization does not take into account the critical differences in children's capacity to deal with stresses and their ability to withstand adversities. These abilities can only be judged by establishing an empathic connection with the child and entering into the child's subjective experience of the events to which he has been exposed.

Anxiety is an indicator of "psychic pain" and may be understood as analogous to physical pain. Physical pain signals a threat to one's physical integrity, while anxiety is a manifestation of a threat to one's psychological integrity. Primary anxieties that threaten the sense of self are the fear of loss of complementary functions. The result of such losses can range from momentary reversible losses of cohesion to feelings of inner disorganization, a loss of the sense of continuity in time and space, or the experience of disintegration. The experience of the loss of cohesion in a precariously established sense of self can be experienced as "disintegration anxiety" in children with a learning disorder. This disintegrative anxiety results not from the fear of physical extinction but from the loss of the sense of humanity. We see it in children with learning disorders whose sense of being different leads them to feel like aliens. Such a feeling is equivalent to a severe psychological injury.

Anxiety may compound the difficulties a child with a learning disorder confronts when trying to make sense of an experience or an event. The unknown, the unexplainable, the magical, may all be sources of anxiety because they are incoherent. The child cannot integrate the experience, a situation that children with learning disorders often encounter prior to being diagnosed. Here again, developmental factors are critical. What may appear mysterious to a younger child may be easily grasped by an adolescent.

For example, a common source of anxiety in children with dyslexia is that associated with the anticipation of having to read aloud in class. These children have compared their reading skills with those of their peers and realize that their performance is far below that of others. While this puzzles them, they may already have given themselves some explanation for the disparity. Usually, an unflattering view of themselves is embedded in the explanation. Consequently, they fear exposing themselves further to the critical judgment of others. In addition, the task of reading is difficult and painful in itself. Even though they may be highly motivated to do well, decoding the words on a page is a slow, laborious process that requires intense concentration. Constant interruptions by teachers or others to correct their mispronunciations or their misreading of words only compound the task for them. The combination of shame, stress, and frustration leads to overwhelming anxiety. As they get older, children develop a variety of strategies to avoid embarrassment. Their repertoire of defenses increases.

A different set of experiences that give rise to anxiety is encountered by children with nonverbal learning disabilities who have difficulty processing visual-spatial information, or children with Asperger's disorder, whose view of the world is fragmented. These children experience a sense of isolation and aloneness that magnifies their feelings of anxiety. Not only do they feel the loss of contact with others, but they also lack a sense of continuity with their own history. Disconnected from the network of their community, they experience being in a state in which no context exists to give them the support they need.

Defenses are usually automatically instituted to deal with anxiety. They represent an effort to rescue oneself from psychological harm. Kohut states, "Defense motivation in analysis will be understood in terms of activities undertaken in the service of psychological survival" (1984, p. 115). These defenses may be triggered by the anxiety generated by the loss of selfobject functions, by the perception of inadequacy, by affective over- or under-stimulation, or by any threat to the stability of the sense of self. They serve the function of maintaining or restoring the sense of cohesion. In this sense, they serve a "self-righting" function, although they do not enhance the person's growth potential. Defenses and defensive styles cannot simply be correlated with the types of deficits from which a patient suffers.

Defenses are those mechanisms used by the child for the purpose of psychological survival or to avoid confrontation with intense psychic pain that can potentially lead to disintegration. But large differences in defenses and defensive styles exist. This is due in part to developmental factors, in part to temperamental factors, and in part to the nature of the learning disorder. The principle that appears to operate developmentally is that children will use whatever is available to them to deal with their anxieties. Some children will act out, while others will withdraw. Some will develop fears, while others will engage in life-endangering activities. Some will lie to get out of the consequences they fear will result from their behaviors, while others will confess readily, enduring the punishments they anticipated. A common defense used by children with learning disorders is disavowal, i.e., acting in disregard of an unpleasant reality while being perfectly capable of assessing the reality itself. In brief, the range and variability of tolerance for anxiety and defenses to deal with that anxiety explain, in part, the great variability in the symptoms that children manifest. The defense structure also accounts, in part, for the difficulty in establishing direct relationships between overt symptoms and underlying dynamics.

The emergence of a disorder of the self may be caused by one of two sets of conditions: The child may respond to his learning disorder with severe distress, in which case self-esteem problems will ensue, or the child's capacity to use complementary functions may be impaired because of the learning disorder (see Kohut & Wolf, 1978).

### Disorders of Self-esteem

At the most superficial level, children with learning disorders often develop awareness of the differences between themselves and other children, and respond to the negative perceptions that caregivers may have of them (Garber, 1988). Most often these differences acquire a negative valence. The children compare themselves to others and find themselves wanting, feel embarrassed, and quickly believe themselves to be inferior to others. This awareness may emerge at a very early age—from the moment that a toddler finds himself unable to perform a task that he expects to be able to perform or sees playmates demonstrate competencies that are beyond his reach. Other children's teasing or criticisms compound these feelings. At times, parents themselves are puzzled that the child seems unable to perform some simple tasks and berate the child for the shortcomings. The child experiences that realization as an injury to his sense of self; he may then feel imperfect or defective. That realization depresses the child's view of himself, producing shame, anxiety, depression, discouragement, or feelings of incompetence. The loss of self-esteem leads to a destabilization in the sense of self-cohesion.

A further complexity is added to these experiences because of the confusion these children feel about their strengths and weaknesses. Children are confronted with the fact that they excel in some areas of functioning while in other areas they utterly fail. The disparity is a source of puzzlement. They are often faced, on the one hand, with tasks that appear easy for others but are immensely difficult for them, while, on the other hand, they see themselves excelling in tasks that appear difficult to others. In light of these experiences, they may conclude that there is something terribly wrong with them or that the difficult tasks are not worth the effort that goes into succeeding in them. These experiences reinforce the child's negative self-image.

In the previous chapters, I outlined some of the specific ways in which these feelings of being different interfere with experiences of selfobject functions. It is easy to imagine how such feelings would interfere with experiences of being mirrored and admired as well as experiences of being connected to others. Such children suffer from narcissistic injuries and begin to associate these experiences with increasing anxiety, which then colors all of their interactions. Some respond to these anxieties and injuries with uncontrolled rage. Those children are labeled as "behavioral problems." Other children may become withdrawn; they may turn to unexpressed fantasies of revenge or fall back on the stance of infantile grandiosity.

## CASE ILLUSTRATION: JAMIE

**Jamie, a nine-and-a-half-year-old third grader, was referred because of mild behavior problems and attentional difficulties. Both of his parents were high-achieving professionals, and a brother three years older was a star pupil. Jamie had assumed the role of the class clown. He disrupted the teacher's efforts at maintaining order and led a group of kids into mischievous stunts. A trial of Ritalin produced no changes in his behavior. Psychological testing revealed a serious dyslexia; he was reading at the beginning first grade level.**

**When I spoke with Jamie, it was obvious that he was a very bright, engaging, fun-loving child. He revealed excellent social skills, which he used both to draw people to him and to get himself out of difficult situations. As he allowed me to probe below the superficial appearance he gave, it became evident that he felt devastated by his school failure. He spoke bitterly of his envy of his brother because of the adulation he got for his success, expressing the feeling that he was entitled to some of the attention his brother got. He made clear that his rambunctiousness in class occurred when he anticipated that he would be asked to read aloud. He felt that his leadership of the group of kids that surrounded him demonstrated to him that he was smarter than any of the kids in his class. It was evident that Jamie seesawed from highs to lows in how he felt about himself. He was always alert to situations that threatened his self-esteem and on the lookout for defensive maneuvers to avoid embarrassment.**

Of the five disorders discussed in Section II, dyslexia, AD/HD, executive function, and nonverbal learning disabilities are most often associated with self-esteem problems. The demands to perform in accord with a certain level of expectation contribute to the child's feeling that he cannot achieve as expected. In addition, some children make unfavorable comparisons between themselves and others that, in spite of any praise they may receive for areas of competence, lead them to feel incompetent. For a child with Asperger's disorder, the issues of self-esteem may be present, but they are not as central to the psychopathology as are the disorganizing factors related to the learning disorder. Often, such children are less self-conscious or introspective and they also tend to act out their problems, thus discharging their anxiety. The consequence is that they appear less concerned about others' expectations of them and about the disparity between their performance and that of others.

## Disorders of Self-cohesion

Children who develop disorders of self-cohesion are more complex and difficult to characterize than those who have self-esteem problems. Their cognitive and affective deficits can interfere with their use of the caregivers' complementary functions and can also interfere in significant ways with their ability to maintain a sense of self-cohesion. These disorders of self-cohesion are most common in children with severe learning disorders, where there is pronounced interference from neuropsychological deficits.

For example, a child with reasoning or visual-spatial problems will find it difficult to integrate his experiences, which will affect his self-cohesion. For that child, the world does not entirely make sense. One consequence is a disruption of self-cohesion. From the child's subjective perspective, the loss of self-cohesion may be experienced as anxiety, depression, or rage.

### CASE ILLUSTRATION: ALEX

**Alex was an 11-year-old fifth grader in a special education classroom in his school. He had been diagnosed as having a language-based learning disability—a central auditory processing problem. Children with this problem test as having at least average intelligence. They have good hearing, but their comprehension capacity is limited because of their inability to process spoken language as quickly or accurately as others. The result is that people in the child's context assume that he can understand what is being said and quickly become puzzled by the child's responses to their verbal communications. Alex became very proficient at giving the impression that he understood perfectly all that was be-**

ing said to him, even though he generally could only extract part of the communication. His responses were, therefore, not on target, and those in his context who did not know of his problem would soon decide that he was either dumb or simply oppositional, not wanting to respond to their communications.

When I saw Alex, he presented as a sweet, gentle, kind young man, who was totally bewildered by the way others treated him. He had no idea why he was in a special education classroom with kids whom he considered to be either more disturbed or less smart than he was. He spoke of feeling terrible and being anxious in social situations. The saving grace for Alex was his loving family. His parents and older brothers and sisters were totally accepting of him. They provided a haven from the cruel world he experienced outside his home. At a subjective level, Alex felt he was smart. He could extract information from reading, but he could not integrate the events in his life in a meaningful way. The world appeared as arbitrary, often unpredictable, and mostly incomprehensible.

Trying to explain verbally to Alex the nature of his difficulties was a difficult and at times futile task. The problem itself interfered with the effort to communicate with him. Furthermore, his sense of self was fragmented, so that the task of integrating the information at an emotional level was especially difficult. The compromise his parents and I had to make was to help him generally understand that there was something that stood in the way of his hearing others properly and that made it difficult for him to know what was going on in relationships with others.

Children with dyslexia may feel devastated by the shame their condition produces and may periodically fragment under that stress. However, a supportive environment or competencies in other areas may attenuate the stresses, so that fragmentation rarely occurs or, if it does, is related to factors other than the dyslexia.

AD/HD may occasionally lead a child to lose his sense of self-cohesion. The neuropsychological disorder often produces a related deficit in the sense of self that involves the capacity for self-regulation. This deficit produces conditions in which the child cannot modulate intense affect states and may not be able to experience the moderating effect of another person's soothing interventions. The result may be a disintegrative loss of control. The child fragments temporarily, but the sense of self-cohesion is eventually restored.

The situation is more complex in children with executive function disorders. A case may be made that the absence of the capacity to organize the world is inevitably accompanied by a profound absence in the capacity to organize self-experience. In such cases, the vulnerability to fragmentation may pose a constant danger. However, the disorder itself, as we shall see, does not necessarily produce deficits in the sense of self that lead to a vulnerability to fragmentation. This issue needs further empirical study.

Children with nonverbal learning disabilities are more prone to a loss of the sense of self-cohesion than those with dyslexia, AD/HD, or executive function disorder. Two sets of issues affect these children's capacity to maintain a sense of self-cohesion, namely, the extent of their neuropsychological deficits and the availability of complementary functions. In the neuropsychological area, there are visual-spatial problems, as well as problems with new situations or transitions from one situation to another, that produce chronic, at times intolerable, anxiety. Added to the stresses this anxiety produces are their difficulties in reading social cues and forming sustained relationships. These difficulties interfere with having others complement their deficits and therefore place them at risk. Consequently, when others are not available, they are left to struggle with few resources with which to cope. Their loss of self-cohesion often manifests in the form of temper tantrums or rage attacks.

As discussed earlier, many children find ways of compensating for their neuropsychological deficits or find others to complement their areas of weakness. For these children the compensations and complementarity become protective factors against the development of psychopathology. Some children find that their dependence on others in the early years permits sufficient growth to occur so that by the time they reach adolescence they have either adapted to their deficits or developed compensatory mechanisms. Some children, however, either do not find ways of compensating or become stuck in their dependence on others. This latter group often find that their dependence on caregivers becomes entwined in serious conflict. This may be due in part to the fact that they have not found the means through which to compensate and in part to the regressive pull the relationship exerts. The adjunctive functions performed by the caregivers are difficult to give up; yet the continued dependence on them is embarrassing to the child and appears inappropriate to the adult. In either case, the child finds himself in desperate need of the function but endangered by the thought of giving it up.

Adolescents are often caught between the developmental requirements of the phase in which they find themselves—the social expectations of conduct that is appropriate to their age—and the realization of
their ineffectiveness in meeting their own expectations of themselves.
Some simply give up and drop out, as we will see in the case of the adolescent with an executive function disorder (Chapter 9). Some turn to
drugs, embrace alternative cultural values, and/or denigrate the value of
academics. When this occurs, serious family conflicts ensue. The caregivers become distraught at their child's self-destructiveness but feel helpless to intervene. For his part, the adolescent often feels that the caregivers are to blame for his dilemmas. They are held responsible for having
provided the missing functions without helping him to develop compensations that would have permitted him to become more successful
on his own.

The results of these failures are often devastating. This is especially
true for those children for whom adjunctive functions were not available
during their growing years. These children confront repeated failures.
They end up perceiving themselves not only as inadequate, but also as
losers who can never make it in society. This group presents therapists
with the greatest challenge. Often, these children are brought to a therapist in mid-adolescence. Some never received adequate testing, with the
result that their learning disorder was never properly diagnosed. There
is pessimism on everyone's part as to what can be done for the child.
Educators may feel that the diagnosis at this age is too late to change the
course of the adolescent's educational career. Their discouragement is
communicated to the parents, who in turn despair that their child will
find success. The depressive atmosphere often engulfs the therapist, who
may become overwhelmed with a feeling of helplessness. Only massive
intervention, both educational and therapeutic, can rescue such a child
from the fate that awaits him.

At times it may appear as though children with learning disorders "distort reality." It is clear that these children often do not fully grasp events
exactly as others do. They filter their experiences through a distinctive
set of neuropsychological functions that keeps them from obtaining complete information about the context. Because the information is incomplete, it is also often erroneous. Yet these children usually carry a conviction that their perceptions are correct and that they are justified in
their responses. They are unaware that their failure to meet the demands
placed on them is due to their deficits rather that to the obstacles that

others place in their path. These children cannot be said to distort reality in the same way that children who suffer from psychotic disorders distort their reality. Within the bounds of their competencies their perceptions are correct; yet from the perspective of others their interpretations of events are clearly disparate from those most people make. This disparity leads to maladaptive responses on their part, responses to which others in the child's context react negatively. Out of step with his context, the child cannot process what is going on and ends up confused and bewildered. The child's fragmentation is the direct consequence of this confusion.

A good example of this problem is found in children with nonverbal learning disabilities. A child with this disorder has visual-spatial problems, so that he fails to process nonverbal signals, such as facial expressions, vocal intonations, or gestures. As a consequence, he misreads social cues, often misinterpreting social contexts. From the perspective of an external observer, the child appears to be "distorting" reality. Yet, from the child's perspective, he is only processing and acting on the information available to him. it. This child's conduct is different from the conduct of a child who transfers patterns established in relationships with caregivers onto others in his current life. The distinction is between a view of reality colored by a neuropsychological deficit and a transference that is motivated by feelings about people in earlier relationships.

In summary, the relationship between disorders of the self and learning disorders varies with the specific disorder, the complementary functions the context provides, and the developmental stage of the child. The relationship is fluid and varies as the context changes and the child develops. Comorbid psychiatric conditions (Axis I, *DSM-IV*) are frequently found alongside learning disorders. These psychiatric conditions are presumed to have different etiologies from learning disorders. Data are not available as to the frequency of the occurrence of a specific comorbid condition with a specific learning disorder and the relationship of each to the other is also unknown. On the other hand, it is likely that a relationship exists between some personality disorders (Axis II, *DSM-IV*) and learning disorders. Learning disorders may contribute significantly to personality disorders, but not all individuals with personality disorders have learning disorders. (See Hooper & Olley, 1996, for a discussion of comorbidity in adults with learning disabilities.)

Anxiety is both an indicator of a loss of self-cohesion and a contributor to it. When a threat to self-cohesion exists, defenses are activated in an attempt at self-rescue. These defenses may manifest as overt symptoms of the child's distress. Disorders of self-cohesion result from self-critical attitudes a child develops in comparing himself to others, resulting in self-esteem problems. In addition, disorders of the self are found either when the child cannot avail himself of the complementary functions caregivers can provide or when those functions are not available to the child.

# 5

# LEARNING DISORDERS AND
# INCOHERENT SELF-NARRATIVES

CHILDREN PRESENT US WITH THEIR current level of integration. To the extent that they are cohesive they can often give a coherent account of themselves through their self-narrative. To the extent to that they are troubled and lack cohesion they often fail to create a coherent narrative out of their life experiences (see Table 5.1). In a sense, their distress arises from the fact that they have been unable to make meaningful what has happened to them. The absence of coherence in their narrative may be in direct proportion to the level of their distress (Cohler, 1982, 1987, 1993). Children experience fragmentation states as a loss of inner organization and the loss of the meanings associated with their experiences. A disorder of the self represents the absence of coherence in the child's self-narrative. Writing of older adults who confront their mortality, Cohler states:

> A sense of psychological well-being in later life is assumed to be associated with enhanced preservation of meaning, expressed as a purposive or coherent life story. Failure to maintain this coherent life story leads to feelings of lowered morale and a sense of personal depletion, as exemplified by the older patient who had lost her sense of personal significance. (1993, p. 108).

Freud introduced the unconscious to make rational sense of his patients' irrational symptoms. Perceiving a fundamental split between the

TABLE 5.1
**Learning Disorders and the Incoherences
in the Self-narrative**

---

1. NARRATIVE INCOHERENCE
   a. Incoherences in the self-narrative represent the child's failure to make sense of episodes within her experiences.
   b. These incoherences are accompanied by feelings of confusion, uncertainty, and lack of comprehension.
   c. They are produced when the child's self-narrative is not concordant with the community's beliefs and values.
2. THE EMERGENCE OF A DISORDER OF THE SELF
   a. A disorder of the self emerges when:
      i. A discordance exists between the personal meanings the child has construed from her experiences and the shared meaning those experiences have for others.
      ii. A conflict between two or more motifs in the self-narrative develops, such as those that result from emplotments or conventionalizations.
      iii. The child's neuropsychological deficits interfere with the ability to integrate the meanings of a set of experiences within the broader self-narrative.
   b. Disruptions in narrative coherence come in a range from partial to substantial incoherences.

---

irreconcilable demands of the drives and the demands of reality, he posited the ego as mediator between the two sets of demands. The ego as a representative of the rational self finds a compromise position that permits the person to adapt. In contrast to this position, which sees human beings as torn apart by internal conflict, self psychology maintains that people's normative mental state is one of unity and coherence. According to this view, there is nothing innately irrational in human beings, although feelings can certainly overrule reason. This model suggests that the conflicts from which human beings suffer are the product not of forces deeply at work in human nature but of deficits from which we all suffer to one degree or another. Our deficits may be the result of an accident of circumstance rather than the result either of instinctual forces or of our evolutionary history. In short, not all conflict is derived from the irrational and not all irrational thoughts or acts are necessarily derived from conflict.

Disorders of the self may manifest in three different types of incoherences in children with learning disorders: (1) incoherences due to discordances between personal and shared meanings; (2) incoherences that result from conflict between irreconcilable motifs, such as those due to the child's emplotment in another's narrative or to the child's attempt at conventionalizing her narrative at the expense of her sense of self; and (3) incoherences that are the product of the failure to integrate experiences because either the child's integrative capacities are overtaxed or the neuropsychological deficits interfere with the integrative task. These three categories do not comprise a comprehensive typology of all the possible types of narrative incoherences that children present. They are simply common examples of such incoherences.

Before turning to a discussion of these three types of disorders, let me address two sets of issues that are central to this perspective, first, what is meant by narrative incoherence, and second, how we differentiate between fantasies and personal meanings in these disorders.

## Incoherences in the Self-narrative

The concept of incoherence raises some major questions: Who is to judge what is incoherent and by what criteria is that judgment to be made? How do we evaluate incoherences from a developmental perspective?

The line between coherence and incoherence is blurred because of differences in perspective. Is a self-narrative incoherent because the patient views it as such or because the therapist considers it to be so? An easy answer to this question is that the narrative is incoherent if the patient and the therapist agree on this point. However, this is not always satisfactory. A child may become distressed because she cannot make sense of an experience that makes perfect sense to the therapist, as in the case of the child who complains that she cannot make friends. In such cases, the narrative the therapist uses to make sense of the child's story is different from the one the child has put together. The therapist finds a different or deeper meaning to the events than the child thought existed. The informed therapist has an explanation for the child's distress and experiences that the child lacks.

Alternatively, some children provide coherent narratives, having explained to themselves what occurred through interpretations given to them by others or by creative connections they have made between disparate events. They may have been called lazy or stupid and criticized for what was interpreted as lack of motivation. Having internalized these criticisms, they embrace these views of themselves. When there is disparity between their narrative and that of the therapist, whose coherence should prevail?

As discussed previously, the coherence of self-narratives cannot be judged by logical criteria. It is a function of the concordance between the personal meanings the child has assigned to events and the shared meanings the context gives to them. When the two sets of meanings are not concordant, the child's understanding clashes with that of the community. Problems arise when the child acts on that understanding, because her responses are perceived by others, including her peers, as being out of step with theirs. For example, a child with an organizational problem may firmly believe that she has no "problems" because subjectively she does not evaluate her disorganization as troublesome. Many of the children I have seen who have this problem will say, when confronted by the chaos in their room, "I know exactly where everything is! If mom cleans up my room, I can't find anything!" The learning disorder does not allow them to perceive that disorder makes for less efficient functioning and they evaluate that disorder positively, finding it to be more desirable than imposed order. The coherence they find in the self-narrative clashes with the caregivers' understanding of what makes sense.

A further complexity arises because of developmental factors. Younger children's capacity to understand causal relationships is less developed than that of older children. Consequently, they will often associate events that are accidentally or temporally linked, believing them to be causally connected. The themes in their self-narrative may incorporate these relationships between events and generalizations made from them. Subjectively, the narrative is coherent, but from the perspective of others it makes little sense. As the child grows older, these seemingly archaic explanations may become modified, elaborated, or embellished. But their nucleus may remain unchanged, leading to beliefs that guide the child's conduct in problematic areas. The age at which such themes crystallize determines, to a degree, whether personal or shared meanings will predominate.

Ultimately, these tensions within the self-narrative are resolved through the therapeutic process. The first steps in therapy require the therapist to immerse himself in the patient's narrative. Once the patient feels that he has been adequately understood, the therapist may share his view of the motives that lead the patient to construct those meanings within the narrative. In making these interpretations, the therapist gives explanations that include factual knowledge about the patient's deficits. The therapist has a body of knowledge that the patient does not possess. By sharing this knowledge the therapist is not simply giving the patient a new narrative but also providing a contextually shared set of meanings derived from that broad base of knowledge. These shared meanings eventually provide the child with an understanding through which to modify her narrative and bring it in line with the shared meanings within the community of which the patient is a part. The information or the interpretations the therapist provides, when incorporated into the patient's narrative, may bring about a shift in the child's attitudes or behaviors. But the reinterpretations are insufficient. For such a shift to occur it must be accompanied by a set of experiences within the transference. The coherence that results is one that the patient will find meaningful within her context.

## Fantasies and Personal Meanings

The explanations children give themselves for events to which they are exposed have traditionally been identified by child therapists as fantasies, because these explanations do not match the reality to which they refer. From this perspective the goal of the therapeutic process is to have the child reveal these explanations, which are then corrected so that they match the probable reality at the time they were formed.

The question this point of view raises is whether it is correct to call the child's communications *fantasies*. Might they not be seen as beliefs to which the child has arrived based on her limited knowledge of the world? If we subscribe to the view that these expressions are fantasies, then we must distinguish the products of a child's imagination from explanations the child has reached about actual events. On the other hand, if we view the explanations as *hypotheses* the child has reached to assist her in interpreting her world, then we are left with the disparity between these hypotheses as personal meanings and the meanings that others in the context share as explanations for the same occurrences. In the latter case, the position to which I subscribe, a distinction may be made between a fantasy and an explanation that is proposed as a hypothesis (Gopnik, Meltzoff, & Kuhl, 1999).

The child's communications are based on the relationship she has established between memories of actual events. Her autobiographical accounts are the product of connections she has established between those events as she experienced them. A fantasy is the product of her imagination. She may make use of memories or knowledge she has acquired to construct an elaborate story, knowing all along that the story is not veridical. The difference between a hypothesis and a fantasy lies in the child's belief that the former is an accurate rendition of what happened, as she recalls it, while the latter is not.

This is similar to the dilemma Spence (1982) presents us when he discusses the distinction between narrative truth and historical truth, which parallels the distinction between personal meanings and shared meanings. If the criterion for the establishment of narrative truth is coherence within the self-narrative, then the self-narrative need not be anchored in the events that gave rise to it. Self-narratives would be no different from fantasies, since they would be indistinguishable from them. There would be no way of establishing their veracity. But if the criterion for the establishment of historical truth of the self-narrative is the correspondence between the explanation and what actually occurred, then a link must exist between what is recalled and what actually occurred—even though what is recalled is a reconstruction of what occurred.

To my mind, the distinction rests on the nature of memory and on the theories of memory function. More light may be shed on this issue as discoveries in the neurosciences add to our understanding of memory function. Therapists, obviously, have no access to the historical events themselves, so they must justify their explanations based on criteria that distinguish between fact and fantasy. Part of the problem lies in the confusion between personal meanings and fantasies. The concept of fantasy in its restricted sense characterizes imaginary or fictitious productions; consequently, the status of the events as nonexistent is not in question.

The construct of personal meaning represents a different form of discourse. Personal meanings represent an interpretation of historical events, however idiosyncratic those interpretations might be. Nonetheless, the interpretations are of actual events. The distinction, therefore, resembles the difference between a novelist and a historian. Unlike a novelist, a historian is constrained by such things as the need to be faithful to the chronology in which the events occurred, and to retain the context and time frames. He cannot add or subtract characters or change the formal relationships that existed among the characters. A brother cannot be a father or a son; the child cannot be born prior to the parents.

Although the elements added to a self-narrative are not found in the events themselves but in the specific meanings the events had to the patient, we cannot call this edition of the events a fantasy without losing much of the meaning and specificity of that concept. An analogy may be drawn with the verdict a jury renders in our system of justice. During litigation, opposing attorneys present two versions of an event to a jury. The task of the jury is to determine which of the two versions is likely to correspond to the historical events themselves. Facts are presented to the jury by both sides, with each side trying to convince the jury of the coherence of its narrative. But at the same time, what is at stake is the truth of what occurred. I believe that as therapists we stand like jury members in relationship to both the narrative the patient presents and to our own. It is our responsibility to balance the tensions between the two stories but be committed to the search for truth rather than simply settle for coherence.

This means that the personal meanings within the patient's narrative can be subjected to modifications through a set of shared experiences or through the revelation of new or additional facts. The therapeutic process, therefore, does not correct a fantasy; rather, it may be said to exchange the patient's personal understanding for a shared understanding. What was formerly unclear to the patient or therapist is modified through the shared set of experiences. The modification is not the substitution of one fantasy for another; rather, it entails the addition of a perspective created within the transference that includes a new set of experiences. The contributions the therapist makes by giving explanations based on his experience and knowledge is balanced by the search for what actually occurred.

In the case of children with learning disorders whose narratives have elements of incoherence, the incoherences are reduced by the experience of having the sources of the disturbances understood. The therapist contributes information about the effects the neuropsychological deficits produce on the patient's view of events. Once the child can grasp the significance and impact of the deficits, a set of shared meanings is created that leads to a reduction in incoherence. The psychodynamic factors at play in the child's problems may then be sorted out from the facts of the deficit and interpreted accordingly.

This is not to negate that children embellish their explanations with fantasies. We have seen this in children's reports of sexual abuse. I would call these embellishments secondary elaborations. A nucleus of truth, in the form of a memory, has been expanded by the addition of fantasies drawn from other sources. Fantasies replace some of the personal meanings. Children may be vulnerable to such secondary elaborations when they have suffered a trauma or when they wish to please an adult.

## Narrative Incoherences and Disorders of the Self

Incoherences in a self-narrative can range from mild to severe. For example, at the milder end of the spectrum is the narrative of a child with dyslexia, who is puzzled by her inability to achieve in spite of her conviction that she is smart. At the other extreme are the incoherences in the narrative of the child with Asperger's disorder, who has great difficulty integrating experiences into her sense of self. For such a child, creating a coherent narrative presents an insuperable task. When asked, she may attempt to give an account of her experiences but her account would be either idiosyncratic or quite incoherent.

Earlier I identified three types of narrative incoherences: incoherences due to discordant personal and shared meanings, those due to conflicts between motifs, and those related to interferences in the integration of events or experiences that learning disorders cause. Let me elaborate on these.

### Discordant Personal and Shared Meanings

Discordant meanings represent inconsistencies between the personal meaning assigned by a child to a set of experiences and how others view the same set of events. In this sense, personal meanings represent idiosyncratic interpretations and views of reality. Discordant meanings are often present in the feelings that children with dyslexia have about themselves as contrasted to the way they may be viewed by others. Although these discordances do not generally lead to serious disorders of the self, they are a source of considerable distress to the child. On the one hand, such children realize that they are smart, often even smarter than many of their peers; on the other, they are confronted with the reality of their failure to achieve. Explaining this discrepancy is often a serious challenge to them. Their puzzlement is often compounded by others' responses to their failures. The effect of the disapproval they get from their caregivers for not applying themselves sufficiently to the task, the criticism they face from teachers who believe them to be lazy, and/or the teasing and derision they get from their peers is a sense of shame and crushing humiliation that pervades their sense of self. Reconciling the two views becomes a formidable, if not impossible, task.

Prior to their initiation into the world of reading, they were relatively happy, carefree children. The motifs organizing their earlier self-narrative were benign or very positive. As one mother reported to me, her child's kindergarten teacher had said to her that one day her child would become president. If the child were to incorporate such a theme into her self-narrative, her subsequent disappointment when confronted with her inability to read would be devastating. When the child also incorporates later experiences into motifs within her self-narrative, she faces the challenge of resolving the confusion created by incompatible motifs.

There is another dimension that is added to this confusion. In an effort to explain the failure to herself, the child creates a script that ties together disparate aspects of her experience into a motif. The motif may include meanings such as "Reading is dumb and unimportant!" or "The teacher is stupid, she doesn't help me!" or "I can get by, I can fool the teacher into thinking I know how to read but pretend that I am too shy to stand up in class to do so." As a hierarchy of such experiences evolves, the child constructs a major motif that may incorporate notions such as "I am smarter than everyone else, but I am not appreciated because I am not my father's favorite!" These personal meanings then act as motives for future action and cause problematic behaviors that may evolve into symptoms. Only when they are uncovered or replaced in therapy as shared meanings can the child be healed of the inner rift. The shared meanings, however, must include an understanding of the source of the dyslexia in a neuropsychological deficit that was responsible for the original failure.

### CASE ILLUSTRATION: JEFF

**Jeff, nine years old, was referred by the neuropsychologist who had diagnosed him as having a nonverbal learning disability. He had serious visual-spatial-organization problems that interfered with his processing of other people's nonverbal social cues. Jeff constantly misinterpreted his caregivers' facial expressions, thinking that they were disapproving, when in fact they were visibly concerned and caring. Similar difficulties were present in peer relationships and in the classroom setting. The teacher, unaware of Jeff's learning disability, tried to control his inappropriate behavior in the classroom by nonverbally signaling her disapproval. The fact that he failed to process her signals and persisted in his behavior led her to feel that he was being oppositional and defiant. She responded by being firmer with him than with the other children, treating him as having a behavior problem.**

Since he missed important aspects of others' communication, Jeff's experience was that people did not like him, that he was punished arbitrarily for things he did not do, and that there must be something terribly wrong with him that he got these responses. During the initial evaluative sessions, Jeff launched into a fantasy about CIA agents who communicated in a secret code that only a few privileged people understood. He detailed the various countries that were infiltrated by the agents and the countermeasures that those countries took to decode the secret messages while at the same time developing their own secret codes that would be unbreakable by the enemy. The symbolic meaning of the fantasy was evident. He lived in a world that used a code of communication that he did not understand. His task was to break this secret code so as to understand and communicate with others in his world. In other words, the personal meaning that he attached to others' messages was directly related to his learning disorder. Had I not known about the nature of his difficulties, I would have taken the fantasy to reflect a strong paranoid suspiciousness of others that helped him defend against the fear of closeness. The opposite was the case. Behind the fantasy lay a deep longing for a close intimate relationship, as he later revealed when he talked of communicating with several imaginary companions who shared the same code and were part of the "agency" he directed. Embedded in this fantasy was a set of personal meanings that reflected his belief about how people communicated with him. The fantasy was "part hypothesis" that explained the reasons for the difficulties he was having understanding others. The incoherences in Jeff's narrative were smoothed over by the explanations he gave himself as to why people responded to him as they did. His disorder of the self reflected both the lack of self-cohesion and incoherence of his self-narrative.

If we look at Jeff from a developmental perspective to understand how he acquired these personal meanings, we can speculate about how he experienced the world from infancy on and how his learning disorder contributed to those meanings. We can imagine Jeff as an infant struggling to focus on and identify the features of his mother's face. His visual-spatial-organizational problems would have prevented him from identifying her visually. In a sense, he would have been like a blind child who had to rely on other sensory modalities to form an attachment to his caregiver. But since his vision was intact his caregiver would have had no way of knowing that he was unable to recognize her. She would have responded with bewilderment at the absence of a connection to her. She might have doubted her mothering skills or her investment in the child. In spite of his learning disorder, Jeff would have detected her intense anxiety. And the disconnection from her would have been heightened because of the barrier the anxiety imposed on him. If by some leap of empathy his caregiver could have overcome her own insecurity and anxiety, the bond between her and Jeff might have been sustained. But Jeff's difficulties were only beginning.

Jeff's learning disorder would systematically affect every other aspect of his life. If he were taken to an unfamiliar environment, a visit to grandparents, for example, the new environment would present him with a booming-buzzing confusion that he would be unable to process. Not only could he not connect with the new faces, but the room, the furniture, the toys with which he might be presented would all enhance his anxiety. Soon his caregivers would find themselves with a screaming, inconsolable child. They would be totally unaware of the reasons for his distress. Such caregivers might learn that Jeff required the safety of familiar context and adapt to his demands. But there would be limits to their ability to protect him from life circumstances.

If we now step aside from Jeff's overt behavioral responses to speculate on how he would have processed and encoded these experiences, we find that he would have begun to attach personal meanings to those experiences, meanings that would be quite different from those that the caregivers were attaching to the events. To him, the world would be a somewhat chaotic place that would be difficult to figure out. But as a child with normal intelligence, he would begin to form representations of those events whose meanings would be personal. He might think of his caregiver as someone who inconsistently attended to his needs. He might begin to believe her to be uncaring or distracted. If he were to become enraged at her because of what he experienced as neglect, the relationship would become more complicated or impaired. Eventually, by the age of four or five, he might decide that mother liked his older sister better, that he was a problem child, and that he must clamor and scream in order to get her attention.

We can obviously extend this discussion, but I hope the point is made that the learning disorder produces circumstances in which the child draws unique personal meanings from his experiences and that these in turn shape his interactions with others. Often, the end result is an incoherent self-narrative and an associated disorder of the self.

### Conflict between Motifs

Of greater interest than the usual conflicts we encounter in children's self-narratives are the conflicts generated by *emplotments* and *conven-*

*tionalization.* These concepts are useful in helping us understand the contribution of the context to the self-narrative and provide a perspective on the way in which children with learning disorders deal with the demands of the environment. Emplotment (Kerby, 1991, p. 3) occurs when the child plays out a role assigned by caregivers that conforms to their expectations of who the child should be. Conventionalization is the process through which a child directs her efforts at having her self-narrative conform to what the community defines as conventional. The child is then in conflict about whether she should conform or pursue her own path. Some children set expectations for themselves even though others have not assigned such expectations to them. When others' expectations conflict with the desires they have to pursue their own life plans, serious conflicts between motifs arise.

Caregivers come to the task of parenting with ready-made narratives of their own, narratives that they have construed from their experiences. The infant may be experienced as a character in their own life's play. While the infant is endowed with a gender as well as with a number of other attributes, the parents carry with them wishes, ideals, and desires that they would like to see realized in the infant's life. Kohut spoke of this phenomenon as the virtual self—the child as a parent desires him or her to be.

Specific narrative motifs are part of some family's traditions; such families have myths that pervade child-rearing and influence the child's narrative. In addition, parents' narratives may get included into the child's narrative. The notion of emplotment is more specific; it involves the active engagement of the child in the preestablished roles of another's narrative. The child configures her experiences into the meanings given by the caregivers. Caregivers structure these meanings into particular scripts that have meaning to them. However, each child edits these scripts, making them conform to meanings that have coherence for her.

The notion of emplotment is particularly relevant to the problems of children with learning disorders. The issues of labeling a child as having a learning disorder illustrate this feature of the self-narrative. Following the diagnosis of a learning disorder, the child is exposed to a set of circumstances in school settings that may be experienced as finding out who she is. The student may be required to have tutorial help that takes her out of regular classes or she may be placed in a special education class. In either case, the student becomes emploted into a system that defines her role in the eyes of her peers and of the educational institution. She is compelled to give up part of who she is by the system in which she participates.

Some students respond by passively conforming or even using the role assignment to accentuate their sense of helplessness and dependence. Others resent and fight the system. They experience such shame that they respond with aggression and rebellious behaviors. They refuse to become emploted into the system; however, they end up being relabeled as oppositional or as having a conduct disorder and thus are shuffled to a different role assignment.

A second feature of the self-narrative is the child's desire to *conventionalize* her narrative into the normative narrative, i.e., the canonical narrative of the social/cultural milieu (Bruner, 1990). The child is slowly exposed to the broader social context through baby-sitters, day care, relatives, school, peers, etc. The challenge to the child is to conventionalize her narrative by having it conform to that of the larger community in which she lives. In order to maintain the selfobject ties to the members of the larger social group, the child may embrace or reject the values that the group maintains. She may modify her narrative to bring it closer to the expectations of those whose opinions are valued.

Each context presents the child with challenges of conventionalization. For instance, each child must integrate the social norms and expectations of gender behaviors into her narrative. In recent years, as the norms have changed and the expression of gender differences has become less stereotypical, it has become possible for gay men and lesbian women to develop conventionalized narratives of their own. This has meant that our society has had to be more accepting of a pluralistic expression of gender preferences and less insistent on a single canonical form.

Individual narratives become conventionalized into normative social narratives. The transition from personal to conventionalized narrative is made through the social rituals prescribed for the person, such as circumcision, bar or bat mitzvah, confirmation, graduation, wedding, etc. The conventionalized narrative becomes part of the person's "social identity." Conventionalized narratives have a culture-specific structure that is prescribed by the community (e.g., Horatio Alger, George Washington, Abe Lincoln, etc., are narratives that approach having "mythological status." They embody a set of values seen as desirable by the social order or culture). Deviations from those prescriptions are labeled aberrations.

If a child appropriates a conventionalized narrative because it is imposed by the caregivers as part of the "virtual self" constructed by the parents, this may lead the child to develop a "false self" (Winnicott, 1960). The child lives out the parents' expectations through the enactment of a specific narrative or of a part in a larger narrative the caregivers dictate.

For children with learning disorders, conventionalization is closely related to the selfobject function of alter-ego that was discussed earlier. While the feeling of kinship to others is a profound issue for patients with learning disorders, the impetus to conventionalize their narratives is driven by the desire to be like others, to eliminate their sense of difference. The cost of conventionalization lies in the negation of a fundamental aspect of the sense of self. The conflict between the negative themes associated with having a learning disorder and the community's perception of what constitutes conventional behaviors may lead to incoherence in their self-narrative.

As we will see, some adolescents struggle against the imposition of requirements to conventionalize their self-narratives until they derive a set of values they can comfortably embrace. The processes involved are complicated by the presence of a learning disorder. The difficulties a child with a learning disorder may have with expectations set by others are at times related to the fear of having to negate some important part of oneself in order to conform. The fear of being molded by others leads the child to actively resist the process. It is as though she faces the dilemma of conforming at the cost of developing a "false self" or rejecting the expectation and being branded as nonconformist. The difficulties these children face in developing a coherent self-narrative are due to the fact that at some level they feel some allegiance to two sets of competing values— the desire to please others and the wish to be true to themselves.

Some children with learning disorders reject efforts at emplotment or conventionalization because they feel that what is expected of them is unattainable. Others reject those efforts because the learning disorder itself defeats the goals set for them. Many in the former group are motivated by the fear of failure, although that fear may be unconscious. Those in the latter group simply do not have the competencies to meet the expectations set for them. In either case, a conflict between the two motifs may lead to symptomatic behaviors.

Some children with AD/HD exemplify the first group of children, while some with executive function disorders exemplify the latter group. Caregivers of children with AD/HD find themselves constantly having to correct, restrain, or inhibit the child's behavior. It is as though they can coexist with the child only by reshaping her behavior. Obviously, this is not done by caregivers simply out of their own need to have the child conform, but because it is their duty as good parents. For their part, the children may initially wish to please their caregivers in order to retain a bond with them. But their impulsivity or hyperactivity overrides those efforts. The children then become caught between their parents' insistence on good behavior and their inability to restrain themselves. If the parents' disapproval or disciplining strategies feel oppressive to the child, then a negative cycle of interactions ensues. Negative approaches by the parents are met with negativism or oppositional behaviors.

When the interactional process is given a personal meaning by the child, the child may brood, feeling that her parents hate her, or interpret their responses as the attention that she craves from them. In either case, the child will act on these interpretations and respond to the parents with further unacceptable behaviors. The child may then turn to tormenting a younger sibling as a way of getting back at the parents for the injustices she feels they are committing. These personal meanings may then become embedded in a script whose central motif is to challenge the caregivers' efforts at emplotment or conventionalization. The child's narrative elaborates those motifs, as they become organizers for the path in life the child will take.

A different set of outcomes awaits children with executive function deficits. For this group of children, there are fewer encounters with the expectations set by caregivers' emplotment or conventionalization prior to adolescence. Most often, during the early years, the children are considered sloppy or disorganized but not symptomatic. These traits are not perceived as being very significant, and their effects do not raise serious concerns for caregivers. However, as the children approach adolescence and the tasks they confront increase in complexity, their efforts at meeting expectations are defeated by their deficits. It is then that more overt conflicts arise between adolescents and their caregivers. The problems at school underscore the limitations of their capacity to achieve. At that point, these adolescents confront a similar set of dilemmas as children with AD/HD. Only now the stakes are much higher. Failures at this level threaten the possibility of success in getting into the desired college or a particular career path. As I will detail in the next chapter on adolescence, the incoherences that result have serious consequences for these adolescents' lives.

### Failure to Integrate Experiences

It is easier to understand how a person exposed to a traumatic experience is unable to integrate its full meaning than it is to understand how a person of average intelligence appears unable to integrate the meaning of a relatively simple human interaction. But that is what happens to some of the children whose neuropsychological deficits impair their capacity to integrate day-to-day experiences. Examples are found among children with central auditory processing disorders, nonverbal learning disabilities, and Asperger's disorder. Commonly, when one listens to a child with a central auditory processing problem or nonverbal learning disability give an account of an incident that occurred in school the previous day, the story appears to make little sense. The sequence of events is jumbled, the central point of the story appears to be missing, and the entire thread that ties the events together is tangled. Only through arduous questioning of the child does an outline of what occurred take shape. In the case of children with Asperger's disorder, the effort at reconstructing an incident appears to be futile. These children are often more interested in a continuing monologue that is unrelated to events in their lives than they are in reporting on day-to-day occurrences. Often the presence of a caregiver is required if one wants clear information about them and events in their lives.

It is evident from these descriptions that this group of children is unable to give a coherent account of their self-narratives. Why this is so is not known. Different factors operate in children in each disorder. Children with central auditory processing difficulties have good intelligence, but their language receptive abilities are impaired. Consequently, what they process is their idiosyncratic explanations of what they believe they heard. In nonverbal learning disabilities and Asperger's disorder, children appear at times to fail in the task of grasping the significance of events in their lives. What appears to be lacking in their reporting is the connection between separate scenes of an event. In the case of children with Asperger's disorder, the deficit appears to be in their inability to understand the motives that lay behind other people's actions. They seem to register the overt behavior but to be mystified as to why people act as they do. A good example is their failure to understand humor. Humor is a complex form of communication because it involves simultaneously processing messages at their surface and deeper levels. Children with Asperger's disorder are concrete in their interpretations of the content of communications and do not grasp the metaphoric elements. Consequently, the meaning of humorous remarks escapes them. This fundamental deficit in the capacity to integrate meanings interferes significantly with the formation of a coherent self-narrative.

CASE ILLUSTRATION: WILLIAM

William, 14½ years old, was referred by the school social worker because she felt that he was underachieving. Over the phone she described
him as a kind, gentle young man who appeared much brighter than his
school performance demonstrated. He was liked by peers, had one or
two close friends, but seemed to restrict his relationships with others.
He had been referred for testing by the school.

*Test results*: The educational psychologist's evaluation indicated that
William was functioning at the lower limits of the superior range of intelligence. Intellectually, a significant disparity of 16 points existed between verbal and nonverbal skills, with higher scores reflected in nonverbal skills (WAIS-R, Verbal I.Q. 112, Performance I.Q. 128, Full Scale
I.Q. 120). William revealed problems in auditory processing and receptive and expressive language. He could not grasp inferential language
and had difficulty with word retrieval. William was unable to process,
retain, and subsequently integrate complete ideas. The information was
originally stored in fragmented form for future retrieval. Because of his
deficit in processing information, he continued to integrate only fragments of information. Although his intelligence was potentially high,
William's deficit in sequencing and retaining language for functional use
had interfered with success. He seemed unable to consistently bring to
learning the procedures necessary for organizing certain information-
processing operations basic to adequate comprehension. His processing ability declined with the increasing complexity of tasks, disclosing
deficits of storage and retrieval that were organizational in nature.
William's auditory problems and his receptive language deficits ad-
versely influenced the coherency of information he heard or read, and
therefore what he integrated for future retrieval. Since he could not hold
onto auditory information long, he could not follow and integrate
lengthy speech or use auditory context well to further develop his vocabulary. He was often unable to use context well in reading in order
to expand his vocabulary and/or enhance comprehension. The deficits
interfered with William's ability to develop a sound, conceptual language
foundation on which higher level cognitive skills could be based.

*Treatment process*: I saw William for almost four years. I report only
on the segment of the work we did together that relates to his language-
processing problem.

When William started treatment, he would report conversations with
his parents or peers that left him puzzled—he could not understand

what was being said to him. His learning disorder had been explained to him; however, he had not integrated how it interfered with communication on a day-to-day basis. He had been taught to tape all of his classes so he could replay the tapes at home to extract from them the content of the lectures. His mother often translated others' communications to him, but in most social situations, where interactions were rapid and shifting, he was at a loss. He also probably lost a great deal of the content in his peers' rapid conversational exchanges, which accentuated his feelings of isolation.

In our sessions, we agreed that I would always be brief in what I said to him. Initially, I would tactfully ask him to repeat his understanding of what I said. We discovered that his anxiety level was often so high that it prevented him from even hearing what was said. Our focus turned to helping him feel less anxious and develop the courage to ask the person to repeat what was said. Once his anxiety became more manageable and he had developed a sufficient level of confidence to manage the situation, we moved on to the next step. This consisted in having him repeat in his own words the gist of what I had said. This technique led to "self-talk," silently telling himself what he had understood.

In one session, during his sophomore year in high school, he expressed an interest in getting a part-time job. He had turned in his application and was told to call back for a response. He revealed that he hated talking to people on the phone because he could never process what was said. If someone called with a message, he left the answering machine on so that he could listen to it rather than pick up the phone. Now he was forced to do what was most difficult for him or lose the opportunity of getting a job. This led to our role-playing in the session what might occur during such a phone conversation. First I played the role of the manager who answered the phone. We had a brief dialogue. Next I asked him to call me at my office from his home so that we could replay the scene. He was so phobic about using the phone that the very thought of having to call me led to a severe anxiety attack. However, since he was highly motivated to get the job, he was able to overcome his anxiety. We had a successful conversation on the phone, which encouraged him to make the call to the manager. Fortunately, the manager was eager to have him come to work and simply told him to come to discuss the hours he would work.

A more emotionally laden situation came in the fall of his junior year. He wanted to ask a girl to a Halloween dance. A friend of the girl told him that she had expressed an interest in him. She had reinforced the interest by giving the friend her phone number so William could call her. We discussed the situation at some length. His anxiety and excitement at the prospect of the date were considerable. No amount of rehearsal appeared to quiet him sufficiently to make the call. Finally, I came up with the idea that he should call her and ask her for her screen name so that they could chat on-line. He liked the idea. Next session, he excitedly reported how relieved both of them had been to chat on-line rather than talk in person. They spent hours chatting on-line and getting to know each other. They got to know each other well enough to be comfortable on the date.

William went on to a college from which he graduated. This college provided him with the supports he needed to deal with his language deficit.

*Discussion*: From a diagnostic perspective, William represents a group of children whose learning disorder does not manifest in overt dysfunctional behaviors. This group of children either withdraws or internalizes their reactions to their problems. Fearing embarrassment, William preferred to suffer quietly rather than create disruptions. The pervasive anxiety from which he suffered in most social situations was the primary symptom of his disorder of the self. While intellectually he understood the nature of his learning disorder, this did not diminish the difficulties he had integrating situations he confronted. His gentle, compliant temperament made him likable and easy to get along with. The major theme of his self-narrative, in some respects, was quite simple: "I do not understand exactly what's going on, but if I smile and keep quiet, people will like me!" The paradox is that, while this theme permitted a measure of coherence, the gaps in his understanding of interactions with others led to incoherences. The accommodation he made to his dilemma was to try to conventionalize his narrative. If he could get a job and have a girlfriend, he could be like others.

William's case is typical of the strategies necessary to deal with this type of language problem. However, I do not wish to give the impression that the treatment consisted of nothing more than providing these adjunctive functions. We addressed many other issues in his life. I have focused on the area of deficits to illustrate his difficulties. He lived in a world where verbal interactions were far more complex than he was able to process. The deficits were not in his intelligence, which was above average, although he was thought not to be very bright because of the way he conducted himself in social situations. But the deficits impaired the type of face-to-face communication on which we are so reliant and take for granted. The "self-talk" he learned helped him compensate for some of the deficits.

In summary, the issues of the coherence or incoherence of the self-narrative cannot be divorced from the correspondence between the account given in the self-narrative and the historical events. A fictitious self-narrative cannot carry the weight required to heal a child's disorder of the self. Shared meanings emerge from the sharing of personal memories of events as understood within the context in which these occurred. The coherence of the narrative is related to those shared meanings and by extension to the view of reality as understood within the context. Learning disorders often interfere with the coherence of the self-narrative, leading to personal meanings that are incomprehensible to others or at variance with shared meanings of the culture. In some children, these incoherences lead to a disorder of the self.

# 6

# LEARNING DISORDERS
# IN ADOLESCENCE

I WAS FIRST CONFRONTED BY the contrast between the ways adolescents and younger children deal with their learning disorders many years ago. I had been seeing a child with multiple learning disabilities for two years. He graduated from eighth grade and went to camp for the summer. Upon his return from camp, as he prepared to enter high school, he announced that he wished to discontinue all tutorial help and wanted nothing to do with the learning disabilities department in his high school. He did not wish to be identified as having a learning disability; instead he wanted to test himself out to see how well he could do without any of the supports he had had. He felt that the supports had only made him dependent, were of little help, and did not permit him to prove how well he could achieve on his own.

His parents and I reacted with consternation and apprehension. However, we were ambivalent as to whether we should try to persuade him to change his mind or let him have his way. After all, his argument, that he wished to test himself, seemed quite convincing. We thought that he might have been right in believing that we had fostered his dependence on tutors. We wondered whether he, in fact, manipulated them to do his work, as his father feared. If he tried and succeeded, the success would give a great boost to his self-confidence. On the other hand, if he failed, the resulting injury might be devastating to him. Besides these questions, there were the practicalities involved. If he withdrew from the high school learning disabilities program and needed to be re-enrolled, accomplishing that would be extremely difficult. Furthermore, good tutors were hard to find. If he gave up his place with his current tutors, he might not be able to return to them, especially his favorite tutor with whom he had worked very closely.

After many such experiences, I learned that any formulas one might devise for understanding children with learning disorders do not apply to adolescence because the developmental tasks of adolescence are quite different and require a different conceptual approach. These tasks compound the difficulties of clarifying the psychodynamics and establishing the relationship between adolescents' learning disorders and the psychopathology they display. The interplay between the responses of the context to the adolescent, the adolescent's developmental tasks, and the learning disorder add a further level of complexity to the inferences to be made from the overt behaviors. Here I discuss only the developmental issues of adolescents with mild to moderate learning disorders. Readers should be aware that, except for brief mention, it is not possible in this space to address the multiple and complex issues surrounding adolescents' different responses to specific learning disorders.

During adolescence, normal developmental issues cloud the manifestations of the neuropsychological deficits. It is as though the importance of the learning disorder recedes into the background and becomes difficult to detect. It is noteworthy that as the adolescent gets older, the learning disorder has an increasingly greater influence on the young adult's career path. In college, the disorder acts as a series of barriers that redirect the adolescent's career interests and achievements. The adolescent's personality consolidation is similarly affected. The choices for the adolescent narrow as he moves on, whether it be in the choice of a subject in which to major, a peer group with whom to socialize, or a set of interests in which to become involved. At times, strengths that may have been dormant emerge and make a major contribution to shaping the young adult's interests and personality. But by the time of graduation from college, the personality of the young adult emerges fairly well stamped by his neuropsychological strengths and weaknesses. The constraints these have imposed on him have a lasting impact. This is not to say that there are no surprises in store; some adolescents succeed even in areas where they once had the greatest difficulties.

In this chapter, I discuss some of the developmental issues that adolescents confront and the impact that a learning disorder has on those issues. Some learning disorders affect only the adolescent's self-esteem; others create more significant problems that lead to a disorder of the self. At times, this impact does not become evident until late adolescence, when a consolidation of what I call the "nuclear sense of self" occurs. The nuclear sense of self represents the culmination of the resolution of adolescent issues. It sets the stage for the transition into adulthood and the articulation of a coherent self-narrative. I begin with a discussion of the concept of the nuclear self and follow that with comments on the specific selfobject deficits that occur in adolescents with learning disorders. Comments on the nuclear sense of self and learning disorders close the theoretical discussion of this chapter.

## The Nuclear Sense of Self

Adolescents arrive at this phase with developmental needs for particular responses from their caregivers. The nature of the selfobject functions required at this stage is different from those of prior phases. The caregivers, who are the vehicles through whom these selfobject functions are performed, are required to play a different role from that played in earlier phases. Their ability to respond to the adolescent's needs is determined not only by the relationship they have had to their child prior to that phase but also by the issues that are activated within them by the adolescent. The issues of their own adolescence may become entwined with their responses to the adolescent.

Adolescents are likely to carry with them unresolved issues or selfobject deficits from prior developmental phases, which add to the complexity of the tasks of this phase. There is also no single path along which all adolescents must travel, no model adolescent phase. Rather, different adolescents will address issues differently and will resolve them in accordance with their endowments and the availability of selfobjects to complement them or to compensate for possible deficits. There is no set script or narrative that guides the adolescent developmental process. Each adolescent must construct a narrative out of past and present experiences. This is particularly true of adolescents with learning disorders (Cohen, 1985; Palombo, 1979, 1988, 1990; Silbar & Palombo, 1991).

In adolescence, a phase-appropriate loosening of the sense of cohesion or of narrative coherence takes place, which may result in experiences of temporary fragmentation. The adolescent processes may lead to a diffuseness in the cohesiveness of the self that challenges the adolescent's effort to reach a sense of equilibrium. The restoration of balance represents the reassessment of the meanings of prior experiences and their integration into a new set of meanings. The capacity for formal operational thought may facilitate the process. Thus, while temporary regressions to older modes of behaving and relating may be seen, these are in sharp contrast to highly mature symbolic forms of thinking that may also be present.

The nuclear self represents the mature form of the sense of self. It is the embodiment of both a sense of self-cohesion and narrative coherence. As we have seen, there is a reciprocal and interactional relationship between self-cohesion and narrative coherence. Each may affect the other, while each parallels the other. As the adolescent approaches adulthood, these two aspects of the sense of self must come together so that a unified sense of self can emerge. Adolescents with learning disorders who have selfobject deficits may fail to develop a consolidated nuclear sense of self. Adolescents whose self-narratives are incoherent may suffer from a similar failure.

## Selfobject Functions and the Nuclear Sense of Self

Let us look at the three sets of selfobjects functions discussed earlier—mirroring functions, idealizing functions and alter-ego functions—as they relate to the development of the nuclear sense of self in adolescents with learning disorders.

### The Mirroring Functions and the Nuclear Self

The mirroring functions are reflected in the self-esteem and feeling of self-worth the adolescent attains. The fact of having a learning deficit is confronted anew in adolescence. This confrontation, no matter how well established the problem might have been, results in a narcissistic injury. The caregivers' well-intentioned praise falls on deaf ears. The adolescent discounts their efforts at support, because the only sources of admiration that count are found in the world outside the household. Respect is a key issue. The sense of being valued is tied to the respect the adolescent desires, as well as to the respect he feels is owed to his caregivers. When this equation is out of balance, the adolescent will not feel respected and will act disrespectfully towards adults.

The egocentrism and exhibitionistic longings typical of early adolescence make the yearnings for mirroring almost impossible to satisfy. These feelings are compounded by the physical changes brought on by puberty, considerable self-consciousness, and the awareness of the body self. The preoccupation with appearances, whether in the direction of obsessive slovenliness or of studied casual "preppiness," is not only dictated by group norms but also driven by the desire to be distinguishable from others and, hence, to be recognized. To be perceived is to have one's existence acknowledged; not to have one's existence acknowledged is equivalent to having one's sense of self negated. The latter can lead to feelings of dissolution or fragmentation. The adolescent feels caught between the embarrassment of openly desiring direct praise and the fear of being flooded by those longings.

For most adolescents, parental responses appear to be of relatively little importance in this regard. At one time, the desire to be valued might have been satisfied through the caregivers' expression of pride and joy in their child's achievements. In adolescence, however, such expressions bring forth unbearable embarrassment. For an adolescent with a learning disorder, such praise is experienced as touching only on appearances rather than on substance. The peer-group's responses are of greater importance. Within the group, praise can take the form of teasing or ridicule, both of which satisfy the longings while enabling adolescents to avoid embarrassment.

## *The Idealizing Functions and the Nuclear Self*

The idealizing selfobject functions in adolescence consist in three sets of experiences: the experience of feeling protected and safe in a trusting relationship, the experience of having the capacity to modulate and regulate affect states, and the acquisition of a set of values and ideals. The presence of a learning disorder may affect all of these. De-idealization of caregivers may result in the rejection of the complementary functions they offer, such as the protection they feel the adolescent requires. Rejection of caregivers' efforts to regulate and modulate tension states may lead either to mood swings and depression or to substance abuse as a substitute regulator. Finally, rebellion against the caregivers' value system may lead either to dropping out of the social context or to turning to delinquent activities.

Preadolescents enter the phase experiencing their parents as globally embodying the functions of protectors, modulators of intense affects, and standard-bearers of all values. In the child's mind, the person of the adult is not distinguished from the function itself; for example, omnipotence may be concretely attributed to the parents. With the onset of the capacity for formal operational thought and the increased capacity to process the meanings of these experiences, a reevaluation of the parents' capacities and functions occurs. The functions can become disassociated from the person performing those functions.

Some adolescents who had previously accepted the complementary functions performed by their caregivers may now regard these as intrusive and infantalizing. These reactions are often based on the adolescents' inability to integrate their own infantile desires into the rest of their self-experience. The result is that the caregivers' interventions are interpreted as negating their more mature efforts. This may result in the denigration and de-idealization of the caregivers. If a massive disillusionment ensues, the adolescent may become depressed and enraged. The injury to the self leads to a conviction that the caregivers intentionally misled or deceived the adolescent. He will blame the caregivers for his underachievement or failure to perform.

The caregivers' response will in part determine the developmental outcome. Caregivers with great needs for their child's admiration and adulation become incapable of tolerating these assaults. They compound the problems by their inability to respond with empathy to the adolescent's desires. Their angry or defensive responses are experienced as further confirmation of the adolescent's perception. If, on the other hand, caregivers can good-naturedly accept the reassessment and shift to an attitude that is respectful of the adolescent, a different outcome becomes possible. The adolescent can retain a selfobject tie to the adult while at the same time gaining a measure of pride and self-respect. Integration of that pride and respect contributes to the consolidation of the nuclear self.

The second set of idealizing functions relates to the modulation of affective intensities and to self-regulation. During latency, children acquire a modicum of self-control and self-discipline, although these require ongoing reinforcement from adults for their stable utilization. Pubertal changes bring shifts in mood states and fluctuations in affect, resulting in a destabilization of the self. Since the caregivers are often seen as unreliable in providing modulating influences, or since, at times, adolescents reject those functions when they are offered, adolescents feel that they are left to their own devices.

An adolescent's depressions and mood swings may be understood as stemming from the loss of the self-comforting functions provided by caregivers. The ubiquitous use of drugs, alcohol, or sex is a manifestation of efforts on the part of the adolescent to medicate himself and recover a comfortable sense of cohesion. In adolescents with learning disabilities what emerges is the absence of ambition and self-confidence or the presence of grandiose and unrealistic expectations of what they can accomplish. At times, disturbances in self-regulation and in the idealization of adults may emerge as a haughty, contemptuous attitude toward the family's value system.

Caregivers are presented with a dilemma that is not easily resolved. If their efforts to regulate their child's distress are ill timed or off the mark, the adolescent feels either infantilized or justified to defy rational limits. If the caregivers themselves are vulnerable in these areas and are unable to regulate themselves or to modulate their own intense feelings, then their responses will be perceived as unempathic, ineffectual, or arbitrary. The injured adolescent will then respond with angry defiance, passive compliance, or withdrawal.

In late adolescence, some of these issues become ritualized. There are social channels that sanction defiant behaviors: "parties" at which it is permissible to get drunk, trash the house or yard of a member of the outgroup, or engage in illegal or dangerous initiation rites. By the time the late adolescent is a freshman in college, alternative rituals are available, such as periods of intense study (e.g., for exams) or concentration on a physical activity that requires hours of practice for mastery. What permits this transformation to take place is the adolescent's beginning integration of the meaning of self-control and self-regulation. These qualities are no longer experienced as emanating from outside sources; rather, they have become an integral part of the adolescent.

The last set of idealizing functions is the acquisition of a value system. In latency and early adolescence, the caregivers have been the providers of a set of moral, social, and cultural values that the child has accepted unquestioningly. Obedience out of a desire to please or fear of disapproval or punishment is linked to the acceptance of the values of compliance and conformity. In peer relations, the acceptance of group norms is motivated more out of considerations of fairness than out of a sense of justice. The reassessment of the values during adolescence is driven at first by the desire to challenge parental authority rather than by disbelief in the values themselves. The selfobject functions associated with authority figures who require conformity are rejected. Paralleling the reevaluation of parental authority is a reevaluation of the content of that authority, that is, the precepts and teachings.

The void creates a challenge that may lead the adolescent to turn to a new set of values or more archaic values, that is, to fuller acceptance of the "traditional" values. The phenomenon of adolescents' embracing either religious or social beliefs that represent even greater conformity than their caregivers had demanded reflects the former outcome. Examples of the latter phenomenon are adolescents who turn to peer groups as substitute idealized selfobjects (e.g., gangs, cults, or fraternities, who come to represent alternatives to parental values). The motive for joining a counterculture group is not always the desire to rebel against parental values; it may also be that the adolescents are attempting to find an ideology that is concordant with their developing lifestyle. A particular group becomes the vehicle through which they can attain that goal. In either case, the selfobject functions have undergone a transformation that leaves a permanent mark on the lives of adolescents.

The extent to which values carried over from latency are rejected, retained, or revised and integrated within a broader set of values to be included within a nuclear self is determined by a number of factors. Among these are the nature of the selfobject experiences to which the adolescent is exposed, the stability and coherence of the latency value system, the effect of shifts in attachment from caregivers to other idealized figures, the blossoming of a particular talent that expands in importance in the adolescent's world, or some accidental factors, such as the death of a close friend, the influence of a boyfriend or girlfriend, or an encounter with a charismatic teacher. This set of values is important for the establishment of a nuclear sense of self because it lays the foundation for the lifestyle and the career goals the adolescent will embrace. When such values are missing, the adolescent with a learning disorder finds himself with few convictions and the inability to decide on a career path.

### The Alter-ego Functions and the Nuclear Self

This set of functions relates to the desire for experiences of kinship with other human beings. The wish to belong to a group of like-minded others, the desire to minimize differences in appearances and ways of thinking from one's group, the easy contagion that permits becoming engulfed in group activities, the exquisite sensitivity to the suffering of those who belong to the group concomitant with harsh cruelty to those who do not belong—all these experiences provide the rich fabric of a subculture to which adolescents feel bound.

Outsiders, characterized as "nerds," "geeks," "spooks," "greasers," and so on, are all considered beyond the pale and utterly inhuman. The bigotry, fanaticism, and elitism that prevail in some adolescent groups may have their roots in the desire to strengthen a vulnerable sense of self. Since difference is often equated with deficiency, the very presence of others who are different becomes a reminder of inner experiences of being deficient. These feelings are also associated with the sense of difference that comes with having a learning disability.

For an adolescent with a learning disorder this set of functions is critical. Feelings of alienation are intensified by the differences the adolescent notices in himself as compared to others. The group dynamics in which adolescents are involved make acceptance into an "in-group" a central issue in their social lives. Since large divisions into groups with well-defined hierarchies exist, belonging to a desirable group becomes the focus of the adolescent's social activities. Embedded in the hierarchy is a set of values that define the acceptable from the unacceptable. Depending on the adolescent's competencies, being part of a specific group can become symbolic of feeling valued or devalued.

Ultimately, feelings of true kinship with others, comfortable acceptance of differences from others, and respect for the values and ideals of others are based on the integration into the adolescent's meaning system of a view of human beings within a social, cultural, and political context that is in harmony with his own sense of history and the narrative that he has constructed to bring a sense of coherence. Self-confidence, self-assurance, and self-respect come as a result of the consolidation of the nuclear self in the context of the attainment of achievements that fulfill of the destiny that the adolescent has chosen for himself.

## The Nuclear Self and the Self-narrative in Adolescence

Reorganization of each person's system of meanings occurs at nodal points in the life cycle. Some of these reorganizations result from specific developmental processes, such as the emergence of language in infancy, while others result from life experiences, whether traumatic or momentous in their significance. The onset of adolescence presents the individual with a challenge to undertake such a major reorganization. One way to conceive of this reorganization is to think of it as consisting of the emergence of a new edition of an old narrative. This new edition begins to take its final shape in late adolescence.

By late adolescence, we observe that several shifts have occurred in the adolescent's sense of self. The painful self-consciousness that was previously noticeable begins to dissipate. The egocentrism and sense of uniqueness give way to more empathic attitudes toward others. Self-regulation becomes more possible and is less dependent on others for reinforcement. Affect states are less labile, mood swings decrease, and a greater capacity for the modulation of these states becomes evident. Greater self-confidence and self-assurance are manifested. The capacity to be assertive without having to be hostile is also observed. Regressions are less frequent and, when they do occur, less severe. There is less need to experiment with fringe activities, such as substance abuse or delinquency, because of peer pressures. Fantasy appears more in the service of creativity or for trial action than for defensive purposes.

A number of factors related to the development of a self-narrative appear to contribute to the processes underlying these changes. First, the advent of formal operational thought at the onset of adolescence plays an important role in the transformation in the adolescent's meaning system. Kohlberg and Gilligan (1972, p. 34) describe the cognitive stage that occurs at that time as reasoning about reasoning. Second, the past is reassessed through the eyes of the present. In some measure, past events are reinterpreted and reintegrated within a set of meanings that did not exist previously. As a result, the adolescent views his childhood in a different light and, depending on his introspective capacities, places a distance between those events and the present. This results in a new perspective. Third, the increased capacity for selfobject experiences at a symbolic rather than concrete level leads to a shift in the meanings that others have, or have had, for the adolescent. The adolescent begins to look beyond the narrow circle of family and peers for selfobject experiences. While seeking avenues for self-actualization, the adolescent searches for values and ideals that are consonant with the rest of his experiences, focusing less on the person as the embodiment of the function and more on the content associated with the function. Finally, the integration of gender role and sexuality into the rest of self-experience acquires an urgency that was not present before. The meanings of femaleness or of maleness, of expression or inhibition of sexuality, become a focal preoccupation.

As a result of these processes, the adolescent begins to construct a coherent narrative that attempts to encompass the totality of self-experiences. If the attempt is successful, unification and consolidation in the sense of cohesion will emerge, along with a different configuration of the self than previously existed. This new configuration may be described as the emergence of a nuclear sense of self. The adolescent is then able to select an avenue through which to express the acquired values, ideals, and ambitions. The adolescent's inner resources may be mobilized to move toward attainment of a life goal. For the adolescent who success-fully completes this phase, a new narrative emerges. At this point it may make sense to speak of an inner program that the person is propelled to actualize. While this process may be thought to be akin to Erikson's (1994) notion of the consolidation of identity, it is different because of the perspective from which adolescent processes are being viewed. The nuclear sense of self is not formed in response to the need for adapta-tion; rather, it occurs irrespective of the adaptive consequences of the adolescent's behavior. Thus, the "unrealistic" attitudes of some youths, which to some adults appear foolish and impractical and represent peren-nial generational struggles, result from the tension between the older generation's exhortations to adolescents to adapt and the adolescents' rebelliousness, which insists on the modification of reality to suit their internal needs—needs that are defined by the nuclear self.

The attainment of a nuclear sense of self does not foreclose the pos-sibility of continual growth in the course of the life cycle. Neither does it guarantee that destabilizations will not occur. Significant life events may lead to amendments to or revisions of a person's guiding narrative. The achievement of the consolidation of the nuclear self may also be cul-ture-bound. In cultures where the exercise of formal operational thought is either not valued or not made possible, a nuclear self may still evolve, although the timing of its emergence and the form it takes may be quite different from that of middle-class Western culture.

## The Nuclear Sense of Self and Learning Disorders

From the adolescent's perspective the importance of the learning disor-der recedes into the background during adolescence, but, in fact, the de-velopmental issues of adolescence accentuate the symptoms associated with the disorders. The self-consciousness that may have been present earlier is heightened by the adolescent's experience of bodily changes. Self-esteem problems become more generalized and the effects of the neuropsychological deficits much more evident to those around the ado-lescent.

An adolescent with dyslexia may have found numerous ways to con-ceal the learning deficits previously. Now the embarrassment of having the deficit is dealt with by displacing it onto other issues. Concerns about appearances such as facial blemishes may be magnified not only because of what they represent but also because they symbolize the hidden deficit. Some adolescents go to the other extreme; rather than hiding themselves because of the deficit they wear their sense of difference from others on their sleeve. Through bizarre modes of dress, hair colors, body piercing, they exhibitionistically say, "I will flaunt my sense of difference by challenging you to be critical of my looks!" Beneath this brash facade is a brittle vulnerability that makes some adolescents respond violently to minimal disapproval. Self-esteem issues are critical for these adolescents.

Adolescents with AD/HD at times display an accentuation of their problems. If they have attentional problems, these may be magnified. If they are hyperactive, they seem to be even more driven than before. If they are impulsive, the consequences of their impulsive behaviors are likely to be much greater than previously. If challenged or provoked, impulsive adolescents act out with no thought whatsoever of the consequences of their actions. Their judgment appears impaired to the point where they can endanger themselves or others by their activities. They will drive recklessly, steal impulsively, or drink to the point where they pass out. When adults respond to such overt acts with anger, adolescents show a seeming lack of concern that can enrage caregivers. Lost in all this turmoil are the motives behind the actions or the deficit that fuels the conduct. These adolescents appear to have a tenuous sense of self-cohesion. They seem to be on the verge of fragmenting and losing control.

Some adolescents with executive function deficits seem to realize early in high school that they will not be able to do the work required of them to graduate. This realization may be unconscious, since at times they seem not to see the connection between their lack of organization and their academic failures. It is as though, in anticipation of what is to come, they have already set a different path for themselves. Some take up the guitar or drums, convinced that their talent will lead them to stardom. Others sense the onset of a severe depression and medicate themselves with drugs or alcohol. Still others drop out of high school, claiming to have no interest in academics. They propose to work but are unable to meet the demands of a regular schedule. Others take off to hitchhike across the country, staying at odd places wherever they can bed down for the night. They call their caregivers only when they get into trouble or are in need of funds, which happens frequently. Adolescents with this disorder struggle to construct a coherent narrative. They know what they need to do to be successful but lack the skills to implement their plans.

Even when their narratives are coherent, their sense of self lacks the structure and cohesion to attain their goals.

In my experience, adolescents with nonverbal learning disabilities seem not to take such tumultuous paths. While many of them have been isolated from peers because of their social problems, they do not manifest the externalizing problems of the other two groups. Their judgment appears not to be so impaired as to make them either expose themselves to dangerous situations or desert academic activities in which they excel. Their emotional issues appear to be much like those of latency-age children, so conformity and acceptable conduct are found more frequently in this group of children than in their peers. This is not to say that their social problems are not a source of concern or of difficulties for them— they are. The difficulties take the form of minor misbehaviors or over-reactions to challenges rather than of major eruptions. Most often, however, they are sad, lonely, and depressed. Self-cohesion and narrative coherence are issues for these adolescents. The reciprocal relationship between a cohesive sense of self and a coherent narrative makes it difficult for them to attain either of them. They experience the incoherences in their self-narratives as distressing, and these incoherences impact their capacity to maintain a sense of self-cohesion.

Adolescents with Asperger's disorder are the most impaired of this entire group. What emerges is an exacerbation of their preexisting problems. Their lack of a sense of self-cohesion and their poor social judgment make them stand out painfully from their peers, even more than before. They are unable to fit into any social group. Often they are teased or harassed; they are almost always excluded from interactions with others, leaving them totally isolated. In classes, they are inappropriate. They not only cannot work up to expectations but their demeanor, their participation, is so out of step from that of their peers that they quickly become the object of derision. Some begin to act out flagrantly in school, disregarding the rules and intruding into others' space. In short, their behaviors violate the expected social norms to the point that school authorities feel compelled to intervene. These behaviors reflect the absence of a coherent narrative to help organize their responses to others. When these problems extend into the home, caregivers are faced with the difficult decision of placing the adolescent in a residential setting. These adolescents suffer from severe disorders of the self.

Since I deal with a clinical population, the picture I have drawn of these five groups of adolescents emphasizes the psychopathology rather than the healthy adaptations some of them may make. Many adolescents with learning disorders may avoid such problems and consequently do not come to the attention of service providers. The absence of data leaves us in the dark as to the proportion of adolescents who encounter serious problems.

During adolescence, the sense of self-cohesion is reciprocal to the establishment of a coherent self-narrative. The nuclear sense of self that emerges in middle to late adolescence is constituted of the totality of the person's experiences, both conscious and unconscious. It is enduring in its stability and has a sense of firmness, intactness, wholeness, and vitality. The coherent self-narrative is the structure that is constituted from the set of meanings that have arisen in the course of development. As the product of one's endowment in tandem with the selfobject experiences, the coherent self-narrative facilitates the integration of affective experience and leads to the structuralization of meaning.

The late adolescent recursively reworks old experiences leading to the formation of the nuclear self. The nuclear sense of self is the set of meanings that have accrued to the person, through which life goals are defined, the means for their attainment examined, and the plans for their pursuit established. This consolidation is the culmination of the increased symbolization of specific selfobject functions. The integration of cognitive strides with affective experiences takes place within the context of the self/selfobject milieu. The selfobject functions that the peer group and caregivers provide represents the context and the means through which cohesion is maintained and the nuclear self is stabilized.

The toll learning disorders take on adolescents varies with the nature of the deficit, the degree to which the deficit was complemented earlier, and the extent to which the adolescent has compensated for the deficit. No direct relations can be established between the severity of the deficit and the severity of the disorder of the self. When deficits are less severe, their impact may initially be less perceptible. The issues of adolescence may, at times, drown out the effect of the deficit, but as the adolescent moves on to college the impact usually becomes obvious again. The choices are narrowed; the options opened to the young adult are fewer. Finally, by the time the young adult graduates from college, the deficits · have left their mark on both his personality and his career choice. The nuclear sense of self, which reflects the consolidation of the mature personality, reflects the scars left by the learning disorder.

# II

# DIAGNOSTIC
# CONSIDERATIONS

# 7

# DYSLEXIA

**D**YSLEXIA IS A SUBTYPE OF the larger category of language-based learning disabilities that is found in children of at least average intelligence whose visual and auditory senses are intact. In order to understanding dyslexia, it is important to place it within the broader range of language disorders to which it belongs. I review language disorders briefly before turning to a discussion of dyslexia. In addition, a distinction is generally made between speech disorders and language disorders. Speech disorders are conditions related to the mechanical production of speech, such as articulation problems, while language disorders are related to the broader cognitive aspects of communication. Our concern in this chapter is with dyslexia as a language disorder, not with speech disorders (see Table 7.1).

Every language is segmented into several components, each of which assists in the study of the language and helps define language disorders. The segments are *phonology, morphology, syntax, semantics,* and *pragmatics.* The study of *phonology* identifies the smallest unit of sound out of which words are composed. The English language is said to have 44 phonemes out of the possible 100 or more sounds that human beings can produce. *Morphology* identifies the units of meaning out of which words are made; these are syllables composed of vowels and consonants. A syllable cannot be a syllable unless it contains a vowel, neither can a word be a word without a vowel. The *syntax* of a language identifies the grammatical rules that speakers must apply to generate meaningful sentences. The *semantics* of the language relates to the meanings associated to the words or sentences used within the language. Finally, language is

**TABLE 7.1**

**Dyslexia**

---

A. CHARACTERISTICS:

    1. *Defining features*: "Dyslexia is one of several distinct learning disabilities. It is a specific language-based disorder of constitutional origin characterized by difficulties in single word decoding, usually reflecting insufficient phonological processing abilities. These difficulties in single word decoding are often unexpected in relation to age and other cognitive and academic abilities: they are not the result of generalized developmental disability or sensory impairment. Dyslexia is manifested by variable difficulty with different forms of language, often including, in addition to problems in reading, a conspicuous problem with acquiring proficiency in writing and spelling" (Orton Dyslexia Society definition adopted by the National Institutes of Health; National Center for Disabilities, 1994).

    2. *Prevalence rates*: Estimates of children in the school population in the U.S. who have reading difficulties range from 20 to 30%. The percentage varies among whites, African-Americans, and other ethnic groups. Only a subset of this group of children is identified as having dyslexia. The disorder may be present in a range from mild to severe and is thought to occur in approximately 3 to 6% of the school age population (Frost & Emery, 1995).

    3. *Sex ratio*: Incidence is the same in males as in females, although boys may be affected slightly more severely than girls (Lyon, 1990, p. 50).

    4. *Coexisting conditions*: At one time dyslexia was thought to be associated with a variety of somatic illnesses, such as allergies. But the association has not been supported by research.

B. DEVELOPMENTAL HISTORY: Usually unremarkable, as most milestones are achieved on time.

C. DISORDERS OF THE SELF: Self-esteem problems are prevalent.

    1. *Presenting symptoms*:

        a. *Academic*: Problems first appear when children begin to read. They have difficulty identifying their letters. They have trouble recognizing and sounding out words. But all have good comprehension of spoken materials. Some appear to be reading, but in reality have memorized the texts of books read to them and have become quite clever at concealing their deficit. Prominent problems with spelling exist.

### TABLE 7.1
### (Continued)

    b. *Social*: No social problems are associated with this learning disorder until the children confront situations in which they are required to complete reading tasks. Their embarrassment at not being able to do what other children do easily may interfere with peer relationships.

    c. *Emotional*: No single set of emotional problems is associated with this learning disability, although the children get embarrassed when asked to perform reading or written tasks. Their repeated embarrassment may eventually lead to self-esteem problems.

  2. *Sense of self-cohesion*: Sense of self-cohesion remains reasonably intact, although self-esteem problems are prevalent.

  3. *Self-narrative coherence*: The self-narrative does not adequately explain the symptoms of the dyslexia unless the child has had that explained to him. Otherwise, the child remains puzzled as to why she cannot read.

D. INTERVENTIONS:

  1. *Remediation*: Systematic phonics instruction by a reading specialist.

  2. *Psychotherapy*: Elective or if indicated because of the secondary effects of the disorders.

---

said to have a *pragmatic* aspect, sometimes referred to as communicative competence, that underlies social usage. This aspect relates to the rules that competent speakers use in communicating with each other and the capacity to evaluate what is contextually relevant. Examples of problems in this area are the inability to understand jokes, literal interpretation of metaphorical expressions, the inappropriate use of questions in social contexts, the injection of irrelevant remarks in conversations or the violation of the rules of turn-taking in conversation. As we will see in Chapter 11, children with Asperger's disorder have serious problems with the use of pragmatic language.

Language-based learning disabilities can occur in the receptive, expressive, or processing domains of verbal language (Bryan & Bryan, 1986; Hallahan, Kauffman, & Lloyd, 1996). The nonverbal domain of communications is discussed separately, and disorders of communication in that domain are often associated with nonverbal learning disabilities rather than language-based learning disabilities. Children who have receptive (verbal) language problems can have difficulties with auditory reception, as in the case of children who have trouble comprehending spoken language, with visual reception, as in children who have reading difficulties, or in both areas. (For an example of an adolescent with a receptive language problem that demonstrates one of the types of problems associated with this deficit, see Chapter 5.) Children who have expressive language problems can have problems with verbal expression, as in the case of children who have difficulty with word retrieval, with written expression, as in the case of children who have difficulty organizing their thoughts to write them down, or both.

Children with language processing disorders have problems conducting operations on and with language signs. For example, we can reason or make inferences because we can process linguistically the information we possess. Difficulties can occur in this capacity, as with children who have central auditory problems. These children can hear perfectly well but have difficulties in decoding what is being said to them. Some children with processing difficulties may have disordered thinking. Their difficulties are in the area of logical sequential thinking, but unlike schizophrenics, who have a thought disorder, they do not have hallucinations or delusions. Other language-based problems occur when children have difficulties with the correct use of syntax, and so are unable to understand or demonstrate good grammatical usage. Others still have difficulty with semantics. They are unable to understand or use the words or sentences appropriate to the content they wished to communicate.

Children with language-based problems may therefore have difficulties with reading, spelling, or writing compositions, with math (which is a language system), or with the social aspects of verbal communication (Toppelberg & Shapiro, 2000).

Dyslexia is a specific type of receptive language problem. It is one of many types of reading disorders. Some children do not learn to read because of the impoverished social and educational conditions in which they find themselves. Those children who do not learn to read because they have a specific neuropsychological deficit are described as having dyslexia. All children with dyslexia are poor readers, but not all poor readers have dyslexia. Although many children with dyslexia have speech problems related to difficulties with speech-sound articulation, these are unrelated to their dyslexia (Beitchman & Young, 1997).

While it would be highly instructive to study many of these language-based disorders with regard to disorders of the self, here I focus on dyslexia because it has been studied in much greater depth than the others. It provides an example of those deficits that interfere with the attainment of self-cohesion or a coherent narrative.

## Explanatory Paradigms

### *Psychoanalytic*

Historically, psychoanalysts believed dyslexia to be a psychogenically based disorder due to intrapsychic conflicts. For example, Rosen, who was at one time the president of the American Psychoanalytic Association, wrote a paper in which he presented this thesis (Rosen, 1955). He described the case of a young adult who was a mathematician and who had dyslexia. Rosen began by setting the context for his views with a discussion of the evolution of written language. The difficulties of patients with dyslexia, he suggested, were associated with the phylogenetic phase in written expression, specifically in the transition between ideographic and syllabic alphabet. He expressed the belief that a specific intrapsychic conflict interfered with a patient's ability to read (which at the time was called strephosymbolia). In the case he presented, the young man's reading problem was attributed to his identification with his mother. The mother represented the "auditory symbols," while the father, with whom he was in competition, represented "visual symbols." The patient's primal scene fantasies (fantasies of his parents having intercourse), which were disturbing and guilt-producing, made it impossible for him to think of the two parents together. Hence, he failed to synthesize the auditory with the visual perceptual modalities. For Rosen, the conflict between the child's feelings about his father and mother led to the inability to read. Interestingly, Rosen felt that he had support for his thesis, because after several years of analysis and of the interpretation of the conflict, the patient did learn to read. He concluded that the problem had to be of psychogenic origin.

A few child analysts still hold to this view. Unfortunately, knowledge about the neurological basis of the disorder is not sufficiently widespread for many of the psychodynamically informed therapists to be aware of different explanations. The problem with Rosen's view is that he causally related two separate and distinct disorders, the neuropsychological and the emotional. The oedipal conflict did not cause the dyslexia, but it may have been that the dyslexia led to the patient's problems with his parents. Rather than being unable to resolve his oedipal feeling about his parents because of his dyslexia, the patient probably felt badly because he could not succeed in his wish to please them. The fact that he eventually learned to read may have been due to the removal, through the analysis, of a secondary inhibition to his effort at trying to learn to read. Educators' experience is that the majority of children with dyslexia eventually do learn to read, although they never become rapid, fluent readers. So with or without treatment the young man might have overcome his reading disability. This is not to say that the treatment did not help him feel better in many other ways, only that it did not remove the cause of the dyslexia.

### Neuropsychological

From a neuropsychological perspective, dyslexia as a type of reading disorders that results from a specific brain dysfunction. This dysfunction prevents a reader from correctly associating the sound of a letter—a phoneme—with its equivalent written symbol. It is a phonological processing disorder. Considerable research is currently being conducted to locate the specific location in the brain involved in this dysfunction.

## Characteristics of the Disorder

*Defining features*: The International Dyslexia Association,* a leading advocacy group for children and adults with dyslexia, defines dyslexia as "one of several distinct learning disabilities. It is a specific language-based disorder of constitutional origin characterized by difficulties in single word decoding, usually reflecting insufficient phonological processing abilities. These difficulties in single word decoding are often unexpected in relation to age and other cognitive and academic abilities: they are not the result of generalized developmental disability or sensory impairment. Dyslexia is manifested by variable difficulty with different forms of language, often including, in addition to problems in reading, a conspicuous problem with acquiring proficiency in writing and spelling" (National Center for Disabilities, 1994).

*Formerly known as the Orton Dyslexia Society.

For reasons that are unclear, children with this disorder are unable to associate specific phonemes with their related written symbols. For example, they are unable to retain the connection between the sound "ma" or "da" with the written syllables *ma* and *da*. This means that, when learning the alphabet, the child cannot associate the sounds of the letters of the alphabet and their related symbols. At times, the problem can be so severe that even if a child memorizes the connection between the sound of a specific letter and its written form, she can no longer identify the letter if the font of the letter is changed. Children therefore have difficulties translating printed words into spoken words. It must be underscored that this disorder does not involve any difficulty in understanding written or spoken language. Children with dyslexia have the capacity for comprehension that is consistent with their intelligence; it is only their ability to read that is affected. Furthermore, while some people have proposed that the problem with dyslexia lies with the child's visual processing of material, there appears to be no systematic research to support this position. The disorder affects not only the capacity to read (decode) but also the capacity to spell (encode), since spelling involves breaking down the word phonetically into its symbols. The disorder is thought to be of genetic origin; however, no specific gene has yet been identified as the cause of the problem. There is clear evidence that it runs in families and that it is heritable.

*Prevalence rate and sex ratio*: While estimates of children in the school population in the U.S. who have reading difficulties range from 20—30%, only a subset of this group of children is identified as having dyslexia. The disorder may be present in a range from mild to severe and is thought to occur in approximately 3 to 6% of the school age-population (Frost & Emery, 1995). The percentage varies between whites, African-Americans and other ethnic groups. At one time it was thought that boys were more prone to have the disorder than girls, but recent research indicates that the distribution is fairly even, although boys may be affected slightly more severely than girls (Lyon, 1990, p. 50).

*Coexisting conditions*: For many years it was believed that dyslexia was associated with deficiencies in the immunological system (allergies and asthma). Research has not substantiated this view (Lyon, 1990, p. 20) except in a small subset of cases. (See Toppelberg & Shapiro, 2000, pp. 149-150, for the comorbidity of the larger category of language disorders with psychiatric disorders.)

## Developmental History

Pennington reports: "Clinically, the preschool histories of some but not all dyslexics contain reports of mild speech delay, articulation difficulties, problems learning letter names or color names, word-finding problems, missequencing syllables ('aminals' for 'animals,' 'donimoes' for 'dominoes'), and problems remembering addresses, phone numbers, and other verbal sequences, including complex directions" (Pennington, 1991, p. 62). A young patient of mine in speaking of his reading disorders told me that he had been diagnosed with "dixlexia."

Since the problem is related to the capacity to read, its effects on a child's development do not emerge until the ages of five, six, or even seven. Up to that point, the development progresses as it would for a child without any disorder. Caregivers do not notice anything very different about their child. She is like their other children. The deficit does not interfere with the care and nurture the child receives.

Problems may be suspected when the child is in preschool because of lack of interest in reading. Caregivers' responses to this will depend on the family's value system and its educational level. The more intellectually oriented and academically inclined the caregivers, the more they will wonder about the child's lack of interest. Often it is rationalized as due to other factors.

By kindergarten concerns begin to be raised by teachers. The picture may be clouded because the child has memorized the books read to her. There might be no suspicion of a problem, although it may be noted that the child is not demonstrating a level of achievement in school comparable to that of her peers. Another problem area that emerges is that of written expression. Since the child has not learned the alphabet, she may have trouble writing down letters. Again the issue is clouded by the fact that the child can copy letters, even though she does not seem able to reproduce them from memory. Issues of motivation, maturity, or willfulness may be raised.

By first grade problems begin to escalate, but they seldom reach the crisis proportions they will later on. The child may begin to act out and verge on becoming a behavior problem. Then the failure to achieve is often attributed to the behavior problems rather than the other way around. What has probably occurred is that a bright child has begun to realize that things that appear to come easily to others are impossible for her. She will find herself placed in embarrassing situations, such as having to read out loud when she cannot. Rather than reveal her ignorance, which is totally baffling to her, she would rather create a distraction, becoming resistant to reading tasks and oppositional in dealing with those who make demands on her. At this point patterns begin to be laid down that are formative for the child's personality. The central issue is the repeated narcissistic injuries the child suffers silently and the defenses she brings to bear to deal with those injuries.

This is not to say that all children respond by acting out. Some hide their shame by withdrawing, or by excelling in an area of strength. A child gifted athletically will focus on that area, minimizing her interest in the academic areas. She may become popular and use her social skills to draw other children to her. Those children who withdraw will not be identified as having a learning problem. Only much later, when many of the basics of learning have been lost, will there be a wake-up call that the child is in trouble.

Most parents and school systems are forgiving of children's antics at first, but as they mature, expectations change. What was formerly considered cute is now seen as obnoxious. By the time the child reaches second or third grade it is no longer possible to ignore the problem. But the reason for the problem may remain obscure to parents and teachers. In a school system that is aware of the causes for academic problems a referral for testing may lead to the identification of the dyslexia. In less sophisticated school systems, the problem will be defined differently.

In two recent studies of adult outcomes of having dyslexia the following picture emerges. Klein and Mannuzza (2000) followed 104 children diagnosed with uncomplicated reading problems 16 years after the initial identification of the learning disorder. Their status was compared with a control group of 129 individuals. They found that of those with reading problems 25% failed to obtain a high school diploma, as compared to 4% in the control group, and fewer than 10% obtained a bachelor's degree. While their employment histories were comparable to those of the control group, they failed to obtain comparable occupational levels. Four percent attained high executive levels, as compared to 40% of the control group. Finally, this group's rate of alcohol and substance use was twice that of the control group.

McNulty (2000) studied in depth the life stories of 12 subjects (8 men and 4 women), ages 25 to 45, who had been diagnosed with dyslexia in childhood. While all the participants were able to compensate to one degree or another for the effects of their reading difficulty on their employment, all reported experiences that they regarded as "traumatic" while growing up. The participants felt themselves to be different from their peers as early as the age of three. They reported failures, difficulties, and feeling misunderstood during their middle school years. When testing confirmed the diagnosis, they felt relief but also confirmed in the feeling that something was wrong with them. Finally, in adulthood some found adequate ways of compensating for their deficit, while others continued to struggle.

## Disorders of the Self

### Presenting Symptoms

*Academic*: In the academic area, children with dyslexia begin to have difficulties with phonological awareness as preschoolers when attempting to learn the alphabet at an age when their peers can master the task. By first grade, they confuse or mispronounce words when trying to read. These errors often mirror their spoken errors. They also make spelling errors that are based on their inability to decode the sounds of the word, have problems rhyming words, and avoid reading either silently or aloud. Pennington (1991, p. 61) states that these children have considerable difficulty with the language games such as Pig Latin. Pig Latin requires the child to drop the initial sound in a word and to add the sound "ay" at the end. Playing it successfully requires good phonological awareness. Some children with dyslexia have difficulty with phonological memory, which interferes with their spelling and their ability to retain word and number sequences. This difficulty may show up as being unable to remember days of the week, the months of the year, the seasons, a series of directions, or a story sequence. It is important to remember that, because of the variability in the children's abilities to decode, some children become less symptomatic as they progress through school; they learn to compensate for their difficulties but seldom become as fluent in reading as their peers.

*Social*: No specific social problems are associated with this disorder (Lamm & Epstein, 1992). Some children, especially boys, may resort to acting out or clowning in the classroom as a way of discharging their anxiety in anticipation of being asked to read aloud. These behaviors are obviously secondary to the embarrassment the children feel. The severity of the problem may be related to the way the context responds to the child's handicap. The more punitive or lacking in understanding the context is, the angrier the child's response. It is noteworthy that these problems tend to dissipate during the summers when the child is not in school (Ryan, 1994).

*Emotional*: In making generalizations about the effects of dyslexia on children's psychodynamics two points must be emphasized: First, it is seldom the case that a child suffers from a pure case of the disorder. Most often children with learning disorders have multiple deficits. This means that the psychodynamics are often clouded by the presence of those other deficits. Second, the kind of response the child receives and the expectations for achievement are important contributors to the child's psychodynamics. But in general, the most frequent emotional problems associated with this disorders are problems of self-esteem.

### The Sense of Self-cohesion

The child's subjective experience of having dyslexia is reciprocal to the responses of others to the child's problem. The child does not perceive herself to have a problem until confronted with expectations that cannot be met. The earliest injuries to the child's sense of self occur when the child becomes self-conscious of her inability to perform as others do. Interferences with the development of the grandiose self emerge. Up to this point, before the child was confronted with failure, she may have felt adequately mirrored by caregivers who responded to her as their special child. Her sense of cohesion remained intact. Her self-esteem was reasonably robust. As she begins to realize that by comparison to other children she does not meet the standards set by important adults, or expectations she has of herself, she begin to ask why. At first, she may discount the value of learning to read. But most bright children feel frustrated that the means through which they can acquire knowledge are closed of. Shame and embarrassment soon lead her to question whether she is as smart as she was made to believe. If much value is placed on being smart, her self-worth comes into question. Her observation of how others respond to her raise different questions. Are her parents just being nice to her in not being critical of her inability to read because she is their child? Are their efforts directed at sparing her the knowledge that she is less smart than other kids? Are teachers unfair, and do they favor others over her for some obscure reason she cannot fathom? How smart is she in reality, if she cannot do the things that others do so easily and so much better than she?

The erosion in self-esteem need not occur as a result of failures in mirroring from others. In fact, parents and teachers may be making every effort to shore up the child's self-esteem by encouraging her or praising her for other attributes. Their failure lies not so much in not sufficiently mirroring her as in not recognizing the existence of the problem. By the time it is recognized, dialogue between the child and adults is already derailed. It is as though the caregivers' empathy is fallible since it was not able to penetrate below the surface of the child's appearance to the core of the child's distress.

As the child suffers, so does her sense of worth. Affirmation that must come from real achievement is not forthcoming. She experiences praise by others at best as false; at worst she feels deceived because she knows what others are unwilling to acknowledge, that there is something terribly wrong with her. The feeling that there is something wrong becomes the focus of an entire set of new dynamics.

A child's sense of humanity comes in part from the feelings of being akin to others and of belonging to a larger community from which she derives her sense of being valued as an individual. Differences between her and others can be experienced as either a blessing or a curse, depending on the value placed upon the sense of difference. A child who is recognized as different because she is the only adopted Korean child in a class of white middle-class children may end up feeling proud of her difference, if the community values her adoption. But in a community that frowns upon that heritage and looks down on the child's parents for the choice they have made, that child will feel devalued and discriminated against. The child with dyslexia is caught in such a dilemma.

As the cases that follow illustrate, selfobject deficits generally occur along the lines of mirroring or alter-ego functions. It is also possible for the idealizing functions to be affected. The child may experience her failure to acquire the skills necessary for reading as resulting from the caregivers' inability to teach her to read. She may then feel disillusioned, become disrespectful, and withdraw or begin acting out.

### Self-narrative Coherence

The incoherences in dyslexic children's narratives are evident in their puzzlement about the circumstances in which they find themselves. From their perspectives, academics have turned out to be unexpectedly hard. Some have great curiosity and wish to learn, but find that extracting information from books is practically impossible. They absorb all they can by listening to and discussing issues with others. But that method of acquiring information leaves large gaps in their knowledge base. What compounds their puzzlement is that they have no clear understanding of the nature of their problem. Through a haze, they perceive their difficulties with reading, but they cannot grasp what makes that activity so difficult for them.

In searching for some coherence, some children dismiss academics as unimportant. Some find much greater pleasure in social interactions and consequently focus their energies in that area. At times, those who are well coordinated direct their energies to excelling in sports. The incoherences in their self-narrative may often be patched over with a variety of rationalizations. However, the self-esteem problems overshadow almost all that they do. Many harbor feelings of incompetence or feel they are deceiving others by giving the appearance of great competence, while beneath the surface they feel incompetent. The disparity between what they feel and how they behave leaves them with large areas of incoherence. If they become highly successful or if they succeed in compensating for their dyslexia through diligence and hard work, the gap in the incoherence may close. They simply explain to themselves that they have used areas of strength to succeed and minimize the feelings they have about their lack of interest in reading.

## Interventions

*Remediation*: Numerous reading specialists are available who can help both adults and children with their dyslexia. These specialists have developed a variety of strategies and techniques and their rate of success is quite high. Nevertheless, most of them caution that, in spite of remediation, the reading rate of someone with dyslexia will not be commensurate with that of someone who does not have that problem.

*Psychotherapy*: The goal of psychotherapy with patients with dyslexia is to address the problems that are secondary to the deficit. The patient must also receive as much adjunctive support as possible during the time she is in therapy. The therapist must be available to collaborate in any way necessary with caregivers, school personnel, or those involved in the remediation.

The overall strategy is to provide the patient with tasks in which she can succeed. Such successes are important in order to build self-confidence—self-confidence that will carry over into the task of learning to read. At first patients may be offered a variety of activities in which they might excel, preferably in non-academic areas. The reason for avoiding academic areas initially is that many patients have developed an aversive response to academic tasks because of past failures. They are therefore unprepared to approach the task for fear that they might fail again. Some children eagerly pursue opportunities to engage in sports or social activities. For others, participation in a children's theater, where they can exercise their good comprehension and verbal expression, gives a boost to self-confidence. Participation in summer programs that may or may not have an academic component is also recommended.

Once patients have developed a better sense of confidence, it is possible to approach the psychological tasks of dealing with the injuries the years have inflicted. The experience in therapy is geared to helping them be valued and appreciated. Concomitantly, explanations are given regarding the nature of their reading difficulties. These explanations are meant to fill in the gaps in the self-narrative. Patients who have been tested have a basic knowledge of the nature of the disorder, but often it has not been processed cognitively and remains unintegrated. The purpose of such discussions in therapy is to permit patients to integrate that understanding and incorporate it into a self-narrative. For this to be accomplished, the therapist must explore the themes the patient has used to organize her understanding of her difficulties. Part of this involves exploring the unconscious dimensions of those themes—dimensions that emerge through enactments, play activities, or flights of fantasy.

Improvements in patients' feelings about themselves occur when they can function adequately academically, have experienced real life successes, and have developed a good understanding of the reading disability. Children who reach this point can go on to be their own advocates as they progress within the educational system.

## CASE ILLUSTRATION: JOEL

*Referral and presenting problem*: **Joel was seven and a half years old when his parents requested a consultation. The second grade teacher had urged them to seek counseling for their son. In first grade, Joel's behavior had progressively deteriorated. He became oppositional and provocative in class. He refused to do any work, insisting that it was "too easy" for him. He kept repeating, "Only babies are asked to do this!" He maintained that he was too smart to be learning to write the alphabet or his name. When the teacher would ask that he read, he would refuse. If she challenged him that he was having trouble reading, he would retort that she was dumb, and in any case it was her fault that he did not know how to read—she was not such a good teacher. Through his behavior he appeared to be constantly seeking attention; he dis-**

rupted the class and often ended up having to spending time in the principal's office.

*Developmental history*: Joel was the only child of parents who adored him. He was the first male grandchild in a large family. This extended group of adults showered much affection and attention on him. He felt cherished and very special. The attention was a great source of enjoyment for him. Expectations were very high, as he was perceived to be a brilliant child who would follow his grandfather's and father's illustrious footsteps. He saw himself as destined for greatness by upholding a family tradition of great achievement. The pride he felt at being a part of his family's lineage was evidenced in the fact that he carried his grandfather's name.

*Test results*: Testing by a reading consultant at age seven revealed that Joel was functioning at a second-to-third pre-primer level in silent reading. He earned a grade equivalent score of 1.4 for vocabulary and 1.5 for comprehension on the Gates-MacGinitie, Primary A, Form 1. He was just starting to use beginning and ending sounds as decoding aids and was still dependent on visual cues to identify words and comprehend sentences. His quick recognition of words was inadequately developed for reading first grade material. When reading material beyond the pre-primer level orally, his meager sight vocabulary and his lack of a consistent method of word attack hampered his reading and slowed his rate considerably (Gray Oral, form B 1.2). He read word by word, did not attempt to analyze unfamiliar words, and had some difficulty keeping his place. Joel was able to identifying all letters in isolation (with some confusion on b–d and p–q). He was able to print most of the alphabet in sequence from memory (forgot I, M, O, Q, T, V and was slow on K and R). However, he did not recall all of the lowercase letters and formed many letters incorrectly.

*Clinical presentation*: When seen diagnostically, Joel presented as a likable, very bright, extremely verbal child who saw himself as very special. He began the conversation much like an adult by talking with great pride about his activities and his family. He showed disdain when asked if he wanted to play with any of the toys that were available; he preferred to sit and talk. At one point, he sat back and crossed his legs conveying an air of superiority that seemed characteristic. When an opportunity arose for him to draw something on a sheet of paper, he scribbled hastily with no apparent intention of producing anything meaningful and then in a rage tore up the paper and threw it on the floor.

I recommended therapy for Joel and saw him twice a week for two years. At first he adamantly refused any tutorial help for his dyslexia. It was only when I suggested that getting the help might make him smarter than the other kids in class that he finally accepted the remediation he needed. One of the major play activities in which he engaged during therapy was that of the constructing an airplane using sheets of paper and wood that he brought with him. During its construction, he felt convinced that he could make it fly. The construction became so big that we had to find a closet in which to store it between sessions. After attempting to fly with it in the office by jumping off the desk, he complained that there was not enough room to prove that it could stay airborne. Eventually, after several failed efforts at flying, he came in one day and started to talk about his progress in school. He made no mention of the plane. I finally asked him what he wanted to do with the plane; he responded that he was no longer interested in it. It was not clear to me whether his grandiosity was modified as he realized the futility of his plan or if he had simply set aside his plans, having rationalized that the circumstances would not permit their actualization.

A break came for the summer, as he went to camp. On his return at the end of the summer, his parents chose to discontinue the treatment because his behavior had improved and he was doing better academically.

*Discussion*: What is notable about Joel's response to his problem is how he resorted to haughty contempt toward adults who offered him help with tasks he could not perform. Having been an indulged child in a family that responded with admiration to his obvious intelligence, it was unbearable for him to think that there might be anything wrong with him. The world was out of step with him, not the other way around. He blamed his teachers for his deficit, refused their assistance, and responded with aggression when his posture was threatened. As long as those feelings could be preserved, Joel could feel cohesive. But this cohesiveness was tenuous, in that it entailed viewing adults as ineffectual. If they could not teach him what he needed to know they were imperfect. Such imperfection meant that they could fail him or were incapable of protecting him. Confronting this belief would be seriously traumatic, since he needed them to be there for him. The only safeguard to his sense of cohesiveness was to rely on himself, as only he had the resources to protect himself. This self-reliance manifested as grandiosity and contempt for adults.

Although some working through of the grandiosity occurred during the therapy, the parents interrupted it. Family dynamics were at play that supported some of Joel's psychopathology. It appears that they needed him to serve selfobject functions for them, and his continuing in therapy was an injury to their pride. As a result, it was not possible to modify the underlying theme in his self-narrative. He never did accept the fact that he had a learning disorder and consequently never integrated that understanding as part of his self narrative. The one positive result came from the tutorial help he received, which resulted in a marked improvement in his ability to read.

As for Joel's self-narrative, its central motif is embedded in the fantasy he chose to play out during the session. The plane he chose to construct represented his sense of self in all its grandiosity. It revealed his belief that he was smart enough to produce a creation that could defy gravity. In addition, it demonstrated that he had little awareness of the unrealistic view he had of himself. The materials out of which the plane was constructed were as flimsy as his own sense of self. They could not accomplish the task for which they were intended; neither could they sustain the weight they were designed to carry.

I went along with the fantasy because it was necessary for someone to accept uncritically the vulnerable view he had of himself. I needed to demonstrate to him that I could empathize with his desire to appear smart and admirable. The collapse of the scheme was a necessary outcome of the therapeutic encounter. Reality had to intervene without my pointing out flaws in the plane or challenging the motif itself. To have done so would have only inflicted further injury by replicating what others in his life did to him. At some level he recognized the failure without having to acknowledge it overtly. His subsequent behavior demonstrated that he could view himself differently and could begin to address the narcissistic injury of having a learning problem without finding it to be an intolerable flaw in himself.

CASE ILLUSTRATION: JUAN

*Referral and presenting problems*: The psychiatrist who was medicating Juan for depression referred him for an evaluation. He was a fifteen-and-a-half-year-old freshman in a large high school in Chicago. The parents had consulted the psychiatrist because of the difficulties into which Juan had gotten himself. In particular, he had been arrested for driving without a license. His parents were also worried that a local gang was actively recruiting him. Some of Juan's friends were gang members, and he had been involved with them in several minor acts of delinquency, for which they had not been caught. Juan had begun to dress like those gang members but recently discontinued at the urging of his girlfriend. He was skipping school and failing most of his academic classes. The referring psychiatrist felt that an improvement in attitude had appeared after Juan began taking medication. He was doing better in school and appeared to be rethinking his involvement with the gang members.

*Developmental history*: Juan's parents gave the following history. He was born in a small town in the southwest. Both his parents were first-generation immigrants who were fluent in English but spoke Spanish at home. They described his early years as unremarkable. He had no health problems and was generally a happy, carefree child. A change occurred when he began first grade. Juan did not like school, and a pattern of misbehavior began. By the end of second grade, the teacher was constantly complaining that Juan was lazy and made no effort to do the schoolwork. The school psychologist who tested him found a reading problem as well as a language-processing problem. These problems were attributed to difficulties with processing visual materials. He was also found to have difficulties in dealing with numbers. No intervention was made because the school did not have the resources to provide special tutoring.

When family relocated to Chicago, Juan entered the third grade and a new school system. On the annual testing given to children, Juan was reading at the first grade level. He was retained in third grade but not retested until he got into fourth grade. At that point, he received some resource help from a tutor who tried to teach him keyboarding on a computer. His teachers, who were bilingual, were less harsh and more understanding of Juan's problems than those in his prior school. However, no remediation for his learning disability was instituted.

In fourth grade, he was placed in a special education class with three girls. Instead of feeling helped, he felt humiliated and became more aggressive. In spite of these behavior problems at school, at home he remained affectionate and obedient. By then, he had lost interest in reading and complained that when he tried to read the words ran together so that he quickly got tired by the effort it took him to read a single page.

In sixth grade he went to junior high school, where he was placed again in a special education class. Academically Juan was far behind his peers. He felt isolated and began to act out even more than before. He tried to resist being placed in the special education class, saying that he would rather to be in a class of children with behavioral disorders than with the "dumb kids." The family tried to obtain some special help for him at a private learning center, but he hated to go there and soon refused. They became convinced that he would never learn the way other children did. By seventh grade, he insisted on being mainstreamed, but he was so far behind academically that he stopped going to school. Signs of depression emerged. He complained that he felt dumb and began talking about wishing he were dead. He made a suicidal gesture by taking half a bottle of aspirin, but his parents did not think it was a serious attempt.

When he entered eighth grade, he was a year older than most of the children in the class. He became more socially outgoing and had some friends, but his parents felt that he "hooked up with the wrong kind of crowd." His best friend was a bully who was in a class for children with behavior disorders. He began to smoke, and they suspected that he was also on drugs. He developed a relationship with a girlfriend who was in the class for children with behavioral disorders. Juan's parents emphasized that he is an affectionate child whom they consider to be strong-willed. They thought that he now wanted to get back on track and improve his self-esteem.

*Testing*: The reading specialist who tested Juan in third grade found the following: Within the area of reading and spelling he demonstrated great difficulty. He was administered the Durrell Analysis of Reading Difficulty, where his oral and silent reading of passages was rated at a low second grade level, with good comprehension. His oral reading of text was characterized by word by word reading, poor enunciation of difficult words, and inadequate word-analysis skills. In silent reading, he read slowly and evidenced marked insecurity. His reading of new or difficult words showed poor use of phonetic analysis in favor of reading words as a whole, by focusing on beginning and ending parts as clues. His spelling errors showed confusion with some vowel sounds and reversals of b and d. His attempt to use phonetic analysis was evidenced here; however, his actual spelling revealed a poor sight vocabulary. More recent testing was not available.

*Clinical presentation*: His mother brought Juan to the appointment. She had previously called to say that Juan would be willing to meet with me, although he expressed a great deal of resistance. He agreed to come for one session and would decide whether to return depending on how he felt about our session.

Juan came casually dressed and immediately became engaged in talking with me. I was surprised at the extent of his openness and ability to share personal information during the 45-minute session.

We began by discussing issues related to his academic performance. He had taken a final exam that morning, and he felt he had done well. He had three finals the next day, for which he felt unprepared. When asked to describe the source of his academic problems, he related them directly to his dyslexia. He described that when he tried to read, the lines on the page ran into each other and that he couldn't distinguish individual words. Reading became impossible. We traced the difficulties in reading back to kindergarten in the southwest. He was in a bilingual school through third grade, which aggravated his problems.

When he moved to junior high school, he was placed in the class with children who were considerably more advanced than he was. He stated that seventh and eighth grade were "the worst years of my life!" Through the years, he had developed a pattern of becoming angry and rebellious, which led to being considered a behavior problem. He turned for friendships to peers who cared little about schoolwork and who were on the fringes of gangs. He described himself as dressing like one of the "gang bangers" and becoming totally disrespectful of all adults, including his parents. After he was finally referred to the psychiatrist who placed him on antidepressants, his mood began to change. He has felt considerably better ever since he started taking medication.

Now the center of his life is the relationship with his girlfriend, with whom he is head over heels in love. He has changed the way he dresses because she requested it. They are part of a group of kids who are not gang members, but most of whom are in the behavioral disorders class. He then went on to describe some of the complications of the relationship with his girlfriend, whom he described as one of six children from a "wealthy family." At this point, he asked if I would assure him that I would keep the information he was about to tell me confidential, which I did. He said that he and his girlfriend had been sexually active for some time. In fact, he thought he got her pregnant a month ago, but both felt relieved when she had a spontaneous miscarriage. Her parents did not know about this aspect of her life.

I returned to the issues around his investment in academics. To this he responded by saying that he would just as soon drop out of school. He was eager to drop out and work so he could get a car. This led us to discuss the issue of his arrest for driving without a license. He minimized the incident by saying that he had a driver's permit that allowed him to drive with an adult in the car, but he got caught because he needed to take his girlfriend home when no adults were around to drive with him. He felt that this was a minor infraction.

As we discussed these problems, he pointed out that he has a terrible temper. He becomes enraged and gets out of control, especially when demands to perform academically frustrate him. On occasion when he has felt frustrated he has put holes in the wall in his room. He felt it strange that often, after having one of those fits, he would feel exhausted and would lie down and sleep for a long time. On waking up later he would feel as though nothing had happened. He was aware that his inability to control his temper was a serious problem and said that he would like to do something about it.

At the close of the session, I thanked him for sharing so much about himself. I asked him to think about whether he wanted to come back to see me.

*Discussion*: Juan presented as a classic example of an adolescent with unremediated dyslexia who turned away from academic interests in anger at the unreasonable demands he felt were being made of him. His rebelliousness was in turn labeled as resistance to learning. Devaluing learning and academic interests, he turned to a group of peers who embraced an alternative lifestyle. By embracing their values he devalued his parents' values and expectations and found an area that was meaningful to him. In addition, his chronic depression fueled his irritability and rage, thus reinforcing his alienation from his family and the school setting. At the time of the interview the medication appeared to have taken the edge off his irritability. He felt better and was less enraged. However, he still could not read or achieve in academic areas at a level commensurate with his intelligence. This reinforced the choices he was making of rejecting school and identifying with peers who did not value school success.

Juan's psychodynamics were different from Joel's. The selfobject function most seriously affected by the neuropsychological deficit was the idealization of adults and the functions associated with that idealization. Juan suffered serious disillusionment in his caregivers and those responsible for his education. His curiosity and desire for learning were denied by his dyslexia. But worst of all, he experienced the failures of his caregivers to provide him with the tools to overcome his deficits as a lack of investment in him. Adults, he felt, did not care that he suffered shame and humiliation in the presence of his classmates. This injury turned to anger and escalated into rage at them. He lost respect for them and all they stood for. It was, therefore, natural for him to gravitate to others who were like him and with whom he could feel less isolated and alienated. The loss of respect led to a denigration of the entire value system associated with his parents.

By losing the connection with adults, he also lost another significant function they performed developmentally—the regulation and modulation of his affect states. Not only could they not provide him with comforting responses, but they also could not serve as regulators for his mood swings. The depression into which he lapsed may originally have been in response to the context, but it then took on a life of its own and turned into a chronic disorder. At that point, he would not allow adults to limit his conduct and lost control of himself.

As for his self-narrative, Juan clearly understood what had happened to him. This understanding provided him with justification for his conduct. To that degree, his narrative had elements of coherence. The incoherences that fueled his rage toward adults were in response to questions such as: "Why was it that they did not help me?" "Why did they allow me to be humiliated in front of my peers?" "How could it be that I, who was as smart as most kids in my class, had to be placed with kids who were significantly less smart than I?" These incoherences were the result of the fact that he could not conventionalize his self-narrative in ways consonant with his parents' expectations.

Most adolescents with learning disorders find it difficult to not respond to such incoherences with frustration and rage. They are not prepared to listen to explanations or rationalizations that adults give them. They are even less receptive to the idea that they have a learning disorder that causes their problems. Juan felt emploted into a self-defeating web from which he could not extricate himself. He felt he was assigned a set of roles that went with being labeled learning disabled and sent to special education. He violently rejected those labels and roles. In the process, he also rejected the alternative of conventionalizing his self-narrative. Since he could not be like others, he would find his own path.

Juan failed to consolidate a nuclear sense of self, which is a critical developmental step (see Chapter 6). Rather than developing a set of career goals or finding a career path that could lead him to success, he was left adrift. Some adolescents in those circumstances embrace a career in criminal activity, thus achieving narrative coherence by incorporating antisocial values into a lifestyle.

As for Juan, he refused to return for further sessions. I was unable to obtain any follow-up to determine what happened to him.

# 8

# ATTENTION-DEFICIT/ HYPERACTIVITY DISORDER

ATTENTION-DEFICIT/HYPERACTIVITY disorder (AD/HD) is a heterogeneous disorder whose symptoms manifest with considerable variation (see Table 8.1). It is the most common condition for which children are referred to mental health centers (Barkley, 1998). In the past few years, public awareness of the prevalence of AD/HD has mushroomed. Articles appear in the popular press almost weekly. CHAAD (Children and Adults with Attention-deficit Disorders), an organization created in 1987, has expanded its membership to the point where it has numerous chapters all over the country. It is devoted to advocacy and to providing an educational forum for people with this disorder.

For many years, neurologists believed that AD/HD was a disorder that affected only children and disappeared with the onset of adolescence. We now know that the disorder frequently persists into adulthood, although its manifestations in adults are, at times, different from its manifestations in children and adolescents. In some adults, the symptoms are continuous, while in others the hyperactivity disappears, but the related symptoms of impulsivity and inattention remain. Many adults are now either diagnosing themselves or being diagnosed and are seeking help for the disorder. The issue of appropriate psychotherapeutic treatment for these adults has now come to the forefront.

**TABLE 8.1**
**Attention-Deficit/Hyperactivity Disorder**

A. CHARACTERISTICS:

   1. *Defining features*:According to *DSM-IV,* there are three components to AD/HD: inattention, impulsivity and hyperactivity. *DSM-IV* identifies three subtypes of AD/HD: combined type; predominantly inattentive type; and predominantly hyperactive-impulsive type.

   2. *Prevalence rates*:The National Institutes of Health studies find that 3 to 5% of all children, perhaps as many as 2 million American children, suffer from the disorder (NIMH, NIH Publication #96-3572, 1994; NIH, 2000). Cantwell states that as "much as 50% of the child psychiatric clinical populations" have attention deficit disorders (Cantwell, 1996, p. 978).

   3. *Sex ratio*:The ratio of male to female ranges from 2:1 to 9:1 (Pennington, 1991, p. 84). Barkley states "epidemiological studies find the proportion to be approximately 3:1 among nonreferred children displaying [these] symptoms" (Barkley, 1989, p. 44).

   4. *Coexisting conditions*: Among those conditions found to coexist with AD/HD are: mood disorders, anxiety disorders, oppositionality and aggression, obsessive-compulsive disorder, executive dysfunction, and substance use disorder.

B. DEVELOPMENTAL HISTORY: Most milestones are achieved on time. Some children's level of activity is noticed to be higher than average at a very early age. Most frequently, the child's hyperactivity manifests around the time he begins to walk.

C. DISORDERS OF THE SELF: Self-esteem problems and problems with impulsivity and self-regulation predominate.

   1. *Presenting symptoms*:

     a. *Academic*:Academic performance may be impaired, but the impairment is secondary to the impulsivity or inattentiveness.

     b. *Social*: Social relationships and relationships within the family may be impaired because of the child's disruptiveness, bossiness, or oppositional behaviors.

     c. *Emotional*: Demoralization and self-esteem problems may be present secondary to the effects of others' reactions to the child's disruptiveness. Problems with self-regulation and affect regulation are often present.

## TABLE 8.1
## (Continued)

2. *Sense of self-cohesion*: Sense of self remains reasonably intact, although self-esteem problems are prevalent. Regulation of affect states, particularly anger, is problematic.
3. *Coherence of self-narrative*: The self-narrative does not adequately explain the symptoms. Children may justify their behaviors by displacing the responsibility for their actions onto others.

D. INTERVENTIONS:
   1. *Remediation*: Stimulant medications are often prescribed for the attenuation of the symptoms. These medications present a complication for children with a coexisting Tourette's disorder because the medication exacerbates the tics. Behavior modification sometimes produces positive results.
   2. *Psychotherapy*: Family therapy or individual therapy may be used selectively, depending on the situation.

---

Public law 94-142 in 1975, which mandated special education services for children with learning disabilities, did not include AD/HD as one of the disabilities, nor did the reauthorization of this legislation as the Individuals with Disabilities Education Act (IDEA) P.L. 101-476, 1990. It was not until March 1999, under pressure from advocacy groups, that the Department of Education revised its regulations and authorized services for patients with AD/HD under Part B of IDEA as "other health impairment" (Department of Education, 1999).

## History

The history of the identification of AD/HD is closely tied to the identification of other learning disabilities, especially dyslexia. In the early 1900s, children with this disorder were thought to suffer from a "morbid deficit in moral control" (Lerner, Lowenthal, & Lerner, 1995, p. 24). Following the outbreak of encephalitis after World War I, children who had been affected by the disease exhibited many of the symptoms, called "postencephalitic behavior disorder," that we now associate with AD/HD. This led researchers to hypothesize that the condition was caused by brain damage. Subsequently the concepts of "minimal brain damage" and "minimal brain dysfunction" (MBD) gained currency. Educators began using these terms to identify this disorder, as well as other disorders now associated with learning disabilities (Barkley, 1990; Lerner et al., 1995).

In the 1960s, a shift occurred when the evidence to support the hypothesis of brain damage did not materialize. The term MBD was discarded and the terms "hyperactive" or "hyperkinetic reaction of childhood disorder" were introduced to describe what was thought to be a syndrome (American Psychiatric Association, 1968). In the 1970s, intensification of the search for causes for the disorder led some to identify environmental factors as causal agents. Food additives and refined sugar were considered the culprits (Feingold, 1976). The popular press contributed considerably to the dissemination of views supportive of this position, but researchers found no support for this hypothesis.

With the appearance of *DSM-III* in 1980, a more empirically based approach began to emerge. The authors of the Manual made a distinction between attention-deficit disorder with hyperactivity (ADDH) and without hyperactivity (ADD/noH). As new evidence was gathered, it became evident that these labels did not cover the various manifestations of the disorder. In the revised version, *DSM-III-R* (American Psychiatric Association, 1987), the two categories were fused into one, attention-deficit/ hyperactivity disorder, with emphasis placed on an empirically based set of categories that gave recognition to the developmental dimensions of the disorder. Unfortunately, the disorder was classified, along with conduct disorder and oppositional defiant disorder, under disruptive behavior disorders. This was rectified with the publication of *DSM-IV* in 1994. The defining features, as spelled out in *DSM-IV*, are given in the section on characteristics of the disorder.

## Explanatory Paradigms

The major explanatory paradigm for the disorder is offered by Barkley's model of "behavioral disinhibition." Barkley considers AD/HD to be a heterogeneous disorder, that is, children ". . . display considerable variation in the degree of the symptoms, the pervasiveness across situations of these problems, and the extent to which other disorders occur in association with it" (Barkley, 1990, p. 3). He finds that many questions may be raised about its being regarded as a clinical syndrome, since the terms "inattention," "impulsivity," and "hyperactivity" lend themselves to such different interpretations. Furthermore, the mechanisms operating behind the behavioral manifestations of the disorder are difficult to identify. For example, inattention may be due to diminished persistence rather than to distractibility. It may be secondary to behavioral disinhibition or the absence of alertness.

Barkley's conceptualization is based on a Skinnerian principle: Attention is not a behavior; it is a relationship between a stimulus and a response. Children with AD/HD have a deficit in the capacity to delay responding to a stimulus. If the relationship between the stimulus and the response is weak, the result is inattention; when the behavior is not maintained, the result is a poor attention span; when the response is too rapid, the result is impulsivity; and when the child cannot wait, the result is the inability to delay gratification. The deficit in behavioral regulation may stem from one or more of the following impairments: (1) diminished sensitivity to behavioral consequences, (2) diminished control of behavior by partial schedules of consequences, and (3) poor rule-governed behavior. Poor rule-governed behavior is involved when children "have problems sustaining responding to experimenter rules and instructions particularly when the instructions are repeated or when the experimenter leaves the setting" (Barkley, 1990, p.45). Poor rule-governed behavior is associated with behavioral disinhibition.

In 1993, Barkley (1993, 1994) proposed a new theory to explain AD/HD. This theory is based on Bronowski's theory of the function that language serves in human development. Language is interposed between the stimulus and the response in such a way as to permit a delay in responding to the stimulus. Children with AD/HD suffer from "disinhibition," i.e., they have a deficit in the capacity to delay responding to stimuli. We will see later that Barkley used this conceptual framework to suggest a method of intervention for children with this disorder.

In 1998, Barkley proposed a further modification of his theory to include the emerging consensus among neuropsychologists that deficits in executive functions play a major role in the disorder. In the Preface to this work, he states: "The cornerstone of this text continues to be that ADHD must be viewed as a developmental disorder of behavioral inhibition, inattention, and self-regulation. New to this volume, however, is the belief that the developmental delay in inhibition gives rise to deficits in the executive functions that subserve self-regulation. . . . It is these secondary deficits that result in the inattentive, distractible, impersistent, and poorly regulated behavior of those with ADHD" (p. ix).

Pennington (1991; Pennington, Bennetto, McAleer, & Roberts, 1996) had already considered AD/HD to be a subgroup of executive function. He questioned whether it is a distinctive syndrome, because the terms "hyperactivity" and "attention" may be too broad to identify a syndrome behaviorally. By identifying subtypes of AD/HD, he tried to establish the relationship between attentional problems and deficits in executive function. Examining the specific cognitive tasks in which children with AD/HD are impaired, he found that the deficits involved in the completion of these tasks reinforce "the hypothesis that the underlying deficit is not in a particular information processing domain, like verbal memory, but in executive functions that regulate all of information processing" (Pennington, 1991, p. 94).

In 1996, Barkley had associated Bronowski's theory and the processes involved in prolongation (delayed responding) to working memory. Since executive functions and working memory are closely related, Barkley's position was compatible with Pennington's. A consensus was evolving that a primary deficit in executive function led to the manifestation of symptom clusters that are identified as AD/HD. However, as Pennington pointed out, the data "hardly provide conclusive evidence for this hypothesis. . . . We do not know if executive function deficits are among the most persistent features of the disorder, although adult outcome studies provide indirect evidence for this view" (Pennington, 1991, p. 96).

Barkley (1998) proposes a "hybrid model" in which self-control and self-regulation are central to an understanding of AD/HD. His fundamental assumption of learning theory's stimulus-response mechanism remains unchanged. The problem does not lie in the inattention given to the stimulus, but rather in the failure to inhibit a response to it. A delay in the inhibition of response disrupts the executive functions associated with self-control. There are four specific sets of executive function that are affected: working memory; internalization of speech (verbal working memory); self-regulation of affect, of motivation, and of arousal; and reconstitution (Barkley, 1998, pp. 225–260). In simple terms, working memory involves keeping events in mind while working at a task and being aware of time; internalization of speech involves reflection, reading comprehension, and moral reasoning; self-regulation involves the regulation of affect states, motivation, and arousal in the service of completing a task; and reconstitution involves the kind of analysis and synthesis of information related to the task at hand. When these executive functions are not efficiently deployed, the result is a disruption in the motor control necessary for the execution of the task. For Barkley the attentional problems associated with the disorders are secondary to the primary executive function deficits. They are related to a lack of persistence in the implementation of goal-directed behaviors.

## Characteristics of the Disorder

*Defining features: DSM-IV* sets out three criteria for the diagnosis of AD/HD (American Psychiatric Association, 1994): *inattention, hyperactivity,* and *impulsivity*. It specifies three types: a combined type in which attentional problems and hyperactivity-impulsivity are present, a predominantly inattentive type, and a predominantly hyperactive-impulsive type. Although these criteria were written primarily for children, the wording is couched in a form that makes them applicable to adults. Among the problems with attention are: not paying close attention to details, being unable to focus on tasks, being easily distracted, having difficulty organizing resources to achieve a goal, not following through on instructions. Examples of how hyperactivity displays itself are: "being on the go" all the time, being hyper-verbal, being restlessness, being unable to relax and enjoy leisure activities. Finally, problems with impulsivity often manifest as impatience, loss of control, interrupting others during conversations, and chronically making hasty decisions before considering all the facts.

*Prevalence rates*: The National Institutes of Health studies find that 3 to 5% of all children, perhaps as many as 2 million American children, suffer from the disorder (NIH, 2000; Neuwirth, 1994). Cantwell states that as "much as 50% of the child psychiatric clinical populations" have attention-deficit disorders (1996, p. 978).

*Sex ratio*: The ratio of male to female ranges from 2:1 to 9:1 (Pennington, 1991, p. 84.) Barkley states "epidemiological studies find the proportion to be approximately 3:1 among nonreferred children displaying [these] symptoms" (Barkley, 1989, p. 44).

*Coexisting conditions*: In the introductory chapter to the book on conditions comorbid with AD/HD, Brown (2000a) proposes that the disorder be considered a "spectrum disorder" rather than a unitary syndrome. Following that assumption, the contributors to the book discuss the comorbidity of AD/ HD with mood disorders, anxiety disorders, oppositionality and aggression, obsessive-compulsive disorder, learning disorders, executive dysfunctions, substance use, and other disorders. Of special interest to us is the chapter by Tannock and Brown (2000) that discusses the comorbidity of attention-deficit disorders with learning disorders. They state, "About 20%–25% of children with ADHD are likely to present with specific learning disorders, with these estimates based on both epidemiological and clinical studies that use rigorous criteria to define ADHD and learning disorders" (p. 238). They cite comorbidity rates of 15%–30% with reading disorders, and 10%–60% with mathematics disorders. Overlaps with disorders of written expression, developmental coordination disorders, and central auditory processing are also found, but no specific prevalence rates are noted.

## Developmental History

*Pregnancy, birth, and infancy*: Some mothers notice an unusual amount of activity in utero. Infants may not establish a regular feeding or sleep cycle. Mothers may experience the infant as fidgety, restless, and nonmolding. The child may overwhelm them, especially if it is a first child. They feel inadequate and frustrated. They feel rejected by the child because their efforts at soothing are unrewarded. Some mothers get depressed and work at trying to overcompensate for those feelings by catering to the child's every wish.

In a study of 25 mothers of 30 children with AD/HD and 8 children with undifferentiated ADD, Segal (1996) sought to determine the nature of the mothering experience. She found that the mothers could be divided into two groups. One group was able to obtain a diagnosis of the child's problem shortly after becoming aware of the problem, while the other group obtained a diagnosis much later. Those in the first group were able to mobilize themselves to acquire knowledge about the condition and to obtain resources to help their child. The second group blundered through the process of mothering their child and struggled to keep connected to the child. Both groups of mothers experienced serious stresses in daily living, which at times led to marital problems. Most mothers chose to limit the size of their families because of the problems they confronted.

In the first and second year, the children's gross motor milestones are often on schedule. Sleep patterns are often problematic. At times, the child is so active that he will climb out the crib, creating serious problems for caregivers who fear for the child's safety. Some caregivers begin setting limits on the child, but these interventions are often counterproductive, since they bring on greater resistance to conformity. The child is generally experienced as unrewarding to parents. While they see their child as "normal," parents find it difficult to respond positively to him. Often they are unable to distinguish behavior that is out of control from behavior that is appropriately intended to produce positive feedback, which disrupts their ability meet the child's need for positive mirroring. No unusual separation problems appear, unless there is a comorbid anxiety disorder.

During the child's third to sixth years, developmental milestones continue to be met but management problems continue. In the area of self-care, the child, although clearly capable of performing the required age-appropriate tasks, needs a great deal of supervision and assistance to actually complete the tasks. Battles develop around starting tasks, going to bed, and being cooperative. Interpersonally the child appears jovial and fun-loving, but caregivers feel a lack of depth in the relationship and the affective tone is frenetic. Clowning behavior is characteristic but becomes less charming as the child gets older. With peers contact and cooperation appear difficult, and others generally shun the child because he is not fun to be with. Often contact with other children becomes overstimulating and situations deteriorate as fighting results and someone gets hurt. The child does better in structured situations where expectations are clear-cut or in one-on-one situations where stimulation is minimal or well-controlled. Some children display fearlessness and aggression, while others are demanding. Many are described as "driven by a motor."

In middle childhood, some children display patterns of lying, petty thievery, and resistance to authority. During these years the labels of conduct disorder and oppositional defiant disorder are often used to describe these children. Some children are accident prone, while others manifest resistance to routines. In general, they do not comply with rules of conduct and expectations set by parents and adults and behave inappropriately in social functions.

In adolescence, some children display symptoms such as sadness, depression, or lack of self-confidence. As a group, adolescents with AD/HD are at greater risk for substance abuse than their peers, and a number manifest antisocial behaviors.

## Disorders of the Self

### Presenting Symptoms

*Academic*: School performance is variable in children with this disorder. In preschool children are often inattentive and aggressive in ways that interfere with socialization and learning. In elementary school, the disorder may interfere with the child's performance, although he may be learning. Gym classes, lunch period, and recess are difficult even if the child is well coordinated; the overstimulation in the unstructured setting leads to diffusely disorganized behavior that is often disruptive or destructive. Teachers often find the child's behavior intolerable, although the parents may or may not be uncomfortable with his behavior at home. Some children say they like school but hate the fact that they cannot demonstrate their competence. Hallowell and Ratey (1994) note the following symptoms: restlessness, underachievement, procrastination, distractibility, blurting things out, flirting with danger, organizational difficulties, operating on multiple channels, hunger for stimulation, intolerance of boredom, low frustration tolerance, and verbal and behavioral impulsivity.

*Social*: Although attentional difficulties may exist, parents often report that the child can sit and watch TV or play a video game for hours. They report a great deal of negativism, to the point where "everything is a hassle," such as getting the child off to school in the morning and keeping track of possessions. They also report that the child has low frustration tolerance, overreacts to stimulation, and has poor impulse control. He has poor relationships with siblings—he is aggressive and hateful toward them, he is jealous, can't share, and stimulates regressive behaviors in them by overstimulating them. The child gets along all right with adults or with younger children, but does not get along with peers. With other children he is aggressive, and he often becomes overstimulated in group situations. Hallowell and Ratey (1994) also note that the tendency in adolescence to self-medicate with drugs is a way of dealing with the dysregulation problems and the inability to self-soothe.

*Emotional*: The child appears unable to experience feelings of contentment or a sense of internal regulation. Interactions with caregivers are not experienced as soothing or comforting. The absence of these experiences leads to selfobject deficits that manifest as the lack of self-control and self-esteem. Caregivers will often seek services for their child at an early age because they find the child's behavior intolerable.

### The Sense of Self-cohesion

The aspect of endowment involved in AD/HD is the neuroregulatory control system (self-control and self-regulation), which is part of the executive functions (Palombo, 1996a, p 245). Because of the neuroregulatory deficits, the patient cannot adequately regulate thought processes, affect states, and/or behaviors. The child's responses are not congruent with the expectations of others in the context. Children with AD/HD are action-oriented and seldom given to introspection about their responses. They react before they have thought about their reactions and respond to others' responses before processing the meaning of those responses. From the child's subjective perspective, others misinterpret the motives behind his responses and perceive the behavior to be defiant, oppositional, or negativistic. The child's responses, at first, are not necessarily motivated by a desire to make life miserable for his caregivers. It is only after interactional patterns are established, in which the child expects to be misunderstood and is made anxious because of his failure to understand, that a vicious cycle of negativism is established. The child's frustration increases and eventually leads to rage or withdrawal.

The dysfunctions of children with AD/HD create conditions in which the capacities for self-regulation and self-soothing are diminished. The child wishes to please and to be accepted by caregivers, but the interactions are so tainted by negative feelings that the specific selfobject functions the child requires are not available. Most affected may be the idealizing function—with its correlated experience of self-soothing and self-regulation. When caregivers are experienced as benignly powerful, they become capable of calming and reassuring a distressed child. However, if caregivers are perceived as harsh, punitive, and arbitrary, their capacity to fulfill such functions is greatly decreased. The capacities for self-regulation and self-soothing cannot be internalized. The child is unable to calm himself and experience pleasurable sense of self-cohesion. Self-discipline and self-control become problematic.

In addition, the negative patterns interfere with the acquisition of the other selfobject functions. Rather than feeling appreciated for his joyful assertiveness, the child experiences the parents as controlling and inhibiting, if not punitive. The positive experiences of pride and admiration are few and far between, since the focus appears to be so much more on limit-setting. The result is a self-centeredness that is reflective of an arrest in this area. The age-appropriate acquisition of standards and values is also impeded. Others are experienced as controlling and punitive, since they seem to be always correcting or punishing and never providing comfort. The child may feel that nothing he does is effective in producing the kind of response he wants. These dynamics are complicated by the parents' own issues, particularly if they have AD/HD (Weiss, Hechman, & Weiss, 2000).

The presenting symptoms vary depending on: the degree of hyperactivity, poor self-image, problems with parents, hypersensitivity, short attention span, inability to concentrate, low frustration tolerance, inability to follow directions, difficulties in school, and poor sibling and peer relationships. Deficits in regulatory functions are seen in negativism, poor self-soothing, poor impulse control, and proneness to overstimulation. Although the parents may try their best to compensate for the child's deficits, they are experienced as punitive and judgmental by the child. The resulting self-esteem problem leads to an underlying depressiveness, against which defenses are erected. The child feels he is bad and that closeness to others is not rewarding

### Coherence of the Self-narrative

A particular type of incoherence characterizes many of the self-narratives of children with AD/HD. They seem unaware of the causes of the difficulties in their lives. In part, this is due to the fact that they are more action-oriented and less introspective than others. They give little thought to their contribution to the difficulties in which they find themselves and most often see external factors as responsible. They do not recognize their impulsivity and their inability to regulate their feelings as problematic. In fact, many children value those traits in themselves. They derive pleasure and excitement from their capacity to respond immediately to situations. They feel justified in given vent to their feelings and are confident that no other response would be appropriate.

These children respond to the consequences of their actions, rather than focus on their contribution to the situation they have created. They are often troubled by the fact that adversities seem to follow them even though they do not seek them out. The themes of their narratives reflect these attitudes. Commonly, one hears: "I don't know why these things happen to me so often and not to others!" "He started the fight, I was only trying to defend myself!" "I never wanted to hurt her feelings—she's just a crybaby!"

Underlying the statements are themes that organize their self-narratives. Some feel that they are victims of circumstance, unjustly accused of being responsible for events they did not cause. Others justify their temper outbursts as caused by the way they are treated by others. They carry a chip on their shoulder. Still others take pride in their aggressiveness and value it as a demonstration of their strength. The incoherences in these narratives reflect a clash between the personal meanings they assign to events and the shared meanings the community confers upon them.

## Interventions

*Diagnosis*: Since the criteria for attentional problems, impulsivity, and hyperactivity are primarily behavioral and involve clinical judgments, diagnosticians must rely on parents' and teachers' reports. Some instruments available to assist in making the diagnosis are the T.O.V.A. (Tests of Variables of Attention) (Greenberg, 1999) and the Conners (1989) rating scale. The T.O.V.A. is a continuous performance test that children take while sitting at a computer and responding to visual stimuli presented on the screen. The test measures response time, errors of omission (inattention), errors of commission (impulsivity/disinhibition), and several other variables. It can be used for children as young as four. It is considered a reliable tool in monitoring the effects of medication. The Conners is a behavior rating scale that provides a reliable measure of parents' and teachers' perceptions of the child's functioning in six problem areas: hyperactivity, conduct problems, emotionality-overindulgence, anxiety-passivity, asociality, and daydreaming/attention (Conners & Wells, 1986).

At times it is difficult to differentiate features that are diagnostic of the condition and personality traits that children incorporate into their style of relating. In those circumstances, it is often difficult to distinguish between the disorder and a related coexisting personality disorder. Often, confirmation of the diagnosis comes indirectly after a regimen of medication is instituted and found to control some of the symptoms.

*Remediation*: Medication, psychotherapy, group therapy, and special education are the most common modes of intervention. Children with hyperactivity are in greatest need of these interventions (Goldberg, 1999; Lerner et al., 1995).

Barkley (1993, 1994; Barkley & Murphy, 1993) suggests a mode of intervention based on Bronowski's model of delayed responding. The Barkley/Bronowski theory of delayed responding states that there are four steps to this process. First, the disinhibition leads to *a failure in prolongation*, that is, a failure to prolong the effects of the signal by symbolically fixing the event mentally, i.e., thinking before acting. Second, *there is a failure to separate feelings from facts*, to separate the personal feelings that an event or experience arouses from its objective content. The third step is *a failure to use self-directed speech* or to use the internalization of language (self-talk) in the service of achieving self-control. Fourth, is *a failure to break apart and recombine information*, to analyze the components of a situation so as to resynthesize them in the service of an adaptive response. Barkley suggests a behavioral-systems approach for dealing with family dynamics as helpful in modifying the behaviors of these children. Yeschin (2000) has proposed a view that combines the psychoanalytic concepts of object relationships theory with these interventions.

One type of remediation is that of parental involvement in behavioral management on a time-limited basis. The goal is to change the parents' style and techniques of addressing the child's problems. This approach uses positive reinforcement of acceptable behaviors and logical consequences for unacceptable behaviors. It favors a unified approach by both parents and a decrease in marital discord. It provides support to the caregivers to help decrease anger, and it provides suggestions for structuring the child's behavior. A carryover of these strategies to the school setting is recommended to provide consistency in the management of behavior.

Stimulant medication is an important adjunct to any intervention.

*Psychotherapy*: Individual psychotherapy for the child has as its goals enhancing self-esteem, improving self-control, minimizing impulsivity, deceasing aggressiveness, and strengthening the capacity for self-regulation.

It is characteristic that in unstructured clinical interviews these children appear to be enjoyable and fun-loving kids with no major problems. In time, they show signs of being controlling and imperious. There may be no evidence of depressiveness but a poor self-image emerges through comments such as "I hate myself!" "I can't do it!" "I always get into trouble!" Although not overtly depressed, these children manifest an underlying sadness, which may mask depression. They may be very talkative, although they will jump around from topic to topic. They generally are very open and forthright in responding to questions. If they begin to engage in an unstructured play activity, overstimulation may take over, followed by regressive disorganization.

### CASE ILLUSTRATION: ADAM

***Referral and presenting problem*: Adam's mother contacted me requesting an evaluation of her son, a nine-year-old fourth grader. He had been seen by a pediatrician who diagnosed him as having AD/HD and placed him on Ritalin. Adam's mother reported that he was preoccupied with fire and with being injured. He had nightmares, feared going to sleep, and was hard to get up in the mornings. He still had difficulties with separation. When anxious he appeared clumsy, and repeatedly he had been hurt in interactions with other kids. His emotional reac-**

tions were always very intense. Adam and his mother got into constant power struggles; when he lost, he collapsed and withdrew for hours in his room.

*Developmental history*: Adam was an active infant who was difficult to comfort. He was a very active toddler, loved exploring his environment, making it difficult for his mother to keep up with him. He walked at one year, swam well by age three, rode a two-wheeler by four. He was developing into a superb athlete.

He started in a developmental nursery at age three and a half. Both mother and father accompanied him and stayed with him initially because of his problems with separation. The school troubles began in first grade, which was very difficult for him. He had two teachers who did not understand him and he acted out a lot. Behavior problems have continued in school ever since.

*Test results*: When Adam was tested at age nine, the results indicated that he had superior overall learning ability. On the WISC-R his Verbal I.Q. was 124, Performance I.Q. was 111, and Full Scale I.Q. was 121. He was found to have a significant weakness in the area of written language, which created a significant discrepancy between his potential for achievement and his current level of achievement in this area. There were deficits in his rate of performance, particularly when a written response under a time constraint was required. He displayed little knowledge of how to organize his thoughts for the purposes of written formulation. A specific learning disability in the area of written expression was found to exist in addition to his attention-deficit disorder.

*Clinical presentation*: I saw Adam for two diagnostic sessions. In these sessions, he appeared as an attractive nine-year-old, who was at first exceedingly anxious and somewhat restless. He was quite verbal as he communicated his anxieties and fears. He indicated some confusion as to what was happening between him and his mother. He felt generally uncomfortable in the school setting, but could not articulate why that was so.

It was hard to evaluate the extent of his attentional problems and to sort out how much of his behavior might be related to the stresses in his current life situation. I recommended to the parents that Adam be seen in once-a-week psychotherapy for an extended evaluation to assess whether or not he could benefit from psychotherapy and suggested meeting with them every other week for supportive work to help with his management.

*Treatment*: After these diagnostic sessions, I recommended that Adam be seen for twice-a-week therapy. The treatment lasted for approximately three years, with interruptions during summers when he went to camp. During the first year of treatment, Adam made remarkable strides in school with the help of the tutoring he was receiving. Concerns about his school achievement and learning disability receded into the background.

In his sessions, Adam chose to talk rather than engage in play activities. Occasionally he would draw while he talked. He impressed me as a very bright and articulate child, who showed remarkable curiosity for his age. He brought a variety of concerns that we discussed extensively. In what follows, I have selected one theme among the many that were discussed. This theme centers on his preoccupation with fire, with injury, and with the issues of power and control.

Adam would often come to sessions with a question that had been on his mind, such as, "Exactly how does a flintlock rifle fire?" "How can you start a fire by rubbing sticks together?" "How is the fuel for the space shuttle boosters rockets ignited?" His curiosity and intelligence led him to ask questions that I found fascinating. He was capable of probing into an issue in such detail that I was often left wishing I had an encyclopedia in my office.

It was easy to lose sight of Adam's emotional issues given the intellectual stimulation he could generate. The central issue was his fascination with and excitement generated around fire and explosions. Fires had a hypnotic effect on him. Given access to matches—forbidden objects—he would hide under his bed and ignite scraps of paper. He and a friend would rummage in the trash in the alley behind his house for articles that would burn more brightly than paper. He looked forward to the Fourth of July even more than to his own birthday. The thought of having access to firecrackers elated him. Somehow, in spite of his parents' efforts to monitor him, he would find ways to buy some. He would hide a stack to use during the rest of the year. These he would use in ways designed to produce the most excitement. Watching M-80s explode was an emotional high. He would come to therapy to report on his exploits, describing in detail how, where, and when he had managed to scare a bunch of girls.

Every so often I would get a frantic call from his mother, who had been called by the school because he was found trading firecrackers or playing with matches. Most frightening of all was the time when mother called me in a panic; she had found two bullets in his pants pockets. We never found out where he got them.

An inquisition would generally follow each of these episodes. Mother and father would question Adam as to where he got the illegal goods.

They would lecture him on the dangers, they would berate him, and finally they would ground him for an unreasonable length of time. Adam's response would invariably be contrite and submissive. He would not protest unless he thought the punishment was excessive. He would agree with them that what he had done was wrong and promise never to repeat it. Then the parents would ask for us all to meet to underscore their disapproval. At those meetings, Adam would be genuinely upset at the distress he was causing his parents, especially his mother. He would tearfully say he was sorry. It was as though he recognized that he had done something impulsively, beyond his control, and now wished there were some way that he could have stopped himself.

My own attitude about all of this was complex. In our individual sessions, I let Adam know that my primary concern was his safety and that of his family. I shared with him that I worried about him and feared that something terrible would happen. However, I also felt it important to share in the experience of excitement he felt with these experiments. I chose to call them experiments because I felt that it was important to focus on what could be learned from them. What I learned was that the excitement he felt was related to a sense of something being out of control within him that required controlling. By creating these situations he was saying nonverbally that there was something explosive in how he felt and wished he could control it. His agreement with his parents as to the dangers of his activities reflected his concern about himself. The firecrackers were a metaphor for his internal state. But the imposition of external restrictions and punishments did not help him internalize the control he needed. A different process was necessary for that to happen. Something had to occur in the transference so that he could acquire that function.

While Adam was already on medication for his AD/HD, his parents clamored for increasing the dosage. I stayed firm in insisting that, while medication helped and was necessary, the work in therapy was critical to his being deflected from those activities. My active interpretations centered around his enjoyment of the forbidden activities and the relationship of that enjoyment to how he felt when not engaged in those activities. I contrasted the sadness and empty feelings that led him to seek out the excitement of watching a fire. At times, he asked for permission to bring matches to the office so that we could watch them together while they burned. I did not give him permission because I felt that doing so would condone and encourage the activity. Instead, I suggested that we think about his desire as an experiment in which we could both participate, much as we would if we discussed a physics or chemistry experiment. He liked that idea and soon his interest turned to science, which he felt could become a career for him. As we discussed great physicists and chemists, his interest in actually lighting fires diminished and his intellectual interest increased.

*Discussion*: I understood the dynamics operating as follows: Adam's AD/HD left him at risk for a failure to develop the regulatory functions that would enable him to acquire self-control. Children like Adam are hampered by the absence of two sets of regulatory function, those with which infants are born and those that are acquired during the maturational process. From birth on, his parents were frustrated in their efforts to soothe and comfort this hyperactive child. His physiological state interfered with the important caregiving function of providing him with comfort through holding, cuddling, rocking, and singing. He was unable to sit still long enough to experience these benign activities.

Adam was essentially deprived of experiences tied to the idealizing selfobject function and the growth that occurs through experiencing that function. This is not because his parents were unable or unwilling to provide them; rather, it is simply that he could not avail himself of them when offered. The situation was compounded by the fact that one of his caregivers—his father—also had AD/HD and could not be experienced by Adam as capable of helping him with the internal overstimulation created by the AD/HD. His father's helplessness in this respect led the child to experience him as ineffectual. Instead, Adam perceived him as harsh, arbitrary, and unempathic. He felt entitled to be enraged at him for that failure, as he perceived it as a personal and intentional response rather than due to circumstances and the father's and son's mutual disability.

Serious consequences followed those dynamics. It is likely that Adam's perception of his father as ineffectual was quite frightening. His father's inability to soothe him or contain his overstimulation led him to feel that his father also could not protect him. Adam's night fears were probably related to these dynamics. Since he could not feel a sense of safety, nighttime and darkness became filled with monsters that he felt endangered his life. A light in the room was insufficient to reassure him that he was safe. He needed the physical presence of one of his parents in order to feel safe. When his parents protested, telling him that they were sitting next door in the living room and that there was nothing to fear, he did not feel reassured. He required the embodied person who was the carrier of the function to be present in order to feel safe, much like a younger child with a separation problem.

In Adam's case, the psychological deficit had to be filled through a transference experience that would allow him to acquire the function. In the therapeutic process, I had to be able to share empathically in the pleasurable excitement of the overstimulation. This sharing conveyed to Adam through nonverbal means that I understood his experience. Combined with his admiration of my knowledge about issues he chose to discuss, this led to the emergence of an idealizing transference. I became someone who could both enjoy how he felt and also help him contain his feelings. I demonstrated my sense of self-control at times when we met as a family. Rather than overreact as his parents did, I took a benign stance, demonstrating my ability to deal with their strong feelings and calm them down, in a way that was beyond their capacity with Adam.

A question might be raised as to why I did not take a firm stand, prohibiting him from the activities and joining the parents in their efforts to have him stop. To my mind, taking such a position would only have repeated for him the situation he experienced with his parents. For one thing, it would be obvious to him that I had no way of enforcing any prohibition. Once he left my office there would be nothing I could do to prevent him from carrying on. But even more important, such a position would have been of little help in supporting his own internal efforts at containing his feelings. Something more powerful had to occur, something he could experience as positive, to help him rescue himself. My sharing these experiences with him permitted him to develop the necessary selfobject functions to deal with his out-of-control feelings.

Eventually, our sessions became more focused on intellectual discussions of how human beings learned to harness the energies of nature to make them useful. It became possible to talk about the constructive uses to which energies could be put. Accompanying these discussions were reports of school projects in which he became involved. He discovered the pleasures of learning and improved his grades, gaining much praise from his teachers and parents. His night fears subsided as he felt more in charge of himself.

The manifest theme in Adam's narrative was that pleasure and excitement are associated with dangerous activities. Fire, firecrackers, even bullets are sources of excitement and danger. Consciously, they appeared to have had no other meanings for him; unconsciously, however, they appeared to represent an inner life that was profoundly significant.

First, the AD/HD produced in him urgent affect states that required discharge into activities. A script was established that being "hyper" meant being in a state of tension relieved only by action. The release was pleasurable in that it brought relief. The association of pleasurable action with reprimands for misbehavior enlarged this script. Later misbehavior was related to being involved in dangerous and forbidden activities. The motif then became that reprimands were an acceptable price to pay for the pleasure derived from forbidden activities. He found a channel for the expression of impulsivity and high energies.

Fascination with fire has complex roots, with much broader social and cultural meanings than can be addressed here. Our interest in Adam's fascination with it lies in finding a symbolic interpretation for the meaning he assigned to it. It is too easy to say that the explosive potential of fire and firecrackers represented an internal state in which he was about to burst with anger and frustration. Such an interpretation is too broad and lacks specificity. The evidence for such an interpretation is lacking. Furthermore, not all children with AD/HD respond by being fascinated with fire. The association with its psychological roots may have been accidental. Perhaps a peer exposed him to these activities and he joined in to retain the friend (his parents often complained that he was being influence by the bad company he kept). Whatever its origins, by the time he came into therapy this motif was central to his self-narrative.

I believe that the discussions he and I had around this topic served to neutralize some of his excitement related to forbidden activities. Together we were able to shift the motif from being the source of enactments to being an intellectual interest he pursued. Consolidated in adolescence and young adulthood, this shift might become integrated into a career path. That would be a best case scenario for Adam.

Mention should be made of my collaborative work with Adam's tutor and his teachers. I attended several school conferences where my role was to help school personnel understand his dynamics and institute interventions that coordinated the work his family and I were doing. This consisted in defining the problem for him as a difficulty in self-control. All of us supported his efforts to acquire such self-control. His lapses were interpreted within that context, although in school natural consequences would follow the lapses. His tutor, teachers, and I communicated frequently to keep each other informed of important developments.

# 9

# EXECUTIVE FUNCTION DISORDERS

BEFORE GRADUATING FROM high school most students must write a major paper. Often called a "theme" assignment, this task is meant to help develop a model for the completion of a research paper. The particular class in which this assignment is given may vary from one high school to the other, although it is usually given in a social studies class. The goal from the teacher's point of view is to have the student learn to approach such tasks in an organized, systematic, logical manner.

The teacher often begins by breaking down the task into steps the student must follow, emphasizing the relationship between the components to the entire theme. The components are made as simple as possible and are assigned as separate units the student must complete on the way to finishing the entire paper. The first step is for the student to choose a topic that is to be the subject of the paper. Sometimes a list of topics is suggested, although often students are given free range as to their choice of subject. Having done that, the student is asked to construct a reasonably comprehensive reading list on the topic. This list is turned in to the teacher, who checks to make sure that the selection made is a proper representation of the material to be covered in the paper. The student is then asked to submit a subset of readings from the list that the student will read, taking notes and collecting data on the subject. Those notes are also turned in to the teacher, who makes suggestions and corrections or requests that the student start over.

### TABLE 9.1
### Executive Function Disorders

---

A. CHARACTERISTICS:

1. *Defining features*: Executive functioning disorders involve a complex set of deficits that include: Difficulties in the initiation, conception and implementation of a plan. These difficulties include the inability to manage time, to organize resources, to self-monitor and self-regulate so as to translate a plan into productive activity that insures its completion.

2. *Prevalence rates*: No data are available on prevalence rates.

3. *Sex ratio*: No data are available on sex ratio.

4. *Coexisting conditions*: AD/HD often accompanies this condition.

B. DEVELOPMENTAL HISTORY: Generally unremarkable, with milestones achieved on time.

C. DISORDERS OF THE SELF: Depending on the severity of the organizational problems, disorders can range from mild disruptions in the capacity for self-regulation to serious disorganization in the sense of self.

1. *Presenting symptoms*:

     a. *Academic*: The child underachieves because homework assignments are lost or not turned in. The child has poor study skills; she is inefficient in doing class assignments and appears scattered and disorganized. The child is described as a procrastinator.

     b. *Social*: Social relationships appear unaffected by the disorders. Although the child can make friends easily, the friendships are hard to sustain because of the child's inability to follow through consistently on plans and failure to take responsibility for activities. As the child gets older, caregivers and teachers become increasingly impatient with the child's disorganization as well as the reasons for the underachievement. Some children become oppositional in reaction to caregivers' attempts at structuring and organizing tasks for them.

     c. *Emotional*: No distinctive emotional problems are associated with this disorder, although a pattern emerges of not being able to put order and sequence into life occurrences. A sense of bewilderment as to why things do not work out overtakes the child and erodes self-esteem. Patients are generally ineffectual in adapting to social and life situations, perhaps reflecting an absence of psychic structure.

## Table 9.1
## (Continued)

2. *Sense of self-cohesion*: The cohesion of the sense of self may be threatened by the disruptions that occur periodically as a result of the neuropsychological deficit.
3. *Self-narrative coherence*: The incoherences in the self-narrative may be covered over with justifications and rationalizations for the disorder. It appears coherent to the child but incoherent to others.

D. INTERVENTIONS:
1. *Remediation*: Intense tutoring to help the child develop habits that minimize the effects of the deficit.
2. *Psychotherapy*: Parent guidance to supply structure for the child. Individual psychotherapy is elective.

---

The student is now ready to outline the main ideas to be dealt with in the paper. Here the task for the teacher is to make sure that the sequence of ideas the student presents is internally logical. Sometimes teachers suggest a format to be followed: a statement of the issues the paper will address in the first paragraph; presentation of the facts; discussion and expression of the student's opinion; and finally conclusion. At this point, the student should be ready to begin the actual writing of the paper. The teacher may have additional suggestions regarding the form of the actual writing, such as how to begin a paragraph, and whether to include charts or other materials to make the exposition easier to follow.

Ideally, once the student has mastered all of these steps and developed the capacity for self-monitoring during the process, she will have learned a model for approaching such tasks in the future. The internalized model will be applicable not only to writing papers but to almost all tasks of a similar nature. The neuropsychological functions that this process reinforces are called "executive functions" (see Table 9.1). Briefly, executive function is the name given to the domain of cognition that is involved in the successful, efficient implementation and completion of a task such as the one described above. In effect, therefore, executive functions are important not just in the completion of an essay but in the implementation of every life task. As Eslinger (1996) states, "executive functions are considered by many scientists to be one of the crowning achievements of human development" (p. 368).

Teachers find that the average student will have few problems with the completion of the task. Most end up turning in their papers and receiving a grade commensurate with their intelligence and with the work they have put into the project. The puzzle centers on a group of bright students, some of whom have stellar intelligence and highly developed verbal skills, who appear unable to complete the task. They get stuck at one level or another and seem unable to move on. Much like the brilliant graduate students who are unable to complete their dissertations, these adolescents cannot put their knowledge into a product. It may be that some of these adolescents have an executive function disorder.

## Explanatory Paradigms

Executive function disorders are not currently included in the list of learning disabilities, partly because this disorder has only recently been recognized to exist in children and partly because it is difficult to diagnose. Denckla (1994) has stated that "executive function is a domain of neurocognitive competence that is a candidate for one of the specified 'psychological processes' presumed, in all definitions of learning disabilities, to underlie discrepancies between general aptitude and academic achievement" (p. 118). Borkowski and Burke (1996) state, "Perhaps the most appealing, yet least understood, aspect of cognition is executive functioning" (p. 235).

There is little consensus among researchers as to the defining features of executive function disorders, although the information-processing and the neuropsychological paradigms present definitions of and hypotheses about them. Each paradigm emphasizes different aspects of mental functioning.

Torgesen (1994), a proponent of the information-processing paradigm, suggests that these children's problems may be best understood as the absence of the capacity to process information metacognitively. *Metacognition* involves the capacity for self-monitoring, self-regulation, and for the selection of the salient factors necessary to complete a task. A distinction is made between *metacognitive knowledge* and *metacognitive behaviors*; that is, while the child may possess the necessary knowledge to complete a task, she seems unable or does not possess the know-how to get the job done. The distinction is based on the difference between the cognitive strategies necessary to understand intellectually what is involved in accomplishing a specific objective and the actual steps necessary to implement the plan and monitor the progress made toward an objective (Wong, 1984).

Levine (1994) describes four types of persistent organizational failures: (1) material-spatial disorganization, which prevents children from dealing effectively with the various equipment needed to be efficient in school, seen in such behaviors as losing things, creating messes among belongings, and not bringing home assignments or not returning them in a timely way; (2) temporal-sequential disorganization, in which children display confusion about time and the sequencing of tasks, such as being late, procrastinating, having trouble allocating time or estimating how long a task will take to complete, and not knowing the order in which a task must be attacked to be completed; (3) transitional disorganization, which does not allow children to shift gears smoothly, resulting in rushing from one activity to the next, having difficulty settling down to do work, or being slow in preparing to leave home for school in the mornings; (4) prospective retrieval disorganization, which involves the inability to remember to do something that had been planned in advance, such as forgetting the deadline of project until the night before or failing to follow through with a promise to finish a task (pp. 138–141).

From a neuropsychological perspective, Denckla (1994, 1996) presents a compelling argument for the relationship between executive function disorders and brain dysfunction. She gives as evidence the data from neurology, where patients with damage to the prefrontal cortex and its interconnected subcortical regions manifest many of the symptoms associated with executive function disorders. She suggests that executive function disorders are domain-general as contrasted with the modular or domain-specific impairments, such as dyslexia. By this she means that, while in the specific learning disabilities a direct association between a set of symptoms and a dysfunction in a specific brain system is hypothesized to exist, such a view is too simplistic for our understanding of executive function disorders. The functions subsumed under executive function are broad and probably widely distributed. Her definition includes "interference control, effortful and flexible organization, and strategic planning" (p. 117).

Pennington (Pennington, Bennetto, McAleer, & Roberts, 1996) focuses on working memory and the demands for inhibition that are involved in the completion of the task. Working memory refers to the memory buffer in which we hold all the information that we need in order to focus and take actions that will assure the completion of the task. We may think of working memory as a virtual space in which necessary information is temporarily held so as to implement a plan. The information is chosen selectively and restricted to the elements relevant to the task at hand. By keeping in mind both the information and the strategies necessary to complete a task, it is possible for the person to see the relationship of the part to the whole and to keep track of her place in the sequence of steps. As for the demand for inhibition, Pennington emphasizes the need to both select and exclude information in order to proceed efficiently with the completion of a task.

It is important to point out that in these various definitions of executive function the focus has been on the cognitive component involved in the completion of tasks. These definitions leave out such important factors as social, emotional, and personality factors, although these contribute significantly to a child's efforts toward completion of the task. In particular, they ignore the factor of motivation, which presents a serious confound in any attempt to distinguish between a person's inability to perform a task and her lack of desire to do so. Distinguishing between a lack of motivation and a neurologically based deficit is a focal diagnostic issue in the assessment of children with this disorder.

## Characteristics of the Disorder

*Defining features*: Lezak (1983) describes in detail four steps that she considers to constitute the behavioral components of executive function: *goal formulation, planning, carrying out goal-directed plans,* and *effective performance.* These steps resemble the familiar ones we encountered in our discussion of teachers instructing students on how to write an essay. Patients with executive function problems may have difficulties in one or more of these areas. She emphasizes the behavioral manifestations of the problem, because she is interested in ways to test for and measure the dysfunction.

1. Goal formulation involves the capacity to conceptualize a plan and the ability to initiate steps to implement it. Procrastination is probably the most prominent symptom of the failure in this capacity.
2. Planning involves the ability to select and bring to bear a number of resources such as materials and skills that will be

necessary to implement the plan. It involves drawing upon a pool of knowledge as well as envisioning the actual steps or obstacles that may lie ahead for the successful completion of the task.

3. Carrying out the activities or implementing the plan involves the translation of the conceptual scheme into a set of behaviors or actions.

4. Effective performance requires the person to inhibit responses to distractions so that tangential factors do not interfere with the attainment of the goal. Furthermore, it requires the resourcefulness and flexibility to find alternative paths to the goal if obstacles are met. Self-monitoring and self-regulation are important psychological functions necessary to stay focused on the task.

*Prevalence rate and sex ratio*: No data are available on the prevalence or sex ratio of this disorder.

*Coexisting conditions*: AD/HD is frequently associated with this condition, although the actual rate of its coexistence is unknown. Some of the symptoms of AD/HD, such impulsivity and inattention, may be present; however, unlike AD/HD, the symptoms associated with executive function disorders do not respond to stimulant medication (Ellenberg, 1999).

## Developmental History

Little is known about the developmental history of children with executive function disorder (Welsh, Pennington, & Groisser, 1991). Clinical data suggest that their development is unremarkable. The literature is also sparse. Welsh and Pennington (1988) report "evidence for the view that frontally mediated executive functions emerge in the first year of life and continue to develop at least until puberty." They believe that "under certain circumstances younger children [under seven years of age] display primitive abilities to control, direct, and regulate their behavior in accordance with external constraints and internal goals" (p. 211). This suggests that they view the capacity for self-control in children as related to executive function. The obverse, that is, a lack of self-control, might suggest a problem in that area, although other causes for the absence of self-control exist. Teachers do not begin to notice symptoms associated with this condition until around third or fourth grade. Up to this point, it is likely that the demands made of the children did not require some of the skills or that others in the context complemented the child's deficit, attributing it to immaturity.

When the child enters seventh and eighth grade, problems escalate. Her output appears severely curtailed. Assignments are not completed or, if completed, not turned in. The child's backpack is a mess of leftover lunches, stained papers, dog-eared books, and miscellaneous forgotten or misplaced items. The disorganization is also reflected in the child's room, where everything is in disarray. Caregivers, failing to distinguish between ordinary untidiness and the absence of organization, often accept this disorganization, attributing it to adolescence. Adolescents may be untidy in their appearance and their possessions, but severe untidiness is often symptomatic of an executive function disorder.

## Disorders of the Self

### Presenting Symptoms

*Academic*: Problems begin to emerge at school around third or fourth grade and escalate as the child progresses to the upper grades. Parents and teachers who do not understand the nature of the problem or do not realize its neurological basis see these children as unmotivated or outright lazy. They feel that the child is simply not making an effort to get done what needs doing. These children rarely come home with their homework; if they have it, they can't get down to the task of getting it done; if caregivers supervise them to be sure it gets done, the homework never seems to get to school or handed to the teacher. If they have a project, they procrastinate until the last hour and then they are in crisis about getting it done. The household is then totally disrupted as everyone tries to get the child organized to finish the project. This occurs in the context of a child who is bright and appears to have the capacity to undertake complex and challenging tasks.

From the teachers' perspective, the tasks are simple and require little effort. If they provide incentives such as a reward system, the child may muster enough energy for a brief period of time to complete some tasks, but failure soon follows. Punishments are quite ineffective. The children, finding themselves caught between their desire to please their caregivers and their inability to perform what is required of them, may lapse into apathy. At times, they respond by turning to other interests as substitutes.

Most children, when first confronted with the problem, will insist that they will do better next time. In fact, the children all seem to do much better at the beginning of a school year. At that point, the external structures are all in place, the expectations are fairly low, the academic content consists primarily of review of the prior year's work. So problems are minimal. But as expectations increase, tasks become more complex, and new material has to be mastered, the structure begins to fall apart. From the children's point of view, there is often little realization that this is happening. So it comes as a surprise when around the time of the first teacher's conferences, they are confronted with an accounting of the homework they have not turned in, the books they have misplaced, and the fact that they are close to failing subjects.

*Social*: At first, the children's capacity for social interaction is generally unaffected by this disorder. To all appearances they appear contented; they have friends, are involved in extracurricular activities, and are well liked by adults. As they get older and enter adolescence, their carelessness, poor habits, and lateness to events begin to wear thin with peers and adults. They increasingly come under criticism, to which they respond with resentment. As they become labeled as irresponsible and unreliable, significant social consequences may ensue. While some peers continue to be friends, others turn away.

On another front, the problems with organization affect their abilities to undertake projects with others. They are shunned as partners in important projects. At times, they may set goals that are totally unrealistic, such as starting a band or basketball team. These plans never materialize, in part because these adolescents seem to have little idea of what it takes to get to the goal, in part because they cannot initiate steps to begin the process. Failures such as these further erode the relationships they have with others. Some end up isolated not because they are socially inept but because maintaining a friendship with them is too hard.

At times, power struggles develop between child and caregiver. The problem then takes the form of oppositional or negativistic behavior on the part of the child. Caregivers are then convinced that the issue is the child's unwillingness to conform to parental expectations. Battles are joined around the issues of conformity, with the result that the relationship becomes disrupted. These battles may center on the children's rooms, which are in total disarray, with clothing and papers all over the floor. Caregivers may attempt to help by offering to put things in order, but the order lasts barely a day. The children will often deny the need for greater order, claiming that they know exactly where everything is, if only it were not touched or put away. The chaos with which they seem to surround themselves does not appear to affect them. The fact that they tend to not keep track of possessions, to lose gloves, hats, coats, books, and other valued objects, further aggravates caregivers.

*Emotional*: Children with executive function disorder, if they have no other major problems, are seldom perceived as having an emotionally based disturbance. Interestingly, self-esteem problems do not seem to surface until preadolescence or adolescence. The children do not evidence any symptoms that would cause concern to caregivers. However, the erosion of the relationship with caregivers may lead some caregivers to seek help in the hope of improving the relationship. Often caregivers question whether or not to complement a child's deficit. They wonder whether they should do less or more for the child. They are caught in a dilemma: If they complement the child's deficits, they will create a dependence and not give the child the opportunity to take responsibility for herself, but if they do not, the child will fail.

### Sense of Self-cohesion

Not infrequently, as adults listen to adolescents' grandiose schemes, they feel considerable skepticism as to whether these can be accomplished. Adults often think to themselves, "When you grow up, you will see how difficult it is to get things done—it is not as easy as you think!" What we as adults are saying to adolescents is, in essence, that their executive function abilities are not sufficiently developed for them to appreciate all the steps that need to be taken and all the difficulties that may clutter their path. At times, we are astonished when they do achieve a goal that we considered to be impossible. Young adults who succeed not only have a vision but also understand the steps that need to be taken to attain their goal and are competent enough to implement their plans. Distinguishing between the child's grandiosity and her true capacities involves an assessment of executive function.

Studies of executive function have focused on the cognitive tasks, ignoring motivational, emotional or social factors. Moreover, the developmental trajectory for the capacity for executive functions remains to be studied. It is difficult to distinguish between a child who is inefficient at the completion of tasks because she is unmotivated from a child who simply lacks the wherewithal to do what is necessary to accomplish that task. One must also consider the possibility that the child who fails does so because she is depressed or because social difficulties interfere with her desire to achieve. Some children are less competitive than others, others subscribe to different sets of values, and still others lack the sufficient resources. In still other children, immaturity contributes to their inability to go forward with the completion of the task. A child might be more interested in playing than in finishing her homework; consequently, she will put less effort into her work than a child who has gone beyond that phase. Since all of these factors enter into a child's productivity, sorting out those that motivate the child from those that are determined by neuropsychological deficits is difficult.

An even more complex set of considerations is related to the question of personality formation. If we look at various problems associated with executive function disorder, we might ask whether the dysfunctional behaviors are related to that person's being ineffectual in dealing with the demands of a complex world or due simply to the context in which she was raised. Such questions, to my mind, represent the leading edge of areas for future exploration. They remain unanswered but at the same time challenge existing personality theories.

Eslinger (1996) states, "Although the models of executive function— have focused primarily on cognitive aspects and specific learning and problem-solving paradigms, the construct of executive function may also encompass a powerful influence of social behavior" (p. 389). He and his colleagues have suggested the concept of "social executor" as a companion construct to executive function in order to conceptualize issues of social dysfunction. He suggests four aspects of the "social and interpersonal behavior that appear to have strong executive features" (p. 390): social self-regulation, social self-awareness, social sensitivity, and social salience. Cognitive functions cannot be separated from social and emotional factors. This implies that an interconnection exists between personality disorders and neurocognitive impairments. It is interesting to note in this connection that some hypothesize that disorders such as autism, schizophrenia, Asperger's, and nonverbal learning disabilities include impairments in executive function.

This discussion would be incomplete without addressing the issues of adjunctive functions and compensation. An entire industry exists to help people become or stay organized. Electronic devices, computer programs, and clever calendars are all intended to help people keep track of tasks so as to complete them successfully. What these provide are adjunctive functions. A common fantasy is that owning one of these devices will help one become organized. My experience leads me to be skeptical about that solution. Disorganized patients who have tried this approach find that, while at first their motivation and enthusiasm enable them to be successful, they soon lose track of the devices themselves and revert back to old habits. Executive function deficits are difficult to compensate. The skills required in order to develop adequate compensations are defeated by the deficit itself. A true compensation would be found if the person either chose an occupation in which organization was not required or became obsessional in performing tasks in the same way every day, never deviating from the routine. A patient of mine who was able to use the latter strategy bitterly complained that, if she deviated in the least from her routine when she got up in the morning, she would find in the evening that she had wasted the day completely. She would get lost in peripheral activities and be unable to return to her tasks. It had taken her some years, with the assistance of a therapist and a coach who tutored her, for her to develop that strategy.

### Self-narrative Coherence

The self-narratives of children with executive function deficits are misleadingly coherent. If there are incoherences, these are due to factors other than their executive function deficits. It is as though they have a blind spot when it comes to perceiving their executive function problems. When they are asked about their problems, these either are not mentioned or, if mentioned, are dismissed as unimportant. They respond as though the issue is of concern to others but not to them. The fact that the problems have a significant impact on their lives seems to escape them. One might say that, since they have never experienced what it is like to be organized or orderly, they have no concept of such activities. This is true even if a caregiver has repeatedly tried to teach the child to be orderly. Only as children progress to high school, where they cannot avoid confronting the problem, do they begin to experience anxiety and puzzlement at their lack of success.

As we will see in the case illustration that follows, Sam, who suffered from a severe form of the disorder, not only fails to see that he has a problem, but constructs a narrative that excludes the necessity for order and organization in his life. He chooses an alternative lifestyle that does not make the kinds of demands the larger community makes of its members. Dropping out of society becomes valued because that lifestyle is simpler and requires little of him.

Not all patients make this choice. Some young adults encounter major obstacles to the path they have chosen. When they cannot overcome these obstacles, they become seriously depressed. The tragedy is that having an explanation of what occurred provides little comfort to them. They are faced with a reality they cannot change—that they do not have adequate skills to cope with some of life's demands.

## Interventions

*Remediation*: Young children can benefit from a tutor who specializes in techniques that maximize whatever organizational strengths the child has. At times, the focus is on "study skills," through which strategies are taught to help the child track school-related activities. A good educational psychologist can provide a set of strategies to be implemented. Some accommodations in the child's environment can also serve a useful function. For example, open shelving on which to put possessions works much better than drawers and cupboards; everything is in the child's view so that forgetting what to do and when to do it is minimized. "To do" lists serve an important adjunctive function, but these must be large and visible and the child has to develop the habit of checking them at regular intervals.

*Psychotherapy*: The issue of whether to recommend psychotherapy for children with this disorder centers around a determination of the problems on which to focus. Both young patients and adults are distressed by the circumstances in which they find themselves. Responding to their request for help often involves engaging them around the issue of their deficit. Helping them understand why they find themselves in those circumstances is enlightening, but it does not help solve the problem. Since the psychological issues are so varied with this group of patients, it is of utmost importance to sort out which of those are directly related to the deficit and which are problems the person would have had regardless of the deficit. If it is clear that the deficit is accompanied by an absence in the development of psychic structure, then psychotherapy is indicated. But if the deficit is producing life problems for the person, then psychotherapy is unlikely to be effective. Some other form of assistance is indicated.

### CASE ILLUSTRATION: SAM

***Referral and presenting problem*: I first heard from Sam's parents when he was 13 years old and beginning eighth grade. A psychologist**

was seeing him, but they wanted a second opinion about his diagnosis and treatment. After several long conversations with Sam's mother on the phone, I obtained a superficial picture of the situation, but because of scheduling problems it was not possible for me to see him. Sam's mother formed an immediate attachment to me, thanked me profusely for the time I had spent with her, and asked to keep me informed of the situation.

Two months later, she called to report that, at the recommendation of the psychologist, Sam was being sent to a boarding school to finish eighth grade. He had been having lots of problems. Although he tested in the very superior range on intelligence and academic tests, his school performance was unacceptably low. Serious conflicts had erupted between him and his parents, to the point that they considered it best to send him to a boarding school where he could be supervised and helped to achieve his potential. Both he and his parents agreed to the recommendation, hoping that the situation might resolve itself.

*Developmental history*: Sam's father was a renowned cardiologist in a prestigious university, who was in demand all over the world. He was caring and available to Sam when he was around, which was seldom. Mother was a talented musician who had given up a promising career to raise their only child.

Sam's early development was unproblematic. He achieved all the milestones early. He learned to read on his own at age three. He was a gregarious child even as early as nursery school. He did very well until third grade. At that point, Sam's parents began to be mildly concerned about his losing personal possessions and the chaotic condition of his room. But having had their child late in life and not having had any other children, they had no point of reference by which to judge and assumed that all children were this way. When teachers brought problems to their attention, they indulgently rationalized that he was a creative child who would not conform to the usual expectations set by a school environment. Although he was musically talented, he seemed uninterested in mastering an instrument. He started piano lessons but seldom practiced. His piano teacher eventually gave up on him; she did not think he had the self-discipline to meet even her minimal expectations.

Problems escalated as the school sought to impress the parents with the seriousness of the situation. By the time he was in fifth grade, he was producing no work, although on tests he was capable of getting all the answers right. He seemed to be operating purely on his native intelligence, absorbing material from listening in class but taking no initiative to learn proactively and expressing no interest in academic pursuits.

By sixth grade, the parents themselves could no longer overlook what was going on. They instituted measures at home and with the school to keep track of Sam's schoolwork. These produced minimal academic results; instead they increased the confrontations between Sam and his mother. The more she tried to monitor his work the more he resisted. She tried cajoling him, and when that failed, threatened punishment. That also failed. Finally, father got involved, but that only produced more chaos as tension in the household became unbearable. Through all this Sam seemed totally puzzled by adults' responses to him. He saw himself as brilliant, as entitled, as capable of doing anything he put his mind to doing, but he simply saw no need to prove himself to anyone. He felt he should be accepted for who he was rather than molded to conform to others' expectations. He cited the example of his father, who had challenged the academic community with his seemingly odd theories, only to be proved right eventually.

When the family finally sought help in seventh grade, Sam was not ready to involve himself in therapy. He saw that as an effort to label him as having a problem, something he could not accept. When he did consent to see the therapist, it was because the therapist had framed the problem as being a "family problem" rather than simply as Sam's problem. The family sessions that followed went nowhere. Sam adamantly stood his ground. He insisted that his parents were being unreasonable in their demands, the school was full of nerds who didn't really know anything, the teachers knew how smart he was but demanded stupid demonstrations of his capacities, and finally, his parents did not know how to raise a child. As a result, the parents' own confidence in their parenting skills was totally undermined, despite the therapist's supportive stance.

Meanwhile, pressures were increasing with the approach of high school; eighth grade loomed on the horizon as a transitional year in which he would either be prepared for high school or perpetuate the current situation. The therapist suggested boarding school as a solution. After a bad start in eighth grade, Sam did not resist the suggestion; he saw the move as an adventure. He was accepted into a prestigious prep school on the basis of his tests rather than his actual performance. Everyone hoped that after a year he would be ready to return home to go to the local high school.

Unfortunately, all did not go well at the boarding school. The first semester was promising. Sam received close supervision on his work, but, being so bright, he charmed his monitors and professors. His teachers in particular enjoyed his ability to challenge the contents they taught, to raise interesting questions and to make important contributions to class discussions. In the meantime, Sam began to gravitate to a group of kids who saw themselves as having special privileges and status in the school. The group thrived on breaking rules and not getting caught. They lived on the edge of what was acceptable. On the surface, they were compliant and conforming, but behind the scenes they denigrated and had contempt for all the school's values. The school principal was aware of the group's existence and made concerted but unsuccessful efforts to break it up. At the end of the school year Sam was told that his behavior was unacceptable. In addition, his grades dropped, although that was attributed to his behavior problems rather than to his lack of organizational skills. He was placed on probation for his returning freshman year in high school.

That summer Sam went to camp for eight weeks. He considered it a wonderful experience because he was with several of the boys from the school. They continued the "club" they had at school with the encouragement of a camp counselor who enjoyed their acting out.

On his return to boarding school as a freshman, Sam was ready to take on the establishment. The austere headmaster no longer intimidated him. He felt that the teachers were pushovers whom he could manipulate into thinking he could do the work even when he failed to produce it. Some of his friends supported him in his activities. The school had prepared itself for the return of the boys and was on the lookout for their antics. A confrontation similar to the one that had occurred between Sam and his parents two years earlier was in the making. He and friends were caught drinking beer on the school grounds. This being his first infraction, the school read him the riot act and warned him that he would be expelled if he violated the rules again.

On his return to school after the Christmas break, the final crisis came. He and another boy were caught smoking marijuana. A stash of pot with some paraphernalia was found in his room. He was informed that he was being expelled. The parents were totally distraught on hearing the news. They pleaded with the headmaster for one more chance. They feared the outcome of his expulsion and his return home where they could not control him. The boarding school had been their last hope for salvaging Sam's academic career—even his future. The headmaster agreed on condition that Sam inform him of where he had gotten the marijuana and the paraphernalia. He confessed to having procured it while at home. This satisfied the headmaster, who placed him on strict probation.

Probation lasted six weeks; then Sam was caught selling marijuana to a classmate. This time there was no reprieve. He was simply sent home. Mother, who had kept in touch with me, called urgently asking for my help. I was able to schedule an appointment at once.

After getting a full history from the parents, my first response was to refer them to an excellent educational psychologist to have Sam tested for a possible learning disability. We discussed whether Sam would be willing to come to see me for an evaluation. They thought they might get him to agree to come once, but they warned that he had been so turned off by the prior experience in therapy that they feared he would not follow through.

*Clinical presentation*: Sam was an engaging young man, who was somewhat contemptuous of the process of therapy but had agreed to come because he was in such trouble. He straightforwardly recounted what had happened at boarding school, giving the facts much as his parents had done. He minimized his involvement in the delinquent activity, excusing it as something everyone his age did. So "nothing was wrong" with what he had done. In effect, he felt that too much had been made of a minor infraction.

When asked about academics, he was utterly self-confident that he could do the work if he wanted to, but saw no need for that. Instead, he went to great lengths in describing to me that he was teaching himself to play the guitar. In fact, he thought he was going to form his own band at school. To him the success of that band was more important than grades.

We discussed realistically whether he would find involvement in therapy useful at this time. He was quite clear that he would not. He was quite honest in saying that if I insisted, as had his parents, he would comply but all that would happen would be that he would entertain me with stories of his exploits at boarding school. I could get paid, but he would get nothing from it. I told him that I would feel dishonest accepting those terms for this involvement. He responded that it was my problem whether I accepted or not. I then explored with him the possibility of his getting some tutorial help to allow him to catch up with schoolwork, but he rejected that as a possibility also. All doors to helping him seemed closed.

When I met again with the parents to review what had transpired, they were very discouraged. We considered the alternative of finding a therapeutic school for Sam; however, that alternative was not a possibility because of the cost and his adamant refusal to go to any other institution. We finally agreed to wait for the results of the testing to make a final decision. In the meantime Sam would attend the local high school.

*Test results*: Sam was 15 years old at the time of testing. He was described as a young man of superior verbal intelligence and at least average overall levels of performance in nonverbal areas (Verbal I.Q. 125; Performance I.Q. 93; Full Scale I.Q. 112). However, the 32-point discrepancy between his Verbal and his Performance I.Q. suggested that these should be considered as separate areas of mental functioning. Sam did not appear able to utilize his full intellectual potential, due to the presence of specific deficits in attention and in nonverbal and motor performance areas. His performance on the WISC-R indicated that he did best when he used language to express what he knew and to comprehend his world. While Sam appeared to have good long- and short-term memory capabilities for the meanings of words and for ideas in context, he had impairments in sequencing. Hence he had trouble retaining the order of perceptual or conceptual stimuli or events or sequencing them to make a logically coherent whole, such as ordering the seasons, formulating cause-and-effect statements, performing multistep numerical and/or symbolic operations, or understanding relations ordered by time sequence. The tests revealed that Sam had a serious executive function problem. The outlook for his academic future looked grim, unless he could involve himself in serious remediation and treatment.

*Waiting for Sam to be ready*: In my next conversation with Sam's mother we agreed that things had to get worse before they could get better. We waited for the next crisis to occur, although we had no plan for how to deal with it when it came.

Once Sam was in high school, his parents lost all control over him. He came and went as he wished. He would leave for school but more often than not fail to arrive there. They seldom knew where he was or with whom he associated. They heard that he spent time with a group who claimed to be forming a band, but no one ever heard them play together. From other parents, they heard that he ran around with a bunch of kids who were heavily into drugs.

When they called me to ask what to do, I often felt at a loss. My only advice to them was that they not do anything that would undermine their relationship with him. I did not believe that tough love would work or that throwing him out onto the streets was wise. Hard as it was, they needed to maintain whatever threads of good feeling connected them to him and him to them. In fact, as long as they could tolerate what he did, he reciprocated by being courteous. He expressed concern for mother's health when she got sick and offered to be of help around the house. But for the most part the relationship was experienced by his parents as exploitive, since he was always demanding money from them for one thing or another. They finally felt they had to limit how much they gave him, although he vehemently protested those limits.

By the beginning of his senior year it was evident that Sam would not be able to graduate from high school with his class. He realized that and informed his parents that he would drop out. His plan was to go with several of his friends to Los Angeles, where they hoped to record an album. When his parents expressed concern about how he and his friends would get to Los Angeles or what they would live on, he reassured them not to worry, he had taken care of all of that. He and a group of friends left in an old car with only a few hundred dollars that he had saved.

It was painful to hear the parents' distress at what they believed to be the loss of their only child. I could only respond by saying that he had to find out for himself what he was looking for. I emphasized that at one time they had a wonderful relationship with him; they needed to hang onto the bare threads of the relationship and to stay available to him during these experiments in living.

A week later, mother called to let me know that Sam had called asking that they immediately send him $500. The car he and his friends were using to get to California broke down in Colorado and they needed the money to repair it. Reluctantly, his parents sent the money and waited to hear from him. Indeed, he called periodically to let them know where he was and how he was doing. He had gotten to Los Angeles on his own, having left his friends behind and picked up a girlfriend along the way.

When next they heard from him, he wanted them to pay the rent on an apartment he was sharing with some other people. He and the girlfriend were still living together. She was working as a waitress, and he had found a job at a record store. His knowledge of music had served him well in this instance. His parents consented to pay his rent, hoping that in this way they could give him some stability. They had other concerns, which he dismissed. He was still covered by their health insurance but had no car insurance and was driving the girlfriend's car.

During the next two years, mother and I kept in touch to develop strategies as to how to respond to Sam's periodic crises. She feared that he would get sick and not have proper medical care; consequently, he was kept on father's health insurance. Periodically, he would move from one apartment to another and ask for money for a deposit, which she usually provided. On one occasion, he got a traffic ticket that he could not pay, and she sent him the money.

We seriously discussed "tough love," which several of her friends were urging her to use. They had almost convinced her that she was "enabling" his dysfunctional behaviors by continuing to support him. My experience has been that such strategies are misguided. If mother were to stop supporting him, he would simply break off the relationship and perhaps never be heard from again. I urged her to maintain the contact as best she could.

Mother and I had agreed that the best outcome we could hope for was to have Sam return home where he would be safe and where they would not have to worry about his getting into trouble. I had dealt with two other similar situations in my practice whose outcome was positive, so I felt hopeful about this possibility.

In the meantime, she prepared the ground by talking to Sam about missing him and wishing he would come home for a visit. She offered him a plane ticket as an incentive. He did come home for Thanksgiving. Both parents tried hard to make the stay as pleasant as possible, although Sam spent most of the time away from home visiting his old haunts. They had evidence that he was continuing to use marijuana, but did not know if he was on any other drugs. Sam refused to extend his visit.

The following winter was a hard one for Sam. First, his girlfriend broke up with him. She expressed disgust at the pigpen he had created in the apartment and was tired of cleaning up after him. He had tried to reform by helping to clean up, but his efforts were insufficient. In a phone call, his mother was able to remind him of his learning disability, saying that she understood how the girlfriend felt but knew that this disorganization was one of his weaknesses. For the first time he was able to admit that he had a problem. In fact, he had struggled trying to correct this problem in order to please his girlfriend but found that he simply didn't have the skills to do it. His mother was able to talk with him about that being a long-standing problem, wishing she could have helped him sooner. At the end of the conversation mother felt that she had gotten closer to him than she had in years.

The next crisis came when Sam was about to the evicted from his apartment for nonpayment of rent. The friends with whom he shared the apartment had disappeared one day and he was left to pay the entire rent, which he could not do. Not having the money, he let a couple of months go by without payment. At this point mother decided that she could not send him the large sum of money he asked for. In part this was because she could not be sure that he would use the money for its intended purpose. She always suspected that some of the money she sent was used for drugs. In this instance, she decided to send a small amount to allow him to find alternative housing. In fact, he ended up crashing at the home of a group of his friends after agreeing to clean up the place for them.

Soon, another crisis broke out. Sam called from jail; he had been arrested for possession of marijuana. He was in a panic as to what to do. In a long series of phone calls between him and his mother, punctuated by phone calls to me, we agreed that they should provide him with a lawyer to try to get him out of jail. This was felt to be an opportunity to insist on his coming home. In an arrangement between the lawyer, the prosecutor, and the judge, an agreement was reached to have him placed on probation but allowed to leave the state to return home. Sam was just turning 20.

Sam returned home a very different person from when he had left three years prior. He had left feeling flushed with confidence in his capacity to be successful. There were no obstacles he felt he could not overcome. His contempt for his parents' values led him to elevate his lifestyle to a higher status than theirs. He felt he could have a better life than they could offer him. Now he looked at the shambles he had made of his life but had no idea of how to pick up the pieces. He put up little resistance to coming to see me when his parents suggested it.

*Treatment begins*: The Sam I saw at this point was quite different from the neatly dressed, well combed, preppie-looking doctor's son I had met some years back. Instead, here was a tall, disheveled man who came carrying a cup of coffee. His hair was shoulder length and looked like it hadn't been washed in weeks. He wore a full beard, the stem on his glasses was held together by a paper clip, the bottoms of his jeans were caked with mud and totally frayed. He could have been a homeless person who had walked in off the street. I felt that his appearance reflected the internal chaos that characterized his sense of self.

In spite of his appearance, once he started talking I found myself totally involved in trying to understand his view of life, which he was eager to share with me. It is difficult to describe the process between us as it occurred during the following weeks and months. Although his mother had to drive him to the sessions because he did not have a valid driver's license, he came willingly, did not need to be reminded by his mother of his appointments, and was quite invested in our times together.

He chose to talk about his reactions to his family, particularly his father, and about his views on the meaning of his existence, delving into philosophical issues and generally attempting to sort out his life. I focused on trying to understand his experiences since he was 12 years old. I felt I had to live through that period with him to help him make sense of his existence. If that were possible, then the idea of his life taking a different course might emerge. If we could construct a coherent narrative out of his experiences, he might begin to feel that what had occurred made sense and consequently might feel better about himself.

From his perspective, he never felt he belonged in his family. He contrasted his mother's neatness and her efforts at maintaining order in the house with his lackadaisical attitude. As he put it, "What's the point of tying your shoelaces every morning if you have to untie them when you take them off at night!" The same thing applied to making his bed, washing his clothes, or picking up his room. The cycle of putting things in order only to create disorder seemed senseless to him. Along with that, he felt that, from early childhood, his outlook on situations was different from that of others. He knew he was smart, he had seen his test scores, but to him knowledge was something you acquired because you had an interest in what you learned. It was unnecessary to take math and science, for example, if all you were interested in was the Civil War. He read everything about the Civil War when they got to that section in social studies class, but failed the course. He said he saw no point in keeping up with his other assignments.

His experience at the boarding school totally reinforced his feeling that society was out of step with him. Here were preppie professors who appeared enthralled at having to teach a bunch of rich kids, but whose lives, to him, seemed empty. He could not see that they were having any fun; they were just driven by a desire to impress the parents of the children there. All they did for him was to make him feel that he had to fit into the identity they had carved for him. He would have had to give up being himself in order to be what they wanted him to be. There was no way he was going to let that happen.

So he joined the group of kids who were intent on thumbing their noses at the established modes of being. He didn't care that adults thought what he did was wrong. Their morality was empty and misguided. With the group he had fun, felt alive, was excited. Reliving those days, he exclaimed, "Sure we drank and smoked. The school never knew how much of that went on. They assumed that the times they caught kids were the only times that it happened, but they were wrong."

I asked about his drug use and how it began. His response was that it came along when he started to drink in eighth grade. One of the kids shared a joint at an eighth grade party. It had such an impact on him— he had never before felt as he did when he took the hit. The rest came easily. The buzz he got from pot helped him through the dreariness of the day. He soon came to crave the high he got and actively pursued smoking regularly. I wondered if he felt his boredom was related to his being depressed, perhaps because he missed home. His response was that it might have been at first. He never actually felt homesick or depressed. What he did feel was that there was nothing that excited him or in which he could feel deeply immersed.

We moved on to discuss what happened after he came home. His return home was both a revelation and a liberation. The revelation came from seeing his parents in a completely new light. He saw his father as enslaved to his work, a man driven to be successful and determined not to lose his standing in the professional community. He could not see the sense of having to struggle so hard. "Why do it?" He could connect more with his mother's creative involvement in music. It was from her that he developed the desire to have his own band. During the years in high school he went to every concert he could. He and his friends would get high, get lost in the music, and feel on top of the world. He got to know every band that played, and met many of the stars by befriending the retinues that surrounded them. Among his friends he became known as a walking encyclopedia of music. Even now people turn to him when they have questions about bands, music, or performers.

In spite of his passion for music, he acknowledged that he had not mastered his guitar. However, he got immersed in playing; he then felt totally lost in the mood he created for himself. He offered to demonstrate by playing on the piano in my study. I was happy to let him do so. What he played were a set of chords that were almost monotonous in their repetitiveness. Their effect was to send me into a trance. A set of nostalgic reveries was evoked in me as I listened. I felt transported into what seemed like an old familiar realm. Fifteen minutes later we were both shaken out of our trance by my realization that the hour had ended and it was time to stop.

In the hours that followed, he talked about many themes that preoccupied him. He recalled how he felt after he left home to go to California. On the way there, he was introduced to reality. He described his panic when the car broke down. Since he could not let the others know how frightened he was, he became determined to appear calm and took charge of the situation by calling home. But internally he felt totally panicked. Hooking up with his girlfriend was the best thing that happened to him. She was caring and loving. For a long time their relationship was not sexual. She just liked to be held by him. It turned out that she was 16 and had run away from home. Attaching herself to him and the group gave her a sense of belonging and security. His description of their relationship reminded me of two children in parallel play. Each played at his or her own game. When their playing overlapped they touched each other; otherwise they went their separate ways.

Sam, over time, gave this account of his thoughts during the time he was away. What was forming in his mind was a view of the world as a place in which one does what one has to do in order to survive, maximizing joy and minimizing pain. The simpler one's life can be made, the better off one is. It was always best to not get upset or bothered by events. One has to take these upsets as a natural part of life that one has to endure. The idea is not to let them affect you. Work and success are part of a different universe of values, removed and foreign from his world—as alien as Mars is from Earth. To engage in such activities would be to give up his freedom, thus becoming trapped in someone else's orbit. By not setting his sights on any goal, he did not risk failure. Achievement would not be measured by where you got but by the inner state you preserved.

With this world view, Sam now settled into a pattern at home. He got up at around 11 o'clock in the morning, had one or two cups of coffee, then retreated to his room to practice his guitar. If pushed by his mother, he would help a little around the house or with shopping. By evening, he would leave the house to go visit his favorite haunts where bands were playing. He would go from one bar to another, drinking and getting high. At times he would meet an old acquaintance, spend time together, then part ways. Marijuana was part of his daily diet; it seemed to help him maintain an inner peace.

On my advice the parents continued to subsidize his lifestyle, at first making minimal demands of him. They were relieved that he was home safe and that they did not have to worry about his getting into serious difficulties. Without pressure, the routine was gradually modified, with Sam taking more responsibility for household chores. He began to help regularly with the grocery shopping and to do some of the heavier work around the house and yard. It took a year for us to feel that Sam's life was sufficiently stabilized so that more demands could be made of him. However, the central issue remained Sam's deficit in his capacity to structure himself.

All did not go smoothly, however. Periodically, Sam's father would become enraged at what he perceived to be Sam's laziness. He would then threaten to cut off Sam's funds, depriving him of his favorite forms of entertainment. Sam would panic and threaten to return to California, never to return home again. His mother would intervene, reminding his father of the goal and of Sam's problems.

In time, I introduced Sam to the idea of getting a job so as to be less dependent on his parents for money. Sam was surprised by my suggestion but agreed with the rationale. This step proved fateful in forcing Sam to confront some of his limitations. He applied at a few places, including some fast-food chains. Soon he found that he was truly unemployable; to his embarrassment even fast-food places would not accept him as he was. He was told to come back after he had a haircut, shaved his beard, and cleaned himself up. He considered doing so but quickly decided it was not worthwhile.

So far, the therapy consisted primarily in being supportive to Sam and his family. While this approach helped stabilize the situation, making for less conflict between Sam and his parents, it did not address the fundamental problem of Sam's executive function deficit. In essence, his personality and sense of self lacked sufficient inner structure for him to be able to function in the real world. Therapy alone could not provide him with the means to build such structure. I decided that consulting a vocational counselor might help him with some strategies to become employable. Since he had also come to realize how far on the fringe of society he had reached, this suggestion was acceptable to him. The damage done by his rejection of the values of society was evident to him, but his sense of self was caught between accepting himself as he was and making changes that would bring him more into the mainstream.

A year later, Sam had consulted a vocational counselor, although little progress had been made with regard to his employability. He was seeing the counselor regularly and had developed a good relationship with her. Sam, his parents, and I agreed that we had accomplished as much as we could in therapy for now. We agreed to cut down our contacts, so that I would be available only on an as-needed basis.

In a follow-up phone call, mother informed me that Sam had settled on not changing himself, although he continued to see the vocational counselor regularly. He and his parents were hoping he would be able to enroll in a junior college to take some courses. First he had to take a proficiency exam to get his high school diploma, a prospect he did not relish. That Christmas I received a card with a note saying that he had passed his high school equivalency test and was taking courses at a community college. He sounded quite happy.

*Discussion*: Clearly, Sam represents a young man with a severe case of executive function disorder. Most children's and adolescents' problems are in the mild to the moderately severe range. I chose Sam's case both to illustrate the degree to which the deficit can impair a person's functions and to alert professionals to the danger of overlooking this disorder.

In his younger years, the disorder did not interfere with Sam's relationships to others. In fact, he seemed to have retained his social skills even in adulthood. The deficit, however, did derail his ability to create a conventional self-narrative. This derailment had reverberations in the selfobject functions he could draw from others. In particular, it affected his ability to idealize the values of his parents and to take a path that was consistent with theirs. One might ask which came first—the de-idealization or his realization that it would be impossible for him to attain the goals associated with his parents' values. A psychogenic explanation would emphasize the former, while a neuropsychologically informed explanation would emphasize the latter. I, of course, favor the latter.

If we try to reconstruct Sam's self-narrative, we begin with a child who thought of himself as brilliant and full of promise. His sense of difference was valued and associated with his creativity. A different set of expectations—that he would follow his father's path and choose a professional career—was laid out for him from what he had for himself. A core motif began to unfold whose script was that it was better to be different and nonconforming than to be emploted in his parents' plan.

Embedded in that motif was the notion that creativity brings with it a sense of enlivenment and excitement, while conformity is dull and boring. Intense affects were attached to each alternative; the latter was scorned while the former was idealized.

In the early years, creativity was reinforced and equally valued by the context. The fact that he felt contemptuous of the day-to-day demands of school was forgiven and minimized. But those qualities did not wear well. When demands began to be made for the accomplishment of specific tasks, Sam confronted his inability to perform the tasks, but he quickly shifted the focus by diminishing their importance. The motif now became elaborated into one that included a devaluation of expectations. The devaluation was at first met by caregivers with gentle reprimands, but soon these escalated to inpatient criticism. What was acceptable in a younger child was perceived as childish in a preadolescent. From Sam's perspective, the greater the pressure he felt to comply, the more resistant he became. The motif changed to defying adults as a way of defining himself. His sense of self began to be shaped around his noncompliance. The academic and social consequences of this motif were dramatic.

It is difficult to characterize what was occurring at the time as being the result of a disorder of the self. Sam's problems did not necessarily represent an internal conflict or a deficit in the sense of self. The behaviors, even if viewed as "symptomatic," could be interpreted as representing a different world view. Sam's rejection of therapy was understandable in that context, in that therapy represented to him an effort to convert him from the belief system he had embraced to one he had rejected. At some level, he must have unconsciously realized that, even if he were to "convert" to a more conventional lifestyle, he would not have the skills to be successful in that world. In a simpler society, Sam would not have had the problems with which he was struggling in our complex society. The motives behind his behavior were not meant to defy society's values; they may instead have reflected the fear of failure. To a degree, we can credit the coherence of Sam's self-narrative for the equanimity with which he confronted adversities. In spite of the many stressful situations he faced, he was able to retain a sense of self-cohesion. He used his intelligence to draw on others' resources to help him survive. He developed a detachment from his surrounding, such that no misadventure became a threat and no rupture in a relationship could wound him very deeply.

In one sense, Sam represents a group of young people who drop out of society. It is unknown how many of those drop out because of deficits similar to those of Sam. These are individuals who may not suffer from coexisting mental illness but who end up on the streets because they cannot cope with the complex society in which we live. The challenge we face is twofold: (1) to find the means to identify these children at the earliest possible age so as to institute remediation programs that might mitigate the effects of their deficits, and (2) for our society to recognize the sources of these individuals' problem so as to institute appropriate measures to rehabilitate them.

# 10

# NONVERBAL LEARNING DISABILITIES

J OHNSON AND MYKLEBUST introduced the concept of nonverbal learning
disabilities into the literature in 1967. In their studies of children with
learning disabilities, they came upon a group of children with common
characteristics who did not have language-based learning disabilities.
They designated this group as having "nonverbal learning disabilities," in-
tending to convey that the children's problems lay in a different domain
than that of verbal language. The problem with this designation is that it
identifies a negative domain rather than a positive set of symptoms. Although misleading, this label gained popularity and remains in use today
(Little, 1993) (see Table 10.1).

## Explanatory Paradigms

Several different lines of research followed Johnson and Myklebust's
work. One was taken by neurologists who identified similarities between
the problems of this group of children and those of children with right
hemisphere dysfunctions resulting from strokes or brain injury. Since the
group of children studied by Johnson and Myklebust did not evidence
actual brain damage, neurologists gave their problems the designation of
"right-hemisphere developmental learning disabilities" (Semrud-Clikeman
& Hynd, 1990; Voeller, 1986, 1995; Weintraub & Mesulam, 1982).

A second line was taken by Rourke (1989, 1995a, 1995b; Rourke &
Tsatsanis, 1995), a neuropsychologist with a long-standing interest in

TABLE 10.1
Nonverbal Learning Disabilities

A. CHARACTERISTICS:

1. *Defining features*: Patients exhibit a complex set of neurocognitive strengths and weaknesses: strengths in rote verbal memory, in reading decoding and spelling; weaknesses in tactile and visual perception and attention, in concept formation, reading comprehension of complex materials, problem solving, and dealing with novel materials; academic problems in math and science; and a pattern of socioemotional difficulties involving the reception and expression of modulated affects and of nonverbal modes of communication.

2. *Prevalence rates*: No data are available on prevalence.

3. *Sex ratio*: Unknown, but clinically the rate of referral to the Rush Neurobehavioral Center is 10:1 boys to girls.

4. *Coexisting conditions*: Chronic anxiety, ADD-like symptoms, and depression.

B. DEVELOPMENTAL HISTORY: As infants they are passive, fail to engage in exploratory play, and do not respond as expected. They appear clumsy and poorly coordinated. They have difficulties interacting with other children in groups. They are unable to form friendships or to sustain being with other children even for brief periods of time without an eruption ensuing.

C. DISORDERS OF THE SELF:

1. *Presenting symptoms*:

   a. *Academic*: They have poor handwriting and are deficient in arithmetic skills. Their reading comprehension is not on a par with their verbal skills, although they are good readers. They have great difficulty with tasks required by art classes. They also have problems with attention, dealing with novel materials, and adjusting to new situations.

   b. *Social*: Their social functioning is often problematic; they interact well with adults but not with peers. They are unable to decode social cues, failing to "read" other people's body language, facial expressions, and vocal intonations. They are inept in social situations.

## TABLE 10.1
## (Continued)

c. *Emotional*: The area of affective communication is problematic. They appear unable to decode feelings associated with prosodic or vocal intonations; they have difficulty reading the feelings conveyed by facial expressions. They have problems in modulating or regulating certain affects; they lose control and have temper tantrums, when frustrated.

2. *Sense of self-cohesion*: The child's sense of self is prone to injury and vulnerable to fragmentation manifested as rage attacks or meltdowns.

3. *Self-narrative coherence*: In their self-narratives they provide explanations for their thoughts and behaviors that exclude the significance of the learning disorders. These self-narratives have elements of incoherence that are rationalized and attributed to the child's experiences.

D. INTERVENTIONS:

1. *Remediation*: Specialized social-skills groups that address problems with social interactions.

2. *Psychotherapy*: Long-term supportive psychotherapy can be helpful.

---

identifying specific subtypes of learning disabilities. From a large sample of children tested in his laboratory, he identified a group of children with common features whom he designated as having a nonverbal learning disability. He found a pattern of neuropsychological strengths and weaknesses, which he proposed were paradigmatic of these children's problems. Interestingly, he too hypothesized that the etiology of the children's problems was to be found in the right hemisphere. Specifically, he thought that a failure in the proper migration of neuronal cells led to a dysfunction in the white matter of the right hemisphere. Rourke collected data to support this hypothesis, finding similar problems in children who have Williams syndrome, callosal agenesis, early hydrocephalus, congenital hypothyroidism, fetal alcohol syndrome, and other conditions. Many of the children with these conditions manifest features of nonverbal learning disabilities. Specific histological research to support the white matter hypothesis remains to be conducted (Rourke, 1995b).

Clinical experience does not fully support Rourke's findings of common features in the group of children he identifies as having a nonverbal learning disability. In clinical studies conducted at the Rush Neurobehavioral Center,* we have seen children who have the neurocognitive and socioemotional profiles that Rourke suggests but do not have the problems in math he indicates should coexist. We have also seen children who have the academic and socioemotional features of the profile but do not have the other neuropsychological problems. These observations raise questions as to whether Rourke's profile is a single entity or a syndrome within which there are subtypes showing different sets of features.

Other researchers have followed a different line altogether. In an attempt to address directly some of the problems that result from efforts to cluster the children under a single label, Denkla, (1983) a pediatric neurologist, proposed a new category of learning disabilities: "social learning disabilities." She suggested that the common features many children present are found in the area of social functioning. These children may or may not have problems in other areas of neurocognitive functioning.

Two other researchers who have focused on the symptoms associated with the social domain of these children are Pennington and Nowicki. Pennington (1991) takes issue with Rourke's definition and supports Denkla's position. He believes that Rourke conflates children from two different types of disorders, those who have problems in the area of spatial cognition and those who have problems in the area of social cognition. The former group of children, he feels, properly may be said to have a nonverbal learning disability, while the latter may be more properly designated as having disorders within the autistic spectrum of disorders. The latter group includes children with Asperger's disorder.

Finally, Nowicki and Duke (1992) are less concerned with the psychopathology of the children than with the problems they generally have in the domain of nonverbal communication. This domain, they feel, has been seriously neglected by educators and ought to be taught much as foreign languages are taught in schools. They coined the term "dyssemia" to describe children who have problems understanding the language of this domain and created a test, the DANVA (Diagnostic Analysis of Nonverbal Accuracy) (Nowicki & Duke, 1994) to help identify children with problems using facial expressions, gestures, tone of voice, and posture or personal space.

---

*The Rush Neurobehavioral Center is a section of the Department of Pediatrics of the Rush–Presbyterian–St. Luke's Medical Center, Chicago.

Here I use Rourke's definition, since it has gained the widest acceptance of all those definitions, although I strongly favor Denkla's and Pennington's explanatory paradigms.

## Characteristics of the Disorder

*Defining features:*Three sets of features characterize the symptoms these
patients display: neuropsychological, academic, and socioemotional.

Neuropsychological features: Rourke (1989, 1995a; Harnadek &
Rourke, 1993) provides a detailed catalog of these children's neuropsychological assets and deficits. He proposes areas of primary deficits in
tactile perception, such as finger agnosia, that is, the inability to identify
which finger is touched in the absence of a visual cue; visual perception,
such as discriminating and recognizing visual details and organizing visual stimuli; deficits in complex psychomotor tasks that require cross-
modal integration of visual perception and motor output, such as putting puzzles together or solving mazes; and dealing with novel materials
and adjusting to new situations. These children also have problems with
problem solving, concept formation, exploratory behavior, and tactile and
visual memory. Concomitant with these difficulties are speech problems
and problems in prosody that lead to speaking in a monotone or with a
singsong voice.

Academic features: Academic problems are in the areas of poor handwriting and deficient skills in arithmetic. While the children are good readers, their reading comprehension is not on a par with their verbal skills.
Art classes are the bane of these children. Many problems emerge in that
setting because the tasks require the capacity for visual-spatial-perceptual
organization these children do not possess. They are either average or
above average in verbal language skills. They have good syntax and good
pragmatics. Most of them have good memories and manifest rote memory verbalizations that make them look much smarter than they actually
are. Characteristically their concepts lack precision. Although they appear
sophisticated, there is shallowness to the content of their expressions. A
child may talk a lot and use a vocabulary that seems advanced for his age,
but the communications are not always well connected and the content
appears superficial. The problem with concept formation limits their
capacity to reason, analyze, and synthesize materials.

Later on, as the child moves to higher grades, reading comprehension
drops. Complex material becomes much harder to grasp, and the con-

cepts related to it are harder to understand. They cannot organize a narrative to pick out the main points from supporting details or the relevant from the irrelevant. They also have difficulty reading between the lines, making inferences, and understanding the double meaning of expressions. Their capacity to give a narrative account of an event is limited. They grasp an aspect of the total picture and miss the broader gestalt. Asked to report on an event, they give an account that appears disconnected and devoid of feeling. It becomes very difficult to reconstruct what has happened from their reports.

Socioemotional features: Lai (1990) adds social/emotional deficits to the features described by Rourke's. She states:

> The concept of "social skills" is a multi-faceted one, consisting of the integration of several capacities, including the interpretation of nonverbal cues in the environment, the ability to experience a range of emotions in differing contextual circumstances, and the development of a flexible repertoire of behaviors to meet the needs of a particular, complex social interaction, among others. (p. 2)

The functioning of children with a nonverbal learning disability in social situations is often problematic. They interact quite well with adults but not with peers. This may be because adults are more predictable in their responses and can be engaged verbally, while their peers are more erratic and respond more nonverbally. Since they are unable to decode social cues involved in "reading" other people's body language, facial expression, and vocal intonations, they are inept in social situations. They seldom make solid eye contact, which may be due to their inability to organize other people's faces. Grasping the subtle nuances of a social situation is difficult: they lack a sense of humor; they do not know when they are being teased; they interpret colloquialisms or metaphorical expressions concretely.

Sometimes these children are seen as rude, although they are not consciously being disrespectful. They will start a conversation with a stranger as though they were old friends, asking personal questions and sharing personal facts too quickly. They do not respect the privacy that we presume others need, nor does their sense of body in space allow them to respect common usual social distances, such as a culturally determined conversational distance.

In contrast to children with Asperger's syndrome, these children appear to crave social contact and to be capable of relating to others. They try reaching out to other people, but their attempts are inept and are often misread. The children then pull back defensively and isolate themselves or become belligerent, though they do not give up the effort to connect. Unlike the "self-involvement" of autistic children, the withdrawal of children with nonverbal learning disabilities is reactive rather than primary.

With peers their play is disruptive. They appear unable to negotiate social interchanges with other kids. Often a caregiver will say, "He just wants to play the way he wants to play. He doesn't want to share in the play." Negotiating and interacting with others is difficult.

Affective communication, which is also problematic, may be discussed from three points of view: reception, expression, and processing of affective information. In the receptive area, children with nonverbal learning disabilities appear unable to decode prosodic or vocal intonations, although their hearing is unimpaired. If their caregiver's voice sounds serious, they may misunderstand the tone of voice as conveying anger. They also have difficulty reading facial expressions and bodily gestures, as though they suffer from a "nonverbal dyslexia" (Badian, 1986, 1992). In the expressive area we see the counterpart of these problems. They do not use body gestures in speaking and so seem wooden and constricted. They do not use vocal intonations when they speak. It is difficult to read their mood from their facial expressions.

We know very little about the ways in which they process affective information. It is not clear whether their problem lies in the area of decoding affective states or in the area of visual processing. They respond to affect-laden situations with sadness, anxiety, or withdrawal, and appear to have problems modulating certain affects. When frustrated, they lose control and have temper tantrums. Their response to most feelings is generalized excitement that is unfocused and lacking in content. To adults these children appear to have no compassion or empathy for others, to lack the feelings about events and people that their peers are capable of having.

*Prevalence rate*: No data are available on the prevalence of this disorder.

*Sex ratio*: No data are available on the sex ratio of male to female children affected by this disorder, although judging from the rate of referral for testing to our medical center the proportion is over 10:1 boys to girls. This figure may be misleading because the general rate of referral of girls is smaller than that of boys.

*Coexisting conditions*: Clinically, the children exhibit a number of psychiatric symptoms related to their deficit, but no epidemiological studies exist that associate specific psychiatric disorders with this learning disorder. At a young age, children express their frustration through motor output such as hand flapping, jumping up and down excitedly, or extreme temper tantrums. They are then mistaken for children who suffer from pervasive developmental disorder, bipolar disorder, Asperger's syndrome, or mild autism. They generally suffer from high levels of anxiety and severe self-esteem problems. They also suffer from depression, obsessive compulsive symptoms, or attentional problems that lead them to be misdiagnosed as having AD/HD.

## Developmental History

No direct observations are available of these children's early development. What is available is reconstructed from the histories given by caregivers.

If the caregivers have had other children, they sense from the very beginning that the child is different, although they are hard put to pinpoint what it is they feel to be different about the child. They find themselves frustrated in their efforts to understand the child and by their inability to decode his cues. Caregivers feel placed in the position of constantly having to correct, limit, or punish the child, who in turn responds with fury at what he experiences as unfair treatment. The family ends up feeling controlled by the child in all its activities. Often caregivers feel guilty, blaming themselves for their failure to parent properly. This frustration may initiate a cycle in which the caregivers feel rejected by the child and in turn distance themselves emotionally from him. Some caregivers are intuitively able to read the child's messages and soon find themselves being the only ones who can communicate effectively with the child. If that does not occur, the difficulties are compounded by the child's increasing demands on the caregiver and inability to cope when the caregiver is absent.

Sometimes caregivers unwittingly contribute to the confusion because of their own personality difficulties and because they themselves have a nonverbal learning disability. The household then appears like that of a family in which each member speaks a different language. While a measure of communication occurs, large areas are fraught with misunderstanding. The levels of frustration, the anger resulting from constant injury, and the lack of gratification in having such a difficult child all contribute to the ensuing chaos.

Caregivers also report that as infants the children were passive, failed to engage in exploratory play, and did not respond as expected. Many did use toddler toys or enjoy coloring or drawing, but they were unable to put puzzles together (Johnson, 1987).

When the children started to walk, their visual-spatial-motor problems emerged clearly. They appeared clumsy and poorly coordinated, to the point where caregivers had to watch them closely because they bumped into furniture, were unsteady on their feet, broke toys, and endangered themselves. Slow to learn from their caregivers' limits and instructions, they appeared unable to understand causal relationships, so that caregivers had to intervene and correct them constantly. In turn, the children responded with frustration and anger. Often, their frustration escalated, so that by the age of two temper tantrums emerged that were much more intense than those that normally occur at this age.

Around the age of three, they went through an initial stage when their speech was difficult to understand because of articulation problems. These problems dissipated, and they then became quite adept at verbal communication. Caregivers reinforced this verbal channel, becoming overreliant on it to communicate with the children.

Their self-help skills did not develop comparably to those of other children their age. They were slow to learn to feed and dress themselves. They did not master tasks such as hand washing or grooming, and had to be helped and reminded to complete these tasks well into latency, when other children were already performing them independently.

In groups, difficulties in interacting with other children became evident. They seemed not to know how to play with others and clung to the caregivers who accompanied them. If their interactive strategies were unsuccessful, they isolated themselves.

By the time they reached kindergarten or first grade, other problems became evident. Although they appeared to be quite bright and had excellent verbal abilities, they had major problems in the area of peer relationships. They were unable to form friendships or to sustain being with other children even for brief periods of time. Academically, they started out having difficulties decoding letters and words, but once they discovered the rules they became good readers. Their writing, however, was illegible, complicated by their small motor and visuospatial difficulties. Arithmetic difficulties emerged once simple computation was introduced.

By the time the child is seven or eight, the full-fledged syndrome is apparent. It is often at this point that children are referred for therapy.

## Disorders of the Self

### *Presenting Problems*

Children with a nonverbal learning disability are generally referred for a variety of problems. Boys are often referred because of behavioral problems, while girls may be referred because of social isolation. Both boys and girls often present with clinical signs of severe anxiety, depression, low self-esteem, attentional problems, and obsessional preoccupations. They perform poorly in some academic areas but adequately in most. Their histories and the clinical impression from diagnostic interviews disclose their social and emotional distress.

*Academic*: The children are seldom referred because of their academic problems. Their problems with arithmetic, poor handwriting, and reading comprehension are often minimized because they appear intelligent and competent. They have difficulty applying their academic skills to new situations, accommodating or adapting to novel or unpredictable situations. They respond to novel situations with distress or anxiety, at times becoming oppositional or aggressive when faced with new tasks. They also have difficulty maintaining a consistent problem-solving approach throughout a task. They tend to lose track of the goal during a task. They have difficulties problem-solving, although they show significantly better reasoning when the problem involves verbal information alone than when social and pragmatic problem-solving is required.

*Social*: The social area is often the focus of concern. As we have seen, they lack basic social skills. In the area of nonverbal communication they display poor eye contact, their facial expressions are muted, neutral, or flat, their tone of voice is soft, flat, not well modulated. They have difficulty reading nonverbal social cues and read social situations poorly. They do not have close friends and have difficulty forming and keeping positive peer relationships. They tend to be bossy, aggressive, and defensive with peers, relying on rules rather than exercising good judgment. In addition, they are socially awkward and inappropriate. They ask personal questions or make inappropriate or irrelevant comments that make others uncomfortable. They also interpret social situations idiosyncratically or in an overpersonalized way.

*Emotional*: They are self-critical, perfectionistic, and express a lack of self-confidence. They tend to feel inadequate and to have low self-esteem. Their considerable anxiety leads them to express irritation, display frustration, unhappiness, or sadness, and appear worried, fidgety, and uncomfortable. They may complain of stomachaches or express worries about bad things happening to people they care about (e.g., family members).

### Sense of Self-cohesion

For the child with a nonverbal learning disability all interactions are fraught with anxiety. This anxiety leads to defenses that in turn lead to symptomatic behaviors. It is possible to conjecture that some of the disorders of the self encountered in these children are related to the distance of their experiences from those who attempt to provide selfobject functions for them.

These children's clinical presentation is complex and difficult to characterize. Their cognitive and affective deficits seem to interfere with the use of selfobject functions caregivers are ready to provide. The children experience the interchanges with caregivers as lacking in empathy. The resulting deficits impose severe limits on the range and depth of connection between child and caregiver. Various disorders of the self emerge as a result of these selfobject deficits, not all of which are distinctive to children with a nonverbal learning disability. Most common are pervasive self-esteem problems, since their deficits expose these children to *constant* narcissistic injuries from which they cannot escape.

Selfobject deficits generate their own set of narcissistic vulnerabilities and symptoms. Characteristic of these vulnerabilities is a propensity for rage attacks and pervasive anxieties. Children with a nonverbal learning disability are prone to express rage as a result of the constant frustration produced by failed communications or to withdraw into silent despair at never being fully appreciated and understood. The injuries they experience do not lead to flagrantly grandiose behaviors, as is common in children with problems that have a different etiology. Instead, the fantasies of children with a nonverbal learning disability are filled with the wish for recognition, fame, and power. In addition, because the children's efforts at communication are defeated, they often become engulfed by a sense of helplessness that leads to pervasive anxiety. This intolerable anxiety leads to a variety of defenses, which in turn lead to symptomatic responses and/or behaviors. But since the meaning of the danger to the child motivates the response and the choice of defenses, no specific set of symptoms can be associated with this anxiety. Often anxiety is alleviated the moment the deficit is filled by someone providing the missing selfobject or adjunctive functions.

Finally, children with more severe forms of the disorder present with a different set of dynamics. For those children the meanings of the experiences are not integrated into the self-narrative and incoherences creep into the story. The psychopathology that emerges results from their incomplete integration of the personal and shared meanings of their experiences. Their responses are chaotic and reflect the absence of an internal sense of cohesion. It is difficult to sort out whether the level of pathology is related to the severity of the deficits, to the unresponsiveness of the environment, or to a combination of these. The picture is often clouded because there is also evidence of other neurological or psychiatric problems (Palombo, 1995, 1996c; Palombo & Berenberg, 1997).

### Self-narrative Coherence

Children with nonverbal learning disabilities appear to have a different world view from others in their community. When the self-narrative includes both shared and personal meanings, the reality of the child is not so radically different from that of others. The differences, subtle and elusive, emerge in the nuances of communicative interchanges. But their emergence is not consciously noticed, so that when the dialogue becomes derailed there is a feeling of frustration and puzzlement as to what occurred. To the extent that a child's self-narrative and construction of reality are concordant with the views of others, the dialogue is maintained and no relational problems arise. The child feels the self-narrative is a coherent story and has a sense of self-cohesion, intactness, and well-being. But when the self-narrative is not concordant with that of others, serious problems arise.

*Adjunctive functions*: Since verbal expressive capacities are an area of strength for children with a nonverbal learning disability, these children can learn to verbally mediate nonverbal tasks. They achieve the goal of completing a task by talking their way through the nonverbal steps. Some children learn that strategy for themselves, while others can gain from being taught it. The limitations of the strategy lie in the children's shortcomings in dealing with abstract conceptual material. Since this capacity is not as well developed as are their verbal expressive capacities, children may be able to verbalize their understanding of what is required but not to perform the expected tasks.

*Remediation*: Two common types of remediation are involvement in a group that focuses on the social interactional problems of the child and the use of strategies to compensate for the deficit in nonverbal communication. Involvement in a social skills group can be useful provided the leaders are aware of the children's special problems. The children cannot learn by observing others or being criticized for what they do. They require a variety of strategies that allow them to process verbally what they should learn.

Other interventions involve preparing the child for new situations, reinforcing thinking about part-whole relationships, enhancing problem-solving capacities, identifying feelings in self and others, debriefing the child to encourage compensations, helping the child manage his anxiety, and encouraging the development of a sense of humor. (See Palombo & Berenberg, 1997, 1999; Thompson, 1997; and Rourke, 1995c, for more details.)

*Psychotherapy*: Patients with a nonverbal learning disability often find themselves in great turmoil. Much of the turmoil is created by their learning deficit, although the secondary effects of the deficit may at times be the source of difficulty. Before recommending therapy clinicians must be clear in determining the area in which they can be of help. Therapists can provide support, in which case patients are grateful to have someone available who understands their plight. These can become long-term cases that go on for years, especially if the therapist performs adjunctive functions that permit the patient to function in the world. The dilemma for therapists is that of justifying such long-term intervention. There is little doubt that often, without this support, the patient would suffer and his functioning might deteriorate. The extent to which interpretations of narrative motifs and their role in the patients' problems is appropriate will depend on many factors that require a refined diagnostic assessment. Evaluating such factors as the age of the patient, his psychological mindedness, and his flexibility and capacity to change will lead to an appropriate decision.

CASE ILLUSTRATION: LILLY*

***Referral and presenting problem***: **Lilly was in the midst of her seventh grade year at a suburban junior high school when her parents first consulted me. She had undergone a neuropsychological evaluation in first grade and had been diagnosed with attention deficit disorder and various learning disabilities. The pediatric neurologist who**

*Lilly was seen by a woman therapist who does not wish to be identified for reasons of confidentiality. The case is presented as her therapist speaking.

had been following her gave her parents my name to consult with about the social withdrawal and rejection that had been worsening since Lilly entered junior high school. At the time of the initial consultation, she was socially isolated both in and out of school. She ate lunch alone and never made contact with other children. Lilly was highly perfectionistic, critical of herself and others, completely overwhelmed by her schoolwork, and subject to tantrums and emotional meltdowns at school and at home. Her parents were hopeful that I could help her to engage with her peers. The emotional issues were a secondary concern, as they felt able to cope with her anxiety and behavior.

*Developmental history*: Lilly is the oldest of two children. She lives with her parents and her sister, Abby, who is six years her junior. Her parents are both professionals and the family enjoys an upper-middle-class lifestyle. Her parents report that she was planned, that there were mild medical complications during pregnancy, and that labor and delivery were normal. She was a "fussy" baby who always had difficulty falling asleep. The fussiness abated once Lilly was mobile. She was verbally precocious and achieved developmental milestones at or before expected ages; however, gross motor skills were never fully mastered and she is described as "uncoordinated." She had no major illnesses or losses as a young child.

Lilly's behavioral and learning difficulties became apparent upon entering school. She was described as inattentive and impulsive. She had difficulty reading, although it was clear that she was very bright. She was easily angered and frequently upset at school. She would occasionally strike out at other children. After the birth of her sister, Lilly was very difficult to manage at home as well. She was verbally and physically aggressive toward her. Her outbursts and tantrums became everyday occurrences.

Lilly was able to establish friendships with children by second grade. While never very socially inclined, she did maintain a few friendships through grade school. Once the girls entered junior high, they joined a larger group that intimidated Lilly. Although her original friends initially welcomed her, eventually they excluded her when she avoided the group and did not fit in. Lilly withdrew from making social contact and relied solely on her family for relationships; however, these relationships were conflictual. Lilly and her dad were never able to develop a sense of mutuality with each other and she tended to avoid him. He seemed to be only peripherally involved in her life. She was very dependent on her mother for assistance with every aspect of life. Her mother had to help her with her schoolwork, calm her upsets, entertain her, and care for her as if she were a young child. Lilly was very jealous and competitive with her younger sister. For example, as a 12-year-old, she would fight with her over whose turn it was to press the elevator button! She teased Abby without mercy but could not understand why she resisted playing with her when she wanted her to. She resented any care or attention that her mother gave to Abby and was threatened by any of her accomplishments.

Lilly had few interests outside of school. She did like singing and art. She was just starting to babysit and had some success with the much younger children in her care. Lilly was able to engage adults, including teachers, with her expansive vocabulary and fund of knowledge, but her emotional immaturity often interfered with their efforts to help her.

*Test results*: Lilly's first testing took place when she was six years old and determined that she had the characteristics of attention deficit disorder with hyperactivity, as well as nonverbal learning disabilities. A second evaluation took place after Lilly started treatment when she was 13. Her cognitive ability was measured to be at the superior range. She showed remarkably high verbal processing and reasoning, problem solving, and conceptual thought, reaching the upper level of the superior range. She showed two areas of relative weakness: one in the nonverbal learning areas and the other in the realm of executive functioning and self-regulatory capacities. Her relative learning weaknesses were in the visuo-perceptual, visual-motor, and organizational areas. She had learned to compensate in these areas by adopting a painfully slow, perfectionistic style and by overreliance on her verbal capacities. These compensations allowed her to score in the average range of functioning. In the social-emotional areas, she showed less capacity for problem-solving and conceptualization than expected—and this was in stark contrast to her abilities in other areas. While able to recognize obvious social cues, she was unable to appreciate more subtle communications. She alternated between an overly mature, pedantic style of relating and a silly, disinhibited style. She was found to have little capacity for empathy and showed little awareness of the person to whom she was relating.

*Clinical presentation*: In the first interview, Lilly stated that she was happy to see me and to talk to me. In a calm intellectual manner, she acknowledged that she needed to make friends and said that was her reason for seeing me. With more emotion and with obvious disdain, she ex-

plained that the girls in her school were too immature for her to relate
to. Emphatically and angrily, she began to argue against the idea that she
had a nonverbal learning disability. She believed that she understood people quite well.

I found Lilly to be an attractive 12-year-old who dressed and wore her
hair in the manner of a much younger child. She talked without apparent reservation or a need to get to know me. It only seemed important that she convince me that she was not impaired, but superior to
her peers. Her posture was poor, her gestures were exaggerated, her facial expressions were either non-expressive or overly expressive, and
her speech had a singsong rhythm to it. She showed little awareness of
herself in space, of the environment, or of me. She seemed unhappy
and lacking in energy. I recommended to the parents that she be seen
twice a week in therapy.

*Treatment summary*: After several interviews similar to the first, I began to wonder how best to help Lilly while respecting her defenses. She
experienced all her difficulties as stemming from external sources and
was unable to acknowledge any vulnerabilities or concerns. She was
able to detail the ways in which people annoyed and/or failed her and
seemed pleased to have an audience and a supportive response. Having
a place to air her grievances seemed to gratify her emotionally, but I
was troubled that I felt distanced by her impersonal stance. I hoped that
my benign interest and support would allow her to access and express
some of her anxieties. However, she seldom paused for me to speak,
and if I interrupted her too soon to point out a problem, she felt criticized and increased her defensive detachment.

After several months, Lilly finally began to report her distress over
her problems with homework. She then talked about getting less than
perfect grades, forgetting to turn in papers, and other school-related
problems. She had no awareness that her reactions, including her regular tantrums at school and daily frantic calls to her mother, were inappropriate responses to her distress. To her, these daily events were
insignificant. It did not occur to her that she could manage herself differently. Gradually, as I gently, repeatedly discussed these reactions with
her, she began to see that they were quite different in their intensity
and quality from those of other children. She began to express embarrassment over her behavior at school. This gave me an opening to discuss how she might manage her feelings differently to avoid this embarrassment. We came up with a plan that if she got upset, she would
ask her teacher to allow her to go to the social worker's office. If she

needed to, she could call her mother from there—in privacy. This plan allowed her to exercise some self-control and at the same time gave her hope that I could be helpful to her.

A major source of distress was related to her expectations about her academic performance. If she performed less than perfectly, she became extremely distressed. She was convinced that anything less than perfection meant failure. As she entered eighth grade the academic challenges became greater than they had been and her anxieties were magnified. It slowly became evident to her that she could not continue to hold onto these expectations. This was especially true as she anticipated the increased workload that she would face in high school. She came to recognize that she depended entirely on academic success for her self-esteem and worth. With help, she recognized that she needed to make some changes to make it in high school without a breakdown.

At this point, she was willing to think about how to engage with her peers and to have a tutor to help her be more focused and efficient in her academic work. She agreed to join a club at school and to begin to sit in the lunchroom with other children. We discussed ways to talk to other children and how to handle her feelings when engaged with them. Eventually, she was able to identify having wishes for a friend and to be like other kids.

The summer before high school, Lilly arranged a shopping date with a girl with whom she had become friendly. She hoped that this girl would help her dress like other girls her age. Her mother and I were thrilled at her interest and her ability to reach out to a peer for help. The trip was a success. She also began a summer school course, which helped diminish her anxiety about the logistics of high school. For example, she needed a lot of practice working a combination lock. With coaching, she made an acquaintance in class and went on a few lunch dates. Meantime, her tutor helped her prepared for the academics. She accepted a slightly less challenging set of classes than she was capable of, finally recognizing that she needed more time to do her work than other students. This was a major concession that reflected a more realistic understanding of herself. She joined a number of organized school activities in addition to her class load. Unfortunately, by the end of her first semester, her anxiety was overwhelming. Her mother could not handle it, and they both turned to me for help. Nightly phone calls to help her prioritize and set limits on her homework proved very helpful. She began to trust me to comfort and reassure her, which lessened her anxiety. After some hesitation, she accepted my advice and considered a consultation for medication. Referral to a psychiatrist proved to be successful and resulted in her being placed on a small dose of an antidepressant, which also helped with the anxiety.

As the crisis of the semester's end passed, Lilly began to examine her feelings about being different from other children and her sadness that she had so much difficulty fitting in. She began to wonder about her life and how she would manage herself. She was seeing how dependent she was on her mother and how childish she was in her demands at home. She was determined to try to use more self-control at home and to try to handle more situations for herself. She even tried to act maturely with her sister and began to recognize that she had issues that were distressing for her, too.

The next summer, she went on a language immersion trip with other adolescents. This trip provided her with more confidence, as she successfully navigated the relationships. By her sophomore year in high school, she had developed a small group of peers, although she continued to struggle to fit in with them. For the most part, she was successful. She managed the academic pressure without too much distress, and even though socially she was on the periphery of her peer group, she no longer had meltdowns when confronted with social setbacks. We contemplated termination as she began to think about college. By summer her family relationships were vastly improved, she felt ready to leave home, and we terminated therapy.

*Discussion*: When Lilly, an exceptionally bright girl with a nonverbal learning disorder, began treatment, she was avoidant, detached, and arrogant. The social demands of junior high school were well beyond her reach. She was immature in her emotional understanding and management of herself. Her actions were appropriate to a much younger child who could not be self-observant or modulate affect states. Academic success was her only source of satisfaction. None of her relationships was satisfying or enjoyable. She was depressed, withdrawn, and anxious.

Initially, she was vulnerable and so well defended that it was difficult for her to develop a complementary relationship with me. As she experienced my understanding of how she felt as emotional support, her distress and anxiety became the focus of the treatment. At first, the transactions between us were more intellectual than experiential. We discussed the sources of her distress and ways in which her unchecked reactions to it worsened her situation. She became more self-reflective and more willing to try to manage her upsets differently. These discussions led her to an understanding of how her narrowed and high expectations were unrealistic and not matched to the demands of school. She began to accept that some of her difficulties could be managed differently and agreed to get help with them. This included interest in developing peer relationships. The verbally mediated understanding of her difficulties expanded as did her motivation to fit in, to manage herself, to engage with her peers, and to have better relationships. She learned to talk to herself as a way of compensating for her difficulties with the processing of nonverbal communication.

Side by side with these intellectual discussions, which are characteristic of work with preadolescents and adolescents, a strong idealizing transference developed. Her perception of me as a calming, soothing influence in her life allowed her to become increasingly reliant on me for suggestions as to how to manage various aspects of her life, in particular her social relationships. She became confident in my ability to help her, and this permitted her to avoid the fragmentations to which she was prone. As she experienced successes, she became more confident and more active in initiating activities on her own.

When she began treatment, the primary theme in Lilly's self-narrative was that she was superior to others, who were less mature than she was. She was haughty and contemptuous of her peers, expressed disdain for them, and rationalized that they did not like her because she was smarter than they were. This required her to set perfectionistic standards that were impossible for her to meet. In spite of these rationalizations, it was evident that she was troubled by the major incoherences in the narrative. She was depressed, embarrassed by her behavior, and unable to regulate herself. As she began to accept her sense of being different from others as not being totally negative, she was able to reach out to peers and to manage her social life better than she had previously. Although a shift occurred in the central theme of her narrative, it was not clear that she had found a substitute theme. It appeared as though that task would be postponed to later, as she developed a nuclear sense of self.

What remains to be seen is the mark that the learning disorder will leave on her future personality development. There appears to be little doubt that she will be successful academically. Her choice of a career will be critical to her future success. A career that depends little on social interactions is more likely to fit her personality than one that requires her to engage in personal negotiations with others. Whether she will become isolated or be able to maintain a small circle of friends may depend on circumstances. If she were to move to a large city where making connections with others is difficult, she may find herself unable to connected with others. Finally, at the personal level, based on my experience with some adults with a nonverbal learning disability and with children who had a parent with the disorder, I would speculate that she may be able to develop an intimate relationship with a partner. Such a partner would need to be a calming and soothing influence on her and help her maintain her sense of self-cohesion.

These are only conjectures. Their usefulness lies in allowing us to learn whether our knowledge is sufficient to predict the path of a person's personality. Based on past experience, I would say we have to be prepared to be surprised. The capacity to compensate and the complementary functions provided by certain contexts sometimes change the course of a young person's life in ways that we cannot foresee.

### CASE ILLUSTRATION: PAT, AN ADULT WITH A NONVERBAL LEARNING DISABILITY

Pat was referred to me by a colleague who had known her for some years. When I first saw her, she was a 40-year-old government employee who had never gone to college but had risen to a supervisory position by virtue of hard work and good native intelligence. Although she had been in several relationships with men, she had never married. The presenting problem was a fear that her drinking was getting out of control. She had never thought of herself as having a drinking problem, although her social life centered on the people in a tavern she frequented. Lately, however, she now found herself drinking alone at home.

In the first session, she announced that she had decided to stop drinking and did not feel she would have a problem with that. Since this was her first experience in therapy, she did not know what else there might be to say; yet, she agreed to once-a-week therapy.

Over the next year, we focused on what appeared to be an underlying depression, which I suggested she had been medicating with the alcohol. She was unable to maintain her resolve not to drink and continued to drink but not immoderately. During that period, she discovered my interest in self psychology and on her own went out and bought Kohut's and Basch's books. An avid reader, she was able to extract the essence of what she read as well as most social work graduate students. Eventually, in the second year of treatment, she discovered that I had published papers; she tracked down some of them. As you will hear in what follows, she read one of my papers on nonverbal learning disabilities and quickly recognized herself as having similar problems. She asked me whether she was correct. I shared that I suspected that she did have such a learning disability but wouldn't make that diagnosis without testing. I referred her to a neuropsychologist[*] who is an expert in this area, and he indeed confirmed the diagnosis.

Rather than describe Pat's treatment, let me share here an essay she wrote during the third year of her once-a-week treatment. This essay represents a sample of voluminous materials she gave me over the years. She often preferred to communicate in written form, as she felt that her anxiety during sessions prevented her from being as open as she could be in the privacy of her home. This document presents Pat's experience of her disability and clearly illustrates the impact it had on her sense of self. It also gives narrative expression to her understanding of what had happened to her.

*In response to Joseph Palombo's*
*"The Effect of Nonverbal Learning Disabilities On Children's*
*Development: Theoretical & Diagnostic Considerations" by Pat J.*

*I have been in psychotherapy with Joseph Palombo for over two years. Recently I read his article "The Effect of Nonverbal Learning Disabilities on Children's Development: Theoretical & Diagnostic Considerations." In December of last year, W. R. [and an intern] administered a battery of 20 tests to me. Early this year, they returned a neuropsychological evaluation. I believe that the following phrase from the evaluation of me sums up my interest in Mr. Palombo's paper: "the cluster of visuo-spatial difficulties and affective processing deficits make up an entity known as nonverbal learning disability."*

*I am a 42-year-old woman. I have never been married and have been physically and financially independent since I was 18. For most of that time, I've worked for a government agency. In the last three years I have accumulated almost a year of college credit, geared more towards my areas of interests than a degree program. The therapy, the schooling, and a recent emergence in cre-*

[*]Warren Rosen, Ph.D., neuropsychologist at the section of Pediatric Psychology, Department of Pediatrics, of the Rush–Presbyterian–St. Luke's Medical Center, tested her.

*ative writing are slowly pulling me out of wherever I spent the first 40 years of my life. The puzzle that Joe and I have been recently trying to solve is how much of my prior (and present) difficulties were related to this nonverbal learning disability and how much to other factors.*

*When I first requested a referral to see a therapist, it was because I was feeling out of control from alcohol abuse. Immediately after I made the call, I stopped drinking. It was at least six weeks later before I met Joe. I now feel that the fifteen years that I spent abusing alcohol was more related to clouding over other issues in my life than an "addiction." I am not presently abstinent, though I don't feel conflicted over my alcohol use. The layer underneath the alcohol use, we labeled dysthymia. (In one of the first sessions with Joe, he explained that for insurance reasons, we needed a diagnosis. I was taking Psych 101, got my hands on a DSM-III-R, and diagnosed myself as having a schizoid personality disorder. He overruled me on that one.)*

*Dysthymia (once I learned what it meant) made sense. Although superficially functioning, I was withdrawn, unmotivated in any direction, energy-less and isolated. (Except, of course, when I was drinking in my friendly neighborhood tavern.)*

*It also made sense diachronically. My mother was and is severely clinically depressed. My father probably could be diagnosed as having a schizoid personality disorder, in that he seems to be devoid of human empathy. They divorced when I was seven and both remarried volatile partners, with their own share of diagnosable symptoms. My childhood was spent continually moving, not only physically, but into almost completely different familial situations. (Kind of a "please pass the kids, syndrome.") My brother, at least until I was fourteen, was the only constant in these ever changing environments.*

*During the first year of treatment, Joe probably did little more than try to fill selfobject functions for me. I couldn't say for sure, because I was only occasionally, emotionally with him. I don't know that this reaction could be labeled as resistance. I immediately liked and trusted him. I wanted to connect with him. But it has always seemed like there is a transparent barrier, perhaps made of Saran Wrap, which acts to mute connections between anyone and myself. Even now, in my relationship with Joe, the barrier is still there, though thankfully, ripped and shredded. Now, he evokes long latent emotions. I respond, with only quiet temper tantrums, in exactly the way he writes on p. 11 [of the article] about children with a nonverbal learning disability. "They respond to affect-laden situations with anxiety, withdrawal or sadness. They appear to have problems in the modulation of certain affects. When frustrated, they lose control and have temper tantrums. Their response to most feelings is one of generalized excitement that is unfocused and lacking in content." Joe goes on to explain the effect this has on the adults around the child. I've probably learned to hide the disorientation I feel when I'm suddenly "attacked" by this sort of disembodied emotion. That's the closest that I could come to describing it, prior to reading Joe's explanation above. It is not a comfortable feeling!*

*So, first we have a layer of substance abuse. Then we have a layer of dysthymia. Then we have a layer of inadequately filled selfobject functions. Now, we have a nonverbal learning disability. Which chicken laid which egg?*

*It was well over a year ago when I first brought up in therapy, a feeling of kinship to something Joe had written about a woman who he believed suffered from, among other things, a nonverbal learning disability (Palombo, 1993). (I was covertly reading his articles from the time I first learned that he was published. After I confided that, he made life easier for me and local librarians by giving me copies.) It was the first time I considered that my inability to remember faces, places and things might come from something other than disinterest, stupidity and/or laziness. It was the first time I considered that there might be a difference between my experience of the world and that of others. It had never come up in therapy before, because I thoroughly believed memory-aid masters who assert that everyone has the ability to develop a photographic memory if they only make an effort. I failed in my effort, so why keep trying. I knew that whenever I found myself in a different environment and with different people, I would only remember the most outstanding characteristics. I had learned to accept that. It wasn't something I would think to bring up in therapy. It was just the way it was. It wasn't something that most therapists would have understood, even if I had brought it up.*

*So, Joe began to explain some of the normal ramifications of a nonverbal learning disability. Some fit, some didn't. My handwriting was terrible as a child, but so are most children's. I spent a lot of time working at it. It is now compulsively legible. I never learned arithmetic tables but I could get around it with a strong understanding of mathematics. (I have never known by rote what 8 × 7 = ?, but I could always figure it out.) I hated art and phys-ed, because they made me feel incompetent. I am only physically organized with efforts of will which soon deteriorate, so my apartment and my work space are frequently in shambles. I bought my condo six years ago. I have never felt capable of put-ting up a picture or decorating, because I fear that I would do it "wrong." I find visual entertainment frustrating. I never know "who is who" in movies. I prefer old westerns, where the good guys always wear white hats. I passionately avoid games such as "Trivial Pursuit." I hate puzzles. They underline what I feel are my inadequacies. Likewise, I don't want to engage in sports which require any kind of eye-hand coordination. (I do like to swim.)*

*These things contributed to my isolation. That brings us to the affective ramifications I've experienced, at least in part, because of this disability.*

*I remember at an early age forcing myself to learn to make and retain eye contact with people, because someone told me that I should. The neuropsychological evaluation included these obser-vations: "She made clear efforts to engage the examiners appro-priately, chatting and sustaining eye contact for long periods of time. Her continuous gaze and lack of nonverbal feedback, such as nodding and smiling during conversation, seemed a bit unnat-ural and might feel somewhat uncomfortable to others." It is un-natural! Although my gaze appears to be into the other's eyes, there is that Saran Wrap shield in between. I don't want either of us to see through "the windows of our souls." I probably won't even remember meeting you, the next time I see you.*

*Although nothing significant in the area was noted (or, I be-lieve, tested for) in the evaluation, I also seem to have a poor oral memory of any affect-laden situation. I tape my sessions with Joe. When I listen to them, even immediately afterwards, I often won-der where I was. In fact I've recently begun to tape anything that I truly care about, because I don't trust my memory in this area any more than I trust my visual memory. Perhaps Joe could fig-ure out if there is a tie-in. It probably has to do with strong affect.*

*I'm presently enrolled in a creative writing course. Most of the work I've done has been slightly fictionalized, personal recounting. As I was re-reading some of it, I was struck by the number of times I alluded to going from one "world" to another or of being in a different "world." In many of Joe's papers, he refers to a feeling of fragmenting or incoherent self-narratives, both from a self-psychological perspective when selfobject functions are not met, and in children with verbal or nonverbal disabilities, which cause them to see the world differently than their caretakers. I believe that I have maintained a reasonably coherent self-narrative because I have been able to fractionalize the world, instead of myself.*

*Each time that I moved, from depressed mother in a rented house, to self-involved father in a roach-ridden apartment, to spending summers with my grandmother, to a house in the suburbs with a new obsessive-compulsive stepmother and younger stepbrothers who I was expected to care for, to an apartment with my depressed mother and volatile stepfather, I experienced "another" world.*

*Each school I was transplanted to (nine, through high school) apparently had different rules. I had nothing to take with me, each time life changed. It seemed that none of the previously learned behavior was applicable to the new situation. I was always starting from scratch.*

*Starting from scratch meant almost complete initial withdrawal. I had to figure this new world out. I had to categorize the new cast of characters. After a time, I usually made one close friend who was also marked as "an outsider." These friends may have acted as buffers, by explaining the parts of the world I didn't understand. Their "outsideness" generally related to overt shyness, being "the fat kid," or coming from "the wrong side of the tracks." Since I never understood any of these concepts, I'm sure that I filled equal needs by just accepting them. Then it was time to move on. We would vow perpetual friendship. For a time, we'd write. But again, I was in a new world that had no connection with the older world. My energy was sapped in learning the new rules. I could not maintain a friendship.*

*Similar withdrawal accompanied new family situations. Actually, by the time I was ten I learned to build a barrier between myself and all new and old family members. In this arena, there was no one to explain the new rules. My brother was just as confused as I was, and four years older. He had the escape of high school and after-school work. I learned to love to read in my bedroom, with my door locked.*

*How does this apply to Joe's paper? I don't believe that in early childhood I had any sense of viewing the world "idiosyncratically," as he refers to. I believe that both my brother and my father share my nonverbal disability. Confusion as to which waitress was ours in a restaurant, which beach we had last been to, which bush bore black raspberries, was shared by all of us. Our responses, though perhaps confusing to those around us, seemed perfectly normal (from p. 9 of Joe's paper, it seems likely that he would not agree that this would be the expected outcome when people live together with shared a nonverbal learning disability). It was only at 10 years old, when my world changed to a completely "different world," that difficulties arose.*

*When my father remarried, he turned me over to my stepmother, and for all practical purpose, withdrew from my life. My brother began high school. Suddenly, everything seemed "idiosyncratic." Looking back on the time, I always thought that it was my step-mother's emotional difficulties that started my own. In light of Joe's paper, it may have been that I was suddenly thrust into a world that was viewed completely differently by those closest to me. Now, there was a lack of cohesion.*

*But however it came about, I had ten years of a reasonably co-herent self-narrative built up. My Aunt Dodie taught psychological testing at the Western Michigan University in Kalamazoo. She used me as a "testing guinea pig" for her class when I was 10. I loved it—wonderful attention! Not only did I score a high I.Q., but I was also assessed to be abnormally well-adjusted, considering the trauma of living through a divorce, an infrequent phenomenon at the time. When my father remarried, I did withdraw. I became hy-pervigilant. But I never disintegrated. It was the world that was different. Not me. All I had to do was keep learning new rules. Sure, it wore me out. Sure, I escaped into mild, chronic depression. Sure, the fifteen-year sojourn in my local tavern gave me a feeling of be-longing that I had never had. But, it seems that in many areas, I was able to compensate, without paying too high a price.*

*I have used two areas of compensation that Joe mentions (p. 18) for as long as I can remember. I almost always "verbally me-*

*diate" nonverbal tasks and "rehearse verbally what is to occur in anticipation of an encounter with a new function." Now, with the knowledge of the disability, I am further able to compensate by unashamedly questioning others in order to aid in the rehearsal. I'm more able to admit that I have no recall of previous meetings with people. (The conclusion that Joe has come to, that says that people with a nonverbal learning disability don't have a good sense of what is a socially acceptable confidence, is a great aid in this area. I just blurt out that I have this peculiar problem and they tell me who they are. Of course, they then may want to run!) Often I used to try to cleverly finesse my way through uncomfortable situations, or more frequently, just avoid them. This isn't uncommon for people, even without my visual memory deficits. The difference was that often I had met these people many times before, not just once. They knew me and things about me. It turned out that I had often had intimate prior conversations with them, but I had no recall. All my memory told me was that, given certain situations, it was probable that I should recognize them. In the last six months, now that I have an understanding of what is going on, I've learned to take notes, write down names with brief descriptions of a memorable peculiarity and rehearse the lists prior to entering a situation when I'm likely to see the same people again. I've learned not to expect to recognize another person as a gestalt until after many meetings. I didn't even recognize a picture of myself taken at a recent work-related meeting.*

*Joe also writes of caretakers' complementing these sorts of disabilities, or being unable to because the child's behavior seems so foreign. When I first read Joe's paper, I wondered whether my impression of my mother's emotional absence could have something to do with my misreading her intentions and because of the disability, I reacted unusually towards her. Maybe so, however other sources do attest to her clinical depression. Likewise, I wondered about my father. If anything, until I was 10 he related more empathically with me than he probably ever has with anyone. After that, I think that I just emotionally outgrew him. Obviously, from this upbringing, there was no chance of someone else performing a complementary function, with the possible exception of the short-term friends that I mentioned, nor any chance of a developing symbiosis.*

*Would it have helped me if I had been diagnosed with a nonverbal learning disability at an early age, even with everything else remaining the same in my upbringing? I have no doubt that it would have, provided I was at an age where I could at least partially understand it. No caretaker could have, but at 10, I think that I would have. This would be where some of the negative affective results could have been avoided. Children born with other sorts of handicaps learn to understand them and are probably less likely to blame themselves for things beyond their control. In the range of possible handicaps, a nonverbal learning disability would certainly not rate highly in its disabling features. Looking back on ways I adjusted to the world, the only truly harmful outcomes came from the elusiveness of the problem. As I said at the beginning, the world translates the effect as being caused by laziness, inattention, or stupidity. It is very similar to the way children with verbal disabilities were looked at prior to the discoveries of such things as dyslexia. With the knowledge that there is a cause outside of my control, I could have learned, at a much earlier age, to modulate the control that I do have, to fit the context.*

*Instead, I reacted by trying to hide my laziness, inattention and stupidity. I withdrew to the extent possible. And, although I'm not sure that Joe follows me on this one, I think that I divided the world rather than myself, thus maintaining a certain coherence. I conceptualize my moves from Chicago to Arlington Heights to Riverside to Evanston (all in the Chicagoland area) as being similar to an untraveled American who only understands English, going from Japan to Australia to Greece. In order to survive, I believed that each situation had to be treated as a "different" world. If, from early on, I had a better understanding of the dynamics of the disability that made this true, maybe I could have applied learning from the past to the present and the future and not forever have felt like "A Stranger in a Strange Land."*

*Discussion*: Many facets of this document deserve comment; however, I will restrict my remarks to two sets of issues: the symptom of withdrawal and isolation as reflective of her efforts to protect her vulnerable sense of self, and the differentiation between unmotivated and motivated conduct as a major source of confusion in the construction of a coherent self-narrative.

The symptom of withdrawal and isolation from others deserves special attention. Among the factors leading to her defenses and symptomatic behaviors was her chronic anxiety, which she medicated with alcohol. The injuries she suffered from others' responses to her and her inability to modulate her affect states led her to feel repeatedly misunderstood, injured, and confused by what occurred. In addition, the absence of alter-ego experiences to provide a linkage with others left her feeling constantly injured and dehumanized, as though she were an alien in this world. She often spoke of feeling like a color-blind person in a world where neither she nor others knew of her color blindness. Everyone, including herself, assumed that she saw what others saw, but when she responded in ways that did not match others' expectations, she saw herself and others saw her as different, if not weird.

Sometimes this sense of alienation leads patients with a nonverbal learning disability to play up their differences rather than hiding them. The deficits become a badge rather than a shortcoming. Some exaggerate the means through which they communicate and, much like people who speak louder when speaking to a foreigner in hopes of being understood, they dramatize their responses, unaware of their inappropriateness. Some turn to oppositional behaviors as a way of defining themselves, thus making it difficult for them to get along with others. Some feel a deep sense of shame, fearing that their deficits are evident to everyone. They isolate themselves, retreat from social contacts, and appear disinterested in people. The devastating deficit in alter-ego selfobject responses manifests as a severe self-esteem problem. In Pat's case, her primary defense was to bury her innermost self behind impenetrable defenses so that she would be invulnerable to further injury. Only in this way could she avoid experiences that would feel devastating to her. This permitted her to maintain an adequate, though shaky, sense of self-cohesion.

Similar difficulties lay in the path to her acquisition of idealizing selfobject functions. Since most selfobject functions are performed nonverbally, they occurred in a domain that was difficult for her to decode. Along the line of idealizing selfobject functions, experiences such as being held safely by a protective caregiver, being reassured by the modulating influence of a caregiver's regulatory interventions, or being admired by a caregiver had a different meaning for her than for others. She misread or could not perceive the affects that her caregivers conveyed. For example, if gestures were misinterpreted, the personal meanings she drew from them would at best only partially reflect what occurred. As a result, she may, in fact, have experienced her mother as unempathic or uncaring. She could not acquire the psychological structures associated with the idealizing selfobject functions. She ended up feeling unsafe and unprotected in ordinary life situations, had difficulties regulating and modulating affects, and was unable to take pride in her own achievements.

Pat's case demonstrates the confusion created in trying to understand oneself in the absence of information regarding the presence of a learning disorder. The division between unmotivated and motived behaviors is totally blurred. The meanings she attached to her experiences were always filtered through the neuropsychological capacities she brought to the events. Her ability to remember, the sensitivity of her sensory system, her capacity to conceptualize, the level of attention she gave to visual-spatial phenomena, and the affects aroused in her by events all colored her experiences so that she perceived the world differently from others. Until her diagnosis was established, Pat struggled to make sense of her life experiences without any information about her neuropsychological deficits. She felt she had a clear perspective on her past, one that attributed many of her difficulties to what had happened to her. Certainly, events in her history gave her ample reason to feel that her mother's depression, her father's coldness, and the many moves to which she was subjected contributed to depression, alcohol abuse, and lack of success in forming long-term relationships.

The problem we confronted in therapy was her incomplete narrative. She attempted to conventionalize her narrative by "normalizing" the events and her responses. Recognition of her differences from others led her to modify her behaviors to make them conform to the perceived norm. She processed these differences as resulting from her not having learned to respond properly, unaware that the sources of her difficulties lay elsewhere. She knew she could not remember faces or attach names to people's faces; she realized that she was not well coordinated, that her handwriting needed improving, that she did not make good eye contact. To all these shortcomings she responded by trying hard to find accommodations, having learned on her own that her verbal strength could help her compensate for her weaknesses. In all these areas she worked hard and succeeded in making up for many of her deficits. The area that remained problematic was social interaction. Although she managed to develop one or two friendships on which she relied for contact with others, she had little awareness of the level of closeness that others could experience but that she could not.

While much in the environment could explain the form her personality eventually took, ignoring the neuropsychological leaves much unexplained. What often remains unexplained in such cases are the differences in children's responses to the same parental environment. Searching for reasons in the different responses that caregivers make to each of their children is often insufficient. One can speculate as to the effect on Pat during her infancy of her inability to recognize faces and its influence on the attachment she formed to her mother or the effect of her not making good eye contact on her mother's ability to respond to Pat as an infant. These and other factors must have played a significant part in the interaction between Pat and her mother. We cannot separate etiological factors from the dynamics; the two are inextricably entwined. The meanings that people extract from their experiences result from the interaction of the two sets of factors.

Developmentally, although Pat's parents may have been willing and able to respond to her needs, serious selfobject deficits developed in part because she could not experience their mirroring, soothing, and comforting. Whatever limitations her parents might have had in their abilities to respond to Pat, her cognitive and affective deficits also interfered with her use of available selfobject functions. She experienced the interchanges as failures in empathy. The resulting selfobject deficits imposed severe limits on the range and depth of her connections with others.

# 11

# ASPERGER'S DISORDER

IN 1944 A VIENNESE psychiatrist named Hans Asperger published a paper entitled "Die Autistischen Psychopathen in Kindersalter," which translates roughly as "The Autistic Psychopathy of Children" (Asperger, 1991). This paper came one year after publication of Leo Kanner's famous paper "Autistic Disturbances of Affective Contact." In contrast to Kanner's paper, which gained immediate recognition, Asperger's paper went unnoticed until 1981, when Lorna Wing translated it and brought it to the attention of English-speaking readers. She also named the disorder Asperger's syndrome. What is remarkable about the oversight of Asperger's paper is that, with some notable exceptions, the children he described were quite similar to those described by Kanner (Wing, 1991). The exceptions point to differences in the two groups of children, both of whom appeared to suffer from some form of autism. While Asperger's disorder is included in *DSM-IV* as a diagnostic entity, there is controversy as to whether, at a conceptual level, the entity should be considered part of the autistic spectrum or a distinctive diagnostic entity related to other social learning disabilities.

The controversy may be traced to differences that Kanner and Asperger observed in the children they studied (Frith, 1991). Kanner observed a group of children who were much younger than the group that Asperger studied. The former highlighted their social isolation, the peculiarities in the language, and the absence of emotional contact with their caregivers. Asperger, on the other hand, saw children who were

## TABLE 11.1
## Asperger's Disorder

A. CHARACTERISTICS:
  1. *Defining features*: *DSM-IV* criteria include the following:
     a. Qualitative impairment in social interaction.
     b. Restricted repetitive and stereotyped patterns of behavior, interests, and activities.
     c. Stereotyped and repetitive motor mannerisms, and
     d. Persistent preoccupation with parts of objects
  2. *Prevalence rates*: Klin and Volkmar quote studies as finding the prevalence rate to be 3.6 per 1,000 (1997, p. 106).
  3. *Sex ratio*: The ratio of male to female is reported to be 4:1.
  4. *Coexisting conditions*: Tentative data, based on case studies, document the presence of depression, obsessive-compulsive disorder, and AD/HD (Klin & Volkmar, 1997, p. 114).
B. DEVELOPMENTAL HISTORY: Wing finds that in infancy and early childhood children with Asperger's lack normal interest in people, their babbling is limited, their shared interests and activities are very reduced, they lack the drive to communicate verbally and nonverbally, speech acquisition is delayed, and they do not engage in imaginative play.
C. DISORDERS OF THE SELF:
  1. *Presenting symptoms*:
     a. *Academic*: The children appear as average or above average in intelligence, often have unusual capacity for rote memorization, and learn to read quite early. They may have difficulties with written work because of their motor problems. As they progress to higher grades, they are less responsive to academic demands and consequently begin to fall behind. This is not because of their inability to do the work, but because they cannot conform to expectations.
     b. *Social*: Their social functioning is impaired as they present as odd, cold, stiff, egocentric and immature. Their capacity for social communication is impaired in the nonverbal area and in the area of pragmatics. In the latter area, they are tangential, engage in long monologues that are unrelated to the context in which they find themselves, and seem to be conducting one-way conversations.

**TABLE 11.1**
**(Continued)**

---

   c. *Emotional:* They appear to lack the capacity for empathy, seem
      not to appreciate that others have feelings and intentions.
2. *Sense of self-cohesion:* They maintain a tenuous sense of self-cohesion and are prone to meltdowns or fragmentation when stressed.
   Among the defenses they use to maintain self-cohesion is that of
   collecting facts in an area where they become expert, although the
   knowledge is not put to any use.
3. *Self-narrative coherence:* The children appear unable to generate a
   self-narrative. This may reflect their fragmented or noncohesive
   sense of self or it may represent their difficulties with pragmatic
   language.
D. INTERVENTIONS:
   1. *Remediation:* Extraordinary interventions are recommended to be-
      gin at an early age. These include occupational therapy, speech ther-
      apy, and socialization groups
   2. *Psychotherapy:* Intervention with mother and child to deal with
      the child's attachment issues, as the child gets older, supportive
      therapy for the family, and possibly individual therapy for the
      child.

---

older than those in Kanner's group, had intact language skills, but had
peculiarities in the area of nonverbal communication. They manifested
unusual interests in peripheral objects. Nevertheless, Asperger felt that
the children formed good attachments to their caregivers and, rather than
interpreting their peculiar interests as pathological, he credited the children with being original, creative thinkers.

The question of whether these two groups of children represent
variants of the same disorder or two distinct disorders remains open. The
different perspectives taken by proponents of each position may be clus-
tered around three different areas of the children's functioning: the cognitive, the affective, and the social. I will discuss each of these briefly, although it is important to keep in mind that some researchers include
some features in their definition that others exclude.

## Explanatory Paradigms

### *Cognitive Features*

The major work done in the area of cognition centers on the construct of "theory of mind" (ToM) (Baron-Cohen, 1997; Baron-Cohen, Tager-Flusberg, & Cohen, 1993). A child is said to have ToM if she understands that other people have minds, that is, if the child is able to understand that mental concepts have referents in the outside world. She is therefore able to attribute to others mental states such as thoughts, feelings, desires, and intentions. This capacity emerges in normal children at around four years of age. A simple test is used to determine whether or not a child has ToM. This test is called the "false belief test." It consists in having the child, the subject of the test, sit before two closed boxes that are distinctively marked. Either a doll or another person is present as an "observer" to the test. The examiner places an object, such as a candy bar, in one of the boxes while the "observer" (the doll or person) watches. The "observer" is then asked to leave the room and the examiner moves the candy bar from one box to the other; meanwhile, the child who is the subject of the test watches. The "observer" is then asked to return to the room. The child is asked to point to the box where the "observer" would look for the candy bar. If the child responds by saying that the "observer" will look for it in the second box (where the candy bar is now placed), that indicates that the child falsely believes that the observer knows that the candy bar has been moved. The child, therefore, does not understand that other people have separate minds and cannot read her mind. The child has a "false belief" about the nature of mind.

Research indicates that children with autism do not develop the capacity for ToM before 11 years of age. Many autistic children never develop that capacity (Mayes & Cohen, 1994). However, children with Asperger's disorder appear to develop ToM at the appropriate time. Yet, if the disorder falls along the autistic spectrum, we would expect that they would be delayed in understanding theory of mind or that ToM would not develop at all. What is unclear is whether the test is valid and gives a correct indication that they have an understanding of intersubjectivity or whether it simply shows that they have the cognitive capacity to solve the problem, even though they do not understand what it is that guides other people's behaviors. If this were the case, this theory of mind test would not be a good criterion for the identification of children with Asperger's disorder. The clinical evidence indicates that children with Asperger's disorder, even those who show ToM on the false belief test, are unable to understand that other people have motives, desires, and beliefs.

Pennington (1991) defines theory of mind as the capacity for inter-subjectivity. The capacity for intersubjectivity—a concept based on Stern's developmental theory—can be traced to the first year, when the capacities for imitation, for the perception of others' emotions, and for communication between the mother and child through joint attention develop. These competencies form the basis for theory of mind, as well as for competent pragmatic verbal communication that begins in the second year. Pennington finds that children with Asperger's disorder have a poor sense of intersubjectivity.

Some researchers on autism find that these children are severely impaired in the area of executive function; it is thought that the impairment also extends to children with Asperger's disorder. However, to date no definitive data exist to affirm or falsify this hypothesis. As we have seen, executive function remains a relatively unexplored area; consequently, future developments may clarify the role it may play in this disorder.

### Affective Features

Those researchers who focus on the affective dimension of children's development find problems in the realms of attachment and empathy (Gillberg, 1992). The data come from clinicians rather than researchers who have conducted systematic studies. Clinicians who collect data from the reports of caregivers are aware of the limitations in the reliability of the information they obtained. This is particularly true when caregivers are required to give historical information about a child's early development for which there is no supporting documentation.

Generally, children with autism are reported to appear normally attached until the ages of 12 to 18 months. At that point caregivers notice a significant absence of emotional attachment. The parents of children with Asperger's disorder do not report similar shifts in their children; rather, they state that the child's attachment progressed normally, but significant interferences in the relationship occurred as the child's behavior deteriorated. My own clinical experience with children with Asperger's disorder is that their capacity for emotional communication is limited. It is difficult to experience a sense of emotional connectedness with them. In fact, I believe that a major differential diagnostic criterion between nonverbal learning disabilities and Asperger's disorder is that it is much easier to make emotional contact with the children with the former disorder than those with the latter.

As to the capacity for empathy, Gillberg (1992) proposes creation of a diagnostic category of children with "disorders of empathy." He suggests that children with Asperger's disorder suffer from such a deficit. The children have diminished interest in engaging others, and their nonresponsiveness to social cues impairs their ability to demonstrate that they understand that others have feelings or that they can identify the feelings others have. However, whether children have deficits in the areas of reception, expression, or processing of affect remains obscure. It is, therefore, difficult to say definitively that the children are impaired in one of these areas, although the indicators are that they process affects quite differently from others.

### Social Features

Finally, with regard to the social domain two main areas of functioning are significant: social communication and the capacity for social reciprocity. There is general agreement that children with Asperger's disorder are impaired in the capacity for give-and-take with others in social situations. They behave as though they have little recognition of the social niceties that are required for even superficial relationships. They are so focused on their own interests that they are oblivious to others. They appear to have little understanding that others have interests, desires, or worries.

Their impairment in social communication is of two kinds. They lack the capacity for nonverbal communication, and they are deficient in the domain of pragmatic language communication. With regard to the former, they manifest many of the features of children with nonverbal learning disability. As a result, some clinicians have diagnosed children with Asperger's as having a nonverbal learning disability. Their impairment in pragmatic language is so significant that it has led one researcher to suggest that it may be the best criterion for identifying children with Asperger's disorder (Bishop, 1989). Descriptively, they act as though conversations consist of monologues rather than dialogues; more accurately, they appear to dialogue with others, but one has the impression that they have scripted the portion of the dialogue assigned to the listener. There is an appearance of communication, but if the listener departs from the script or wishes to change the topic, the communication breaks down. The child with Asperger's disorder continues talking as though the listener is engaged, long after the listener has given every indication of the wish to discontinue the conversation.

Asperger's disorder is far from being understood or completely validated as a diagnostic entity. It remains an open question whether it is a distinct entity from autism or whether it falls on the spectrum of autistic disorders. As a distinct entity, it might be considered a disorder of social cognition associated with an impaired capacity for affective communication. This would leave unexplained the autistic features the children display. If it were considered part of the autistic spectrum, the features that distinguish this disorder from autism itself, such as the presence of motor problems and problems in nonverbal communication, along with high performance on verbal scales, would have to be explained (Volkmar, Klin, & Cohen, 1997, p. 24).

## Characteristics of the Disorder

*Defining features*: The governing definition of Asperger's disorder in use today is that of the *DSM-IV*. It specifies that at least two of four symptoms of the following impairments in social interaction occur: (1) marked impairment in the use of multiple nonverbal behaviors such as eye-to-eye gaze, facial expression, posture, and gestures to regulate social interaction; (2) failure to develop peer relationships appropriate to developmental level; (3) a lack of spontaneous seeking to share enjoyment, interests, or achievements with other people; (4) lack of social or emotional reciprocity. One of four symptoms of the following restricted repetitive and stereotyped patterns of behavior, interest, and activities be present: (1) encompassing preoccupation with one or more stereotyped and restricted patterns of interest that is abnormal either in intensity or focus; (2) apparently inflexible adherence to specific, nonfunctional routines or rituals; (3) stereotyped and repetitive motor mannerisms; (4) persistent preoccupation with parts of objects.

In essence, these criteria combine some of the symptoms of children with nonverbal learning disabilities and high functioning autism. The criteria include the presence of a significant impairment in the area of social functioning, but no significant delay in language acquisition or in cognitive development and self-help skills. (See Table 11.1 and Atwood, 1998.)

The disorder is thought to be familial and probably genetically transmitted. The indications are that this is a lifelong disorder (Tantam, 1988, p. 71). Currently, no specific neuropsychological tests are available to establish the diagnosis of Asperger's disorder.

*Prevalence rate and sex ratio*: Klin and Volkmar (1997, p. 106) quote studies finding the prevalence rate to be 3.6 per 1,000 and the ratio of male to female 4:1.

*Coexisting conditions*: Tentative data, based on case studies, document the presence of depression, obsessive-compulsive disorder, and AD/HD (Klin & Volkmar, 1997, p. 114).

## Developmental History

The first thing to note about the group of children identified as having Asperger's disorder is the great variability that exists among the symptoms of different children. Not every child has all the features of the disorder. Many children exhibit more severe symptoms in one domain of functioning than in another. The variability may exist in part because of differences in temperamental traits, intellectual capacity, capacity to make emotional contact, and area of special interest.

Little is known about these children's early development. Some parents report that the child manifested no unusual traits until she began to interact with other children. Other parents note peculiarities in eye contact as well as emotional disconnectedness. Most children have difficulties mastering motor tasks. They are often clumsy or poorly coordinated. They do not manifest the same sensory problems that children with autism display such as insensibility to heat and cold or indifference to pain. Most children acquire language in a timely fashion. They develop good vocabularies and grammatical usage. However, their speech patterns may be odd or pedantic. In interaction with caregivers, they often do not display affection, cannot be playful, and appear to lack a sense of humor. The unusual capacity for recall of factual material appears quite early and impresses caregivers as a sign of good intelligence.

Problems emerge when the children are exposed to other children. The demand for social interaction quickly exposes their deficits. Being unable to participate in the imaginative play of other children, they isolate themselves and engage in mechanical repetitive activities. At this stage another pattern often emerges, that of noncompliant or negativistic behavior. Caregivers often get caught up in trying to limit the child's

behavior because it is inappropriate or destructive.The child appears not
to understand the demands for social conformity and resists the caregivers' attempts to shape the behavior to make it conform to appropriate expectations. Often the child's resistance is interpreted as disobedi-
ence or defiance, with the result that caregivers quickly get caught in
power struggles that create major disruptions within the family. Caregivers may at this point seek the help of professionals, but unless they
find someone familiar with Asperger's disorder they are likely to be given
advice more appropriate to a child who is a behavior problem than to a
child with a significant disorder. By latency, the child's presentation is
much as the earlier description given.


## Disorders of the Self

### *Presenting Problems*

By early to middle latency, when a child is referred for evaluation, the
family may or may not have obtained an accurate diagnosis. It is important to note that the descriptions that follow represent the features of
moderately severe to severe cases of the disorder, since I want to alert
clinicians to the range of symptoms children present. Severity is not prog-
nostic of the outcome of the disorder; in fact, it is not unusual for the diagnosis to change by the time a child reaches adolescence.

*Academic*:The child appears to be of at least average intelligence and
is well equipped to perform the tasks that his teachers require. Academically, the child generally does well until the demands of complex assignments begin to tax her capacities. At that time, teachers' reports indicate
that the child is seriously underachieving. Classroom work is seldom completed, and homework is not turned in unless the child is supervised by
caregivers and prompted to do so. Handwriting may be poor or sloppy,
and the child has difficulty remaining on task. In addition, moderate to severe behavior problems become evident.These further impair the child's
learning process.Yet, in spite of these difficulties, the child appears to acquire knowledge and performs on tests within age limits. Many teachers
tell caregivers that they suspect that the child has AD/HD. Caregivers report amazement at the child's memory and describe with pride the extent
to which the child has acquired knowledge in a narrow area.The child
may have memorized the names of all presidents and vice presidents, along
with the names of their wives and children, and have detailed knowledge

that would interest only historians. This encyclopedic knowledge seems to serve no specific purpose; rather, it is an end in itself. The child is reported to be concrete and to lack common sense. For example, when a 12-year-old overheard his mother say that she had to go to a wedding rehearsal dinner, the child asked, "Why do you have to rehearse how to eat?"

*Social*: Social problems are ubiquitous. In interactions with peers numerous problems arise. The child is unable to play with other children or share in their activities. Imaginative play appears foreign, as the child cannot enter into the pretend role-playing involved in such games. The child does not seem to understand the rules of games and responds with frustration when they are enforced. Often, peers perceive the child as odd or weird. These impressions are often reinforced by the child's responses to peers, especially when the child appears to be malicious or destructive for no reason at all. Often the child prefers to isolate herself from others to avoid both their negative responses and the frustrations that invariably result from interactions. However, this does not mean that the child does not desire contact with other children; often, in fact, children with Asperger's complain that they have no friends and wish they could play with others. What stands out is that they have no understanding that their own behavior is problematic and contributes to the negative interactions with others.

Interactions with other children are made all the more difficult by the child's problems in nonverbal communication and in the pragmatic use of language. The absence of appropriate eye contact, of facial expressions, of vocal intonation and other modes of nonverbal communication makes it difficult for others to decode the child's communications and feeling states. As described in the previous section, the problems in pragmatic language usage also raise significant barriers to social interactions. The child's communications appear decontextualized, so that others feel they are coming into the middle of a conversation with no clue as to the relevance of what the child is talking about it. The absence of any acknowledgment on the child's part that she is aware that the listener is interested or uninterested makes the interaction totally one-sided. Since children with Asperger's are unable to contextualize the events in their life, most are unable to provide coherent narratives about events they have experienced, stories they have read, or incidents that have occurred with other peers. In addition, they often have problems making transitions from one activity to another; they do not do well in new situations. They have difficulty negotiating with peers in situations that challenge their adaptability and demand flexibility.

Family and caregivers often complain that the children are defiant, negativistic, or oppositional. They report that at times the child resorts to violence if the caregiver insists on the completion of tasks. The child's stance may not be motivated by rebelliousness or a desire to challenge his parents; more likely, it is a response to the complexity of the expectations for performance. The child's resistance may be due to anxiety or the failure to understand what is being requested. Often, what confuses parents is the fact that the child's intelligence leads them to believe that she is quite capable of understanding their requests but refuses to comply.

*Emotional*: In the area of emotional functioning, one finds significant problems. In appearance, the child presents as cold, stiff, and emotionally aloof. When feelings are expressed, they are inappropriate or exaggerated. The child either gets overstimulated and excited or has a tantrum. She appears to engage in few activities that are truly enjoyable. Caregivers express puzzlement at the fact that at times these children will notice minimal shifts in mother's emotional state and ask "What is wrong?" while at other times they appear oblivious to the stresses they cause her. As for empathy, this is a difficult issue to assess. However, whether in play or in conversation, they manifest little shared enjoyment or reciprocity of feeling. They do not seem to take pride in their accomplishments or express joy at occasions such as parties and birthdays.

### Sense of Self-cohesion

Subjectively, the child experiences the external and internal worlds in highly idiosyncratic, distorted ways and attempts to integrate those perceptions into her sense of self. These attempts either fail because the task cannot be accomplished or, if successful, lead to peculiar ways of thinking that manifest as eccentric personality traits. The sense of self-cohesion is tenuous and unstable. When stressed, these children are prone to meltdowns or fragmentation. The child with Asperger's struggles to come to grips with an environment experienced as chaotic, ill defined, and poorly organized. She experiences adults as demanding and intrusive. Adults' reactions seem bewilderingly unrelated to the child's own experience. The child's distress may escalate, resulting in attacks of rage and temper tantrums.

From a subjective perspective, the child does not experience the deficiency as such; rather, she experiences a sense of disorganization and absence of cohesion. Since she is unaware of the missing structures she so desperately needs to cope with the world, the child experiences the parents as failing to provide feelings of cohesion. The deficiencies in the child's basic sense of organization lead to feelings of being chronically on the edge of an anxiety-filled abyss: the fear is of fragmentation and of the loss of what little sense of cohesion may exist.

The child may attempt to reestablish a tenuous sense of cohesion through a variety of defensive maneuvers that may have proved successful at some time. Withdrawing into the exploration of the world of facts is one of the major defensive operations utilized; collecting and storing information becomes the tenuous center around which to organize oneself. The child may also regress to clinging helplessness and infantile forms of behavior that serve to alleviate anxiety and distress. Other behaviors may express disintegrative forces at work in the child or the fragments of the sense of self.

As for selfobject functions, the sense of comfort that adults usually provide cannot be experienced because of the interferences that come from within the child. The child cannot take in the selfobject functions because her inner turmoil overwhelms any efforts to be soothed and comforted. The predominant issue for the child is psychological survival at the level of self-cohesion. What little cohesion actually exists is often the result of defensive operations and so tainted by the immense deficits. Fears of being overwhelmed by feelings of fragmentation or anxious depletion leave little room for development of a sense of self-esteem. Only when cohesion can be reestablished can self-esteem issues be addressed.

Sometimes the caregivers' special sensitivities lead them to respond in ways that fill in the child's missing functions. In those instances, the child's reliance on the caregivers becomes inordinate. What started out as a sensitively benign response to the child's deficiency becomes problematic because of the extent of the deficits. Caregivers can seldom fill in the functions long enough and well enough for the child to sustain a sense of self-cohesion.

*Adjunctive functions and compensations:* As we will see in the case illustrations that follow, these children are often heavily dependent on the adjunctive functions that caregivers and others provide for their survival. Since they seldom internalize or acquire these functions, complications arise in adolescence when they respond negatively to their dependent states. Their age-appropriate but unrealistic wishes to be less dependent on their caregivers lead to a disruption in the relationship. Serious deterioration can occur, to the point where the caregivers find themselves unable to tolerate the disruptions the child causes. At this time, caregivers often begin to explore alternative living arrangements for the young adult. A few adolescents resign themselves to the need for their caregivers and settle within the family, expressing no wish to change their circumstances. In either case the caregivers find themselves having to make long-term plans for the care of their child.

Compensatory functions may develop in adolescents who are compliant and can tolerate taking direction from others. Their skill level determines the complexity of the tasks with which they can deal. Some eventually find a career path in which they can use their abilities, but social difficulties persist.

## Self-narrative Coherence

It is difficult to speak of these children's self-narratives or even of organizing motifs, because of major disruptions in their capacity to organize their experiences into scripts and themes. Consequently, we seldom hear from these children a reasonably sequenced account of how they experienced or felt about a set of events. What we get is a series of disconnected episodes. Here, the question is not whether their narrative is incoherent or coherent, but rather whether they are able to stitch together the threads of their lives meaningfully to tell a listener about it. Their deficits interfere with their capacity to introspect, so that they are unable to report on matters on which they have reflected.

There are good reasons why they have such difficulties formulating a self-narrative. First, their sense of self is so fragmented that it is difficult for them to give a meaningful history of themselves. They may be able to chronicle events in their lives by giving factual details, but such a chronicle is different from giving a history. A history presumes that the events have been meaningfully related to each other. Establishing such relationships involves making connections between events. It is this process that eludes these children. It is as though their experiences are composed of a series of vividly remembered still photographs.

Second, their difficulties with pragmatic language interfere with their communicative competence. Since they are unable to contextualize their communications, they cannot give listeners enough clues about their frame of reference or the transitions they are making between topics to allow the listener to follow what they are saying. The experience of the listener is that of coming into the middle of a conversation and of being unable to orient herself as to what is going on.

Third, they have a problem selecting what is relevant from what is irrelevant in their communications. The listener is left wondering what the child wishes to say. The theory of relevance has been advanced to indicate that in ordinary discourse we automatically screen out elements that are irrelevant to the topic at hand or to the point we are trying to make (Happe, 1991). This makes it possible for a listener to infer our thoughts and intentions and not be confused by the noise created by other distracting ideas. When such a screen is not applied within a dialogue, a failure in communication ensues. It is as though we are witness to another person's stream of consciousness. Children with Asperger's disorder are unable to apply the rules of relevance to their communications.

Fourth, the affects that guide a listener as to what a speaker is feeling are missing in their communications. It is not that their affects are inappropriate but that they are absent; if they are present, they do not seem to clarify what the child is communicating.

These four sets of difficulties reflect not only language deficits but also the absence of internal psychological structure that is indicative of a cohesive sense of self. With no capacity for cohesiveness, there is limited capacity to generate a narrative about oneself.

## Interventions

*Remediation*: Most children with Asperger's disorder require aggressive multiple interventions to assist in their adjustment at the earliest age possible. The earlier intervention begins and the more extensive it is, the more optimistic one can be about the outcome. Recommended interventions include occupational therapy to help with sensory-integration problems that are common in these children, speech therapy to address their problems in pragmatic language and social communication, and social skills training either in individual or group modalities to help them with the problems that arise due to their social ineptness. Any special interests they have should be explored and encouraged. In school these children may be placed in self-contained special education classes, but such placements have their drawbacks, the major one being that the child is deprived of the opportunity to socialize with peers and develop skills in those areas. In addition, special education classes sometimes expose children to the disruptive behaviors of other disturbed children. If the child is mainstreamed, an aide may be required to help mediate the demands made by being in regular classroom, as well as problems with transitions between activities. These children will also require individualized tutoring to assist with their writing skills or other learning problems. Experience suggests that such multiple interventions can positively affect the child's adjustment.

*Psychotherapy*: Psychotherapy plays a variable role in the life of a child with Asperger's disorder. A distinction must be made between therapeutic interventions designed to support the child's caregivers and those directly involving the child. Chapter 14 addresses at length the work that may be done with caregivers. The goal of individual treatment is to help the child establish and maintain a stable sense of cohesion. That goal may be achieved only if the child can develop a set of compensatory structures to make up for the deficit.

## CASE ILLUSTRATION: EMILY

*Referral and presenting problem*: Emily, age four and a half, was referred by a pediatric neurologist, who requested an evaluation to determine whether she might benefit from therapy. She was diagnosed as having a pervasive developmental disorder and serious problems in pragmatic language.

She was observed in the school setting by the school social worker, who saw her as intense, engaging in constant, repeated behaviors clearly suggesting hyperactivity. She was not oppositional or defiant, but restless, squirmy, overactive, and so distractible that any change in noise level or physical movement would cause her to divert her attention, even so far as to go over to the new stimuli, thus distracting others. The teacher was concerned because Emily's conversation seemed unusual and consisted largely of repetitions and echoing.

*Developmental history*: According to her mother, the pregnancy with Emily was normal, but her heart rate dropped during labor. The APGARS were 9 and 9. As an infant, Emily had no trouble with sleeping, sucking, swallowing, or chewing. She did not roll over until seven months old, but she sat alone by five months. She did not walk alone until 15 $\frac{3}{4}$ months or climb onto the couch until age three. She also began to pedal a tricycle at that time. Emily's mother reported slow gross motor development in general. By age three, Emily had walked up stairs, but she then stopped and would no longer walk up stairs. She was not yet toilet trained at the time of the initial consultation.

Mother reported that Emily was listening to stories by 10 months. She said her first word at seven months, had many words by one year, and was putting two words together by 15 months. She related that Emily had not been affectionate as a baby. Ritualistic behavior at bedtime began at that time and became a serious problem.

Emily's preschool teacher described her at age three and a half as a child who very much liked to please. She was fascinated with water play. She loved to simply turn on the faucet and let the water run as she held her hands under its flow. If allowed, she would stay with that activity for an inordinately long time. She also loved the drinking fountain. Emily would not only drink the icy-cold water but also splash her hands in it. She would fill up her mouth with water at the fountain, run down the hall and spit it on the teacher, another child, or on the toys being played with on the carpet. Outdoors, she would take toys from the sandbox and fill them up with water. At first, she was just interested in dumping the water out and watching the flow, feeling and listening it. Later she began to throw water on others as they exited or entered through the back door. When Emily got excited, she ran about on her tiptoes while wiggling her arms and fingers. This was especially noticed in the music room, when the children marched about to drums, cymbals, and bells. She loved music and would stay in the group while music was being played.

Storytime was extremely difficult for her. She could not sit and listen to a story, no matter how short. She became very disruptive to the class. She very seldom sat in the special circle but ran about dumping baskets of toys, kicking them about, pulling books off shelves, stepping and jumping on them. Emily enjoyed the kitchen area, where she would meticulously set the play table with plates, forks, cups, etc., and after working on this for as long as five minutes, take her arm and swoosh the entire contents on to the floor—often with so much force that items would fly through the air and sometimes hurt another child. Emily had to be watched very closely during free play as she often got so excited that she would start running about the room with an object in hand and hit children on their heads, backs, and shoulders.

Emily had an excellent memory, a superior vocabulary, and good syntax. But the "shape" of her dialogue was dysfunctional. She was usually not responsive to open-ended questions, although she would respond to those that required factual answers. She would initiate dialogue, but the content was not clearly relevant to the context. She seemed to associate loosely to events that she brought up in the conversation. Exchanges with her were disjointed and lacked an intelligible flow. At times, she would gesture to indicate that she had some thought, but

would not respond when asked to share it. Often she would begin talking as though someone had been part of an earlier silent conversation
she was having.

*Test results*: A speech and language specialist who tested Emily at
age three years six months reported that Emily's language was excellent for her age. There was no evidence of articulation or auditory
discrimination problems. Her prosody was appropriate but limited.
She had a broad vocabulary and could use words both referentially
to point out things in the environment and semantically to refer to
socially established meanings. Similarly, her syntactic competence
was appropriate, both receptively and expressively. The major area
of deficit was in pragmatics, i.e., the use of language. Simpler, earlier
uses were in evidence, e.g., instrumental/regulatory ("I want x"; "you
take my gum"), whereas the interactional/relational and self-directive
uses were absent or used only rarely. The examiner heard no narration or description of past or future events. Her mother had worked
with Emily on phatic language, e.g., "please," "thank you," greetings,
and "yes," "you know what?," but instances of these were rare or
absent. Equally unusual were uses of language to seek out others (personal function), to inform them of her feelings (emotive/expressive
function), or to share ideas (conative/informative function). The uses
of language to set up contexts or to articulate and solve problems were
also absent. These functions were most noticeable in the absence of
conversational ability.

In summary, Emily's language structures were receptively and expressively at or beyond age level. However, her language usage reflected
her deficits in social relatedness, especially seen in the limited spontaneous expression of affective prosody and in the limited range of
language functions (pragmatics). These strengths and the nature of the
restriction in social-interpersonal uses ruled out a specific language
disability. Cognitively, Emily seemed very bright. When asked how old
she was, she held up three fingers. She knew her alphabet and seemed
to have concepts and categories commensurate with her receptive vocabulary. As far as the examiner could observe (and without specific
testing), her cognitive competence in terms of play, problem solving,
use of objects, perception and memory, etc., seemed age-appropriate.
There were no reasons for concern about her intelligence.
Inconsistencies in performance involving attention, completing tasks
(e.g., putting pocketbook away), role playing, and so forth, could be
attributed to social rather than cognitive deficits.

*Clinical presentation*: In the first session, Emily came in with her mother as prearranged. She paced around the room aimlessly while her mother and I talked. Periodically, she would echo a portion of the conversation her mother and I were having. At one point, when I turned to ask her about what she had heard, she came up close to me and started singing, "Rock-a-bye-baby." Her mother indicated that Emily liked to have that sung to her at bedtime. By then, Emily was draped over my lap. I picked her up and put her on my lap. She lay down as though about to go to sleep while lustily singing the entire song. It was as though she was play-acting a rehearsed scene and I was another actor in the scene. She knew her lines, but there was something wrong with the connection with me that made the enactment seems out of context. When I attempted to elicit a more related response, she pulled away, jumped off my lap, and started pacing the room while continuing to sing the song, seemingly contented to play by herself. As long as I responded to her script, we could be together, but if I modified my responses so that they did not conform to her script, I could not be a part of the interaction. Her mother confirmed my reactions. She related that Emily would often take on the role of a TV character. When another child came to the house to play, she would start playing that character. As long as the other child conformed to the script that Emily had in mind, they got along. If the other child wanted to modify the fantasy, Emily would get upset and refuse to play.

During the second session, when her mother was not in the room, the following dialogue occurred.

Emily throws her head back and closes her eyes, saying, "Wash hair!"

Therapist: "You're thinking about your hair being washed!"

She: "Why do you have to close your eyes?"

Therapist: "So the soap won't get in your eyes?"

She: "Here, you do it!" She indicates that I should throw my head back. "I'll wash your hair—pretend!" I follow her instructions; she gets behind me and touches my head.

She: "Now, you do it to me." Nudges me to get off my chair so she can sit while I do her hair.

I follow her instructions but before I so much as touch her head she gets up. She moves across the room and repeats the gesture of washing her hair.

She: "Sometimes people with dirty hair don't have it washed!"

It is now evident to me that she's talking about something she observed at a hairdresser's.

I respond, "That's right."

She: "Teenagers don't have their hair washed!"

Therapist: "That's right!"

She: "Do you fly in airplanes?"

Therapist: "Yes!"

She: "Do your ears hurt?"

Therapist: "Yes!"

She: "Do you chew gum?"

Therapist: "I open my mouth and swallow, that helps."

She: "If you chew gum it's the same as if you chew gum."

Therapist: "I think so! Have you been on a plane?"

No response.

She: "Will your birthday be soon?"

The session was being held in August and I had told her earlier that my birthday was in July.

Therapist: "Do you mean when will my birthday come again?"

She: "You said July!"

Therapist: "July was last month. Do you know what month this is?"

She: "Will your birthday be soon?"

Therapist: "No, it just passed."

She: "Then you will have a half birthday."

Therapist: "In a few months!"

She was silently thoughtful for a while, paced around the room, then went to the toy cabinet.

*Discussion*: What was striking about these exchanges was that Emily's experiences appeared quite disconnected from any affects. The disjointed conversation of the second session made me wonder about the scripts she had developed. One of the phenomena observed in children with autistic spectrum disorders is what language specialists call "scripting." Scripting involves the incorporation into ordinary conversation of exchanges the child has heard between others either in her context or on television. The conversation with the child has the external appearance of a dialogue, but the content is not meaningful. The child has imported elements of other dialogues into the exchange, much as Emily spoke of hair washing or birthdays, ignoring the fact that these had little to do with what was going on between us.

Given these disruptions, it is practically impossible to interpret the communications as metaphorical expressions of the child's sense of self, except as they represent a fragmented sense of self. What we observe is the state of her inner being in its disjointed and disconnected form.

Furthermore, the nonverbal dimension of communication is absent, so we lack information that might help in decoding what she is saying and linking the scripts she relates with the meanings others attach to the experience. She seems to link events so haphazardly as to make intelligible conversation impossible. The scripts have personal meaning, but they lack the shared meaning.

Some years later, when Emily was 11, a colleague who was testing her asked her parents' permission to give me an update on Emily's situation. In first grade, she had been diagnosed as having Asperger's disorder. Her mother had devoted herself to providing Emily with as many sources of remediation and stimulation as possible. Major efforts were directed at having her learn to identify feelings in herself and others. By the time my colleague evaluated her he found her to display more of the features of a child with a nonverbal learning disability than those of a child with Asperger's disorder.

## CASE ILLUSTRATION: BARRY

*Referral and presenting problems*: Barry was 11 years old at the time of referral. His parents asked for help because of a history of school problems. The school was complaining that he had serious behavior problems. The parents stated that everything had to revolve around Barry, everything had to be on his terms; he was rigid, would not bend on any aspect of his behavior; he had no respect for authority. Teachers avoided confrontations because he had major meltdowns when even small infractions were gently brought to his attention. He then got so upset that a great deal of time had to be spent in calming him down. Academically, teachers complained that he seemed inattentive but usually knew the answers, his handwriting was almost illegible, but reading was not a problem. In gym, his poor eye-hand coordination tripped him up. He did not do well with friends.

Barry was described as a child with "awkward" language. He had always had difficulties expressing ideas, having learned English almost as if it was a foreign language. His parents were concerned that he now seemed more "out of touch" than he had been in previous years and was not as well focused.

Barry was currently in a learning disabilities program for one to two hours a day. He had repeated kindergarten and attended a self-contained learning disabilities program during first grade. He continued in the learning disabilities program with mainstreaming into the regular pro-

gram from second grade on. In addition to his learning disabilities placement, he received special tutoring and counseling from the school psychologist.

*Developmental history*: In addition to language delays, Barry was a
late walker and seemed to have difficulty in visual-motor tasks. Attentional problems were also evident early on, with daydreaming-like
behavior since age two. On the other hand, his parents always found
him to be an easy child to be around. He was affectionate and had
adapted well to family activities, although he seemed to be especially
self-absorbed or preoccupied. He seemed to want to interact with others but was always an outsider socially. His parents felt that this might
have been due in part to difficulties he had expressing himself. His
parents were particularly concerned about Barry's peer relationships
and general social functioning. They also reported that, while watching television, Barry frequently asked his brother to explain what was
happening. He had trouble understanding the social nuances of interpersonal interactions; he did not have friends and spent the summer playing mostly by himself. In addition, he had a long history of
being annoyed by certain noises, smells, and sounds. His parents worried that these particular sensitivities kept him from eating enough.
In spite of these difficulties, Barry was seen as a kind, sensitive boy
who liked to please, displayed curiosity about his world, and very
much enjoyed writing and reading fiction (especially Stephen King
novels).

*Test results*: Barry had his first evaluation by a neurologist at four
years of age. The neurologist found that he had fine and gross motor
delays, low muscle tone, low confidence level, and fears of climbing. In
addition, his attention was poor, he "stared off" into space, was over-
active/exuberant. The diagnosis given at the time was attention deficit
disorder. Occupational therapy was recommended.

Multiple evaluations followed; all came to similar conclusions. Trials
of Ritalin produced no improvement. Occupational therapy that lasted
for years led to improved motor control in some areas.

The psychologist who tested him at age 10 reported that the psychoeducational testing revealed a 38-point discrepancy between his verbal and performance I.Q. on the WISC III, with the performance I.Q. being 82. In the nonverbal areas he was found to have poor spatial
relations, poor visual-motor integration, poor visual figure/ground discrimination, poor visual closure, and poor spatial construction. He was
given a diagnosis of a nonverbal learning disability.

Barry maintained only fleeting eye contact with the examiner who tested him. He held his body somewhat rigidly in the chair and looked slightly away as he expounded at length on topics of interest to him—usually in the categories of science and history. Whereas Barry allowed himself to be interrupted by a remark or comment from the examiner, left unchecked he continued talking in a monologue rather than a dialogue. Even when pausing for the examiner's interruption, Barry picked up the thread of his earlier remarks rather than respond to the observation of the examiner. His verbosity was also evident when he was answering test questions: he often used sophisticated vocabulary and syntax when a single-word reply was all that was required. His speech was characterized by an aprosodic quality, although he was able to change pitch, which he appeared to use as a substitute for inflection. This was most evident when Barry commented on his own test performance as items grew more challenging for him. He often remarked, "Oh, I can't figure this out!" when working with stimulus items such as blocks, cards, or puzzle parts. He also grimaced, flapped his hands, or talked quietly to himself when his efforts did not yield the hoped-for results. These behaviors were also evident at times when Barry did not appear anxious. He responded readily to the examiner's invitation to take breaks and demonstrated a repertoire of behaviors that appeared to be soothing to him. These included leaving his chair to move about the room or talking about his leisure-time pursuits of Legos and reading. He also proved able to assess his own readiness to return to the assessment, stating "Let's finish this now."

His teacher reported that he was easily diverted from tasks and that his behavior was often somewhat inappropriate (e.g., "makes unrelated comments, interrupts"). He was extremely disorganized and required close monitoring by teachers in order to accomplish schoolwork. Although he seemed to have good basic academic skills in most areas, areas of relative weakness were in math, written expression, organization, and study skills. Despite his inability to take responsibility for work completion, he obeyed rules and was respectful. Difficulties in relating to peers seemed to stem from inability to follow rules and social conventions.

*Clinical presentation*: The following is a summary of Barry's second diagnostic session.

He walked in casually, as though he had known me for a long time, sat down, and started talking about events of the past week. He seemed familiar with the therapy process but treated me as though I were his last therapist. He started to tell me about a visit to the zoo as though he were continuing a conversation we had been having, making reference to events that occurred during the visit as though I were familiar with them. He then started talking about dinosaurs, a favorite subject, demonstrating that he had read and knew a great deal about them. Next he described in detail a novel he had read. I had a hard time following the plot, although I was impressed by his great memory for facts.

After he was done with that, he went on to the themes we had covered the previous week, his visit to the Space Center. We talked about the mission to Jupiter. He again impressed me with his knowledge about the planets. But almost in mid-sentence he asked, "What if the earth was a living thing?" After I re-grouped from the sudden transition, I tried to engage him around what he meant. It was evident that he had a very hard time with the concept. I tried to help with an analogy, but he could not carry on a fantasy of what it would be like to think of the earth as a huge plant!

He gave up, switched to talking about planets, but again he seemed more concerned with a recital of facts that with having a meaningful conversation. I tried to see if he could engage in a reciprocal exchange by asking him what he thought about a space station. But this did not produce a response. Instead, he shifted to talking about basketball and the Bulls, going through a recital of statistics about each player. He then switched to talking about being on a basketball team. I asked if he had made any friends with the members of the team. He responded that he was too tired after the games to do anything with the other kids. He then perseverated until the end of the session on how exhausting it was to play and how super tired he was after every game.

At the end of the session, as he rejoined his mother, he asked her about how tired he was after each game. His mother responded gently by saying that sometimes he was tired but not every time. Barry tried to continue the conversation with her as she and I were trying to negotiate a time for the next appointment. He had to be told to wait until we were through to continue the conversation.

*Discussion*: This case illustrates the conceptual problem involved in the diagnostic label of Asperger's disorder. Is this a child with Asperger's disorder or is it more accurate to say that he has a social learning disability? He made little mention of relationships and appeared to have little investment in them. I felt no sense of connection with him. The social skills he displayed seemed rote and unnatural.

*DSM-IV* specifies that the child have elements of both a nonverbal learning disability and autism to qualify for this diagnosis. In this case the autistic elements appear much less prominent than they were in the previous case. In addition, my clinical experience is that with aggressive interventions some children cease to manifest the autistic symptomatology. In at least two cases about whom I was consulted, the child manifested many signs of autism up to the age of four. By the age of 11 or 12 the children were diagnosed as having nonverbal learning disabilities. However, their relationships lacked the capacity for intimacy that children with this disorder manifest. Their social problems were quite prominent. We are, therefore, left with the question of whether a distinct category of "social learning disability" might not be appropriately defined and clinically useful.

Children with autistic spectrum disorders, including Asperger's disorder, remain a puzzle. Until we learn more about the brain functions involved in social interactions and relationships, it may be that we will not be able solve this puzzle.

# III

# TREATMENT
# CONSIDERATIONS

# 12

# DECIDING WHEN TO TREAT

BEFORE INSTITUTING ANY plan for the treatment of a child with a learning disorder, it is essential that a clear diagnosis be made of the child's neuropsychological strengths and weaknesses through psychoeducational or neuropsychological testing. While it is possible for a therapist to arrive at a clinical diagnosis from behavioral observations, these observations alone are insufficient to establish a definitive diagnosis. Therapists need to have a clear idea of the child's specific strengths or deficits, which such testing can provide. If available, projective testing can be very helpful, provided the diagnostician appreciates that visual-spatial problems will affect the child's perceptions and consequently his responses to visually presented projective materials such as Rorschach and Thematic Apperception Test (TAT) cards. If these problems are not taken into consideration, the protocols will often be interpreted as presenting a much more pathological picture than might actually be the case.

Experience teaches us that there is no clear correlation between the "diagnosis" and treatability. Too many variables are involved to permit a simple correlation. The following are some measures that may be used in the appraisal of a child's treatability:

1. *Psychological mindedness.* This includes the child's capacity to think about feelings, to see possible relationships between feelings, attitudes and behaviors, to be aware of fantasies, and to be able to introspect upon these. These are qualities that make up the therapeutic process and add to the ease with which it can

249

be carried on. Intelligence and the capacity for abstraction also play a role.

2. *Capacity to tolerate frustration, pain and depression.* The therapeutic process is inherently a painful one. The very fact that children have to confront past injuries, deal with intense yearnings, and experience feelings of depletion and emptiness makes it inevitable that a level of discomfort will be evoked. Confronting and working through these feelings requires a degree of courage and fortitude. These qualities assist the child in taking risks and in not being dismayed by what is uncovered.

3. *Capacity to recover from regressions.* The management of the regressive flow induced in a child by the process is the responsibility of the therapist. There are times when regressions overtake a child, who has difficulty recovering his former functioning. Recovering from such conditions requires more that empathic interpretations by the therapist. It involves supporting the child's efforts to overcome the regressive pull. Some children are better able to perform this task than others. Some experience their regression with desperation and cannot pull themselves out of it. The resiliency a child possesses will determine the outcome.

4. *Capacity to give up defenses and symptoms and to tolerate resulting destabilizations.* It is a clinical fact that some children tend to cling to their defenses and to their symptoms with rigidity and tenacity. Their vulnerability appears to be such that no matter how delicately the issues are approached by the therapist, they experience the interventions as injuries. It is true that at such times a response may indicate the child's lack of readiness to move on. However, when a child has been in treatment for a prolonged period of time, the question arises as to the child's capacity to make changes.

These are a few of the factors that should be kept in mind in making a determination of a child's treatability. This is not to say that a scale can be constructed with which to measure each child's capacity; rather, the overall impression determines the total assessment.

The issue of recommending individual psychotherapy is complex. The primary consideration is the usefulness of such an approach to children with these types of difficulties. Most of these children are in a good deal of pain. However, they often feel that it is the world around them that needs modifying—not them. This view is not motivated by resistance to acknowledging the existence of problems; rather, it reflects an inability to make the transition from their point of view to that of others. Often the children feel an unmovable conviction as to the correctness of their perspective; it may be impossible to win them over to a different one. These considerations aside, the real question is whether a therapeutic relationship can effect any change that will lead to the alleviation of the child's symptoms. Ultimately, the decision to recommend individual psychotherapy must be made on the basis of the clinical judgment that the child can form an alliance with the therapist and that the process can help the child achieve some of the following goals:

1. manage the anxiety and depression he experiences (a recent study of five- and six-year-olds found that children's play narratives are predictive of whether they will develop anxiety later in childhood [Warren, Emde, & Sroufe, 2000]),
2. attain a cognitive understanding of his neurocognitive deficits and their impact,
3. learn to decode social situations by observing some of the different ways he experiences others and the ways others experience him,
4. break out of patterns of withdrawal and isolation by establishing a dialogue of shared meanings with the therapist,
5. deal with some of the repetitive narcissistic injuries that result from miscommunications with others.

Unless some of these goals are attainable, individual psychotherapy is not indicated. In addition, there are circumstances under which it would be wise to either defer or forgo making a recommendation for individual therapy. Among these circumstances are the following:

1. If the child is functioning adequately because the parents are currently providing sufficient complementarity, and if he is receiving and making use of a variety of interventions, such as tutoring, occupational therapy, and other supports, then it is advisable to schedule periodic reevaluations to determine whether the child is doing well or is in need of intervention.
2. If, following diagnosis, the child needs to experience some successes in academic areas prior to beginning to deal with the injuries and pain caused by his deficits, then a period of psy-

choeducational intervention is indicated prior to instituting treatment.

3. If the child is currently receiving support from several resources and many professionals are involved, the addition of still another person in the child's life may be experienced either as a burden or as someone who is indistinguishable from others. Treatment should then be postponed to a more propitious time. Under these circumstances, providing guidance to the parents may have a greater overall impact than seeing the child individually.

4. If the child's defenses are well integrated into his personality structure, so that he is functioning reasonably well within the narrow confines of the domain he has chosen, then, although it would appear that the child has arrived at a premature closure to his development, it may be best to leave well enough alone and postpone intervening.

5. If the family's dynamics or circumstances are such that the child's involvement in treatment may threaten a tenuous balance, either a different modality or a postponement of treatment is recommended.

6. If the therapist feels shut out by the child, so that no matter how hard the therapist tries to enter the child's world no access seems available, the wisdom of psychotherapeutic intervention at that moment ought to be evaluated carefully. Alternatives such as educational therapy, art therapy, dance therapy, children's theater, or other interventions need to be considered. After the child has had some successes and positive experiences in other contexts, he may be ready for the task of examining what he does that contributes to derailing dialogues.

## The Therapeutic Dialogue

A fundamental tenet of psychodynamic approaches to treatment is that diagnostic assessment is an ongoing process. What this means in the treatment of children with learning disorders is that the therapist must be constantly alert to the role of the context and the child's competencies in any material he presents, whether it is historical material, reports on the child's current life, or responses to the therapist. By keeping this framework in mind, the therapist should be able to distinguish whether, on the one hand, the child is motivated by psychodynamic factors or, on the other, his conduct reflects neuropsychological factors.

I conceive of the exchanges between child and therapist as a therapeutic dialogue that begins with the initial evaluation and continues
throughout the entire treatment. It requires that the therapist immerse
himself empathically in the child's experience and narrative. For the therapist to understand the child's motives and the personal meanings embedded within the child's narrative, he must create an atmosphere that
is conducive to having the child share his most intimate thoughts and
feelings. The dialogue is engaged when the child feels it is safe to communicate his feelings and when a set of shared meanings is created between the child and the therapist.

At first, the child presents, verbally or nonverbally, his incomplete
and/or often incoherent narrative. The therapist constructs his own interpretation of that narrative by including an understanding of the nature of the neuropsychological deficits, the child's context, and their impact on the child's development. The process then takes the form of an
exchange of narratives between the child and the therapist. Eventually,
child and therapist coconstruct a narrative that incorporates aspects of
both narratives. This occurs within the context of a set of experiences
in which the child enacts aspects of his past.

### The Therapist's Contribution to the Dialogue

The therapist brings to the clinical setting his world view as well as a
set of personal and shared meanings woven into a narrative. These include the therapist's theoretical framework and his beliefs as to what is
curative about the process. The "data" that the child presents are interpreted and shaped by these factors. While the therapist may wish to make
the "data" fit into his narrative, he has to apply restraint and discipline
by allowing for the possibility that the child may have drawn entirely different meanings from those events than he would have drawn. The therapist must then build a set of meanings into his narrative through which
the personal meanings of the child's narrative can be translated and understood. The child's narrative is understood by the therapist through the
therapist's own narrative construction.

From the initial moments of the encounter, the therapist engages in
dialogue with the child at a variety of levels, nonverbal as well as verbal,
affective as well as cognitive. The particular content around which the
dialogue occurs has conscious and unconscious dimensions. Latency age
children communicate primarily through the metaphors of play and fantasy. As child therapists our primary tools are toys and materials that lend

themselves to maximizing the child's ability to communicate. I recommend the exclusion of games from the clinical setting, except possibly for checkers, because the introduction of games that structure the relationship between the participants interferes with the free flow of fantasies. Games shift the focus to issues of competition, competence in playing the game, and other extraneous factors. The exception to the rule is checkers, since this game is effective in engaging some children whose expressive capacities are initially limited or inhibited. Even then, when the child chooses to play checkers, I quickly shift the structure of the game by suggesting that we play "give-away-checkers." This game reverses the rules, making the "winner" the "loser," that is, the person who gives away the most checkers is the winner. This moves the game away from its traditional function and turns it into a fun, if confusing, activity. Children respond with confusion at first, but soon relax and invent all kinds of variations to the rules. This loosens the structure of the activity and allows us to enter into the realm of fantasy.

Once fantasies are elicited through play, drawing, or dialogue, the therapist's task is to understand the meaning of the activity. Having a clear grasp of the child's context and neuropsychological strengths and weaknesses allows the therapist to interpret the content of the fantasies as allegories in which the child is the protagonist. These allegories represent the child's unfolding self-narrative. Themes emerge that give an indication of the areas with which the child is struggling. As the child assigns the therapist a role in these stories, elements of the transference are highlighted. These give a clue to the significance others may have played in the child's life. During this phase of the treatment, it is essential that the therapist not guide the development of the story. Introducing other characters or intruding into the unfolding content will vitiate the course of the child's story and contaminate it with the therapist's own.

This dialogue produces a shared experience, which at first may have personal meanings for each of the participants. This shared experience explicitly or implicitly becomes the focus of a discussion in which therapist and child test out whether their meanings are indeed shared. From a developmental perspective this discussion begins to reveal the extent to which the child has personalized meanings and the extent to which child and therapist can work together to translate these personalized meanings into meanings that are comprehensible to both.

Finally, the therapist's interventions may range from silent sharing to verbal comments reflective of the process within the dialogue. Which of these is introduced depends on what appears appropriate at that moment. Technique may play a role in what is done, but, as we shall see, the process dictates technique, not the other way around. The thrust of the exchanges is to permit something to occur that not only is different from what has occurred in the child's past, but also enables the child to give new meanings to old experiences through their integration in his sense of self. I wish to underscore that understanding the child is a necessary condition to entering into the child's world and creating the condition that makes it possible to form an alliance. But understanding the child, in the absence of a shared experience of what the child feels, leads to an intellectual exercise that is of limited therapeutic usefulness. By the same token, having a shared experience of the meanings may have therapeutic value but does not further the child's integration of those experience into his self-narrative.

Therapy, then, as an applied science or as "practice," is an interpretive activity through which the therapist reads the signs and symptoms the child brings and arrives at a narrative that "explains" what he observes. As an interpretive activity the narrative goes beyond the phenomena at hand to what is hidden. The task for the therapist is to reveal to the child what is hidden by providing explanations that fill the gaps in the phenomena and extend understanding to include a broader set of shared meanings. In particular, the therapist is responsible for providing explanations of the ways in which the symptoms caused by the learning disorder have contributed to the personal meanings the child has attached to events. These explanatory interventions bear a complex relationship to the initial narrative the child presents. This is in part because the child has faith that the narrative being created has greater efficacy to heal than the one he possessed. The therapist understands both the old and the new narrative and can translate the child's narrative into the one that is endowed with the power to bring about the experience of self-cohesion. The narrative the therapist possesses also includes prescriptions that can bring about a result that is desired by the child. The child's narrative alone could not bring about that result. Another way of thinking about this is that the therapist's narrative is coherent with, and capable of being assimilated into, the numerous other narratives to which the culture subscribes. It is more encompassing, not more "correct."

### The Child's Contribution to the Dialogue

The child's unfolding narrative reveals the motifs that have organized his self-narrative. It uncovers feelings associated with past experiences, some of which remain unintegrated. Within this dialogue, what is replicated is the child's inner world, with all the meanings attached to it. At times the mere fact of sharing a meaningful experience can provide relief for the child. The sense of isolation and aloneness is dissolved. Having originally experienced the events in the absence of selfobjects that could be responsive, the child lived alone with the pain. The opportunity to now have someone participate in the retrieval of those events and to resonate with the meanings they had may in itself be curative. Such experiences facilitate the integration of the affects associated with that experience, and lend meaning to them even though they may not be fully integrated into the child's self-narrative. The child may begin to feel restored and healing can occur.

The relationship between the therapeutic dialogue and the dialogue that has occurred with caregivers during development is complex. At a psychodynamic level the dialogue in the here-and-now reflects the personal meanings that were encoded by the child from past experiences. It also reflects aspects of the narrative motifs that have become embedded during development. To that extent the child sees the present through the past. At the developmental level the dialogue and the unintegrated meanings have left gaps in the narrative and are evident only in the incoherences that are noted in the process. Furthermore, the child's cognitive competencies and temperamental traits continue to operate with whatever compensations he has developed. The drive for complementarity in the areas where deficits exist manifests itself in the present.

A tension arises between the child's perspective and that of the therapist. This is related to the personal meanings and expectations that the child brings and the therapist must understand. This tension is revealed when child and therapist do not share the same meanings of events that occurred to the child. The child sees aspects of the present through his neuropsychological deficits and his past. At first, the therapist does not share this perspective. The reinterpretations given by the therapist serve as points of departure for the child to engage in the dialogue.

### Nonverbal Communication during the Dialogue

Nonverbal communication plays a critical role in the therapeutic dialogue, particularly with children who communicate primarily through play. It is important to begin by making some distinction between preverbal and nonverbal means of expression. The importance of this distinction is found in the meanings given to a child's communication and the source to which an enactment may be attributed. Confusions arise from the failure to make a distinction between preverbal and nonverbal forms of communication in at least two areas relevant to clinical practice. One source of confusion stems from a belief that events that cannot be verbalized and hence are nonverbal must have originated in the preverbal period. A second source results from the belief that all nonverbal communication must be capable of being translated verbally.

It is a truism that all preverbal communication is nonverbal, but not all nonverbal communication is preverbal. Developmentally all exchanges between caregiver and infant occur both preverbally and nonverbally until the infant acquires verbal language. Preverbal experiences are encoded nonverbally. They are stored in implicit (or procedural) memory as either iconic or indexical signs. Facial expressions, which represent how people feel, are an example of iconic signs. Gestures are examples of indexical signs; they point to something beyond themselves. As Winnicott (1960) brought to our attention, the earliest dialogue between caregiver and infant occurs through gestures. He conceptualized transitional phenomena as emerging in the preverbal period but extending into adulthood in the form of a nonverbal language that is expressed through dance, music, graphic arts, theatrical activities, etc.

Prior to the acquisition of language, children use gesture to communicate in two different ways: (1) when they point to an object, they are declaring that the object is present; (2) when they reach toward an object that is out of reach, they are requesting that object. As children acquire verbal language these nonverbal modes are integrated smoothly into their communicative styles. Much of the content of the nonverbal style appears to be acquired through identification with caregivers.

Nonverbal signals, e.g., gaze, posture, gestures, and facial expression, are conveyed and received primarily through the visual channels. We look at people's facial expressions; we track their gaze, whether or not they are making eye contact; we take note of their gestures and posture as significant in their emphasis of a point or in reflecting their general mood. The second important modality involves the auditory channel, of which prosody is a major mode of communication. Prosody is the vocal intonation with which we express ourselves. Some people's voices are highly inflected while others' are relatively uninflected.

As children acquire language, these nonverbal modes are integrated smoothly into their communicative styles. Kohut's (1971, 1977, 1984) self-object functions result from the encoding of iconic signs rather than from verbal encoding of experiences. Grandiosity, omnipotence, and idealization as constructs are verbal articulations of these nonverbal experiences.

As we have seen from the discussion of explicit and implicit memory, the verbal and the nonverbal are two separate domains of communication that extend throughout the life span. After the acquisition of verbal language these nonverbal signs continue to exist within a nonverbal language system. They need not be translated into verbal signs to retain their meaning. The nonverbal domain parallels and is entwined with the verbal domain; it is neither more primitive nor more infantile. It extends into adulthood and ranges beyond transitional phenomena. The concept of "primary process" has been used to describe the domain of the dynamic unconscious, that is, the aspect of our mental lives that is repressed because it is primitive and unacceptable. As unconscious content, primary process is also nonverbal. This has led to the traditional view that interpreting the unconscious, translating its contents into verbal language, helps to bring the unacceptable into consciousness and resolve internal conflicts. While primary process is nonverbal, not all nonverbal processes are part of primary process.

For the therapist, the goal of therapy is not necessarily to translate the nonverbal into verbal content. Such a view presupposes that healing occurs only when "primary process" nonverbal unconscious contents are verbally translated and brought into conscious awareness. The goal of therapy, to my mind, is to help children integrate affect states that are overwhelming and unintegrated into a coherent self-narrative. As I discussed earlier, these unintegrated affect states are a source of incoherences in the child's narrative. Since children favor nonverbal forms of expression, the goal is attainable by creating a dialogue that uses these modes of communication to assist in the integration of those affects.

Effective child therapists are expert at decoding nonverbal communications. Nonverbal modes—play, drawings, pantomime—are part of the medium through which the dialogue with children is conducted and affects are expressed. All too often the meaning of a play sequence is misinterpreted because of the therapist's desire to articulate verbally what the child seeks to express. Such misunderstandings can only lead to the derailment of the dialogue. To insist that children grasp verbally the essence of the dialogue in which they are engaged is like asking that they learn a foreign language before engaging in the therapeutic dialogue. The role of interpretation is not limited to verbal explanations; there are, in addition, nonverbal messages implicitly communicated to the child. Therapeutic verbal and nonverbal communications may serve to create new meaning for experiences or to place events in a context that is different from that conceived by the child. These interventions not only provide symbolic reinforcement of the therapist as someone who has shared the experience with the child but also have a healing effect (Lyons-Ruth, 1998; Stern, 1998).

# 13

# THE THERAPEUTIC PROCESS

Giving a written description of the therapeutic process is like offering a course on anatomy to someone trying to understand the meaning of life. The dissection of the live process of therapy fails to convey the essence of the interaction. Yet, writing about therapy is a necessary evil, not only because it is important to tell others what we do, but also because it imposes upon us the discipline of conceptualizing and articulating what we do. Whether we think of ourselves as scientists wishing to arrive at the laws that guide human behavior or as historians reconstructing the motives that drive patients, we must examine the instruments through which these ends are achieved.

Therapy with children and adolescents with learning disorders is, in some respects, no different from therapy with any child. In other respects it is quite different. The major difference is that the therapist brings to the process a perspective that is informed by the contributions the context and the child's competencies make to the child's psychodynamics. In this chapter, I do not undertake to develop a model of the therapeutic process. A model implies a set of standard techniques that are applicable to all patients. While such techniques may exist, the creative aspect of the therapeutic process cannot be captured by such an approach. This is especially true for work with children with learning disorders, where the modes of interaction involve play, drawing, fantasy games, and an entire repertoire of nonverbal modes of communication. In addition, treatment with these children necessitates work with their parents, their teachers, tutors, and other professionals who are closely involved with them.

The goal of the therapeutic process is twofold: (1) *to engage the child in an experience* in which she can relive an old pattern of interaction and create a new pattern in which feelings are deeply engaged and made more meaningful, and (2) *to cocreate a narrative with the child* that helps her understand her strengths and weaknesses, what happened to her historically, and how to use that knowledge in dealing with future situations. The first set of transactions is directed at strengthening the cohesiveness of the child's sense of self, while the second is intended to help her integrate past experiences into her self-narrative. As stated in the previous chapter, experience without understanding may be beneficial but is limited because it leaves the person in the dark as to what exactly occurred and what strategies to consciously bring to bear in future situations. Understanding without an experience in which to anchor the understanding is pure intellectual knowledge. Such knowledge may be helpful, but it may not immunize the child from responding, both affectively and behaviorally, in old ways to current situations.

In the transference, the child unconsciously relives old patterns with little understanding of the motives for her conduct. As new experiences occur between the therapist and child, the therapist has an opportunity to reframe the child's understanding of her self-narrative and can help her create an entirely new self-narrative. Having an understanding for her conduct—that is, having a narrative interpretation that ties disparate events together—provides a road map that serves as a guide for the child. This is a necessary component of the therapeutic process. The therapist's interpretations or explanations serve to reveal the nature of the patterns and help the child begin to build new patterns for conduct. As the child informs the therapist of the narrative themes that shape the enactments, the therapist gains an understanding of the explanation the child has given to herself for her conduct.

In order to understand the treatment process with these children, I introduce the term *moments** to describe nodal aspects of the process

---

*I initially borrowed the term *moments* from Pine (1985) (see his Chapter 4, Moments and Backgrounds in the Developmental Process, pp. 38-53), although I give the concept a different interpretation from his. Recently, I discovered that the term is being used by the Process of Change Study Group, Boston, of which Daniel Stern and Louis Sander, among others, are members. This group (Sander, 1998) uses the term "moments of meeting." Their use of the term is different from either Pine's or mine.

at different phases of the treatment. These moments consist of specific interactions in the dialogue between therapist and child. During this dialogue feelings associated with past experiences and narrative themes emerge. Those moments do not necessarily occur sequentially but arise episodically; they become organizing events that capture for the therapist the essence of the issues with which the child is struggling. As such, they present opportunities for the therapist to intervene through supportive statements, interpretations, or other interventions.

## Moments

The therapeutic dialogue with children with learning disorders may be deconstructed as series of moments (Pine, 1985) in which nodal occurrences are in the foreground of the interaction. By foreground I mean that the dialogue is experienced as having an ebb and flow during which attention gets focused on a particular set of affect-laden and meaningful interactions. Therapists often theorize that the therapeutic process unfolds in an orderly sequential way and that the movement is from one phase to another—from beginning to middle to termination phase. This sequential approach does not sufficiently appreciate the fluid, dynamic, and untidy nature of the dialogue with a child with a learning disorder. In speaking of different *moments* it is possible to view the process as malleable, oscillating from one position to another. The three moments to which I will refer are *concordant moments, complementary moments,* and *disjunctive moments* (Palombo, 1985; Racker, 1968, 1972).

Concordant moments are episodes that occur when the foreground issues are related to the therapist's efforts at maintaining a connection with the child and at creating an environment of safety and confidence. Under the concordant moments, I subsume those issues that have traditionally been classified as pertaining to the therapist's empathy for the child, the creation and maintenance of a holding environment, and the fostering of a working alliance between child and therapist.

Complementary moments are episodes that occur when the foreground is occupied by the *transference* or *nontransference* dimensions of the process. In those moments when the transference elements are activated, the motifs of the child's narrative emerge to shape the interaction between the child and the therapist. The therapist must be open to experiencing those motifs and understanding the impact they have had on the child's life. Motifs from the therapist's narrative also arise within the therapist in response to the child's motifs. These inevitably intrude into the process; they are part and parcel of the exchanges. They cannot be understood as undesirable; rather, it is through the interplay between the two sets of motifs that a better understanding of the child's communications occurs. At times, nontransferential elements are activated that are related to the child's neuropsychological deficits. In those moments, the child may be seeking adjunctive functions from the therapist. The search for complementarity is motivated by the child's inability to function adequately without that assistance. The therapeutic dilemma for the therapist lies in how to respond to what the child perceives that she needs.

Disjunctive moments are episodes during which disruptions in the dialogue occur. The disruptions may be due to factors related to the therapist or the child. When such a disjunction occurs the treatment is in crisis; it is essential that the therapist heal the rupture and reestablish the concordance between himself and the child. It is my view that in those moments the therapeutic process engages both child and therapist at the deepest levels of their senses of self. Countertransference reactions that stem from the therapist's own problems are subsumed under disjunctions; however, the concept is meant to include a much broader set of contributors to the disruptions that occur between child and therapist.

### Concordant Moments: Immersion into the Child's Experience and Narrative

The therapeutic process begins with the establishment of concordant moments in which the therapist's efforts are directed at understanding the child's psychic reality, or the meanings of what she reports. By becoming immersed in the child's view of the world and resonating with the child's experiences, thoughts, feelings, and memories, the therapist enters that reality. The child must experience the therapist as being attuned to her feelings and responsively appreciative of their significance. Through his attuned responsiveness, the therapist begins to understand the meanings to the child of what she brings to the sessions. As the therapist experiences what the child experiences, he conveys, directly or indirectly, the assurance to the child that the clinical setting is a safe place in which no intentional harm will be inflicted.

*Empathy*. Kohut defined empathy as the tool through which we vicariously introspect our way into a patient's experience (Kohut, 1959).

Stern enlarged the definition to include the experience of affect attunement (Stern, 1984). Stolorow emphasized the more cognitive aspect of
understanding the meaning of an experience to a patient (Stolorow,
Brandchaft, & Atwood, 1987). Each of these definitions underscores the
role of nonverbal communication in the clinical process. When we at-
tune ourselves to patients or resonate with their emotional state, we use
nonverbal clues to guide us in our understanding of the child's experience. We listen to patients' verbalizations, but we also note their facial
expressions, the direction of their gaze, their prosody, body posture, and
other cues that enhance our capacity to enter into their experience. We
form impressions of the child's self state through reading these nonverbal cues and respond to them with appropriate verbal and nonverbal
interventions.

Empathy, as a tool for gathering data about the child's experience, is
used to read nonverbal communications while experiencing with the
child what he feels. We do not need to translate the child's nonverbal
feelings into words for us to understand what the child is communicating. Through empathy we can tap into areas of the personality to which
the child's verbalization may not give us access. Understanding a child's
experience occurs through an understanding of the personal and shared
meanings she derived from those experiences.

An important step in the empathic process is that of matching affective states. The concepts of attunement, alignment, and resonance describe a process by which caregivers attempt to match the affective state
of an infant. This capacity to grasp or to understand is rooted not simply
in cognition, but also in the contextual relations experienced by, and affective states evoked in, the child. One determinant of the meaning of
an utterance is the context. The therapist's alignment with the child's affect state while grasping the meaning of the experience to the child defines an act of empathy.

The reliability of any information acquired through empathic observation is constrained by the limits of the therapist's capacity to be attuned to and understand another person's experiences. Therapists face
a difficult problem in their attempts to empathize with the experience
of a child with a neuropsychological deficit. If the therapist has no knowledge of learning disorders he may grasp intuitively the source of some
of the child's struggles but will not understand their origins as related
to neuropsychological deficits.

During the decades when psychodynamically oriented therapists
had no knowledge of neuropsychological deficits, much good thera-

peutic work occurred. However, the work was incomplete because the paradigm did not account for these deficits. A detailed understanding of the nature of those deficits is essential to gaining an empathic understanding of the child's struggles. Empathizing with the child who has dyslexia presents therapists with a very different experience from empathizing with the child who has Asperger's disorder. Neglecting to incorporate an understanding of each of those disorders will lead to a failure to understand the child.

I am reminded of an adolescent with severe dyslexia who was failing most of his high school subjects. He often came to sessions angry that he had to be in treatment for his problems. He would open the sessions with contemptuous remarks about my waiting room magazine selection, the office furniture, or even my car. He compared me to his father's therapist, who had a larger office, more expensive furniture, and an expensive car. It was a hard for me not to feel annoyed and injured by these contemptuous remarks. The temptation to respond defensively or to retaliate for the child's attacks was also hard to control. Only after I could take these assaults in stride could I point out to the adolescent how badly he must be feeling because of his failures and how he dealt with his disappointment in himself by directing his anger at me. The contrast he drew between his father's therapist and me paralleled how he felt. He felt that others were much better endowed and more competent that he was. Had I not known of his dyslexia, I might have interpreted his comments as motivated by other dynamics, such as oedipal competitiveness or narcissistic self-centeredness.

During concordant moments the therapist seeks to establish an environment in which the child can feel safe and understood. A number of factors enter into the creation of such an environment. The therapist conveys a sense of caring and concern by his demeanor and attitude, as well as a readiness to be responsive and helpful. Such a stance is characteristic of the "holding environment" (Winnicott, 1965, p. 240). Additionally, this position has been described as a "working relationship" (Keith, 1975). By being nonjudgmental, by assuring the child of the confidentiality of all transactions, and by consistently trying to maintain a perspective that is from within the child's experience, the therapist establishes an alliance with the child. By being open and receptive to feelings, the therapist strives to permit the child to experience an optimal level of intimacy. The therapist's depth of understanding is related to his knowledge of the effects of the learning disorder on the child's development and personality and his ability to convey that understanding to the child. A therapist who lacks that knowledge is prevented from fully empathizing with the child and understanding her psychodynamics (Ornstein, 1976, 1981, 1986).

The atmosphere created in the clinical setting is always dictated by the standards of social propriety consistent with the cultural context in which the therapy is conducted. It assumes an unqualified acceptance of and respect for the child. This demeanor is not just part of the empathic stance that is proper for the conduct of the therapy but also implied by the code of conduct to which society, and the professional code of ethics, subscribe. Deviations from such standards can, in more serious forms, represent a betrayal of the child's trust. At times minor deviations from social propriety, such as not acknowledging a significant event in the child's life or refusing to respond to questions but not explaining why, insert into the setting an element of artificiality that cannot help but bring discomfort and/or embarrassment to the child. The deviations may be perceived as reflective of the therapist's detachment or wish to exert power. Since the therapist owes the child safety and respect as a condition of therapy, these deviations should be explained to her. Failure to adhere to these standards may introduce an iatrogenic element that will add to the child's suffering.

Finally, maintaining a concordant position is at times equivalent to being available to share meaningful affective experiences. Such responses raise the hope in her that the therapist will acknowledge and respond to her unsatisfied longings. For the therapist to allow himself to be so experienced requires the discipline of keeping his own longings into the background. This disciplined self-denial constitutes the essence of professional integrity.

*Concordant responses.* It is possible to conceptualize a variety of concordant responses that constitute therapeutic interventions, primarily either supportive remarks that indicate to the child that the therapist understands or remarks directed at the enhancement of the alliance. Most children with learning disorders begin treatment with some initial resistances, which must be recognized and worked through. These resistances are often motivated by the fear that their problems will be dealt with much as they have been by others. The empathic atmosphere may raise children's hopes and transference expectations, although they are likely to remain wary that their fear will be realized. Time and acquaintance with the therapist can help work through some of these resistances, and their articulation through interpretations, which convey a general understanding of their source, may speed the process along.

Occasionally interpretations of a child's resistance to the establishment of a concordant position might also be made. Adolescents, for example, are often resistant to the process itself, experiencing the therapist's attempt to be empathic with their experience as intrusive. They seem to actively repel any effort at being understood. Such patients drag their heels into treatment, resentfully complying with caregivers' wishes. Their engagement is initially quite difficult. Rather than responding to these patients in an adversarial way, therapists might think of them as one would of children who are burn victims and require physical therapy in order to be rehabilitated. The therapeutic process itself is agonizingly painful and may even appear to be traumatizing. Keeping their distress in mind makes it easier to respond with gentle firmness, rather than harshly and punitively. The resistance must be addressed with the utmost sensitivity. General interpretations consisting of no more than a comment about the distrust of adults may be more effective than other means.

Once these initial resistances are addressed the process may unfold. Some of the archaic selfobject needs begin to surface as the transference develops, and what Ornstein (1990, p. 51; see also 1981, 1983, 1986) calls the "curative fantasy" becomes activated. This fantasy, which is often unconscious, embodies within it the unfulfilled longings contained within the deficient self. Another way to think of this fantasy is to understand it as the activation of the child's hope for self-restoration. The hope is that at last relief from the chronic suffering is in sight—something will change things radically for the better.

## Complementary Moments

In earlier chapters, I wrote of the complementary functions children with learning disorders use to maintain a sense of self-cohesion; I referred to selfobject as well as adjunctive functions. In the context of the treatment process, I return to the construct of complementarity and extend its meaning to describe part of what occurs between the child and the therapist. The application of this construct to the therapeutic process highlights the parallels between therapy and the functions that parents perform to enhance the child's growth and development. It also sheds light on the replication of those patterns in the transference.

A complementary moment may be said to occur when the therapist replicates the childhood context as the child experienced it. One set of complementary moments is related to the *transference of selfobject func-*

*tions and narrative themes*; the other is related to the performance of adjunctive functions by the therapist, which I designate as a *nontransference reaction.* Let me first discuss those moments that are related to the transference dimension, and then deal with those that are related to the nontransference dimension or the search for adjunctive functions.

*Selfobject transferences and narrative themes.* Broadly speaking, transference is the perception of the present from a particular perspective in the past. It is the arena in which the child reenacts and reexperiences old selfobject needs and themes from his narrative.

With regard to selfobject needs, if we were to contrast Kohut's view with Freud's, we might say that Freud understood patients as wanting something forbidden in the transference (the oedipal object), while Kohut saw them as wanting something they needed (selfobject functions). Selfobject transference then is the evocation of the archaic, infantile experiences that resulted from the frustration of selfobject needs. The revival is the reawakening of the uncompleted developmental sequence, not the reemergence or reenactment of an unresolved conflict.

What is recreated is not the selfobject deficit itself—it would make no sense to speak of the rearousal of something that does not exist— but the desire for particular kinds of responses or the disavowed feelings related to those deficits. The positive transference is the expectation that the new relationship will in some magical fashion provide the patient with the longed-for selfobject functions, that the current relationship will provide what was missed or will repair the injury produced by past events. The negative transference is the expectation that the therapist will respond as others had responded in the past. The child will then be retraumatized. I will deal with the latter aspect of the transference in the section on disjunctive moments.

From the perspective of the child's self-narrative, the transference represents the enactment of the motifs that have organized her experiences. The form the enactment takes reflects the way in which the incoherences in the narrative organized the child's life historically. The clinical setting is, then, a microcosm of the child's current life. It reflects the child's organizing motifs in the here-and-now. Those dynamics reflect the unintegrated personal meanings the child has retained. Enactments often represent the best integration the child has made of her experiences. They represent the "psychic reality" or the narrative interpretation of the child's past. In this sense the historical reality may not have been distorted, because the experience was integrated within the cognitive-affective givens of the child. What makes these experiences problematic now is not that they are fantasies, but rather that they represent a view of reality that has remained walled off from the rest of the child's system of meanings and so has not been integrated with them into a coherent view. The walling-off itself may have been due to an attempt at either repression or of disavowal of the affect.

Since I have dealt as some length in the case illustrations with selfobject transferences, let me focus here on two particular narrative themes I have frequently encountered in the transferences of children with learning disorders: emplotment and conventionalization.

*Emplotment.* The concept of emplotment (Kerby, 1991) is used in narrative theory to delineate the ways in which patients become characters in other persons' narratives or become engulfed by their own expectations of how their self-narrative ought to unfold. As we have seen in Chapter 5, children can become emploted in their caregivers' narratives when they try to conform to their expectations. They may take on the motifs of the narratives of those they wish to please. Caregivers' self-narratives include the meaning the child has for them as well as the role the child is to play in their lives. In effect, the parents experience their infant as a character in their own plot. If the child appropriates these attitudes and behaviors and includes them as subplots within her narrative, she thus becomes emploted into the caregivers' narrative characterizations of her.

Emplotments occur when the child finds it necessary to conform to the narrative themes of others in her context. Children with learning disorders have a great need for others to complement their deficits. At times, the price they have to pay is high: not only must they perform selfobject functions for others, but they must also conform to their expectations. While it is true that many children resist such expectations by rebelling against those who require them, some collapse into compliant conformity. Those who rebel come to the notice of adults more frequently because of their noisy protests. But the compliant ones often fade into the background and are written off as lazy, unmotivated, or simply not bright enough to perform the tasks demanded of them. These children accommodate to their context by trying to become as invisible as possible.

Not all emplotments involve such withdrawals. Some children act out a parent's unconscious assignment of a particular role. A parent may identify the child with a sibling who died young or was a childhood rival. The child's behavior then appears to mimic that of the assigned surrogate.

The sources of these behaviors are often obscured by the fact that they are subtly shaped by the caregivers' unconscious expectations. For example, an eight-year-old child with dyslexia whose testing placed him within the average range of intelligence was referred because his school performance was so much lower than his capacities. His second grade teacher thought he was retarded. During an extended evaluation, the mother revealed that she had a younger brother who had Down syndrome. This brother had required much attention from her parents, who were determined to give him every opportunity to feel valued. My patient's mother interpreted their behavior as disinterest in her and a sign that the parents favored her brother. Her resentment toward her brother, however, was fraught with guilt. When she was assigned duties for his care, she felt both responsible to act as a caring older sister and deeply resentful that she had to give of herself to this rival for her parents' attention.

When her son was born, she was unambivalent in her love for him. But as developmental deficits emerged and he required more and more of her, her old ambivalent feelings toward her brother began to surface. She struggled against these feelings with increasing guilt; however, in spite of her best efforts, she began to treat her child as she had treated her retarded brother. For the boy's part, he needed his mother to fulfill complementary functions, and the only way he felt he could stay connected to her was through close compliance with what he perceived to be her expectations. The net result was that he became emploted in his mother's narrative by representing his mother's brother, whom he unconsciously mimicked by presenting himself as less smart than he actually was.

In the transference, this child seemed desperate to find a role he could play in the therapist's life. He persistently asked for details about the therapist's family. When given a few facts, he tried to fit himself into the family constellation. He imagined that my other patients were my children and that he was their sibling. He would ask me if I preferred them to him, and if they were smarter than he. My responses were that he wished he could be as loved by his mother as he imagined me to love my other patients. I also pointed out that he could not imagine himself to be smarter than they were, a comment that he met with disbelief. It was only after his parents could integrate the fact that the dyslexia stood in the way of his accomplishing more academically that their perceptions of him changed. He was then able to integrate the understanding of having a reading problem as not being equated with being retarded. As the family dynamics shifted, his self-perception changed and he could begin to use tutorial help to learn to read.

*Conventionalization*. Society presents each individual with a set of "predesigned" narrative themes and expects its members to embrace them. Each patient must integrate some social norms, expectations, and behaviors into her self-narrative or suffer some consequence for defying. Children feel pressured to conventionalize their narratives by making then approximate the normative narrative, i.e., the canonical narrative of the social/cultural milieu (Bruner, 1990). The child is confronted with the task of integrating the shared meanings of the context into her self-narrative. In order to maintain selfobject ties to the members of the larger social group, she must embrace or reject the values that the group maintains, to modify her narrative to bring it closer to the expectations of those whose opinions are valued.

The issue of conventionalization is closely related to alter-ego selfobject functions. As we have seen, children with learning disorders often feel themselves to be foreigners in the context in which they are raised; yet they desperately wish to be part of the peer group. They see acceptance by the group as minimizing their sense of strangeness. The desire to conventionalize their narratives leads them to try to be as others expect them to be. There are numerous ways in which children manifest the desire to conventionalize their narratives. By conforming to how others dress, how they talk, the activities in which they engage, or even the drugs they use, they try to join a group of peers that is considered "cool." Acceptance by that group of erases the sense of difference and normalizes their behavior.

For Sam (p. 175), the adolescent with an executive function disorder, the barriers to conventionalization were too great to overcome. When he discovered that he would be unable to follow the expectations set by his social context, he rejected the path of conventionalization and embraced a different one. In treatment, he struggled with the conflict between two sets of values—the one to which he subscribed and that of his parents. The path to success as defined by his parents was blocked by what he experienced as an insurmountable barrier. Yet the other path became increasingly unsatisfactory. On the one hand, he perceived me as part of the establishment, while on the other he appreciated my acceptance of his sense of being different from others. In the context of my valuing her as a person, he began to acknowledge some of his limitations and to move in the direction of mainstream activities.

## CASE ILLUSTRATION: JIM

The case of Jim presents the obverse of Sam's. Jim was desperate to attain a conventionalized self-narrative. This included an adamant refusal to involve himself in therapy, because that would have accentuated his sense of difference.

Jim was an obese high school freshman who had a history of receptive language problems and impairments in auditory memory and auditory processing. His ability to understand verbal communications was impaired, as was his ability to extract information from reading, although he did not have dyslexia. While he heard clearly what was said to him and could process simple verbal communications, he had difficulty fully understanding other people's spoken words if they were not couched in simple sentences. Even with the assistance of a tutor, he struggled to get Cs in courses that involved listening to teachers' lectures. In math, or in subjects that did not involve reading, he consistently got high grades. His perception of himself, in his high-achieving family, was that of someone who would never attain the level of success reached by his parents and siblings. Consequently, he was chronically depressed and had lapsed into a passive stance in which he took no initiative in any activity. His preferred form of entertainment was playing video games, at which he had become quite expert. In addition, he had resorted to eating as a way to comfort himself and was unable to control his food intake. He was more than 60 lbs. overweight, although his large frame masked his obesity so that he looked like an ideal football player.

Jim's father, who had a similar physique, came from a large family in which he had to fend for himself. He was able to become highly successful by being aggressively competitive. While he intellectually understood his son's problems, he felt utterly frustrated by Jim's passivity. He would become enraged whenever he saw Jim watching TV, munching on snacks, or playing video games. To him, Jim was a lazy slug who would never amount to much. He developed the approach of "motivating" Jim by berating him, presenting him with the image of failure unless he did something with himself now to become like other kids. He constantly compared Jim with his high-achieving siblings, tried to restrict his food intake and TV watching, and pushed him to engage in sports. Jim inevitably responded by increasing his food intake and putting even less effort into homework than usual.

When Jim entered high school, his father decided that the solution to the problem was for Jim to try out for football. He felt that participation in football would not only involve him in a healthy athletic program but also encourage him to become more assertive. Jim hated the idea. Being fearful of body contact and not well coordinated, he saw only failure and humiliation ahead of him. However, he felt caught between his own desire to remain regressed and his desire to please his father and gain his approval and affection. For his part, his father dangled the prospect of more fun times together should Jim comply and threatened to withdraw all together from Jim if he did not. Finally, Jim's resistance was overcome by the gains he felt he would be making in pleasing his father.

Football turned out to be a painful but bearable experience for Jim. The coach was impressed by Jim's size and saw him as a promising linebacker who could contribute to the team's success. He took a great interest in Jim's training, praised him for the efforts he made, and rewarded him by publicly recognizing any success on the field. The rest of the team became equally invested in Jim's success since they needed him; they made him an integral part of the group and accepted him as one of their own. Jim began to make efforts to "be like the others." He saw his salvation as lying in the direction of conventionalizing his behavior so that he appeared to be more "normal." He began to daydream of being a star on the football team, thereby shaping his identity into one that would conform to others' expectations of him.

By embracing a conventionalized theme, that of the heroic football player, Jim was able to find an avenue of success that helped restore a measure of self-esteem in an activity into which he had been pushed. While the initial impetus for his trying out for football was a desire to please his father, his involvement was transformed by the responses he got from his coach and teammates. The desire to be like others and to be accepted as part of the group became a powerful force for his continued involvement in football, in spite of his initial fearfulness and his lack of aggressiveness.

We might speculate as to the type of transference that would have developed had Jim become engaged in treatment. We would expect that Jim's resistance would be in the forefront of the initial work. He would need to be engaged at a level that was acceptable to him. The first priority would be to establish an alliance with him in which he could see the therapist as understanding and supportive. One way such a relationship could have been achieved would have been by focusing on the difficulties Jim was having in his academic work. In this connection, it would be important to find out how well he understood the limitation his learning disorder imposed on his capacity to achieve. Addressing this issue would be complicated by his receptive language problem. As in the case of William (p. 101), who had a similar problem, care would be needed in communicating with him verbally, to make sure he understood what was said.

In time, it might have been possible to develop an alliance. The hard work would come with the unfolding of the transference. Expecting the therapist to be as critical and deprecating of him as his father had been, Jim would be acutely sensitive to any negative overtones he might pick up from the therapist's interventions. At the same time, he would be wondering what he needed to do to please the therapist so as to be perceived as a "normal kid."

In the positive transference, the therapist would be responding to Jim's desire to "not have any problems." The issue would be engaged around the meaning Jim attached to having a learning disorder. If he could come to accept that, could he then feel that it did not detract from who he was, and could he feel himself to be different from others without seeing that as a stigma? If those questions could be answered positively, he would escape from the need to seek acceptance by conventionalizing his self-narrative and be freed to find his own path in life.

*Nontransferences.* Not all conduct by a child in the clinical setting is motivated by unconscious factors. Some conduct is the product of the child's neuropsychological deficit. In treating children with learning disorders, therapists confront a major confounding factor, that of making a distinction between a child's responses based on transference and those based on the child's search for adjunctive functions. While sharp differentiations cannot be made, some distinctions are possible that will help therapists in making interventions. As we have seen, children have emotional and learning disorders. They suffer from two types of deficits that often cannot be distinguished: selfobject deficits and neurocognitive deficits. Each has its own history and its own associated set of symptoms. Each leads the child to look to others to fill in these deficits. Neurocognitive deficits do not result from disruption in relationships but from the child's endowment or innate givens. Selfobject deficits arise from the complex interplay between what the child brings to the relationship and the responses of significant others to what they experience the child as expressing. In addition, the child, through his innate givens, contributes significantly to the shape of the relationship with caregivers. Unaware of the child's deficits, caregivers respond to him from the belief that their responses address what the child requires. The failure in the dialogue results in the child's experiencing the parents as unempathic. The therapist must be attuned to the subtle or not so subtle miscommunications that inevitably arise in the transference and replicate these patterns.

Since, as therapists, our focus is always on the transference, the question can be posed as follows: Can we as therapists distinguish between behaviors that are "brain driven" (hence, unmotivated) from behaviors that are motivated by conscious or unconscious factors and hence will manifest as transference reactions? If we were able to answer this question, we would be well on our way to defining appropriate interventions and gaining a better understanding of these children.

At times therapists modify their techniques to respond to specific needs of children with learning disorders. A dilemma is created for the therapist when the child's request requires a departure from what is considered acceptable. For example, a child with a handwriting problem may bring her homework to the session and wish to dictate her work to the therapist. Or, a child may ask that the therapist write a note excusing her from a gym activity that is particularly embarrassing because the child feels exposed and humiliated. The response to these requests must take into account the child's struggles and the issues being addressed. It is not inappropriate to comply with such demands if they serve to demonstrate to the child that the therapist understands the difficulties she is facing.

The child has little or no awareness of her own deficits; therefore, the burden falls upon the therapist to make the distinction and to make a response based on the child's needs. Problems arise less at the extremes than in the middle ground. When a child clearly transfers onto the therapist attitudes that were not invoked by the therapist and manifests patterns of interaction that occurred with significant others, such episodes bear the clear imprint of transference. But when a child asks the therapist to accompany him to the bathroom because the corridors the child has to negotiate to get to the destination are totally disorienting, it is an injustice to the child to attribute such a request to regressive motives or transference. The request does have meanings to the child based on past interactions, but in most situations these meanings are not clear-cut. The therapist's focus and the context must help determine the proper intervention. Ultimately, observing the results of the interpretations of such behaviors permits the therapist to differentiate between transference and nontransference requests. An interpretation may attenuate the

effects of selfobject deficits, but it cannot modify the cognitive deficits—
only compensations or new skills can do that.

## Disjunctive Moments

A disjunction may be said to occur when the child ceases to feel understood by the therapist. The therapist may also feel that he does not understand the child. The situation need not be symmetrical. At such points
the child may withdraw, become enraged, express disillusionment with the
progress of the therapy, or actively seek to reengage the therapist in the
process. For the therapist these indicators are flags that something is seriously amiss in the dialogue. While the reactions may be part of the larger
transference, they cannot be ignored. The repair of the disruption must take
precedence over the reconstruction of the pattern of response. (See also
Atwood & Stolorow, 1984, p. 47 on *intersubjective disjunctions.*)

Several factors contribute to the creation of disjunctions or derail-
ments in the dialogue. These may emanate from three sources:

1. *Negative transference reactions* result from the nature of the
   child's dynamics and recreate experiences in the child's past.

2. *Transferences of the therapist to the child* are the traditional
   countertransferences that have been discussed at length in the
   literature and which I will address in relation to the special problems that occur in the treatment of children with learning disorders.

3. *Nontransferential areas of the therapist's functioning* include
   disruptions created by the therapist's theoretical orientation,
   lack of experience, interferences due to supervision, personal
   life events, neuropsychological strengths and weaknesses, and
   other factors.

*Negative transferences.* Children tend to anticipate that a retraumatization will occur in the therapeutic relationship. The negative transference becomes activated when the child experiences the therapist as the
embodiment of past negative relationships. The conditions for such a re-
activation are often found in a "seed" of reality in the interaction with
the therapist, the result of some small, inadvertent responses on the part
of the therapist. Such responses are experienced by the child as intentional, or even maliciously inflicted, injuries, as the concrete manifestations of her fear of retraumatization.

In the complementary interplay, a nucleus of reality is embedded in the activity or the personality of the therapist, to which the child attaches great meaning. This sets off negative expectations. Since such incidents are an inevitable part of the process and reflect the child's dynamics, they provide an opportunity for therapeutic work. What is required is that the therapist acknowledge his contribution to the disjunction. This affirmation of the nucleus of reality in what occurred allows the empathic bridge to be rebuilt. Following that reconnection it may then be possible to comment to the child about the intensity of her response and its possible transference character. Usually what emerges is that the episode represents a reenactment of a segment of the child's past experience that is now available for possible interpretation. This ebb and flow in the process is one of the major components of the curative dimension. The therapist shifts from a disjunctive to a concordant position back to a complementary one. The shifts are an inevitable part of the treatment process. Healing the disjunction is essential to the treatment.

A disjunction may be triggered when the therapist is perceived as threatening, assaultive, or destructive. The therapist may experience the attribution of such feelings as threatening to his own sense of cohesion. The feelings are alien, not in keeping with the view the therapist has of himself. The therapist may then make a concerted effort to disabuse the child of her notions by pointing out the reality that the attributions are not correct. The child experiences these efforts as evidence that the therapist does not understand. The disjunctive gap widens. It is then not even necessary for the therapist to do anything that conforms to the child's expectations for the child to feel misunderstood.

## CASE ILLUSTRATION: ASHLEY

A therapist came to consult me about a case with which he was having difficulty. He described Ashley as an attractive, angelic looking child of eight, who had been referred because of serious behavior problems at school, although her behavior at home seemed to be well within acceptable bounds. She was diagnosed with AD/HD. The parents had a terrible marital relationship; they had been feuding with each other for years. They seemed unable or unwilling to break the impasse by either working on their relationship or separating.

In the course of twice-a-week treatment, Ashley became more and more contemptuous of her therapist. She ordered him around like a slave, demeaning him by her humiliating insistence that the messes she created be cleaned up by him as she gleefully watched. She developed the disconcerting habit of walking into the office and greeting the therapist by giving him the finger and saying "Hello, you f—." The therapist felt helpless and bewildered as to how to respond to the greeting and to the disrespect. If he did not comply with Ashley's wishes, she would throw a tantrum, screaming, kicking, and spitting in his face. Yet if he did comply he felt totally devastated at being placed in such an abject position. When at one point he complained about her name-calling, she responded that names are only words and can hurt no one. Wouldn't he rather be called names than be kicked or spat upon? While he recognized that Ashley was replicating with him what she probably witnessed at home, the therapist's rage at the constant injury suffered at the hands of this child mounted until he felt his therapeutic effectiveness was totally defeated. He eventually requested that treatment be terminated since he could not see how he could be of help to this child.

In consultation to discuss the impasse, we determined that the concordant position could not be maintained because the therapist's vulnerability to the assaults would not permit him to resolve the child's negative transference. As the consultant, I recommended that the case be transferred to another therapist. What the therapist discovered during the course of the consultation was that Ashley's assaultive behaviors brought up the teasing and taunting he suffered from peers in grade school because of his poor coordination. He had never worked through his embarrassment or his rage at his peers for these assaults. Ashley's parents had dealt with her hyperactivity as misbehavior that required strong reprimands and punishment to control. In the therapy, she replicated the way she had been treated. Unfortunately, rather than responding therapeutically, the therapist became enraged and paralyzed in dealing with the negative transference.

*Countertransference.* A different type of disjunction occurs when the child's own internal chaos produces a contagious anxiety in the therapist. The therapist may feel assaulted and overwhelmed. Because he feels alone and unable to help the child, he may cast about for measures other than those the relationship provides, such as medication or possible hospitalization. It may not always be clear which, if any, of these measures are in fact indicated. What confuses the issue is the helplessness the therapist feels and the effect it has in clouding his therapeutic judgment. Some therapists tend to respond with resentment and rage, as though the child is intentionally tormenting them and making them feel inadequate. Other therapists find their grandiosity stimulated and take charge of such situations with much alacrity and zeal; they become directive and intrusive in the child's life. Obviously, in these instances the burden falls on the therapist to deal with the feelings the child has stimulated.

## CASE ILLUSTRATION: KEVIN

Kevin was a sturdy seven-year-old boy who had been referred because of serious behavior problems. He was diagnosed with AD/HD, for which he was on Ritalin and in a special education class in his school. He was impulsive, disorganized, and at times intensely provocative. He seemed to know his therapist's vulnerabilities and had acquired the knack of provoking instantaneous rage reactions. At one point in the course of treatment Kevin would walk by the therapist and then totally unexpectedly lunge toward him and hit him in the genitals. Although the therapist tried to anticipate these assaults, he was not always quick enough to fend them off or defend himself against them. He would repeatedly be exposed to both humiliation and physical pain. On occasion he would become so enraged at Kevin that he would grab him and feel himself almost enough out of control to have hit him. Fortunately, the therapist was able to observe the process closely enough to realize that these assaults were not totally unexpected. Instead, they occurred most often when the child felt on the verge of disintegrative anxiety caused by something that had occurred either in the prior session or in his environment. The complementary positions of the therapist were leading to disjunctive responses.

In consultation, the therapist realized that his own helplessness was reminiscent of physical abuse he had suffered as a child at the hands of an older brother. He became aware of his countertransference and was able to maintain a therapeutic stance. His realization led to an exploration of the management of Kevin's disruptive behavior at home. After several sessions with the parents, they were able to reveal that between the ages of two and five Kevin was cared for by a housekeeper while his mother was working. The parents began to suspect that she might be either physically or sexually abusing him when his behavior grew increasingly out of control. When they discovered a bruise on Kevin's arm, they immediately dismissed her. Kevin never talked or complained about her, which they surmised was because she might have threatened him if he reported what she did to him.

After these revelations, the therapist was able to empathize with Kevin's victimization. Kevin was doing to the therapist what he experienced as having been done to him. It was then possible for the therapist to share with Kevin his parents' suspicion and to have the parents also talk to Kevin, expressing their concern and sadness at what might have happened. While Kevin never could talk about any of this, the assaultive behavior stopped.

Trying to explain to the child the contribution of the learning disorder to the disruptive pattern without making the child feel that he is being blamed for what occurred requires considerable tact. In Kevin's case, there is no doubt that his overactivity made him a very difficult child to control. While this did not justify physical abuse, it raised the question of how to help him understand that his behavior had an impact on others, and that others' responses were in part related to that impact.

The therapist began by explaining to Kevin that when he got out of control, bad things happened—people did not like it and could not be nice to him. Once he understood that, his therapist was able to discuss with him the internal disruption caused by his overactivity, that is, while he felt excited and stimulated when he got hyper, it was difficult for him to settle down and feel good after that. Kevin could then acknowledge that it was difficult for him to stop himself, especially after the medication wore off. At that point, the therapist engaged him and his mother in a discussion of how she could intervene to stop things from escalating without his getting enraged at her. Since he could now accept her interventions without associating them with the physical assaults of the housekeeper, it became possible to restore a measure of calm to his life.

*Other disjunctions.* Some authors have written about difficult patients (Groves, 1978; Martin, 1975; Winnicott, 1949) to illustrate the fact that some patients are capable of evoking exceptionally intense positive or negative feelings in therapists. With them the threat of a disjunctive response always seems imminent. These are patients whom therapists come to dislike or even hate. Some children produce anxiety at the prospect of their arrival: they are physically or verbally assaultive; they heap invectives and obscenities on the therapist; they are obnoxious, contemptuous, and disrespectful. These children provoke, enrage, and push therapists to the limit of their tolerance. They also have the capacity to distort what occurs in the treatment and, adding insult to injury, report the distortions to their parents under the guise that the therapist is mistreating them. With these children, therapists find themselves trapped between desires to retaliate or to terminate the treatment.

When therapists attempt to treat such hostile or neglected children, they reach the very limits of their capacities for concordant responses. Serious ruptures inevitably occur, and the boundaries of what is usually considered appropriate are overstepped. It is as though therapists leave the safe confines of traditional technique and habitual responses and jump into the turbulent reality of the child's life, responding as others do in the child's life.

These cases raise a question about how much of the disjunction is caused by the child's difficult behaviors and how much results from the therapist's failure to understand the child, who in turn rages at the therapist. While this may not be true of all difficult patients, among several cases of children and adults referred to me because their therapy had failed, a common reason for the failure was that the therapists did not understand the nature of their patients' disorders. To those therapists, the patients were difficult, impossible to treat, or could not benefit from treatment. The therapists appeared to have little insight into the motives behind their patients' conduct. This is not to say that the patients did not have personality problems that made them difficult to treat. I only want to emphasize that when patients are not understood, they will, at times, respond with rage at the therapist and appear not amenable to treatment.

Child therapists who hold onto psychoanalytic theories that fail to take into account the effects of neuropsychological deficits on development often arrive at an impasse with their patients. They are handicapped by their incomplete understanding of the psychodynamics of their patients. The disjunctions that result are caused by an outdated or deficient paradigm.

As therapists, we must look not only at patients' contributions to the process, but also at our own. The sources of our contributions are not limited to our personalities but extend to our theoretical orientation, our belief system, and our self-narratives. Ignoring the significance of these factors in the therapeutic process is as detrimental to the process as ignoring the contribution of the context to the child's adjustment. We are imperfect beings, not unlike our patients. We have our share of difficulties, and some of us have learning disorders similar to those of our patients. The empathy we confer on patients ought also to be turned back onto ourselves. We too are in need of others to complement us and to serve as adjuncts. What we cannot do is turn to our patients for these.

Ruptures in the therapeutic process inevitably occur. Once they occur and the child's rage is mobilized, the therapist must focus on the interventions that will bridge the chasm that has been created. The tasks of healing the rupture, of remaining available as a selfobject, and of restoring the capacity to listen to the child are crucial. Ultimately the flow of empathy between the child and therapist must be reestablished if treatment is to continue.

In summary, in this chapter I have attempted to illustrate a perspective through which to understand the treatment process with children with learning disorders. Treatment is an encounter between a child whose personal narrative inadequately organizes her responses to the world and a therapist who attempts to understand and modify the child's narrative. This goal is achieved through a process in which the child experiences being understood and has her perceptions validated. Once there is a set of shared experiences, it becomes possible for the child to experience the differences between the therapist's responses and those of others. A set of shared meanings is created that helps the child reframe her understanding of the problems. Evidence for greater integration of the child's experiences is found in the greater coherence of her self-narrative. Themes that formerly reflected the assignment of personal meanings to some experiences now encompass shared meanings that have grown out of the child's maturation and experiences in therapy. The child's rehabilitation and restoration to better function can be credited to the combination of greater parental understanding, appropriate school programming, improved social functioning, and the therapist's educative, corrective, and interpretive efforts.

# 14

# WORKING WITH PARENTS

WHILE MOST CHILD therapists would agree that working with the parents of children in therapy is essential to the success of the intervention, few references exist in the literature on this aspect of the treatment. This may be because this topic does not lend itself to being formulated into general principles. Much of what is written comes in the form of illustrative vignettes. In this chapter, I refer to "working with parents" as a modality distinct from family therapy, which conceptualizes occurrences within the family differently from what I suggest here. I present a specific approach to helping the parents of a child with a learning disorder who is impaired in his functioning and/or relationships (see Siskind, 1997).

My focus is on the relationship a therapist forms with the child's parents. The complexity of this relationship deserves examination and characterization in a systematic way. The usual categories assigned to a relationship between therapist and patient do not seem to apply in this situation. The aim of the relationship is not to have the parents form and resolve a transference to the therapist in which they deal with their past. On the other hand, the relationship is more than a "real," i.e., nontransferential relationship, in which the therapist acts as counselor, advisor, or parent surrogate. Something of all these elements exists. Yet, to the ex-

I would like to express my gratitude to Anne H. Berenberg for permission to use in this chapter part of a previously co-authored paper (Palombo & Berenberg, 1999).

tent that this is so, ambiguities in the role of the therapist will cloud aspects of the process.

The goal of work with parents whose child has a learning disorder is to provide the necessary support to facilitate their difficult task. This goal may be accomplished whether or not both parents are seen, whether or not the child is in treatment, and whether or not the parents themselves are in individual, couples, or family treatment.

## The Context

Before discussing the treatment approach with parents, I would like to set out a framework within which to understand the parent/child relationship. As we have seen, children with learning disorders tend to require two sets of psychological functions from caregivers. Both sets of functions serve to complement the child's immature or deficient sense of self. On the one hand, the caregivers are mediators or translators who help the child understand and cope with events around him by providing adjunctive functions. On the other hand, caregivers provide selfobject functions, that is, the necessary emotional nurture and support for the child to progress developmentally.

A concept that is helpful in considering the interactions between the child with a learning disorder and his caregivers is that of *goodness of fit* (Chess & Thomas, 1986). Each partner in the dyad contributes to fit through ongoing interactions that either help the dyad to mesh into a smoothly functioning unit or impede the caregiving process. Chess and Thomas focus on the specific ways in which temperament contributes to the functioning of the dyad. The fit between the child's and caregiver's temperaments either enhances or interferes with a child's healthy development. A good fit can mitigate the temperamental factors that make a child difficult to care for; a poor fit can result in negative caregiver-infant interactions.

We can extend this analysis to the relationship between caregivers and children with learning disorders. The goodness of fit is dependent in part upon a caregiver's ability to decode the child's communications in the absence of clear clues as to the child's deficits. From the point of view of the child, the caregiver's ability to respond is vital to healthy development. Some caregivers are better at reading these signs than others. They are able to understand the few signals a child gives. However, for caregivers who have deficits in the same areas as their children, the situation is full of pitfalls. They are handicapped in their efforts at making a "good fit" with their child. Since the child is similarly impaired, empathic responses may never develop or become disrupted and negative interactions dominate. Whether or not the caregiver has a learning disorder, the caregiver or the child may interpret the failure in communication as unwillingness on the part of the other to communicate or understand. The stage is then set for the child to respond negatively. As a consequence, some children become oppositional, while others become intensely anxious and withdraw, feeling defeated. These self-defeating patterns becoming entrenched themes that carry over into other relationships.

There is, therefore, a reciprocal relationship in the contributions the child and caregiver make to failures in the dialogue. Children with learning disorders are not just passive recipients of parental empathy or attunement. They are also active interpreters of the context in which the empathy is made available, is withheld, or is unavailable. This means that there is no predictable correlation between a caregiver's empathy and the child's integration of the experience of the moment. The idea that the very presence of an empathic caregiver guarantees the child's utilization of the selfobject functions offered is erroneous. The activity of the *recipient* of the attunement, his or her ability to understanding the interaction, is just as critical as the provider's capacity to respond empathically. The child's endowment and prior experiences shape his perceptions. As we have seen, these experiences are encoded into *scripts* (Tomkins, 1979, 1987) that lay down interactional patterns that guide the child's future responses. The child molds the relationship with the caregivers as well as being molded by the caregivers' responses.

The elements in the formation of a complementary relation include the goodness or poorness of fit between caregiver and child, the capacity of caregivers to provide and the ability of the child to utilize selfobject functions, and the sensitivity of the caregivers in becoming attuned to the child's experiences as well as the child's communicative competencies in conveying those experiences to others. To the extent that caregivers can assist the child in dealing with maturational tasks the child confronts, the child will experience the context as benign and be able to function at a cohesive level. For many children the positive interdependence that develops with others safeguards the sense of self-cohesion and enhances the potential for maturation. To the extent that caregivers and others cannot complement the child's deficits, the child may be defeated in his efforts to deal successfully with the maturational tasks. He will fail to integrate the meanings of those experiences.

I have mentioned the difficult dilemmas that confront caregivers in their efforts to complement their child. On the one hand, if a caregiver devotes herself to complementing a child's deficits, a complex relationship evolves. The child may become extremely dependent on the caregiver, making it impossible for the caregiver to distinguish what the child can or cannot do. A caregiver who is exquisitely sensitive and responsive to the child's distress may find that the child has become totally dependent on her. The caregiver intuitively reads the child's messages and soon finds that she is the only one able to communicate effectively with the child. A symbiotic tie may then evolve. When placement in day care or preschool becomes necessary, the child may display severe separation anxiety. Teachers may accuse these caregivers of fostering the child's dependence or not permitting the child to become autonomous. Their motives in responding to the child are brought into question, and their confidence in their parenting is shaken. It is important to recognize that the caregivers' responses often are motivated by the child's survival needs and not necessarily by their unconscious needs to maintain the child's helpless state.

This dependence is further complicated by the anxiety and uncertainty the caregiver feels about how to proceed. On the other hand, if the caregiver is unable to complement the function or refrains from responding, either the child fails or his coping capacities are taxed maximally. The child develops serious behavioral problems, withdraws feeling defeated by the environment, or simply fragments. The caregivers are then experienced as unempathic, negligent, or uncaring. This is not to say that all behavior problems result from dilemmas such as these; the same outcome may be reached by other paths.

Most caregivers cannot avoid these problems of complementarity. Often they will either provide functions for the child or get into power struggles by insisting that the child perform tasks, not realizing that the child is often unable to do so. At times, caregivers will vacillate between two extremes. Understanding the dynamics that drive these interactions and the nature of the child's deficits at the earliest possible stages of development is essential. Since that understanding is often not possible before the ages of three or four, clinical judgment must be exercised as to how best to proceed in those early years. Clinical experience leads me to recommend that for young children it is better to allow the symbiosis between caregiver and child to form, reserving attempts to resolve the dependence for a later time when the nature of the deficits is clearly identified and the child has matured sufficiently to cope with the challenges the environment presents. Ultimately, the goal for any caregiver who provides complementary functions for the child is to permit the child to develop compensatory functions that will take over the functions the caregiver provides.

## The Therapeutic Process

Caregivers who seek help or advice from a therapist are turning to an expert for clarification of a condition they wish to modify or do not understand. They may be seeking information, a diagnosis, guidance as to how to proceed, or simply a consultation to get the therapist's thinking on the problem they face. The therapist may view their request in different ways. He may be mindful of the caregivers' real need to be informed of the nature of the child's problems but also cognizant that other meanings may underlie the request. The request may shed light on the interaction between caregivers and child. This aspect of the process may be conceptualized as providing caregivers with information that enhances the coherence of their self-narrative. Since their responses to the child, based on their understanding of the motives behind the child's actions, are ineffective, they cannot form a coherent account of their experiences with this child. The information therapists provide, as well as the interventions they recommend, must serve to integrate the caregivers' understanding (Silver, 1989).

For example, caregivers may come requesting assistance with the disruptions their child creates around homework time. The child is described as resistant, throwing tantrums, and experiencing meltdowns. The caregivers may be perceived as wanting to know why the child is having such problems, or they may want practical advice as to how to manage the child so as to minimize these disruptions. On the other hand, they may wish the therapist to align himself with them in reprimanding the child for his misbehavior. The therapist is perceived as expert, caregiver, surrogate, and/or authority figure. The knowledge and experience the therapist possesses and shares are drawn from a coherent understanding he has of the child's motives. By sharing this understanding, the therapist is amending the caregivers' understanding and lending coherence to their narrative. What did not make sense to them can now be seen as comprehensible.

Some child therapists prefer to retain the ambiguity of their position so as to maximize the effectiveness of future interventions. By so doing they allow caregivers to form transferences. At times, caregivers come with ready-made transferences. They may have been referred to this particular therapist because of his reputation or because a friend had a good experience with him. They expect someone whose expertise is valued. A positive transference may emerge; however, how it will unfold is not known. Because knowing about this unexpressed transference is valuable, some therapists make a point of obtaining detailed histories on the caregivers themselves so as to anticipate what might occur. This practice is no longer widespread, in part because many caregivers react negatively to a therapist's probing into their lives when the issue is their child's problems, not theirs. Therapists are therefore thrown back on their intuition and must infer from caregivers' reactions the nature of the emerging transference.

I believe it is essential for therapists to keep in mind these subtle unarticulated transferences for two reasons. First, the therapist needs to avoid a negative reaction from the parents that would threaten the alliance necessary to support the work with them and their child. Second, the knowledge these transferences provide can be useful in understanding the caregiver-child relationship. The therapist can be much more effective in suggesting interventions if he takes into account what a caregiver brings to the caregiving process that may affect the relationship with the child.

## CASE ILLUSTRATION: SAUL

This instructive example illustrates how my failure to take such a parent's transference into account led to the failure of the case. The parents came to consult with me around the problems of their 10-year-old son, Saul. He had been diagnosed with ADD. He was a difficult child to manage because he was overactive, could never sit still, disrupted family meals, and seemed to mercilessly tease his seven-year-old sister. The parents had consulted me some years earlier about Saul. After a brief contact and a good outcome they had felt very satisfied with the intervention. Their return now was colored by similar expectations. Mother especially felt that I could use my influence on Saul to make him stop teasing his sister.

After the usual evaluation, I recommended once-a-week treatment for Saul, mentioning that I might want to see him with his sister after he and I had established an alliance. In his therapy Saul bitterly complained that the reason he teases his sister is to get back at his mother for treating him unfairly. He felt he had clear evidence that she favored his sister and gave numerous examples of her doing so. As I understood Saul, he had been the center of the family's attention up to the age of three when his sister was born. His mother had devoted herself to him, managing his hyperactivity by engaging him in active play and enjoying a very close, warm relationship. With the arrival of his sister, she not only turned her attention to the new baby, but also became hostile and punitive toward Saul. She found the baby much more gratifying than her overactive son. Saul's father was aware of the shift, and in joint sessions with Saul he confirmed Saul's story. He had tried to redress the balance in the family's dynamics by developing closer ties with his son, but that only aggravated the situation. His wife became convinced that he favored Saul over his daughter and became even more punitive toward Saul.

This insight only intensified Saul's rage at his mother. He could not forgive her for her unfairness. Although Saul's hyperactivity was partly responsible for many of the disruptions he created, he could have avoided some of these disruptions had he wished to do so. My efforts during joint sessions with mother and Saul produced little change in either of them. What I failed to recognize and what eventually lead to the undoing of my efforts was another set of dynamics that his mother brought to the situation of which I was unaware.

Only too late, I learned that she was the younger sister of a brother who was the favorite in the family. He was considered perfect in every respect; he was a star athlete, an excellent student, charming socially, and beloved by everyone. However, no one saw his other side, which he kept hidden from all but his sister—he was sneaky, lied often, and constantly tormented her. When she complained about it, he denied doing anything to her, instead accusing her of trying to get him into trouble because she was jealous of him. Since everyone else perceived him as the good child, no one believed her. She grew up in his shadow, hating him and unable to defend herself against him.

Now she saw the potential for the dynamics of her family of origin to be repeated and became determined that it would not happen. But, even though she was aware of the differences between her family of origin and her current family, she could not modify her reactions. It appeared that she saw her responses to Saul as an opportunity to pay back her brother for what he had done to her. Saul stood for her brother; she seemed unable to see him in another way.

My error lay in not knowing about those dynamics early enough. Prior to learning about them from Saul's father, I had decided to meet with

Saul and his mother to see if I could help modify her rage at him. I was puzzled by her responses, but I also identified with Saul's plight. I found myself lecturing her about the unfairness of her position. While she acknowledged that I was right, she was adamant that Saul had to change before she would.

A critical incident occurred after a session when I was asked for a change in Saul's appointment time. I was willing to accommodate him because this change was related to an important school activity. I started to negotiate the change in time with his mother, only to discover that every alternative I proposed was rejected by her. I finally suggested an early morning time, which she could have accommodated. But that change involved the minor inconvenience of having Saul's father take the daughter to school instead of her doing so. The choice she was being asked to make was between bringing Saul for therapy or taking her daughter to school. She flatly said that she would not give up taking her daughter to school. Saul wailed that his mother had just proved again her preference for his sister over him. She coldly confirmed that it was so, saying that it was because he was such a terrible child. I could not contain my frustration and said to her that she was really being unfair. With that she said that I did not understand and that she did not feel that I had been of any help to them, since Saul had not changed a bit since coming to see me. She thought the treatment should be discontinued.

She and her husband came the following week for a final session. It was then that I learned more of her history. It became evident that I had come to represent her parents who sided with her older brother, never giving her the benefit of a doubt. By then the damage had already been done and I could no longer be effective in my work with the family. The mother's negative transference was irreversible. They terminated my work with Saul.

I conceive of work with parents of children with learning disorders as a partnership in which the goals are as follows: to give parents the necessary support to feel that they are not alone in dealing with their difficult child; to provide them with information that will allow them to understand the reasons behind their child's behaviors; and to supply them with a set of specific strategies to use when confronted with difficult behaviors. The goal is to create conditions that will permit parents to form complementary relationships with their child, enhance the child's capacity to form compensatory structures, and ultimately increase the child's capacity to cope with his or her environment. Parents are encouraged to cultivate positive feelings for their child and maximize the child's strengths.

In many instances, parents have had prior consultations or testing for their child and have felt blamed for their child's problems by the results. If the disabilities were not diagnosed correctly, evaluators may have conveyed that the child's behaviors were the result of the family dynamics or trauma to which the child was inadvertently exposed. Many parents who have had such experiences approach later evaluations with suspicion and defensiveness. They come prepared for criticism, ready to resist suggestions for testing and viewing the process either as unnecessary or as endangering because it may expose their own vulnerabilities. Some parents are so guilt ridden to begin with that they anticipate the worst from the diagnostician. At times they may feel they have contributed to the child's problems because they themselves have similar problems. The issue of helping parents who may be suspected of having a learning disorder must be dealt with separately.

The approach most helpful to all parents is one of respectful compassion for their plight. Children with disabilities are difficult to nurture. Conveying to caregivers an attitude of concern for their child forms the basis for the emerging alliance. When therapists treat caregivers as they would a colleague or a close friend who asks for counsel, they are not likely to be considered to be part of the problem; rather, their help will be solicited in finding better ways of coping with the child. Before caregivers can begin to appreciate the positive aspects and strengths the child possesses, they may need to express the full weight of their sadness at having such a child and the disruption that having such a child creates. They will need some preparation for the fact that even though help is now at hand, the chronicity of the child's disorder ensures that problems will arise at every turn. They will continue to face the constant frustration of never being able to anticipate precisely when a problem will arise. Often this will occur when they least expect it. Crises may develop at the least opportune moment or when the family should be joyously celebrating an event. Their energies will often be drained by the effort it takes to stabilize situations or avoid emergencies. As the child grows, the nature of the difficulties will change. Each developmental step will be accompanied by a plethora of new challenges. Although these declarations may sound overly pessimistic, their effect is to convey a deep understanding of what caregivers confront, thus forming a bond of empathy with their distress. This will serve as a model for the empathy they will later be able to feel for their distressed child and for the bond they will form with him or her.

Sometimes the downward cycle of disappointment and despair takes such a toll that considerable work is necessary to help caregivers identify and respond to their child's positive qualities. Often, because of the pervasiveness of the child's problems, they have been totally preoccupied with managing as best they can, by focusing entirely on the child's weaknesses. For them to come to the point where they can value the child's identity and can nurture his strengths requires a change in the way they view their child. Once that occurs they can begin the process of building a positive relationship. When the cycle is broken and the disruptions diminish, caregivers can express their love of, and devotion to, their child. The child's qualities that at one time were seen as irritants can now be appreciated for their adaptive qualities. A child's perseverance or wonderful memory for facts or love of music, which may at one time have been used defensively by the child to keep people at a distance, now can be put to good service in achieving desirable goals.

## CASE ILLUSTRATION: JONATHAN

Jonathan, age six, was referred for therapy by the school social worker, who regarded him as inordinately attached to his mother. She perceived his mother to be so overinvolved with him that she thought a symbiotic relationship existed.

Jonathan was diagnosed at age three as suffering from a pervasive developmental disorder. The mother, who had been a teacher, refused to accept the diagnosis, feeling that her child was not that disturbed. However, she complied with the school's recommendation that Jonathan be placed in a therapeutic nursery. At that school, he was dealt with as a "symbiotic psychotic" child who needed to separate from his mother and whose mother needed to be helped to separate from him. This approach did little to alleviate the problems.

At age five educational testing revealed a severe auditory processing problem. His delayed language and his lack of comprehension of verbally expressed materials were found to be related to this deficit. He was found to have relied on nonverbal cues to respond to people. The testing revealed a significant area of strength in visual processing. A program was instituted through which visual cues were provided to complement auditory materials.

At the time of the referral he had made a great deal of progress in most academic areas, but his social functioning remained immature and at times inappropriate. In my evaluation it became clear that the so-called symbiotic attachment was related to the fact that mother had intuitively attuned herself to Jonathan's needs and had complemented his deficits in the auditory areas through nonverbal exchanges. He, of course, was able to understand her and became dependent for his survival on her directions. When I gave mother this explanation of their interactions, she broke into tears—finally someone understood! She had felt terribly guilty at the thought that she might have been damaging her child, yet had been unable to change her approach since it appeared to be the correct response to his demands.

Given this understanding of the child's dynamics, I recommended that he be seen for once-a-week therapy, with mother being seen once a month for child guidance (cf. Vigilante, 1983). I also supported the school's decision that he be placed in first grade rather than in a special education class, since this child's needs for improved social skills could be better served in a regular classroom than in the self-contained special classroom.

I saw Jonathan for a year, at the end of which he was doing well enough that he no longer needed to be seen in therapy. I felt the resources of the family could be better used in having him interact with other children in a group. Jonathan had become less dependent on his mother. Having learned to compensate for his deficits through his strong visual processing capacities, he no longer relied as much on his mother's complementary functions.

I heard from Jonathan's mother on and off through the years, since she remained grateful for my affirmation of her efforts to support her child. She described him as doing very well in all academic areas. However, the social area remained problematic. He had only a couple of friends on whom he relied a great deal for his social activities. His social judgment remained faulty, and he stood out in a crowd as awkward and clumsy. At home he was close to all family members and was a very lovable child.

## Educational Focus

Caregivers are entitled to the best explanation available of their child's problem. To the extent possible, it is desirable to give caregivers general advice on the management of the child and on ways to provide the child with positive experiences (Garber, 1988, 1991). When caregivers are given an understanding of the nature of the child's deficits and the ways in which these deficits impact his life, they often experience considerable relief at finally having answers to their questions. They begin to make connections between situations and the child's deficits. Their narrative of what is occurring is enhanced and made more coherent. Often they will seek to educate themselves about the disorder. If they feel comfortable in joining a group of parents of children with similar problems, they may find support in learning that they are not alone in their struggles. Sharing their experiences and learning from others can alleviate their anxieties and dispel their confusions. It can also help them learn different strategies for dealing with some of the child's difficult behaviors.

Providing caregivers with information about their child's deficits also involves the larger task of reframing their understanding of their child's behaviors. Caregivers come with many different views as to why their child behaves as he does. They started out with the expectation that this child's endowment was no different from that of their other children. But when they used the same child-rearing methods as with their other children, they found that these did not work. Frustrated and confused, they tried different strategies. They then feared being caught treating one child differently and charged with favoritism by their other children. For these caregivers it is important to convey that this child *is* different from their other children and requires special management because of his impairment. The specifics of the deficit can be clarified with examples from the results of the testing and with reading materials (Miller & Sammons, 1999).

Other caregivers, caught up in the vicious cycle of oppositional behavior, may believe that their child is responding as he does because of inadequate socialization or simple meanness. For these caregivers, reframing the child's difficulties involves a slow and systematic demonstration of the ways in which the child's impairment leads to failures in communication that the child interprets as lack of caring. Changing this type of interaction presents one of the most challenging tasks in work with caregivers.

## Intervention Strategies for Caregivers

Every situation is different and therefore requires individualized strategies. Strategies must be tuned to the child's particular topography of deficits and strengths, to the temperament and personality of the caregivers, and to the history of their interaction. Some caregivers prefer addressing specific incidents and learning what went wrong, so that they can tailor their future responses based on their new understanding. Other caregivers focus on relationship problems, wishing to facilitate social exchanges for their child. Still others expect the therapist to provide specific interventions that will relieve problem situations. Clinicians often find themselves using a combination of approaches. Since each approach has validity and is applicable to different aspects of the child's deficits, different strategies must found that are applicable to each situations.

It is important to help caregivers realize the scope of their child's difficulties. When hearing about learning disabilities, most people think of dyslexia, which is a focal disability that affects only a sector of the child's life. Other sectors, such as playing with friends or relationships with caregivers, may be unaffected by the disability. In striking contrast, nonverbal learning disabilities permeate every aspect of the child's life, from the time the child gets up in the morning until bedtime. For example, as the child tries to judge how much toothpaste to put on the toothbrush, visual-spatial problems interfere with the task. Problems intrude in the classroom, where he may struggle with math or the nuances of fiction reading comprehension. At recess the child may be confused by the experience of twenty-odd moving bodies rapidly giving off multiple social cues. At the dinner table, negotiating the crosscurrents of family signals presents challenges of its own. Every step in the developmental path presents new challenges for the child as he displays different behaviors and variations on old themes.

Once caregivers can see how pervasively a learning disorder affects a child's life, they can be helped to hone in on the particulars of their child's experience. It is usually productive to examine their child's everyday life with an eye to the demands made upon him. Much as the caregivers of a physically challenged child need to assess the environment to see the obstacles to their child's functioning, so too must the caregivers of a child with learning disorder identify the impediments in their child's world. Caregivers can then introduce appropriate modifications. They can ask themselves questions such as, What is entailed in this child's walk to school? Older siblings may have easily managed the task at this age, but is it realistic to expect that this child can manage it on his own? On written work, does the child always get mixed up when there are too many math problems on a page? When school is over, is there a large group of neighborhood children with whom the child must cope or is the child enrolled in a loosely run after-school care program that overtaxes his meager social resources? Is he expected to manage playing with more than one child at a time on play dates? Even when playing with one friend, does he need some planned activities and adult input to keep things running smoothly? Such a careful inventory helps to define what the stress points are for this particular child in this particular family. This enables the therapist and caregivers to find starting points for specific intervention.

As caregivers talk about the difficulties and challenges their child presents, it sometimes becomes apparent that over the years their patience has worn thin. They may have become irritated by the child's inability to modify his behaviors in spite of numerous attempts. When difficult situations are reviewed to see what goes wrong, they can be reinterpreted. The contributions of the child's deficits to the interaction can be highlighted in a way that has not been apparent to the caregivers before. Then the problems can be seen as arising from a failure in communication rather than being solely attributable to a willful, defiant child.

It is essential to nurture the positives in the caregivers' relationship to and interactions with their child. This occurs on two different levels. As one thinks about the child's difficulties, it is always important to help the caregivers remember that there are other aspects of the child that they value and cherish. These provide the foundation for building the child's self-esteem. Caregivers may admire their child's capacities for verbal expression. They may take pleasure in the child's theater performances, where he has learned to gesture appropriately or use proper vocal expression to give emphasis to a set of feelings. Even some things about the child that are irritating, such as a child's perseveration, may contain within them the seeds of something positive, such as perseverance.

A further consideration is that, in any interventions with the child, it is important to build on success. The child needs to know what he is doing right. For children with a learning disorder, it is particularly important to verbalize an appreciation of their gains—no matter how minor—in order to solidify them. Empty praise, such as the mindless "That's great!" in response to every drawing the child makes, is not useful, because it cheapens real praise and because it is not specific enough to foster strengths or accomplishments. It is only confusing. Commenting on the use of different colors or the added detail in the drawing, however, nurture the child's growth. Genuine positive responses keep the child moving forward. And as the caregivers notice what is going right, they can also begin to feel better about their own caregiving.

In offering specific interventions for caregivers, two goals are kept in mind: to increase the child's coping capacities and to enhance his self-esteem. An awareness of the issues facing this child in this family situation will guide the therapist and caregivers as to where to begin. Some strategies will be more useful for some children than for others, and the order in which they are introduced will vary from child to child. The therapist tailor-makes the interventions in accordance with what is required by the problematic situation. And while the therapist provides information to caregivers, he is also mindful of the parallel process, through which the therapist models for the caregivers the strategies they can adopt with their child. Bringing the parallel process to caregivers' awareness often helps them integrate the intervention.

Interventions should not be thought of as discrete techniques to apply to children or situations without regard to the total context. Many of these interventions might be applied simultaneously or in combination with others. Of greater importance than interventions as strategies is the mind-set from which they stem. Caregivers who get immersed into their child's modes of functioning will find themselves using these techniques flexibly and creatively. Their sense of oneness with their child will lead to the establishment of complementarity.

## What Is in Store for My Child?

Finally, caregivers will often raise concerns about their child's future. They want to know whether the condition will handicap their child permanently. Except in cases of extreme deficits, the answers to these questions should be framed in the most optimistic light. Children's capacities for adaptation, for compensation, and for maturation must be emphasized. The younger the child is at the time of diagnosis, the more aggressive the interventions can be and the more optimistic the outcome. We have seen good outcomes with many children who at a young age appeared so vulnerable or disadvantaged by their deficits that there was little hope expressed that they could become well-functioning adults. While systematic follow-up research remains to be done in this area, our clinical experience leads us to take a hopeful attitude.

There appear to be nodal points in the course of maturation that present opportunities for forward leaps. It is unclear whether these leaps occur because of neurological maturation or because greater psychological integration occurs when the child attains the stage of formal operational thought or for some other reason. One nodal point appears at around age 17, when the adolescent is a junior in high school. At that point the motivation to achieve academically drives some adolescents forward. Successes result in greater self-confidence and a different perspective on social relationships. For others, a nodal point is reached in the sophomore or junior year in college. A sudden flowering of the personality appears to occur. The awkwardness diminishes, a career choice is made, the young adult becomes more self-directed toward a goal, and all the elements of the personality appear to come together to make for personal success. Others are really late bloomers; these are children whose caregivers truly despair will ever make it. Yet at around age 27 or 28, a transformation occurs. New possibilities open up for the young adult. If the caregivers do not totally give up and if they have not alienated the young man or woman by taking a "tough-love" approach, the young adult may accept their support as he finds his way toward a constructive goal. It is essential that the caregivers make every effort to maintain a positive relationship with their child. No matter how alienating the child's behavior may be, if the bond is maintained hope is kept alive and the child will eventually respond. That is the message we try to convey to the caregivers of these children.

# 15

# SUMMARY AND CONCLUSION

THREE MAJOR THEMES HAVE organized this discussion of the relationship between learning disorders and disorders of the self in this work. By drawing on self psychology's understanding of a child's subjective experiences, I have sought to explore (1) the effects of neuropsychological deficits or weaknesses on a child's development, (2) the factors that give rise to a disorder of the self when a child has such deficits or weaknesses, and (3) the modifications of the way the treatment process is conceptualized when a child has a learning disorder.

From a developmental perspective, I began with the assumption that each child is born within a context and brings to that context a set of neuropsychological strengths and weaknesses. At the experiential level, a dominant motive that drives the interaction between these two factors is the wish to maintain a sense of self-cohesion that forms the foundation for a coherent self-narrative.

With regard to the psychopathology, Freud moved from his original position of coupling pathology to external events to securing it to the personal meanings his patients assigned to their experiences. Kohut, on the other hand, linked disorders of the self to the deficits produced by the failure to develop selfobject functions. I propose an addition to both these perspectives. The interactions between the context and neuropsychological deficits can either contribute to or act as protective factors against the development of a disorder of the self.

Finally, every clinical theory articulates principles that explain the manner in which therapeutic results are attained. For Freud the bright light of reason and reality brought back health. For Kohut the responsive

experience of a new relationships that provide selfobject functions restored health. To this perspective I have added the idea that the restoration of self-cohesion involves not only the restorative effect of a positive
experience, but also the acquisition of a self-narrative that can give explanatory coherence to the child's life events.

It is not advisable to develop a model technique and apply it to all
cases. Such a technique would stultify the creative nature of the process
and of the engagement in the dialogue. The fluid ebb and flow of the engagement is fundamental to this approach. A clinical theory can outline
the principles that guide the conduct of the therapeutic process; however, clinical practice involves a set of activities on the part of the therapist that do not lend themselves to systematic description. This perspective leads me to conceptualize the therapeutic encounter as
composed of moments—concordant, complementary, and disjunctive—
in which the therapist and child live through a set of experiences and
arrive at an understanding of their meaning.

When children with learning disorders enter treatment, adults usually
determine the goals to be set. Adults often conceive of the goals as the
removal of symptoms, a change in the child's personality, a lessened
vulnerability to injury, a diminished proneness to acting out. From the
therapist's perspective, the goal is the restoration of self-cohesion and
the establishment of coherence in the child's self-narrative.

The dialogue between the child and the therapist becomes engaged
when a set of shared experiences emerge, making it possible for both
to understand the meanings of what the child has experienced. If successful, this endeavor helps the child attain greater cohesion and a
deeper understanding than previously existed. The construction of a new
narrative serves the child and therapist as an orienting text that reframes
the meaning of past experiences, shedding new light on old stories or
revising these in such a manner as to give them new meaning. Upon
completion of the autobiographical task, the child's sense of cohesion
is strengthened and the nuclear self can give expression to life goals and
ambitions. As Saari has stated, the therapeutic process "involves the organizing of old meanings into newly constructed consciousness. What
is curative is not so much the recovery of deeply rooted repressed material but the reordering of structures that underlie personal meaning
and the symbolic capacities of the individual so that new meanings can
be differentiated, constructed or abstracted" (1986, p. 27).

Termination of the treatment comes as a logical conclusion to the dialogue. The child feels ready to go on with life in a joyous, optimistic

mood. The future is ahead, and the road to further self-discovery, self-fulfillment, and achievement is open. It is then that one can speak of a termination that is experienced as a triumph, rather than as the mournful loss of one's symptoms. The relationship between child and therapist has served to open the channel to the future rather than merely setting aside the past.

In conclusion, this work has presented an overview of many of the issues involved in understanding the relationship between learning disorders and disorders of the self. In order to present such an overview, it was necessary to condense the discussion of many of these issues and to refrain from exploring fully the complex interrelationships that exist between many of the factors that produce these disorders of the self. Furthermore, it was impossible to detail in the discussion of each of the learning disorders and the case presentations all the ramifications of each factor. This economy in presentation, while necessary to give the reader a chance to absorb the "big picture," may also leave the correct impression that much was left unsaid and some discussions were incomplete. I plead guilty to those charges.

In some ways, this work lays out a program for future study. I envision the tasks to which further research should be devoted to be the following:

1. The development of means to identify learning disorders and to devise ways to access the child's subjective experiences of those deficits at the earliest stages of development. This task requires the development of diagnostic instruments that would permit the identification of learning disorders and techniques to access the child's experience at a much earlier age than is now possible.

2. The study of factors that lead to the emergence of disorders of the self. The identification of the specific factors in the context and in the child's neuropsychological deficits may permit a fuller understanding of the failures that occur in their interaction and lead to the emergence of a disorder of the self. As I suggested earlier, it may be valuable to gain a greater understanding of the relationship between a learning disorder and Axis II personality disorders by identifying the specific role that learning disorders play in personality formation. Two related issues that deserve attention are the comorbidity of psychiatric conditions with learning disorders and the factors that protect against the risk of developing disorders of the self.

3. The issue of treatability requires considerable discussion. It is incorrect to assume that treatability is negatively correlated with the severity of the learning disorders and/or the disorder of the self. The criteria for treatability are unfortunately far from being fully understood. Some children with severe learning disorders benefit from aggressive interventions, while others who are less impaired and more cohesive cannot approach the task of therapy. There appear to be some personality traits that make it possible for some children and adolescents to benefit from treatment. It would be of great benefit to identify those traits.

4. The knowledge we acquire from these studies can provide strategies for interventions and remediation that take into account the child's subjective experience. Many of the interventions currently used ignore either the child's subjective experience or the contribution of the neuropsychological deficits to the child's problems. Some therapists direct their interventions to the modification of the child's behavior, with little understanding of the underlying dynamics that generate the behaviors. The walls between the disciplines involved in dealing with these children must be brought down so that each discipline can benefit from the contributions made by the others.

5. The incidence of learning disorders in adults is thought to be as frequent as that found in children. Emerging data indicate that the majority of adults with such disorders remain undiagnosed, since school systems were not mandated to test children suspected of having such disorders when these adults were in the primary grades. Many of these adults suffer from disorders of the self. Some have learned to hide their disabilities but bear the scars these produced in earlier years. Some, in spite of success in their careers, feel great shame and feel deficient in some vague and undefined aspect of their sense of self. Others have learned to compensate for or bypass the effects of their disabilities and find satisfaction in their success. An understanding of these adults' early development, as well as how they coped with their learning disorder, would be highly instructive in devising better plans for their care and for that of future generations of children (Orenstein, 2000).

# REFERENCES

Aaron, P. G., Phillips, S., & Larsen, S. (1988). Specific reading disability in historically famous persons. *Journal of Learning Disabilities, 21*(9), 523-538.

Abrams, J. C. (1987). The National Joint Committee on Learning Disabilities: History mission process. *Journal of Learning Disabilities, 20*(2), 102-108.

American Academy of Child and Adolescent Psychiatry. (1998). Summary of the practice parameters for the psychiatric assessment of infants and toddlers (0-36 months). *Journal of the American Academy of Child and Adolescent Psychiatry, 37*(1), 127-132.

American Psychiatric Association. (1968). *Diagnostic and statistical manual of mental disorders* (2nd ed.). Washington, DC: Author.

American Psychiatric Association. (1987). *Diagnostic and statistical manual of mental disorders* (3rd ed. rev.). Washington, DC: Author.

American Psychiatric Association. (1994). *DSM-IV: Diagnostic and statistical manual of mental disorders* (4th ed.). Washington DC: Author.

Andrulonis, P. A., Glueck, B. C., Stroeble, C. F., Vogel, N. G., & Shapiro, A. L. (1980). Organic brain dysfunction and the borderline syndrome. *Psychiatric Clinics of North America, 4*(1), 47-66.

Anthony, E. J. (1987). Risk, vulnerability, and resilience: An overview. In E. J. Anthony & B. J. Cohler (Eds.), *The invulnerable child* (pp. 3-48). New York: Guilford.

Asperger, H. (1991). "Autistic psychoapthy" in childhood. (U. Frith, Trans.). In U. Frith (Ed.), *Autism and Asperger syndrome* (pp. 37-92). Cambridge: Cambridge University Press.

Atwood, G. E., & Stolorow, R. D. (1984). *Structures of subjectivity: Explorations in psychoanalytic phenomenology*. New York: Analytic Press.

Atwood, T. (1998). *Asperger's Syndrome: A guide for parents and professionals*. London: Jessica Kinsley Publishers.

Ayres, A. J. (1977). *Sensory integration and learning disorders*. Los Angeles, CA: Western Psychological Services.

Badian, N. A. (1986). Nonverbal disorders of learning: The reverse of dyslexia? *Annals of Dyslexia, 36*, 253-269.

Badian, N. A. (1992). Nonverbal learning disability school behavior and dyslexia. *Annals of Dyslexia, 42*, 159-178.

Barkley, R. A. (1989). Attention deficit-hyperactivity disorder. In E. J. Mash & R. A. Barkley (Eds.), *Treatment of childhood disorders* (pp. 39-72). New York: Guilford.

303

Barkley, R. A. (1990). *Attention-deficit hyperactivity disorder: A handbook for diagnosis and treatment*. New York: Guilford.

Barkley, R. A. (1993). A new theory of ADHD. *The ADHD Report, 1*(5), 1–12.

Barkley, R. A. (1994). More on the new theory of ADHD. *The ADHD Report, 2*(2), 1–12.

Barkley, R. A. (1996). Critical issues in research on attention. In G. R. Lyon & N. A. Krasnegor (Eds.), *Attention, memory, and executive function* (pp. 45–56). Baltimore, MD: Paul H. Brookes.

Barkley, R. A. (1997). *ADHD and the nature of self-control*. New York: Guilford.

Barkley, R. A. (1998). *Attention-deficit hyperactivity disorder: A handbook for diagnosis and treatment* (2nd ed.). New York: Guilford.

Barkley, R. A. (2000). Genetics of childhood disorders: XVII. ADHD, Part 1: The executive function of ADHD. *Journal of the American Academy of Child and Adolescent Psychiatry, 39*(8), 1064–1068.

Barkley, R. A., & Murphy, K. (1993). Guidelines for written clinical reports concerning ADHD Adults. *ADHD Report, 1*(5), 8–9.

Baron-Cohen, S. (1997). *Mindblindness: An essay on autism and theory of mind*. Cambridge, MA: The MIT Press.

Baron-Cohen, S., Tager-Flusberg, H., & Cohen, D. J. (Eds.). (1993). *Understanding other minds: Perspectives from autism*. Oxford: Oxford University Press.

Basch, M. F. (1975). Perception consciousness and Freud's Project. *Annual of Psychoanalysis* (Vol. 3, pp. 3–19). New York: International Universities Press.

Basch, M. F. (1976). Psychoanalysis and communication science, *Annual of Psychoanalysis* (Vol. 4, pp. 385–421). New York: International Universities Press.

Basch, M. F. (1983). The concept of self: An operational definition. In B. Lee & G. G. Noam (Eds.), *Developmental approaches to the self* (pp. 7–58). New York: Plenum.

Beitchman, J. H., & Young, A. R. (1997). Learning disorders with a special emphasis on reading disorders: A review of the past 10 years. *Journal of the American Academy of Child and Adolescent Psychiatry, 36*(8), 1020–1032.

Berg, M. (1992). Learning disabilities in children with borderline personality disorder. *Bulletin of the Menninger Clinic, 56*, 379–392.

Bishop, D. V. M. (1989). Autism, Asperger's syndrome and semantic-pragmatic disorder: Where are the boundaries? *British Journal of Disorders of Communication, 24*, 107–121.

Borkowski, J. G., & Burke, J. E. (1996). Theories, models, and measurements of executive functioning: An information processing perspective. In G. R. Lyon & N. A. Krasnegor (Eds.), *Attention, memory, and executive function* (pp. 235–261). Baltimore, MD: Paul H. Brookes.

Brandell, J. R. (2000). *Of mice and metaphors: Therapeutic story telling in children*. New York: Basic Books.

Brown, T. E. (2000a). Emerging understanding of attention-deficit disorders and comormidities. In T. E. Brown (Ed.), *Attention-deficit disorders and comorbidities in children, adolescents, and adults* (pp. 3–55). Washington, DC: American Psychiatric Press.

Brown, T. E. (Ed.). (2000b). *Attention-deficit disorders and comorbidities in children, adolescents, and adults*. Washington, DC: American Psychiatric Press.

Bruner, J. S. (1983). *Child's talk: Learning to use language*. New York: Norton.

Bruner, J. S. (1987). Life as narrative. *Social Research, 54*(1), 11–32.

Bruner, J. S. (1990). *Acts of meaning*. Cambridge: Harvard University Press.

Bryan, T. H., & Bryan, J. H. (1986). *Understanding learning disabilities* (3rd ed.). New York: Alfred Publishing.

Cantwell, D. P. (1996). Attention deficit disorder: A review of the past 10 years. *Journal of the American Academy of Child and Adolescent Psychiatry, 35*(8), 978–987.

Chess, S., & Thomas, A. (1977). Temperamental individuality: From childhood to adolescence. *Journal of the American Academy of Child Psychiatry, 16*(2), 218-226.

Chess, S., & Thomas, A. (1986). *Temperament in clinical practice*. New York: Guilford.

Chethic, M. (1979). The borderline child. In J. D. Noshpitz (Ed.), *The handbook of child psychiatry* (Vol. 2, pp. 304-320). New York: Basic Books.

Cohen, J. (1985). Learning disabilities and adolescence: Developmental considerations. *Adolescent Psychiatry* (Vol. 12, pp. 177-196). Chicago: University of Chicago Press.

Cohler, B. J. (1982). Personal narrative and life course. In P. Baltes & O. G. Brins (Eds.), *Life-span development and behavior* (Vol. 4, pp. 205-241). New York: Academic.

Cohler, B. J. (1987). Adversity, resilience, and the study of lives. In E. J. Anthony & B. J. Cohler (Eds.), *The invulnerable child* (pp. 363-424). New York: Guilford.

Cohler, B. J. (1993). Aging, morale, and meaning: The nexus of narrative. In T. R. Cole & W. A. Achenbaum (Eds.), *Voices and visions of aging: toward a clinical gerontology* (pp. 107-133). New York: Springer.

Cohler, B. J. (1996). Suicide, life course, and life story. In J. L. Pearson & Y. Conwell (Eds.), *Suicide and aging: International perspectives* (pp. 65-85). New York: Springer.

Cohler, B. J. (1998). Psychoanalysis, the life story, and aging: Creating new meanings within narratives of lived experience. In J. Lomranz (Ed.), *Handbook of aging and mental health: An integrative approach* (pp. 255-280). New York: Plenum.

Cohler, B. J., & Freeman, M. (1993). Psychoanalysis and the developmental narrative. In G. H. Pollock & S. L. Greenspan (Eds.), *The course of life. Volume 5: Early adulthood* (pp. 99-177). Madison, CT: International Universities Press.

Cohler, B. J., & Galatzer-Levy, R. M. (1988). Self, meaning, and morale across the second half of life. In R. C. Nemiroff (Ed.), *Psychoanalytic perspectives on age and aging* (pp. 214-263). New York: Basic Books.

Colapietro, V. M. (1989). *Pierce's approach to the self: A semiotic perspective on human subjectivity*. Albany: State University of New York Press.

Conners, C. K. (1989). *Conners Teachers Rating Scale-28 (CTRS-28)*. Tonawanda, NY: Multi-Health Systems.

Conners, C. K., & Wells, K. C. (1986). *Hyperkinetic children: A neuropsychological approach*. Beverly Hills: Sage.

Coplin, J. W., & Morgan, B. S. (1988). Learning disabilities: A multidimensional perspective. *Journal of Learning Disabilities, 21*(10), 614-622.

Cosden, M., Elliott, K., Noble, S., & Kelemen, E. (1999). Self-understanding and self-esteem in children with learning disabilities. *Learning Disabilities Quarterly, 22*(4), 279-290.

Daelhler, M. W., & Bukatko, D. (1985). *Cognitive development*. New York: Knopf.

Denckla, M. B. (1983). The neuropsychology of social-emotional learning disabilities. *Archives of Neurology, 40*, 461-462.

Denckla, M. B. (1994). Measurement of executive function. In G. R. Lyon (Ed.), *Frames of reference for the assessment of learning disabilities* (pp. 117-142). Baltimore, MD: Paul H. Brookes.

Denckla, M. B. (1996). A theory and model of executive function: A neuropsychological perspective. In G. R. Lyon & N. A. Krasnegor (Eds.), *Attention, memory, and executive function* (pp. 263-278). Baltimore, MD: Paul H. Brookes.

Department of Education. (March 12, 1999). Rules and Regulations. *Federal Register, 64,* 12422.

Egan, J., & Kernberg, P. L. (1984). Pathological narcissism in childhood. *Journal of the American Psychoanalytic Association, 32*, 39-62.

Eichenbaum, H., & Bodkin, J. A. (2000). Belief and knowledge as distinct forms of memory. In D. L. Schacter, & E. Scarry (Eds.), *Memory, brain, and belief* (pp. 176-207). Cambridge, MA: Harvard University Press.

Ellenberg, L. (1999). Executive functions in children with learning disabilities and attention deficit disorder. In J.A. Incorvaia, B. S. Mark-Goldstein, & D.Tessmer (Eds.), *Understanding, diagnosing, and treating AD/HD in children and adolescents: An integrative approach* (pp. 197-219). Northdale, NJ: Aronson.

Erikson, E. H. (1994). *Identity and the life cycle*. New York: Norton.

Eslinger, P. J. (1996). Conceptualizing, describing, and measuring components of executive function: A summary. In G. R. Lyon & N. A. Krasnegor (Eds.), *Attention, memory, and executive function* (pp. 367-395). Baltimore: Paul H. Brookes.

Famularo, R., Kinscherff, R., & Fenton, T. (1991). Posttraumatic stress disorder among children clinically diagnosed as borderline personality disorder. *Journal of Nervous and Mental Diseases, 179*(7), 428-431.

Farrar, M. J., & Goodman, G. S. (1990). Developmental differences in the relation between scripts and episodic memory: Do they exist? In R. Fivush & J. A. Hudson (Eds.) *Knowing and remembering young children* (pp. 30-64). New York: Cambridge University Press.

Feingold, B. F. (1976). Hyperkinesis and learning disabilities linked to the ingestion of artificial food colors and flavors. *Journal of Learning Disabilities, 9*(9), 551-559.

Fraiberg, S. H. (1964). Studies in the ego development of the congenitally blind child. *Psychoanalytic Study of the Child* (Vol. 19, pp. 113-169). New York: International Universities Press.

Fraiberg, S. H. (1977). Congenital sensory and motor deficits and ego formation. *Annual of Psychoanalysis* (Vol. 5, pp. 169-194). New York: International Universities Press.

Freedman, D. A. (1981). The effect of sensory and other deficits in children and on their experience of people. *Journal of the American Psychoanalytic Association, 29*(4), 831-868.

Freud, A. (1962). Assessment of childhood disturbances. *Psychoanalytic Study of the Child* (Vol. 17, pp. 149-158). New York: International Universities Press.

Freud, A. (1965). *Normality and pathology in childhood*. New York: International Universities Press.

Freud, A. (1983). Problems of pathogenesis: Introduction to the discussion, *The Psychoanalytic Study of the Child* (Vol. 38, pp. 383-387). New Haven: Yale University Press.

Freud, S. (1895). Studies on hysteria. In J. Strachey (Ed. and Trans.), *The Standard edition of the complete psychological works of Sigmund Freud* (Vol. 2). New York: Norton.

Freud, S. (1912). The dynamics of the transference. In J. Strachey (Ed. and Trans.), *The Standard edition of the complete psychological works of Sigmund Freud* (Vol. 12). New York: Norton.

Fries, M. E., Nelson, M. C., & Woolf, P. J. (1980). Developmental and etiological factors in the treatment of character disorders with archaic ego functions. *Psychoanalytic Review, 67*(3), 337-352.

Frith, U. (Ed.). (1991). *Autism and Asperger syndrome*. Cambridge, England: Cambridge University Press.

Frost, J. A., & Emery, M. J. (1995). Academic interventions for children with dyslexia who have phonological core deficits. *ERIC Digest E539* (ERIC Identifier: ED385095 ed., Vol. 2000).

Garber, B. (1988). The emotional implications of learning disabilities: A theoretical integration, *The Annual of Psychoanalysis* (Vol. XVI, pp. 111-128). Madison, CT: International Universities Press.

Garber, B. (1991). The analysis of a learning-disabled child. In A. Goldberg (Ed.), *Annual of Psychoanalysis* (Vol. 19, pp. 127-150). Hillsdale, NJ: Analytic Press.

Gathercole, S. E. (1998). The development of memory. *Journal of Child Psychology and Psychiatry, 39*(1), 3–27.

Gazzaniga, M. S. (1988). *Mind matters: How mind and brain interact to create our conscious lives*. Boston: Houghton Mifflin.

Giffin, M. (1965). *The diagnosis and treatment of perceptually handicapped children: A variation on an enigma*. Unpublished manuscript.

Gillberg, C. L. (1992). Autism and autistic-like conditions: Subclasses among disorders of empathy. *Journal of Child Psychology and Psychiatry, 33*(5), 813–842.

Goldberg, M. J. (1999). AD/HD—approaching the millennium: New understanding, new technologies, new therapeutic interventions. In J. A. Incorvaia, B. S. Mark-Goldstein, & D. Tessmer (Eds.), *Understanding, diagnosing, and treating AD/HD in children and adolescents: An integrative approach* (pp. 489–512). Northdale, NJ: Aronson.

Gopnik, A., Meltzoff, A. N., & Kuhl, P. K. (1999). *The scientist in the crib: Minds, brains, and how children learn*. New York: Morrow.

Greenberg, L. (1999). Using the T.O.V.A. in the diagnosis and treatment of attention disorders. In J. A. Incorvaia, B. S. Mark-Goldstein, & D. Tessmer (Eds.), *Understanding, diagnosing, and treating AD/HD in children and adolescents: An integrative approach* (pp. 151–182). Northdale, NJ: Aronson.

Greenspan, S. I. (1981). *Psychopathology and adaptation in infancy and early childhood*. Madison, CT: International Universities Press.

Greenspan, S. I. (1988). The development of the ego: Insights from clinical work with infants and young children. *Journal of the American Psychoanalytic Association, 36*(1), 3–55.

Greenspan, S. I. (1989a). The development of the ego: Biological and environmental specificity in the psychopathological developmental process and the selection and construction of ego defenses. *Journal of the American Psychoanalytic Association, 37*(3), 639–686.

Greenspan, S. I. (1989b). *The development of the ego: Implications for personality theory, psychopathology, and the psychotherapeutic process*. Madison, CT: International Universities Press.

Greenspan, S. I. (2000). *Clinical practice guidelines: Redefining the standards of care for infants, children, and families with special needs*. Bethesda, MD: Interdisciplinary Council on Developmental and Learning Disorders Press.

Greenspan, S. I., & Meisels, S. (Dec. 4, 1993). *Toward a new vision for the developmental assessment of infants and young children. A work in progress from the ZERO TO THREE/National Center for Clinical Infant Programs Work Group on Developmental Assessment*. Paper presented at the ZERO TO THREE/National Center for Clinical Infant Programs' Eighth Biennial National Training Institute, Washington DC.

Groves, J. E. (1978, April). Taking care of the hateful patient. *New England Journal of Medicine, 298*(16): 883–887.

Gregg, N., & Scott, S. S. (2000). Definition and documentation: Theory, measurement, and the courts. *Journal of Learning Disabilities, 33*(1): 5–13.

Hadley, J. (1989). The sensual-sexual motivational system. In J. Lichtenberg (Ed.), *Psychoanalysis and motivation* (pp. 217–252). Hillsdale, NJ: Analytic Press.

Hallahan, D. P., Kauffman, J. M., & Lloyd, J. W. (1996). *Introduction to learning disabilities* (2nd ed.). New Jersey: Prentice-Hall, Inc.

Hallowell, E. M., & Ratey, J. J. (1994). *Driven to distraction: Recognizing and coping with attention deficit disorder from childhood through adulthood*. New York: Simon and Schuster.

Halprin, J. M. (1996). Conceptualizing, describing, and measuring components of attention: A summary. In G. R. Lyon & N. A. Krasnegor (Eds.), *Attention, memory, and executive function*. Baltimore: Paul H. Brookes.

Hammill, D. D. (1993). A brief look at the learning disabilities movement in the United States. *Journal of Learning Disabilities, 26*(5), 295-310.

Hammill, D. D., & Bryant, B. R. (1998). *Learning disabilities diagnostic inventory: A method to help identify intrinsic processing disorders in children and adolescents. Examiner's Manual.* Austin, TX: Pro-Ed.

Hammill, D. D., Leigh, J. E., McNutt, G., & Larsen, S. C. (1987). A new definition of learning disabilities. *Journal of Learning Disabilities, 20*(2), 109-113.

Happe, F. G. E. (1991). The autobiographical writings of three Asperger syndrome adults: Problems of interpretation and implications for theory. In U. Frith (Ed.), *Autism and Asperger syndrome* (pp. 207-241). Cambridge, England: Cambridge University Press.

Harnadek, C. S., & Rourke, B. P. (1993). Principal identifying features of the syndrome of nonverbal learning disabilities in children. *Journal of Learning Disabilities, 27*(3), 144-154.

Hooper, S. R., & Olley, J. G. (1996). Psychological comorbidity in adults with learning disabilities. In N. Gregg, C. Hoy, & A.F. Gay (Eds.), *Adults with learning disabilities* (pp. 162-183).

Johnson, D. J. (1987). Nonverbal learning disabilities. *Pediatric Annals, 16*(2), 133-141.

Johnson, D. J., & Myklebust, H. R. (1967). *Learning disabilities: Educational principles and practices.* New York: Grune & Stratton.

Kandel, E. R. (1998). A new intellectual framework for psychiatry. *American Journal of Psychiatry, 155*(4), 457-469.

Kanner, L. (1943). Autistic disturbances of affective contact. *Nervous Child, 2*, 217-250.

Kavale, K. A., & Forness, S. R. (2000). What definitions of learning disability say and don't say. *Journal of Learning Disabilities, 33*(3), 239-256.

Keith, C. R. (1975). The therapeutic alliance in child psychotherapy. *Journal of Child Psychiatry, 7*, 31-43.

Kerby, A. P. (1991). *Narrative and the self.* Bloomington: Indiana University Press.

Klein, R. G., & Mannuzza, S. (2000). Children with uncomplicated reading disorders grow up: A prospective follow-up into adulthood. In L. L. Greenhill (Ed.), *Learning disabilities: Implications for psychiatric treatment* (pp. 1-31). Washington, DC: American Psychiatric Press, Inc.

Klin, A., & Volkmar, F. R. (1997). Asperger's syndrome. In D. Cohen & F. R. Volkmar (Eds.), *Handbook of autism and pervasive developmental disorders* (pp. 94-122). New York: Wiley.

Klitzing, K. V. (2000). Gender-specific characteristics of 5-year-olds' play narratives and associations with behavior ratings. *Journal of the American Academy of Child and Adolescent Psychiatry, 39*(8), 1017-1023.

Kohlberg, L., & Gilligan, C. (1972). The adolescent as a philosopher. In J. Kagan & R. Coles (Eds.), *Twelve to sixteen: Early adolescence.* New York: Norton.

Kohut, H. (1959). Introspection, empathy and psychoanalysis. *Journal of the American Psychoanalytic Association, 7*(459-483).

Kohut, H. (1971). *The analysis of the self.* New York: International Universities Press.

Kohut, H. (1977). *The restoration of the self.* New York: International Universities Press.

Kohut, H. (1978). Remarks about the formation of the self: Letter to a student regarding some principles of psychoanalytic research. In P. H. Ornstein (Ed.), *The search for the self: Selected writings of Heinz Kohut 1950-78* (pp. 737-770). New York: International Universities Press.

Kohut, H. (1984). *How does analysis cure?* Chicago: The University of Chicago Press.

Kohut, H. (1991). Four basic concepts in self psychology (1979). In P. H. Ornstein (Ed.), *The search for the self: Selected writings of Heinz Kohut 1978-81* (pp. 447-470). New York: International Universities Press.

Kohut, H., & Wolf, E.S. (1978). The disorders of the self and their treatment: An outline. *International Journal of Psycho-Analysis, 59,* 413–425.

Lai, Z. C. (1990). *A proposed neural circuitry underlying the processing of emotional cues derived from a syndrome of social skill impairment: A functional evolutionary architectonic perspective.* Unpublished doctoral dissertation, University of Minnesota, Minneapolis.

Lamm, O., & Epstein, R. (1992). Specific reading impairments—Are they to be associated with emotional difficulties? *Journal of Learning Disabilities, 25*(9), 605–615.

Leckman, J. F., & Mayes, L. C. (1998). Understanding developmental psychopathology: How useful are evolutionary accounts? *Journal of the American Academy of Child and Adolescent Psychiatry, 37*(10), 1011–1021.

Lerner, J. W., Lowenthal, B., & Lerner, S. R. (1995). *Attention deficit disorders: Assessment and teaching.* Pacific Grove, CA.: Brooks/Cole.

Levin, F. M. (1991). *Mapping the mind.* Hillsdale, N.J.: Analytic Press.

Levine, M. (1994). *Educational care: A system for understanding and helping children with learning problems at home and in school.* Cambridge, MA: Educators Publishing Service.

Lezak, M. D. (1983). *Neuropsychological assessment.* New York: Oxford University Press.

Lichtenberg, J. D. (1983). *Psychoanalysis and infant research.* Hillsdale, NJ: Analytic Press.

Lichtenberg, J. D. (1989). *Psychoanalysis and motivation.* Hillsdale, NJ: Analytic Press.

Lichtenberg, J. D., & Wolf, E. (1997). General principles of self psychology: A position statement. *Journal of the American Psychoanalytic Association, 45*(2), 531–543.

Little, S. S. (1993). Nonverbal learning disabilities and socioemotional functioning: A review of the recent literature. *Journal of Learning Disabilities, 26*(10), 653–665.

Lofgren, D. P., Bemporad, J., King, J., Lindem, B. S., & O'Driscoll, G. (1991). A prospective follow-up study of so-called borderline children. *American Journal of Psychiatry, 148*(11), 1541–1547.

Lyon, R. G. (1990). *Research in learning disabilities: Research directions.* Unpublished manuscript.

Lyons-Ruth, K. (1998). Implicit relational knowing: Its role in development and psychoanalytic treatment. *Infant Mental Health Journal, 19*(3), 282–289.

Mahler, M. S. (1968). *On human symbiosis and the vicissitudes of individuation.* New York: International Universities Press.

Mahler, M. S., Pine, F., & Bergman, A. (1975). *The psychological birth of the human infant.* New York: Basic Books.

Martin, P. A. (1975). The obnoxious patient. In P. L. Giovacchini (Ed.), *Tactics and techniques in psychoanalytic therapy* (Vol. 2, pp. 96–204). New York: Aronson.

Mayes, L. C. (1999). Clocks, engines, and quarks—Love, dreams, and genes: What makes development happen? In A. J. Solnit (Ed.), *Psychoanalytic Study of the Child* (Vol. 54, pp. 169–192). New Haven: Yale University Press.

Mayes, L. C., & Cohen, D. J. (1994). Experiencing self and others: Contributions from studies of autism to the psychoanalytic theory of social development. *Journal of the American Psychoanalytic Association, 42,* 191–218.

McNulty, M. A. (2000). *The life stories of adults diagnosed with dyslexia as children.* Unpublished qualitative study, Institute for Clinical Social Work, Chicago, IL.

Miller, A. (1981). *Prisoners of childhood.* New York: Basic Books.

Miller, L. (1991, March/April). Psychotherapy of the brain-injured patient: Principles and practices. *Journal of Cognitive Rehabilitation,* pp. 24–30.

Miller, L. (1992, January/February). Cognitive rehabilitation, cognitive therapy, and cognitive style: Toward an integrative model of personality and psychotherapy. *Journal of Cognitive Rehabilitation*, pp. 18–29.

Miller, N., & Sammons, C. C. (1999). *Everybody's different: Understanding and changing our reactions to disabilities*. Baltimore, Paul H. Brookes.

Morvitz, E., & Motta, R. W. (1992). Predictors of self-esteem: The roles of parent-child perceptions, achievement, and class placement. *Journal of Learning Disabilities, 25*(1), 72–80.

Murphy, J. P. (1990). *Pragmatism: From Peirce to Davidson, with an introduction by Richard Rorty*. Boulder: Westview Press.

National Center for Learning Disabilities. (1994). What is dyslexia? Washington, DC: Author.

National Information Center for Children and Youth with Disabilities. (1999). *Fact Sheet Number 7* (FS7). Washington, DC: Author.

National Institutes of Health (2000). National Institutes of Health consensus development conference statement: Diagnosis and treatment of attention-deficit/hyperactivity disorder (ADHD). *Journal of the American Academy of Child and Adolescent Psychiatry, 39*(2), 182–193.

Nelson, K. (1992). Emergence of autobiographical memory at age 4. *Human Development, 35*, 172–177.

Nelson, K. (1993). The psychological and social origins of autobiographical memory. *Psychological Science, 4*(1), 7–14.

Nelson, K. (1994). Long-term retention of memory for preverbal experience: Evidence and implications. *Memory, 2*(4), 467–475.

Nelson, K. (2000). Memory and belief in development. In D. L. Schacter & E. Scarry (Eds.), *Memory, brain, and belief*. Cambridge, MA: Harvard University Press.

Neuwirth, S. (1994). *National Institutes of Health Publication no. 96-3572*. Bethesda, MD: Author.

Nowicki, S., & Duke, M. P. (1992). *Helping the child who doesn't fit in*. Atlanta: Peachtree Publishers.

Nowicki, S., & Duke, M. P. (1994). Individual differences in the nonverbal communication of affect: The diagnostic analysis of nonverbal accuracy scale. *Journal of Nonverbal Behavior, 18*(1), 9–35.

Olds, D., & Cooper, A. M. (1997). Dialogue with other sciences: Opportunities for mutual gain. *International Journal of Psycho-Analysis, 78*, 219–225.

Orenstein, M. (2000). *Smart but stuck: What every therapist needs to know about learning disabilities and imprisoned intelligence*. New York: Haworth.

Ornstein, A. (1976). Making contact with the inner world of the child: Toward a theory of psychoanalytic psychotherapy with children. *Comprehensive Psychiatry, 7*(1), 3–36.

Ornstein, A. (1981). Self-pathology in childhood: Developmental and clinical considerations. *Psychiatric Clinics of North America, 4*(3), 435–453.

Ornstein, A. (1983). An idealizing transference of the oedipal phase. In J. Lichtenberg & S. Kaplan (Eds.), *Reflections on self psychology* (pp. 135–148). Hillsdale, NJ: Analytic Press.

Ornstein, A. (1986). Supportive psychotherapy: A contemporary view. *Clinical Social Work Journal, 14*(1), 14–30.

Ornstein, A. (1990). Selfobject transferences and the process of working through. In A. Goldberg (Ed.), *Progress in self psychology: The realities of transference*. Hillsdale, NJ: Analytic Press.

Osman, B. B. (2000). Learning disabilities and the risk of psychiatric disorders in children and adolescents. In L. L. Greenhill (Ed.), *Learning disabilities: Implications for psychiatric treatment* (pp. 33–57). Washington, DC: American Psychiatric Press, Inc.

Pally, R. (1997a). I. How brain development is shaped by genetic and environmental factors. *International Journal of Psycho-Analysis, 78,* 587-593.

Pally, R. (1997b). II. How brain actively constructs perceptions. *International Journal of Psycho-Analysis, 78,* 1021-1030.

Pally, R. (1997c). Memory: Brain systems that link past, present and future. *International Journal of Psycho-Analysis, 78,* 1223-1234.

Pally, R. (1998a). Bilaterality: Hemispheric specialization and integration. *International Journal of Psycho-analysis, 79,* 565-578.

Pally, R. (1998b). Emotional processing: The mind-body connection. *International Journal of Psycho-analysis, 79,* 349-362.

Palombo, J. (1976). Theories of narcissism and the practice of clinical social work. *Clinical Social Work Journal, 4*(3), 147-161.

Palombo, J. (1979). Perceptual deficits and self-esteem in adolescence. *Clinical Social Work Journal, 7*(1), 34-61.

Palombo, J. (1982). Critical review of the concept of the borderline child. *Clinical Social Work Journal, 10*(4), 246-164.

Palombo, J. (1983). Borderline conditions: A perspective from self psychology. *Clinical Social Work Journal, 11*(4), 323-338.

Palombo, J. (1985). Self psychology and countertransference in the treatment of children. *Child and Adolescent Social Work Journal, 2*(1), 36-48.

Palombo, J. (1985). The treatment of borderline neurocognitively impaired children: A perspective from self psychology. *Clinical Social Work Journal, 13*(2), 117-128.

Palombo, J. (1987). Selfobject transferences in the treatment of borderline neurocognitively impaired children. In J. S. Grotstein, M. F. Solomon, & J. A. Lang (Eds.), *The borderline patient* (pp. 317-346). Hillsdale, NJ: Analytic Press.

Palombo, J. (1988). Adolescent development: A view from self psychology. *Child and Adolescent Social Work Journal, 5*(3), 171-186.

Palombo, J. (1990). The cohesive self, the nuclear self, and development in late adolescence. In S. C. Feinstein (Ed.), *Adolescent psychiatry* (Vol. 17, pp. 338-359). Chicago: University of Chicago Press.

Palombo, J. (1991). Neurocognitive differences, self cohesion, and incoherent self narratives. *Child and Adolescent Social Work Journal, 8*(6), 449-472.

Palombo, J. (April 24, 1992). *Learning disabilities in children: Developmental, diagnostic and treatment considerations.* Paper presented at the Fourth National Health Policy Forum, Healthy children: Obstacles and opportunities, Washington, DC.

Palombo, J. (1993). Neurocognitive deficits, developmental distortions, and incoherent narratives. *Psychoanalytic Inquiry, 13*(1), 85-102.

Palombo, J. (1994). Incoherent self-narratives and disorders of the self in children with learning disabilities. *Smith College Studies in Social Work, 64*(2), 129-152.

Palombo, J. (1995). Psychodynamic and relational problems of children with nonverbal learning disabilities. In B. S. Mark & J. A. Incorvaia (Ed.), *The handbook of infant, child, and adolescent psychotherapy: A guide to diagnosis and treatment* (Vol. 1, pp. 147-176). Northdale, NJ: Aronson.

Palombo, J. (1996a). Discussion of "A self-psychological approach to Attention deficit/hyperactivity disorders in adults: A paradigm to integrate the biopsychosocial model of psychiatric illness." In A. Goldberg (Ed.), *Basic ideas reconsidered* (Vol. 12, pp. 243-248). Hillsdale, NJ: Analytic Press.

Palombo, J. (1996b). Paradigms, metaphors, and narratives: Stories we tell about development. *Journal of Analytic Social Work, 4*(3), 31-59.

Palombo, J. (1996c). The diagnosis and treatment of children with nonverbal learning disabilities. *Child and Adolescent Social Work Journal, 13*(4), 311-332.

Palombo, J. (2000). Psychoanalysis: A house divided. *Psychoanalytic Social Work*, 7(1) 1-26

Palombo, J., & Berenberg, A. H. (1997). Psychotherapy for children with nonverbal learning disabilities. In B. S. Mark & J. A. Incorvaia (Eds.), *The handbook of infant, child and adolescent psychotherapy: New directions in integrative treatment* (Vol. 2, pp. 25-68). Northvale, NJ: Aronson.

Palombo, J., & Berenberg, A. H. (1999). Working with parents of children with nonverbal learning disabilities: A conceptual and intervention model. In J. A. Incorvaia, B. S. Mark-Goldstein, & D. Tessmer (Eds.), *Understanding, diagnosing, and treating AD/HD in children and adolescents: An integrative approach*. Northvale, NJ: Aronson.

Palombo, J., & Feigon, J. (1984). Borderline personality in childhood and its relationship to neurocognitive deficits. *Child and Adolescent Social Work Journal, 1*(1), 18-33.

Pennington, B. F. (1991). *Diagnosing learning disorders: A neuropsychological framework*. New York: Guilford.

Pennington, B., F., Bennetto, L., McAleer, O., & Roberts, R. J. (1996). Executive functions and working memory. In G. R. Lyon & N. A. Krasnegor (Eds.), *Attention, memory, and executive function* (pp. 327-348). Baltimore: Paul H. Brookes Pub.

Piaget, J. (1972). *The principles of genetic epistemology*. New York: Basic Books.

Pickar, D. B. (1986). Psychosocial aspects of learning disabilities: A review of research. *Bulletin of the Menninger Clinic, 50*(1), 22-32.

Pine, F. (1985). *Developmental theory and clinical practice*. New Haven: Yale University Press.

Racker, H. (1968). *Transference and countertransference*. New York: International Universities Press.

Racker, H. (1972). The meaning and uses of countertransference. *Psychoanalytic Quarterly, 41*, 487-506.

Robinson, K. S. (Ed.). (1983). *The borderline child: Approaches to etiology, diagnosis, and treatment*. New York: McGraw-Hill.

Rosen, V. H. (1955). Stephosymbolia: An intrapsychic disturbance of the synthetic function of the ego. *Psychoanalytic Study of the Child* (Vol. 10, pp. 83-99). New York: International Universities Press.

Rosenberger, J. (1988). Self psychology as a theoretical base for understanding the impact of learning disabilities. *Child and Adolescent Social Work Journal, 5*(1), 269-280.

Rothstein, A. A., & Glenn, J. (1999). *Learning disabilities and psychic conflict: A psychoanalytic casebook*. Madison, CT: International Universities Press.

Rothstein, A., Benjamin, L., Crosby, M., & Eisenstadt, K. (1988). *Learning disorders: An integration of neuropsychological and psychoanalytic considerations*. Madison, CT: International Universities Press.

Rourke, B. P. (1989). *Nonverbal learning disabilities: The syndrome and the model*. New York: Guilford.

Rourke, B. P. (1995a). Introduction: The NLD syndrome and the white matter model. In B. P. Rourke (Ed.), *Syndrome of nonverbal learning disabilities: Neurodevelopmental manifestations*. New York: Guilford.

Rourke, B. P. (Ed.). (1995b). *Syndrome of nonverbal learning disabilities: Neurodevelopmental manifestations*. New York: Guilford.

Rourke, B. P. (1995c). Appendix: Treatment program for the child with NLD. In B. P. Rourke (Ed.), *Syndrome of nonverbal learning disabilities: Neurodevelopmental manifestations* (pp. 497-508). New York: Guilford.

Rourke, B. P., & Furerst, D. R. (1991). *Learning disabilities and psychosocial functions: A neuropsychological perspective*. New York: Guilford.

Rourke, B. P., & Tsatsanis, K. D. (1995). Syndrome of nonverbal learning disabilities: Psycholinguistic assets and deficits. *Topics in Language Disorders, 16*(2), 3-44.

Ryan, M. (1994). The other sixteen hours: The social and emotional problems of dyslexia. Baltimore, MD: Orton Dyslexia Society.

Saari, C. (1986). *Clinical social work treatment: How does it work?* New York: Gardner.

Saari, C. (1991). *The creation of meaning in clinical social work.* New York: Guilford.

Sander, L. (1998). Intervention that effect change in psychotherapy: A model based on infant research. *Infant Mental Health Journal, 19*(3), 280-281.

Schacter, D. L. (1996). *Searching for memory: The brain, the mind, and the past.* New York: Basic Books.

Schafer, R. (1980). Narration in the psychoanalytic dialogue. In W. J. T. Mitchell (Ed.), *On narrative* (pp. 25-50). Chicago: University of Chicago Press.

Schafer, R. (1981). *Narrative actions in psychoanalysis.* Worchester, MA: Clark University Press.

Schafer, R. (1983). *The analytic attitude.* New York: Basic Books.

Schafer, R. (1992). *Retelling a life: Narration and dialogue in psychoanalysis.* New York: Basic Books.

Schore, A. N. (1994). *Affect regulation and the origin of the self: The neurobiology of emotional development.* Hillsdale, NJ: Erlbaum.

Segal, E. (1996). *Mothering a child with attention-deficit hyperactivity disorder: Learned mothering.* Unpublished qualitative research, Institute for Clinical Social Work, Chicago, IL.

Semrud-Clikeman, M., & Hynd, G. W. (1990). Right hemisphere dysfunction in nonverbal learning disabilities: Social, academic and adaptive functioning in adults and children. *Psychological Bulletin, 107*(2), 196-209.

Shane, E. (1984). Self psychology: A new conceptualization for the understanding of learning-disabled children. In P. E. Stepansky (Ed.), *Kohut's legacy: Contributions to self psychology* (pp. 191-202). Hillsdale, NJ: Analytic Press.

Silbar, S., & Palombo, J. (1991). A discordant consolidation of the self in a late adolescent male. *Child and Adolescent Social Work Journal, 8,* 17-32.

Silver, L. B. (1989). Psychological and family problems associated with learning disabilities: Assessment and intervention. *Journal of the American Academy of Child and Adolescent Psychiatry, 28*(3), 319-325.

Siskind, D. (1997). *Working with parents: Establishing the essential alliance in child psychotherapy and consultation.* Northvale, NJ: Aronson.

Spence, D. P. (1982). *Narrative truth and historical truth.* New York: Norton.

Spence, D. P. (1986a). Narrative smoothing and clinical wisdom. In T. R. Sarbin (Ed.), *Narrative psychology: The storied nature of human conduct* (pp. 211-232). New York: Praeger.

Spence, D. P. (1986b). When interpretation masquerades as explanation. *Journal of the American Psychoanalytic Association, 34*(1), 3-22.

Spence, D. P. (1987). *The Freudian metaphor: Toward a paradigm change in psychoanalysis.* New York: Norton.

Spence, D. P. (1990). The rhetorical voice of psychoanalysis. *Journal of the American Psychoanalytic Association, 38*(3), 579-605.

Spitz, R. A. (1945). "Hospitalism": An inquiry into the genesis of psychiatric conditions in early childhood. *Psychoanalytic Study of the Child* (Vol. 1, pp. 53-74). New York International Universities Press.

Spitz, R. A. (1946). Hospitalism: A follow-up report. *Psychoanalytic Study of the Child* (Vol. 2, pp. 113-117). New York International Universities Press.

Spitz, R. A. (1951). The psychogenic diseases in infancy: An attempt at their etiologic classification. *Psychoanalytic Study of the Child* (Vol. 6, pp. 225-275). New York International Universities Press.

Stern, D. N. (1984). Affect attunement. In J. D. Call, E. Galenson & R. L. Tyson (Eds.), *Frontiers of infant psychiatry* (pp. 3–14). New York: Basic Books.

Stern, D. N. (1985). *The interpersonal world of the infant.* New York: Basic Books.

Stern, D. N. (1989a). Developmental prerequisites for the sense of narrated self. In A. M. Cooper, O. F. Kernberg, & E. S. Person (Eds.), *Psychoanalysis: Toward the second century* (pp. 168–178). New Haven: Yale University Press.

Stern, D. N. (1989b). The representation of relational patterns: Developmental considerations. In R. N. Emde & A. Sameroff (Eds.), *Relationship disturbances in early childhood: A developmental approach* (pp. 52–69). New York: Basic Books.

Stern, D. N. (1998). The process of therapeutic change involving implicit knowledge: Some implications of developmental observations for adult psychotherapy. *Infant Mental Health Journal, 198*(3), 300–308.

Stolorow, R. D., Brandchaft, B., & Atwood, G. (1987). *Psychoanalytic treatment: An intersubjective approach.* Hillsdale, NJ: Analytic Press.

Strang, J. D., & Casey, J. E. (1994). The psychological impact of learning disabilities: a development neuropsychological perspective. In L. F. Koziol & C. E. Stout (Eds.), *The neuropsychology of mental disorders: A practical guide* (pp. 171–186). Springfield, IL: C. C. Thomas.

Tannock, R., & Brown, T. E. (2000). Attention-deficit disorders with learning disorders in children and adolescents. In T. E. Brown (Ed.), *Attention-deficit disorders and comorbidities in children, adolescents, and adults* (pp. 231–295). Washington, DC: American Psychiatric Press, Inc.

Tantam, D. (1988). Annotation: Asperger's syndrome. *Journal of Child Psychology and Psychiatry, 29*(3), 245–255.

Thompson, S. (1997). *The source for nonverbal disorders.* East Moline, IL: LinguiSystems.

Tomkins, S. S. (1979). Script theory: Differential magnification of affects. In H. E. Howe & R. A. Dienstbier (Eds.), *Nebraska symposium on motivation* (Vol. 36, pp. 201–236).

Tomkins, S. S. (1987). Script theory. In J. Aronogg, A. I. Rabin, & R. A. Zucker (Eds.), *The emergence of personality* (pp. 147–216). New York: Springer.

Toppelberg, C. O., & Shapiro, T. (2000). Language disorders: A 10-year research update review. *Journal of the American Academy of Child and Adolescent Psychiatry, 39*(2), 143–152.

Torgesen, J. K. (1994). Issues in the assessment of executive function: An information-processing perspective. In G. R. Lyon (Ed.), *Frames of reference for the assessment of learning disabilities: New views on measurement issues.* (pp. 143–162). Baltimore: Paul H. Brookes.

Vail, P. L. (1989). The gifted learning disabled child. In L. B. Silver (Ed.), *The assessment of learning disabilities: Preschool through adulthood college* (pp. 135–159). New York: Little, Brown & Co.

Vaughn, S., & Haager, D. (1994). Social competence as a multifaceted construct: How do students with learning disabilities fare? *Learning Disability Quarterly, 17,* 253–266.

Vigilante, F. W. (1983). *Working with families of learning disabled children.* Washington, DC: Child Welfare League of America.

Voeller, K. K. S. (1986). Right-hemisphere deficits syndrome in children. *American Journal of Psychiatry, 143*(8), 1004–1009.

Voeller, K. K. S. (1995). Clinical neurologic aspects of right-hemisphere deficit syndrome. *Journal of Child Neurology, 10*(1), Supplement.

Volkmar, F. R., Klin, A., & Cohen, D. J. (1997). Diagnosis and classification of autism and related conditions: Consensus and issues. In D. Cohen & F. R. Volkmar (Eds.), *Handbook of autism and pervasive developmental disorders* (pp. 5-40). New York: Wiley.

Vygotsky, L. (1986). *Thought and language.* (Alex Korzulin, Trans.). Cambridge, MA: MIT Press.

Warren, S. L., Emde, R. N., & Sroufe, L. A. (2000). Internal representations: Predicting anxiety from children's play narratives. *Journal of the American Academic of Child and Adolescent Psychiatry, 39*(1), 100-107.

Weil, A. P. (1970). The basic core. *Psychoanalytic Study of the Child, 25,* 442-460.

Weil, A. P. (1973a). Children with minimal brain dysfunction: Diagnostic and therapeutic considerations. In S. G. Samir & A. C. Nitzburg (Eds.), *Children with learning problems* (pp. 551-568). New York: Brunner/Mazel.

Weil, A. P. (1973b). Ego strengthening prior to analysis. *Psychoanalytic Study of the Child* (Vol. 28, pp. 289-301).

Weil, A. P. (1977). Learning disturbances with special consideration of dyslexia. *Child Mental Health, 5*(1), 52-66.

Weil, A. P. (1978). Maturational variations and genetic-dynamic issues. *Journal of the American Psychoanalytic Association, 26*(3), 461-492.

Weil, A. P. (1985). Thoughts about early pathology. *Journal of the American Psychoanalytic Association, 33*(2), 335-352.

Weintraub, S., & Mesulam, M. (1982). Developmental learning disabilities of the right hemisphere: Emotional, interpersonal and cognitive components. *Archives of Neurology, 40,* 463-468.

Weiss, M., Hechman, L., & Weiss, G. (2000). ADHD in parents. *Journal of the American Academy of Child and Adolescent Psychiatry, 39*(8), 1059-1061.

Welsh, M. C., & Pennington, B. F. (1988). Assessing frontal lobe functioning in children: Views from developmental psychology. *Developmental Neuropsychology, 4*(3), 199-230.

Welsh, M. C., Pennington, B. F., & Groisser, D. B. (1991). A normative-developmental study of executive function: A window on prefrontal function in children. *Developmental Neuropsychology, 7*(2), 131-149.

Wender, P. H. (1972). The minimal brain syndrome in children: The syndrome and its relevance for psychiatry. *Journal of Nervous and Mental Disorders, 155,* 55-71.

Wing, L. (1991). The relationship between Asperger's syndrome and Kanner's autism. In U. Frith (Ed.), *Autism and Asperger syndrome* (pp. 93-121). Cambridge, England: Cambridge University Press.

Winnicott, D. W. (1949). Hate in the countertransference. *International Journal of Psycho-Analysis, 30,* 69-74.

Winnicott, D. W. (1960). Ego distortion in terms of true and false self. In D. W. Winnicott (Ed.), *The maturational processes and the facilitating environment* (pp. 140-152). New York: International Universities Press.

Winnicott, D. W. (1965). *The maturational processes and the facilitating environment.* New York: International Universities Press.

Wolf, E. S. (1988). *Treating the self: Elements of clinical self psychology.* New York: Guilford.

Wong, B. Y. L. (1984). Metacognition and learning disabilities. In T. G. Waller, D. Forrest, & E. MacKinon (Eds.), *Metacognition, cognition and human performance.* New York: Academic Press.

Yeschin, N. J. (2000). A new understanding of attention deficit hyperactivity disorder: Alternate concepts and interventions. *Child and Adolescent Social Work Journal, 17*(3), 227-245.

# INDEX

Aaron, P. G., 44
Abrams, J. C., 16
adjunctive functions
  for developing self-cohesion, 30
  for maintaining self-cohesion, 26, 27–28,
    36–38, 74
  for managing deficits
    in Asperger's disorder, 233–34
    in executive function disorder,
      173–74
  for managing nonverbal learning
    disabilities, 202–3
  providing in therapy, 268
    case illustration, 103
  seeking from the therapist, 263
adolescence, learning disorders in, 105–18
adolescents
  with executive function deficits, responses
    to expectations of caregivers, 99
  responses to developmental
    requirements, 82
adults, learning disorders in, 302
affective communication
  in Asperger's disorder, 228
  in nonverbal learning disabilities, 193
affective dimension
  in Asperger's disorder, 226–27
  of the development process, 5
*Affect Regulation and the Origin of the Self*
  (Schore), 21
affects
  as analogues of experiences, 50
  categorical, of innate scripts, 50
  integration into the sense of self, 26
  self-regulation of, 148
affect states
  absence of, in Asperger's disorder, 235
  attunement to, as empathy, 263–64

modulation of
  in attention deficit/hyperactivity
    disorder, 56
  by caregivers, 33–34
age, and sense of self, response to adversity,
  74–75
agency, sense of, and self-narrative, 64
alcohol use, by dyslexic adults, 129
alienation
  of adolescents with learning disabilities, 113
  of children with learning disabilities, 35
  in nonverbal learning disabilities, resulting
    behaviors, 219
alliance, enhancement of, with concordant
  responses in therapy, 266–67
alter-ego functions, 35–36
  and conventionalization, 271
  effects of lack of, 219
  and the nuclear self, 112–13
  relationship with conventionalization, 98
Andrulonis, P. A., 12
Anthony, E. J., 31
anxiety
  and hearing, in auditory processing
    deficit, 102
  as an indicator of psychic pain, 75
  about interactions, in nonverbal learning
    disabilities, 201
  managing in therapy, 251
  problems with, in children with learning
    disorders, 3
  as a response to threatened loss of
    self-cohesion, 73–74, 83–84
arousal, self-regulation of, in attention
  deficit/hyperactivity disorder, 148
Asperger, H., 222
Asperger's disorder, 222–45
  anxiety accompanying, 76

317